Joshua, Judges, and Ruth

Westminster Bible Companion

Series Editors

Patrick D. Miller
David L. Bartlett

Joshua, Judges, and Ruth

CAROLYN PRESSLER

Westminster John Knox Press
LOUISVILLE • LONDON

Scripture quotations, unless otherwise indicated, are from the New Revised Standard Version of the Bible, copyright © 1989 by the Division of Christian Education of the National Council of the Churches of Christ in the U.S.A., and used by permission.

Book design by Publishers' WorkGroup
Cover design by Drew Stevens

First edition
Published by Westminster John Knox Press
Louisville, Kentucky

This book is printed on acid-free paper that meets the American National Standards Institute Z39.48 standard. ∞

PRINTED IN THE UNITED STATES OF AMERICA

02 03 04 05 06 07 08 09 10 11—10 9 8 7 6 5 4 3 2 1

Library of Congress Cataloging-in-Publication Data is on file at the Library of Congress, Washington, D.C.

ISBN 0-664-25526-4

Contents

Series Foreword

This series of study guides to the Bible is offered to the church and more specifically to the laity. In daily devotions, in church school classes, and in listening to the preached word, individual Christians turn to the Bible for a sustaining word, a challenging word, and a sense of direction. The word that scripture brings may be highly personal as one deals with the demands and surprises, the joys and sorrows, of daily life. It also may have broader dimensions as people wrestle with moral and theological issues that involve us all. In every congregation and denomination, controversies arise that send ministry and laity alike back to the Word of God to find direction for dealing with difficult matters that confront us.

A significant number of lay women and men in the church also find themselves called to the service of teaching. Most of the time they will be teaching the Bible. In many churches, the primary sustained attention to the Bible and the discovery of its riches for our lives have come from the ongoing teaching of the Bible by persons who have not engaged in formal theological education. They have been willing, and often eager, to study the Bible in order to help others drink from its living water.

This volume is part of a series of books, the Westminster Bible Companion, intended to help the laity of the church read the Bible more clearly and intelligently. Whether such reading is for personal direction or for the teaching of others, the reader cannot avoid the difficulties of trying to understand these words from long ago. The scriptures are clear and clearly available to everyone as they call us to faith in the God who is revealed in Jesus Christ and as they offer to every human being the word of salvation. No companion volumes are necessary in order to hear such words truly. Yet every reader of scripture who pauses to ponder and think further about any text has questions that are not immediately answerable simply by reading the text of scripture. Such questions may be about historical and geographical details or about words that are obscure or so loaded with meaning that one cannot tell at a glance what is at stake. They may be about the fundamental meaning of a passage or about what connection a particular text might have to our contemporary world. Or a teacher preparing for a church school class may simply want to know: What should I say about this biblical passage when I have to teach it next Sunday? It is our hope that these volumes, written by teachers and pastors with long experience studying and teaching the Bible in the church, will help members of the church who want and need to study the Bible with their questions.

The New Revised Standard Version of the Bible is the basis for the interpretive comments that each author provides. The NRSV text is presented at the beginning of the discussion so that the reader may have at hand in a single volume both the scripture passage and the exposition of its meaning. In some instances, where inclusion of the entire passage is not necessary for understanding either the text or the interpreter's discussion, the presentation of the NSRV text may be abbreviated.

We hope this series will serve the community of faith, opening the Word of God to all the people, so that they may be sustained and guided by it.

Introduction to Joshua and Judges

A student once commented that to study the Bible was to enter into a conversation that had been going on for several thousand years about the most important questions we could ever ask. *Who is God? How does God act in our lives? Who are we and how are we to act as God's faithful people?* That student had a good grasp of the dialogical nature of the Scriptures. The books that form the subject of this commentary, Joshua, Judges, and Ruth, represent many voices reflecting on Israel's earliest days in its land. This centuries-long conversation about Israel's beginnings has produced narratives that are less an academic history than a people's colorful, complex stories told to probe or proclaim a nation's identity and its faith. Ruth represents a somewhat different voice in the dialogue than Judges and Joshua, and merits a separate introduction (see pp. 261–64). Here, we introduce Joshua and Judges.

THE DEUTERONOMISTIC HISTORY

Joshua and Judges belong to a massive story of Israel's life on the land that also includes the books of 1 Samuel and 2 Samuel and 1 Kings and 2 Kings. Because its authors seem to have taken Deuteronomy as the cornerstone of their worldview, as well as the introduction to their compilation, biblical scholars refer to Joshua through 2 Kings as the "Deuteronomistic History" and to its authors as the "Deuteronomistic Historians."

Moses and Israel come to the edge of the promised land (Deuteronomy), and the Deuteronomistic History takes up the story with Israel's emergence in the land, portrayed as a conquest (Joshua). The account then moves to stories about the settlement period (Judges), followed by accounts of the reigns of David and Solomon (1 Samuel–1 Kings 11), the divided monarchy, and finally about the Babylonian conquest of Judah and exile from the land (1 and 2 Kings).

The Deuteronomistic account of Israel and its land incorporates memories and reflections of numerous people who told and retold Israel's traditions at different periods of time. The compilers who shaped it used an array of earlier traditions in their work: spy stories, battle reports, hero legends, songs, liturgies, confessions, and administrative lists, reflecting a range of perspectives on what it meant for Israel to be the people of God. As an artist makes a collage by putting different objects and scraps together to form a particular picture, the Deuteronomistic Historians pieced together myriad diverse traditions in order to depict their particular views of Israel's story. They added speeches and narratives in order to clarify the main shape of their work and convey their message. The result reflects both the viewpoints of earlier materials and the compilers who reused them.

Moreover, the overarching history went through at least two major editions. The final form of Deuteronomistic work was finished no earlier than the sixth century B.C.E., when the events reported in the last chapter of 2 Kings occurred. Most American scholars believe that an earlier, late seventh-century version was compiled by supporters of Judah's King Josiah (his think tank, as it were).

Josiah was a reformer bent on reestablishing the kingdom as it had been in its glory days and on centralizing and purifying its national religion. For 150 years before Josiah came to the throne, Assyria, a huge empire whose heartland was north and east of Judah (in the northern parts of modern-day Iraq and Iran) dominated Judah along with the entire region. By the late seventh century, weakened by internal struggles, Assyria began to lose its grip over the western lands, including Judah. Josiah seized the chance to reassert national independence. He attempted to bring the northern kingdom of Israel, separate from Judah since the tenth century, back under the rule of the Davidic kings, then sought to throw off Assyrian domination of the newly expanded Judah. In a move that considered both politics and religion, Josiah resolved to centralize worship in Jerusalem. The main emphases of Josiah's reform (2 Kings 22–23) find parallels in the key themes of Deuteronomy and the Deuteronomistic History. Many scholars believe that initially Deuteronomy, then later the Deuteronomistic History, were first compiled by Josiah's supporters to bolster his reform. That theory sheds light on the Deuteronomists' stress on hierarchical, centralized leadership, their insistence that God fights for Israel, and the saber-rattling tone of their work.

Just a few decades after the heady, optimistic days of Josiah's nationalistic expansion and religious reform, all hopes of national resurgence were dashed. Babylon rose to dominate the region. Judah twice attempted to resist Babylonian rule, and Babylon twice put down the rebellion. The second conquest, in 587 B.C.E., was a devastating defeat for Judah. Babylon burned the temple to the ground, razed Jerusalem and the surrounding countryside, and put an end to the Davidic kingship. The Babylonian king dragged the elite of Judah into exile and subjected the remaining population to his rule.

Both at home and in exile, the surviving Judeans asked agonized questions. *Had their God, Yahweh, been defeated? Or was Yahweh fickle?* Perhaps their God, in anger, had rejected them forever. The circle of thinkers whose predecessors compiled the Josianic edition of the Deuteronomistic History edited it to respond to the conquered Judean's questions. The Deuteronomists explained that Judah's suffering was not evidence of the defeat or the injustice of God, but the result of Israel's sin. Exile was Yahweh's just punishment. The historians wove into that explanation a thread of hope. The exile was a consequence of God's judgment, but divine mercy extends beyond divine wrath.

The Deuteronomists, then, sought to address existential issues, not to create a collection of materials for the national archives. While much of the material in their work is historical, their primary purpose was not to record exactly what happened, but to ask and answer questions like, "Who is Israel?" "How is God at work in Israel's history?" and "Why has Israel suffered, if Yahweh is just?" A driving practical purpose shaped the work of both the Josianic and the exilic compilers. They urged Judah to reform, to turn again to its covenant God so that the nation might be renewed in Josiah's time, or, in the exilic period, restored.

Joshua and Judges as Chapters of the Deuteronomistic History

Joshua and Judges are the first two chapters of the Deuteronomistic History. The first half of Joshua tells the story of Israel's emergence on the land, which it recalls as a rapid, unified conquest. The second half of Joshua recounts the apportionment of territory to each of the tribes. Both the conquest and the apportionment narratives served to assert Judah's claim to its land, a claim it was rarely able to take for granted. The book of Judges describes the tribes' struggle to settle the allotted territory in the face of external threat and internal sin.

Theologically, the two books assert the justice of God. When Israel is faithful, God is faithful. Divine wrath and judgment are not the result of

Yahweh's caprice, but of Israel's sin. Joshua illustrates the first part of that statement: Israel is obedient; its leader, Joshua, is faithful; and God fulfills God's promises, giving Israel the land.

Judges depicts the other side of the equation. Israel repeatedly forgets Yahweh and worships false gods. God, angered by the people's betrayal, withdraws aid, "selling them into the hands" of aggressive nations around them. When suffering Israel cries out in pain, God relents and raises up a deliverer. But complacent Israel again betrays its relationship with its covenant God. The authors depict not just an ongoing cycle, but a downward spiral. The weight of Israel's sin eventually results in utter social chaos.

Yet finally, according to the compilers of Judges, what drives history is neither Israel's faithfulness nor its sin. Ultimately, the tension that matters in this story is between divine judgment and divine mercy. The Deuteronomists are clear: Sin does have consequences; God cannot and will not allow human rebellion against God to continue. Nonetheless, these theologians also insist that judgment is not the final word. Divine mercy reaches beyond righteous wrath.

Within the overarching themes of faithfulness, faithlessness, wrath, and mercy, the compilers wrestle with a range of issues. In the context of Assyrian domination and, later, humiliating defeat and exile, the Deuteronomists grappled with the nature of Israel's identity. Is Israel defined by ethnicity or by faith? The dominant voice of Joshua and Judges defines the people ethnically. In their anxiety to avoid assimilation to Assyrian and later Babylonian culture, the Deuteronomists urged Israel to avoid contact with other peoples and their religions. The compilers' concern for maintaining Israelite identity resulted in the grisly belief that nascent Israel should have killed all the indigenous people of the land of Canaan.

Other perspectives temper the xenophobia of the dominant Deuteronomistic voice. Joshua and Judges tell of outsiders becoming insiders. The non-Israelites Rahab and Jael rescue the Israelites from their enemies. Israel enters with indigenous people into covenants that, although against Deuteronomic law, are upheld by Joshua and uncensored by the narrator. The books also tell stories of insiders becoming outsiders by rebelling against divine law or violating social custom. Finally, these stories suggest that membership in Israel is determined not by biology but by faith.

Leadership is also a key Deuteronomistic concern. The book of Joshua presents centralized leadership as a model of faithfulness. Joshua, Moses' successor, is in command. Consistently, the divine word is mediated through Joshua. God speaks to Joshua, who speaks to the tribes, who then obey.

Leadership takes a different form in the book of Judges, in which leaders arise as they are needed. For the most part, they are military deliverers. The book is called "Judges" because many of the leaders it describes are said "to judge" Israel. However, the Hebrew verb, much broader than its English translation, means "to lead." Of the various deliverers in the book of Judges, only Deborah is a judge in the legal sense.

Like Joshua, the deliverers are under the rule of God. They are charismatic—that is, divinely chosen and empowered. Finally, however, the Deuteronomistic editors find charismatic, ad hoc leadership inadequate. As the book progresses, the deliverers are increasingly flawed. Samson, the final judge, is little more than a brawling womanizer. By the end of the book, there is no judge, no leader. The editors ascribe the complete social and religious breakdown narrated in the concluding chapters of Judges to the absence of a king in Israel. The stage is set for God's new act of mercy: the establishment of an Israelite king.

This commentary highlights a dialectic found in the Deuteronomistic view of divine providence: God's will is knowable and unknowable, expected and surprising. The Deuteronomists' tenet that God rewards obedience and curses disobedience is tempered by their belief that Israelite sin is nonetheless met by God's mercy. A countervoice challenges the view that Israelites are divinely chosen to the exclusion and even destruction of others. The first to confess Yahweh's sovereignty in the Holy Land is not an Israelite warrior but a Canaanite whore. Expectations of who God can and will use as agents are also overturned in the book of Judges. Among the divinely appointed deliverers are a female military advisor, a left-handed assassin, and an outcast brigand. Finally, human expectations or conventions do not limit God. The Deuteronomists trace predictable patterns in Israelite history, but they also tell of a free God, whose spirit "blows where it chooses" (John 3:8).

IMPLICATIONS FOR INTERPRETATION

The understanding that the Scriptures are the product of a centuries-long "conversation" and thus reflect diverse perspectives has a number of implications for interpretation. First, listening for countervoices as well as dominant themes is important. Second, understanding Joshua and Judges as theological and political literature rather than as merely historical reports suggests that one should listen for their theological message more than for their historicity, although history is not irrelevant. Reading a story in light

of its historical context often brings its meaning into sharper focus. Different points in this commentary consider what a passage would have
meant to its seventh-century audience or to the exiled and colonized
Judeans/exiles of the sixth century B.C.E. The "truth" of a passage is not
necessarily limited to its historical veracity. This exposition focuses more
on what passages teach about God than on what they say about specific
events.

Joshua

1. Setting the Stage
Joshua 1

The first chapter of Joshua marks a momentous transition in Israel's history as conceived by the Deuteronomists. The era of Moses is over; the era of Joshua has begun. Under Joshua, the Israelite's time of landlessness also comes to an end. Israel is about to enter Canaan: a longed-for transition. The gift of land represents fulfillment of God's promise to Abraham, the climax and goal of the deliverance from Egypt. After centuries of slavery and decades of wilderness wanderings, the gift of land is a home, a blessing, and a concrete expression of salvation. Yet this transition time is also a time of crisis. Security in the land will come only after fierce battles that the tribes must fight without their great and trusted leader, Moses. "Never," according to the Deuteronomists, had "there arisen a prophet in Israel like Moses, whom the LORD knew face to face" (Deut. 34:10). But now, Moses is dead.

The first chapter of Joshua is almost entirely a Deuteronomistic composition, written to demarcate and introduce the period of the conquest. With Joshua 23, another Deuteronomistic passage, the chapter frames the traditions found in the book and helps shape the readers' responses to them. The chapter looks both backwards and forwards. It looks back to Deuteronomy, taking up Israel's story directly from Deuteronomy 34, which narrates Moses' death. Indeed, almost all of Joshua 1 is comprised of quotes and paraphrases from the previous book. The chapter also looks forward, introducing the main characters, structure, themes, and even tensions that are found throughout Joshua, and stressing the decisive shift that has occurred in Israel's history.

The chapter thus plays a key role in shaping the book of Joshua and the overarching history to which Joshua belongs. The themes it raises—warfare, land, leadership, the unity of the people, and the faithfulness of God—are found throughout the book. Joshua 1 also speaks a theological word in its own right. The verses from Deuteronomy are knit together in a way that stresses continuity in the midst of newness and change. Above all, the chapter affirms that the source of both continuity and newness is God, whose word initiates a new epoch for Israel, and whose unchanging faithfulness is the basis for confidence in times of newness and change. Joshua makes clear that the proper response to God's faithfulness is "strong and courageous" obedience.

1:1 After the death of Moses the servant of the LORD, the LORD spoke to Joshua son of Nun, Moses' assistant, saying, 2 "My servant Moses is dead. Now proceed to cross the Jordan, you and all this people, into the land that I am giving to them, to the Israelites. 3 Every place that the sole of your foot will tread upon I have given to you, as I promised to Moses. 4 From the wilderness and the Lebanon as far as the great river, the river Euphrates, all the land of the Hittites, to the Great Sea in the west shall be your territory. 5 No one shall be able to stand against you all the days of your life. As I was with Moses, so I will be with you; I will not fail you or forsake you. 6 Be strong and courageous; for you shall put this people in possession of the land that I swore to their ancestors to give them. 7 Only be strong and very courageous, being careful to act in accordance with all the law that my servant Moses commanded you; do not turn from it to the right hand or to the left, so that you may be successful wherever you go. 8 This book of the law shall not depart out of your mouth; you shall meditate on it day and night, so that you may be careful to act in accordance with all that is written in it. For then you shall make your way prosperous, and then you shall be successful. 9 I hereby command you: Be strong and courageous; do not be frightened or dismayed, for the LORD your God is with you wherever you go."

10 Then Joshua commanded the officers of the people, 11 "Pass through the camp, and command the people: 'Prepare your provisions; for in three days you are to cross over the Jordan, to go in to take possession of the land that the LORD your God gives you to possess.'"

12 To the Reubenites, the Gadites, and the half-tribe of Manasseh Joshua said, 13 "Remember the word that Moses the servant of the LORD commanded you, saying, 'The LORD your God is providing you a place of rest, and will give you this land.' 14 Your wives, your little ones, and your livestock shall remain in the land that Moses gave you beyond the Jordan. But all the warriors among you shall cross over armed before your kindred and shall help them, 15 until the LORD gives rest to your kindred as well as to you, and they too take possession of the land that the LORD your God is giving them. Then you shall return to your own land and take possession of it, the land that Moses the servant of the LORD gave you beyond the Jordan to the east."

16 They answered Joshua: "All that you have commanded us we will do, and wherever you send us we will go. 17 Just as we obeyed Moses in all things, so we will obey you. Only may the LORD your God be with you, as

he was with Moses! [18] **Whoever rebels against your orders and disobeys your words, whatever you command, shall be put to death. Only be strong and courageous."**

Continuity and change are already signaled in the first verse of the chapter. The close tie between verse 1 and Deuteronomy 34 suggests continuity, while the phrase "After the death of X" is a formula the Deuteronomists use to mark a new historical period. The beginning of the time of the Judges is indicated by the words, "After the death of Joshua" (Judg. 1:1); the story of the Davidic monarchy starts, "After the death of Saul" (2 Sam. 1:1). The formative years in the wilderness end, and the time of conquest begins "after the death of Moses."

The first verse also suggests that Joshua will be Moses' successor, but not his equal. Moses' epithet, "the Servant of Yahweh [the LORD]," is used to honor Israel's most venerated leaders. The title is given to the patriarchs, Abraham, Isaac, and Jacob; and to kings, particularly David. Joshua himself will be called "Servant of the LORD" (Josh. 24:29). First and foremost, the phrase is used of Moses. In the story of Israel, Moses is *the* servant of Yahweh. As the book of Joshua opens, Moses is dead, but his presence is still felt strongly. God's gift of the land is grounded in the divine promise to Moses; God's promise to be with Joshua is compared to God's presence with Moses. It is Moses' law on which Joshua is to meditate, and Moses' command that he reiterates to the Eastern tribes. The tribes promise to obey Joshua as they obeyed Moses.

Joshua is elevated in this chapter and throughout the book as the sole legitimate successor of Moses, but he is not of Moses' stature. The distinction is already apparent in verse 1. Moses is "the servant of the LORD"; Joshua is the "assistant" of Moses. The word translated "assistant" is used to refer to the ministry of priests and to the personal service of apprentices, disciples, or attendants. Elisha is Elijah's "assistant"; the word also is used to describe the relationship of one of David's concubines to the king. The three Pentateuchal texts that refer to Joshua as Moses' "assistant" portray him as a rather overly zealous, albeit favored, disciple (Num. 11:28–29; Exod. 24:12–14; 33:7–11). Like Moses, Joshua's authority is grounded in the authorizing presence of God, but it is also rooted in adherence to the traditions of Moses (Josh. 1:7–8).

That the subject of Joshua 1:1 is Yahweh is vitally important. God is the first speaker and actor in the book; God continues to be the key agent behind all that happens. The word of God initiates and sustains Israel's life in the land.

GOD'S SPEECH TO JOSHUA
Joshua 1:2–9

The introduction to the commentary noted that the compilers of the book of Joshua used speeches to unify and interpret the older traditions they brought together into their massive story of Israel's life on the land. The first of these speeches is God's exhortation and command to Joshua. According to the Deuteronomists, God's word initiates the conquest of Canaan, just as God's word drives all of Israel's history. And God's encouraging, directing, and accompanying presence provides the basis of confidence in transition and crisis.

Commissioning of Joshua

The speech confirms the transfer of authority from Moses to Joshua (vv. 6, 9). Joshua has already been designated Moses' successor by four texts in Deuteronomy. Norbert Lohfink demonstrates that the passages, though similarly worded, actually serve different functions (Lohfink, 1994, 234–47). God commands Moses to commission Joshua in Deuteronomy 1:38 and 3:28. In the presence of all Israel, in the midst of a solemn covenant ceremony, the commission is carried out first by Moses (Deut. 31:7–8) and then by God (Deut. 31:23). In Joshua 1:2–9, the Lord instructs Joshua to begin exercising the leadership to which he has been appointed.

The commissioning in Joshua 1 follows closely a set pattern found in the Deuteronomic texts. The first part of the pattern are *words of encouragement*, "Be strong and courageous." The words are both exhortation and command. They speak to an attitude, a willingness to step out into the future that God makes available. Divine agency does not call for passivity but for bold and courageous action.

The second element is the *designation of a specific task for which the leader is commissioned*. The formula does not commission people to office in general, but rather appoints them to a specific task. Leadership is not a matter of position, privilege, or status, but of task and responsibility.

The tasks assigned to Joshua include leading the invasion, distributing the land, and observing Mosaic law. Joshua is to lead the invasion and conquest of Israel. "Cross over" belongs to the language of conquest. The Hebrew word translated "people" in this and many other contexts has the more specific meaning of "army." God instructs Joshua to begin the invasion of Canaan. After the conquest, Joshua is to divide the land among the tribes. The Hebrew word translated "put . . . in possession" often (though not always) means "apportion." The assignments God gives to Joshua, first to conquer and then to apportion the land, correspond to the two major sections of the book of Joshua. Chapters 2–11 deal with preparations for war and battle; chapters 13–21 address division of the land.

Finally, God gives Joshua a less-expected assignment: to "meditate" on Moses' law "day and night." After the words, "Be strong and courageous," one might expect to hear the command to occupy the land. Instead the command is to observe the law—indeed, to be so familiar with the law that it becomes second nature (Miller, 1990, 221). This command gives Joshua's role a royal flavor; in Deuteronomy 17:14–20 the king is to study the law "all the days of his life." It also emphasizes that successful occupation of the land depends neither on power nor on strategy, but on faithful observance of Mosaic law. "This book of the law" (Josh. 1:8) refers in the first place to Deuteronomy. "Torah" later came to mean the first five books of the Bible.

Indeed, faithful observance of the law seems to take the place of military conquest of the land. Lawson Stone has demonstrated that this third task is not simply added on to the first two. It serves to reinterpret them. The editor who inserted verses 7–9 also appears to have added passages in Joshua 8 and 23 that stress observing Mosaic law. The passages function to convert the military language of the book into what Stone calls "a massive metaphor" for observing Torah. Much like "Onward Christian Soldiers" exhorts Christians to "march as if to war" for their faith, an exilic editor has called the Judeans to "occupy the law" (Stone, 1991, 36).

The third element of the commissioning formula is the *promise of divine presence and aid*. God reassures Joshua of God's presence and assistance with lavish repetition: "As I was with Moses, so I will be with you; I will not fail you or forsake you." "[T]he LORD your God is with you wherever you go" (vv. 5, 9). The capacity to be strong and courageous and the ability to accomplish the assigned tasks are grounded in one fundamental fact: God is with Joshua. God is with us. Later, the tribes' response to Joshua's leadership (v. 17) demonstrates that divine presence is the only essential factor of a leader's authority. Joshua will put Israel in possession of its land not by merit nor by strategies—nor even, finally, by his own obedience—but by the powerful, effective presence of God.

The Gift of the Land

God's promise to give Israel the land is drawn from Deuteronomy 11:24–25. The land that Israel is about to conquer is first of all a *gift*.

God is *giving* (Josh. 1:2), has already *given* them (v. 3) the land. The different tenses speak to different aspects of the same reality. The land is a divine gift. The participle "giving" expresses ongoing action. The land is never received or possessed once and for all. Israel will continue to depend upon its God for the gift of land. Yet Yahweh also says of the land, "I have given" it to you—even before the Israelites have set foot on it. God has determined to make this land Israel's, and God's power and constancy is such that what God has decided is, in effect, already an accomplished fact.

The land is Israel's by *promise* (vv. 3, 6). Joshua and Israel's occupation of the land is the culmination of a long history of God and this people. Land is central to God's promise to the ancestors (Josh. 1:6, see Gen. 15:18), a promise reaffirmed to Moses (Josh. 1:5).

As we learn from the description of the tasks to which Joshua is commissioned, the land *given* and *promised* must also be taken. Joshua is to lead the people in the conquest of their promised gift of land. This intertwining of human and divine action is characteristic of God's way with the world.

The text gives an idealistic description of the land God gives to Israel to conquer. The territory delineated by the boundaries set out in verse 4, from the wilderness of the Negeb Desert in the south and east, to the Euphrates River in the northeast, to the Mediterranean Sea in the west, includes the whole of Syria and Palestine. (The reference to the "land of the Hittites" was probably added later, and refers to the fact that the Hittite empire at one time controlled much of Syria and Palestine.) The idealized description reflects the memory of the land once briefly under King David's sway rather than any realistic description of the territory that comprised Judah and Israel. The description of the territory allotted to the tribes in Joshua 13–21 provides a smaller, more realistic picture of Israelite land, without the inclusion of Syrian territory.

The description of the land and the reassurance that God will give it to Israel provide further clues into the leadership theology underlying the book of Joshua. The Hebrew language has different words for the pronoun "you"; some are singular, some are plural, and they are not used randomly. The Deuteronomists have used the plural "all of you," when speaking of the gift of the land. The *gift* is for all the people. The *task*, the responsibility, and therefore the needed words of assurance, however, are concentrated on Joshua. The Deuteronomic view of leadership stresses responsibility rather than power and privilege.

JOSHUA'S SPEECHES TO THE TRIBES
Joshua 1:10–15

God's speech to Joshua is followed by two brief speeches by Joshua to the people. The first, verses 10–11, made to all the tribes, emphasizes Joshua's obedience and sets out clearly the chain of command. The second, verses 12–15, addresses the tribes settled east of the Jordan and also raises two themes: the unity of Israel and the concept of "rest."

Joshua acts immediately on God's command. Told to cross the Jordan, he turns and instructs the officers to prepare to enter Canaan. Joshua is presented as a model of faithful leadership. Throughout the book, his obedience is demonstrated by the pattern found in this first speech to the tribes. God commands Joshua, Joshua commands the people, and the people obey.

The notion of "obedience," once central to faith, has fallen into disfavor in many segments of the church. The type of rote obedience that makes people less rather than more fully human is not the kind of obedience that Joshua 1 suggests. In Joshua, obedience has to do with listening to and responding to God's word with strength and courage. In obedience, Joshua takes risks, relying on the trustworthiness of the divine promise. His obedience manifests in moving forward to possess the land, the blessing and responsibility, that God opens up for God's people. To be sure, the military content of Joshua and Israel's obedient action in chapters 2–11 is rightly problematic for most contemporary Christians. Nonetheless, the book does have something to teach us about the bold, active, enlivening character of obedience.

The Deuteronomists' understanding of the proper chain of command is apparent in verses 10–11. God has commanded Joshua. Joshua obeys by issuing orders to his officers. The Hebrew word translated "officers" has a broad range of meaning, including civic officials and, as is most likely the case in verse 10, military leaders. The officers in turn command the people (in this case, probably the army). Biblical historians rightly note that the chain of command resembles a monarchical rather than tribal form of government.

The shift from Yahweh's speech to Joshua's speech represents a refocusing from general instruction and exhortation to imminently practical concerns. Joshua commands the officers to have the people prepare food for the journey into Canaan. The divine word is worked out in mundane details. Joshua's speech to the Reubenites, Gadites, and the half-tribe of Manasseh presupposes knowledge of the Deuteronomic account of the

tribes' conquest of land east of the Jordan (Deut. 3:1–22). According to
that story, the Amorite Kings Sihon and Og came out against Israel and
were defeated in battle. Moses gave the conquered territories to Reuben,
Gad, and one of the clans of Manasseh. The land grant was made with the
condition that the eastern tribes accompany their kin in the effort to conquer the land west of the Jordan.

In the context of Joshua 1, the summons to these two-and-a-half tribes
to fulfill their promise serves to underscore the unity of Israel. "All this
people" (v. 2) fight together for the promised land.

Joshua's second speech raises another theme, "rest," that threads its
way throughout the Deuteronomistic History. As the term is used in
Joshua through 2 Kings, it has to do with national security, an end of
warfare, and peaceful life on the land. "Land," we noted, is understood as
a concrete expression of divine blessing and even salvation. "Rest" is the
fulfillment of life on the land and is the goal of all the warfare and struggle narrated in the book of Joshua. "Rest" is even the Deuteronomic
understanding of what theologians call "eschatology," that is, the concept
of ultimate fulfillment at the end of time. For a little nation regularly subjugated by rapacious empires and frequently devastated by war, to live in
peace and security in a land of their own must have seemed something like
heaven.

THE PEOPLE'S RESPONSE
Joshua 1:16–18

The eastern tribes' response to Joshua is the last of the speeches comprising Joshua 1. The chapter closes with the peoples' pledge of total allegiance, with a caveat. In words that echo God's speech (vv. 5, 7), the tribes
assert that they will obey Joshua absolutely *only* if God is with him.
Presumably, evidence of God's presence comes from success in battle.
Echoing the divine exhortation, the tribes urge Joshua to be strong and
courageous. The eastern tribes' response functions as a response on behalf
of all the tribes. With this pledge of obedience, the people accept Joshua's
leadership. The transfer of authority from Moses to Joshua, begun in verse
1, is complete.

Joshua 1 introduces several themes that play a key role in the remainder of the book. These themes include land, the unity of the people, warfare, leadership, law, and the faithfulness of the Lord.

Land plays a central role in Joshua. Joshua 1 begins to develop a theology of land that is found throughout the book. The gift of the land is the concrete expression of divine blessing, the culmination of God's saving acts. This gift is also the context of the relationship between God and Israel, and a crucial factor in Israel's identity. The land is promised and given, not earned. But neither promise nor gift are unconditional. Israel can lose its land. The word "only" in verse 7 signifies the condition upon which the gift of land is given: "only" be careful to act in accordance with Mosaic Torah. Land and the blessing it represents are Israel's not by its own merit nor by its might, but by divine disposition. What is given can be taken away if Israel flouts the God who has given it the land.

The *unity of Israel* is central to the book of Joshua. The whole of Israel, acting in consort, conquers the land. Despite their secure possession of territory, the eastern tribes agree to cross the Jordan and fight alongside their brothers. The theme develops through Joshua with language that stresses unity. Terms like "the whole congregation of Israel," "all Israel," "all the assembly," and "all the tribes of Israel" are repeated throughout the book. The theme is also carried by persistent references to the tribes settled east of the Jordan (see especially Josh. 22). The compilers want to make sure their audience understands that the Gadites, Reubenites, and the half tribe of Manasseh belong to Israel.

Repeated references to the eastern tribes suggest a countertheme in Joshua, that of geographical and ethnic division and pluralism. The Deuteronomists take pains to assert the unity of Israel, but their very emphasis indicates that unity could not be taken for granted. Israel's claim to the territories traditionally assigned to Gad, Reuben, and the eastern clans of Manasseh was rarely unchallenged; in the time of Josiah, it was more vision than reality. The compilers' struggle with pluralism and division in relationship to the unity and identity of Israel is also seen in the stories about different ethnic groups such as Rahab's family (Josh. 2:1–24; 6:22–25) and the Gibeonites (Josh. 9).

The *warlike* character of the book of Joshua emerges in martial language such as "cross over" and "fear not," and especially in Joshua's reminder to the eastern tribes that they had agreed that their warriors would "cross over armed" to help take the land (v. 14). Nonetheless, in chapter 1, the absence of more extended, stronger military language is perhaps as striking as the martial references that are found. The chapter introduces a book whose primary subject is the conquest of land and that repeatedly reports the annihilation of indigenous populations. Yet the chapter is preoccupied not with military stratagems but with the faithfulness of God, the obedience of Joshua and the people, the transfer of leadership, and the observance of Torah.

A clear, centralized model of *leadership* emerges from the chapter. Israel is depicted as one people united under one leader who mediates the word and will of God. Israel's faithfulness to Yahweh is expressed by the obedience of the leader who, in turn, the people must obey (v. 18).

Dangers are inherent in this model of leadership. As noted above, the model of leadership in Joshua, which supports centralization of power, was shaped in part by the political needs of Josiah's government. As introduced in Joshua 1, the Deuteronomistic theology of leadership includes constraints against a despotic use of power. The leader's task is to enable the people to claim God's gift and challenge to them. God's command to Joshua to heed Mosaic Torah sets leadership under the rule of law, precluding any legitimate use of despotic power. Finally, the people must accept the authority of the leader. The transfer of leadership from Moses to Joshua is complete only when the tribes offer Joshua their allegiance. The condition for that allegiance is the perception that God is with the leader. The leader must be a servant of God.

God's instructions to Joshua highlight the theme of *law*, Torah (vv. 7–8). Law is a central concern of the Deuteronomists. Among Christians, "Torah" or "law" is among the most misunderstood concepts in the Pentateuch. Christians often contrast law with grace, identifying it with a God of wrath. That view, while common, is not biblical. Ancient Israel understands law as a concrete expression of what it means to "love . . . God with all your heart" (Deut. 6:5). Law gives shape to the life of faith, drawing the parameters within which healthy communal existence is possible. According to Deuteronomy 6:20–25, the purpose of the law is "for our lasting good, so as to keep us alive." The Psalms reverberate with love of Torah. In language very similar to Joshua 1:7–8, Psalm 1 proclaims, "Happy are those . . ." whose "delight is in the law of the LORD, and on his law . . . meditate day and night. They are like trees planted by streams of water . . ." (vv. 1a, 2–3). Torah is extolled in Psalm 19: "The law of the LORD is perfect, reviving the soul; the decrees of the LORD are sure, making wise the simple; the precepts of the LORD are right, rejoicing the heart; the commandment of the LORD is clear, enlightening the eyes. . . . More to be desired . . . than gold, even much fine gold . . ." (vv. 7–8, 10a). The Bible does not regard law as burden or wrath, but as gift.

The theme upon which all the rest of the theology of Joshua is based is the *faithfulness of God*. God's word is at the beginning of the chapter, initiating the new era in Israel's history. God's promised presence and assistance are the foundation of Joshua's courage and capacity and the basis of the people's obedient response to him. God promised and gives the land. God is the agent behind all that happens to bring Israel into existence. The response of Joshua and the people to their giving, commanding, initiating God is "strong and courageous" faith, a willingness to walk into new land in lively obedience and trust in their Lord.

2. The Outsider's Faith
Joshua 2

The Deuteronomistic writers' primary intent for the first chapter of Joshua was to introduce the themes and characters of the book. The text seems to reflect the perspective of an elite albeit reform-minded group of thinkers from the highest echelons of Judean society, a perspective that dominates the book. The tale of Rahab and the spies (Josh. 2) continues important aspects of the plot and the faith introduced in Joshua 1; at the same time, the Rahab story introduces an alternative voice, a voice from the margins, that broadens what could otherwise be an overly narrow understanding of Israel and its faith.

God's command to Joshua to proceed to lead his troops across the Jordan (Josh. 1:2) initiates the conquest. That plot continues in Joshua 2, as Joshua sends spies into Canaan to prepare for the invasion. The faith that shapes Joshua 1—that Israel's God is the one who moves history forward—is upheld by Rahab's confession that Yahweh is God of heaven and earth (2:11). Rahab's word also confirm the divine promise to give Israel Canaan's land (2:9).

So far, so orthodox. Nevertheless, if the story of Rahab upholds orthodox faith, it does so in a most unorthodox way. Rahab, the character who declares faith in the sole sovereignty of Israel's God, is not an Israelite at all, but a Canaanite, an "outsider." Rahab, the hero who saves the spies, enabling their mission to succeed and the conquest to continue, is a prostitute: morally suspect, outcast, despised. The narrative of the conquest of the Canaanites and the life of the chosen people in their land begins with the faithful words and saving deeds of a Canaanite whore.

The presence of alternate voices in the Rahab story stems in part from the diverse storytellers and editors who have helped to shape it. The story of Rahab and the spies had a long, complex history before assuming its current shape and place in the book of Joshua. Most scholars believe that the core of the story was an old folk tale, passed down from storyteller to storyteller, quite independent of the traditions about Joshua and Jericho, but just what the ancient tale included is hard to say. Perhaps the story told of a prostitute who outwitted a king to protect customers accused of espionage. Perhaps a woman helped spies find a hidden way for their army to enter her city. (Such a story is found in Judges 1:23–25, a passage that in many ways resembles Joshua 2.) In any case, the tale's humor attests to its folk origins, as do several of its motifs: the harlot with a heart of gold; the trickster who wins by wit, not power; the underdog who bests a powerful lord. All are typical folkloric themes.

The compiler of chapters 2–11 has incorporated Rahab's tale into the conquest narratives by placing the spies under Joshua's command and setting the story in Jericho. The conclusion of Rahab's story became linked to the fall of Jericho, which it does not fit overly well. In that context, the story serves as an oracle declaring that Yahweh has authorized the battle of Jericho and promised Israel victory. Israelite holy war ideology held that such an oracle was a necessary prerequisite to battle.

In the context of Joshua 2–12, the story also raises questions about Israel's identity. Is membership in Israel determined by ethnicity or by faith? The presence of "outsiders" like Rahab and the Gibeonites (chap. 9) who believe and obey Yahweh, on the one hand, and the story of the "insider" Achan's disobedience (chap. 7) bear witness to Israel's ongoing struggle to define who comprises the people of God.

Finally, the Deuteronomists, Josiah's theologians, expanded Rahab's speech (see Introduction to the commentary, pp. 1–3). The Canaanite prostitute is shown preaching from the book of Deuteronomy. Her story serves the Deuteronomists' message: Even a harlot, the lowest of the low, acknowledges the reign of Israel's God; even a Canaanite declares that their land has been given to Israel. The orthodox perspective that has given Joshua 2 its final shape does not silence the voice of the ancient story, a voice that comes from the people, the powerless, the poor. Rahab's story stands as a challenge and correction to the book's violent, elitist, or ethnocentric dimensions.

A long history of telling and retelling the Rahab/spy tale has resulted in a few glitches. For example, Rahab seems to hide the spies twice (vv. 4, 6). The spies appear to negotiate the terms of their oath as they dangle from the rope by which Rahab is lowering them from her roof to the ground. Nonetheless, the main story line is clear. The narrative is framed by the commissioning (v. 1) and report (vv. 23–24) of the spies. The main body of the account has three scenes, each focusing on a conversation. The first sketches Rahab's encounter with the king's messengers (vv. 2–7); the second, Rahab's confession of faith and covenant with the spies (vv. 8–14); and the third, the spies' renegotiation of their oath and escape (vv. 15–24).

2:1 Then Joshua son of Nun sent two men secretly from Shittim as spies, saying, "Go, view the land, especially Jericho." So they went, and entered the house of a prostitute whose name was Rahab, and spent the night there. [2] The king of Jericho was told, "Some Israelites have come here tonight to search out the land." [3] Then the king of Jericho sent orders to Rahab, "Bring out the men who have come to you, who entered your house, for they have come only to search out the whole land." [4] But the woman took the two men and hid them. Then she said, "True, the men came to me, but I did not know where they came from. [5] And when it was time to close the gate at dark, the men went out. Where the men went I do not know. Pursue them quickly, for you can overtake them." [6] She had, however, brought them up to the roof and hidden them with the stalks of flax that she had laid out on the roof. [7] So the men pursued them on the way to the Jordan as far as the fords. As soon as the pursuers had gone out, the gate was shut.

[8] Before they went to sleep, she came up to them on the roof [9] and said to the men: "I know that the LORD has given you the land, and that dread of you has fallen on us, and that all the inhabitants of the land melt in fear before you. [10] For we have heard how the LORD dried up the water of the Red Sea before you when you came out of Egypt, and what you did to the two kings of the Amorites that were beyond the Jordan, to Sihon and Og, whom you utterly destroyed. [11] As soon as we heard it, our hearts melted, and there was no courage left in any of us because of you. The LORD your God is indeed God in heaven above and on earth below. [12] Now then, since I have dealt kindly with you, swear to me by the LORD that you in turn will deal kindly with my family. Give me a sign of good faith [13] that you will spare my father and mother, my brothers and sisters, and all who belong to them, and deliver our lives from death." [14] The men said to her, "Our life for yours! If you do not tell this business of ours, then we will deal kindly and faithfully with you when the LORD gives us the land."

[15] Then she let them down by a rope through the window, for her house was on the outer side of the city wall and she resided within the wall itself. [16] She said to them, "Go toward the hill country, so that the pursuers may not come upon you. Hide yourselves there three days, until the pursuers have returned; then afterward you may go your way." [17] The men said to her, "We will be released from this oath that you have made us swear to you [18] if we invade the land and you do not tie this crimson cord in the window through which you let us down, and you do not gather into your house your father and mother, your brothers, and all your family. [19] If any of you go out of the doors of your house into the street, they shall be responsible for their own death, and we shall be innocent; but if a hand is laid upon any who are with you in

the house, we shall bear the responsibility for their death. [20] But if you tell this business of ours, then we shall be released from this oath that you made us swear to you." [21] She said, "According to your words, so be it." She sent them away and they departed. Then she tied the crimson cord in the window.

[22] They departed and went into the hill country and stayed there three days, until the pursuers returned. The pursuers had searched all along the way and found nothing. [23] Then the two men came down again from the hill country. They crossed over, came to Joshua son of Nun, and told him all that had happened to them. [24] They said to Joshua, "Truly the LORD has given all the land into our hands; moreover all the inhabitants of the land melt in fear before us."

The first verse of the narrative introduces its audience to the kind of story they are about to encounter, its settings, and its main characters. The narrative genre found in Joshua 2 is familiar to modern as well as ancient readers. It is a spy story. The commissioning of spies (v. 1) is a common motif in biblical conquest narratives. The espionage rarely has to do with military tactics (but see Judg. 1:23–25). More often, the spies' reports function as oracles, providing information about the quality of the land and the possibility of capturing it (see, for example, Judg. 18:2–6). Such is the case here.

The initial setting of the story is Shittim, which tradition understood as the tribes' last campsite before crossing the border. The exact location of Shittim is unknown; it is most often identified as one of two archaeological sites located east of the Jordan River, opposite Jericho. The traditions associated with Shittim are not altogether positive. Numbers 25 remembers Shittim as the place where Israelite men prostituted themselves with foreign women who led them to worship foreign deities. Joshua 2 reverses (and redeems) that memory. The journey of the two Israelite men from Shittim to Jericho involves a foreign woman, a prostitute, but she will lead them to renewed faith in Israel's God.

Verse 1 introduces the main actors: two nameless spies and a harlot, Rahab. The meaning of the Hebrew word *rahab* is "wide." The significance of the name is debated. Some scholars believe that the name was taken from a group of non-Israelites called Rahabites who lived in the vicinity of Jericho. Others propose that the name was chosen to recall the "good and broad (*rahab*) land." Still others suggest that the word *rahab* was a coarse term for a woman or a prostitute, something like the English word "broad." In any case, Rahab is the only character besides Joshua named in the story.

Interpreters are frequently puzzled and even distressed by the presence of a harlot in the role of deliverer, especially since she is uncensored by the text. From as early as the first century C.E., some commentators have sought to show that the Hebrew word normally translated "prostitute" should be interpreted as "innkeeper" when it refers to Rahab. The Hebrew text, however, provides no basis for translating the word in any but its usual sense. Other interpreters, especially recent ones, have recognized that Rahab was a prostitute, but have rejected the idea that she is a deliverer or hero. Several recent commentators describe her as "entrapping," "mastering," or "humiliating" the spies. Her request that the Israelites refrain from murdering her and her family is interpreted as an unreasonable or unfair demand. Such interpretations seem to reflect the readers' opinions of prostitutes, foreigners, or women more than they reflect the textual evidence.

In any case, the New Testament authors clearly understood Rahab as both a prostitute and a hero. The author of Hebrews includes "Rahab the prostitute" in the list of those saved by faith (Heb. 11:31). James, arguing that "faith apart from works is barren" (James 2:20), provides just two examples of saints whose faith was "brought to completion by . . . works": "our ancestor Abraham" and "Rahab the prostitute" (2:21–22, 25). Jewish traditions also exalt Rahab as a model of the faithful. Ancient Jewish legends maintain that Rahab converted to Judaism, married Joshua, and gave birth to a long line of priests and prophets, including Jeremiah and Ezekiel.

Indeed, the fact that Rahab is a prostitute is integral to the story; as some commentators rightly note, her profession is important to its plausibility on several levels, explaining why the spies could possibly hope to come and go unobserved and why Rahab could claim not to know anything about her visitors. Most ancient Near Eastern women were subject to the authority of their fathers or husbands; Rahab's profession explains how she happened to have autonomy to be able to shelter the spies. Rahab's status as a prostitute is also important to understanding why this Canaanite would help Israelites planning to invade her city. We tend to consider prostitution as a moral issue. Then as now, prostitution is far more a matter of economics. In a majority of cases, poverty and a lack of any other means of survival force women to sell their bodies. In the ancient Near East, prostituted women were tolerated because they were necessary for men's satisfaction, but they were despised. They were not outlawed, but they were outcast (Bird, 1989, 120). As an economically marginalized social outcast, Rahab would have little reason to be loyal to the city's rulers. According to the biblical story, the Israelite tribes were also economically and socially marginal: escaped slaves, landless wanderers. It is not implausible that a destitute woman like Rahab would identify more with the poor Israelites than with the rich lords of Jericho.

Most important, Rahab's profession is essential to the theological message of the passage. The story has to do with the difference between human expectations and divine decisions. A strong thread running throughout the Scriptures insists that God's choice of agents is not determined by social respectability or power, that God has "brought down the powerful from their thrones, and lifted up the lowly" (Luke 1:52). Rahab, a Canaanite, a woman, and a prostitute, is three times "other," three times despised. Yet she is a deliverer of Israel, the first in the promised land to confess the sovereignty of God.

Rahab stands in a long line of faithful foreign women who save or serve Israel. Pharaoh's daughter rescues baby Moses from the water (Exod. 2:5–10); the Midianite, Zipporah, again saves Moses' life (Exod. 4:24–26). Ruth, a Moabite woman, serves as a model of covenantal loyalty, redeems Naomi from her barrenness, and gives birth to the line of David. These women challenge the stereotype of non-Israelite temptresses. At the very beginning of a book that seems to equate ethnic cleansing and obedience, Rahab serves as a reminder that Israelite identity is defined by faith, not ethnicity.

Joshua depicts Israelite society as a man's world. Its primary concerns are war and land distribution, institutions dominated by men. The story of Rahab and the spies shows that God works through both women and men. Moreover, the story shows God at work through a woman whom society deems morally and sexually suspect. Yet that woman, along with Tamar, who dressed as a prostitute to seduce her father-in-law, and Ruth, who lay down at Boaz's "feet" in the middle of the night, are named as ancestors of Jesus (Matt. 1:5). Rahab, Ruth, and Tamar stand over against human stereotypes and judgments about who is or is not fit to bear the divine word.

The first scene of the body of the narrative pits the prostitute's wit against the king's power. The king of Jericho has spies of his own, who are not slow to discover the presence of suspicious strangers. When his messengers come to arrest the spies, Rahab allays their suspicions by acknowledging the men had indeed been there. She then uses her profession as protective coloring. How could a whore be expected to know where her customers are from or where they plan to go when they leave her? She sends the messengers off on a wild goose chase.

The storytellers' choice of a hiding place is plausible. Middle Eastern houses typically had flat roofs that could be used for storage. As it now stands, the tale is condensed; we are not told how Rahab could have known the spies' whereabouts had been discovered, so that she hid them before the king's men arrived. The story moves back and forth between Rahab's hiding the Israelites (vv. 4, 6) and denying any knowledge of them to the messengers (vv. 4b, 5, 7). The contrast emphasizes the foolishness of the king's men and the wiliness of the woman. Rahab uses trickery, the power of the powerless, to outwit the king.

The scene shifts to the roof, to the encounter between Rahab and the spies (vv. 8–14). The heart of the chapter is Rahab's confession. Her declaration, worded in the language of the great confessions of Israel's faith, supports Deuteronomistic orthodoxy. Rahab's assertion that dread has befallen the inhabitants of the land, who melt in fear before Israel's God (v. 9) echoes the song of Moses, one of Israel's ancient and foundational hymns: "All the inhabitants of Canaan melted away. Terror and dread fell upon them" (Exod. 15:15–16). Rahab's proclamation of the sovereignty of Yahweh is couched in the words of Deuteronomy: "The LORD is God in heaven above and on the earth beneath" (Deut. 4:39). Her assertion that God has given Israel the land reiterates the divine promise found in Joshua 1:3–5. Moreover, her speech presupposes a traditional Israelite understanding of "holy war" according to which God is the Divine Warrior who spreads panic among Israel's enemies. Rahab's request to spare her life and the life of her family presupposes a key tenet of the Deuteronomistic understanding of war—that is, that Israel was to exterminate the defeated Canaanites.

The unorthodox character of the speech lies not in what is said, but in who says it. Deuteronomic law mandates that Israel shall put to death all inhabitants of the land, all Canaanites, lest they teach Israel to "do all the abhorrent things that they do for their gods" (Deut. 20:16–18). The spies are the first Israelites to encounter a Canaanite; that Canaanite proceeds to declare faith in Yahweh, Israel's God. Israel is absolutely prohibited from making treaties with the inhabitants of the land; the oath that Rahab elicits from the spies bears the marks of covenant. Israel is to "utterly destroy" the peoples of Canaan (Deut. 7:2); the first reference to "utter destruction" (*herem*) is made by Rahab (v. 10) in the context of requesting and being granted an exception to the ban. The covenant, the exception to the ban, is not only granted; it is upheld by Joshua (6:22) and uncensored by any biblical text.

In the final scene of the story, Rahab helps the spies escape a locked city by lowering them out a window (vv. 15–22). The ploy works because her house is built against or in the city walls. The latter presupposes that the fortifications of the town consisted of casement walls, double walls that were sometimes filled with rubble, but other times partitioned off for dwellings. The location of Rahab's house is also symbolic. She lives on the margins of the community, both literally and figuratively.

As the spies make their way down the rope, Rahab continues to instruct them. The pursuers have gone east, toward the Israelite camp; Rahab sends the men west, to the low barren hills beyond Jericho, where they can wait until the hunt has died down. (The three days mentioned in verse 16 should probably be interpreted rather loosely as "a few days" to fit with the chronology of Joshua 1:11 and 3:2.) The spies reaffirm their oath to save Rahab and her family, but hedge it with conditions: that she bind a cord in the window, that she and her family remain in the house, and that she keep the spies' visit a secret. Perhaps, feeling more secure once they are off Rahab's roof, they remember Moses' prohibition against any such oath. The crimson cord has been the subject of much speculation. Perhaps the storytellers chose it to symbolize the covenant between Rahab and the spies because of a wordplay; the Hebrew word translated "cord" is a homonym of the word for "hope." Perhaps it is simply a sign marking a brothel, the ancient Near Eastern equivalent of a red-light district (Bird, 1989, 130). The spies eventually return to the east bank of the Jordan and report to Joshua, using words taken from Rahab's speech (2:9).

3. Miracles and Memory: Crossing the Jordan
Joshua 3–4

God has commanded Joshua to "proceed to cross the Jordan" (Josh. 1:2). In chapters 3 and 4, that command is carried out. But what a crossing! The waters part, pile up in heaps, and the people march across the dry riverbed in a great liturgical procession. The miraculous and liturgical ways in which the crossing is portrayed express the deep significance of the event for Israel, exalt Joshua, and, above all, exalt Yahweh. The narrative leaves no question that the crossing and all it signifies are God's accomplishments.

Two issues require attention prior to commenting on the passage: the liturgical character of the narrative and its repetitive, disjointed quality. The spies' positive report and the divine command to take the land prepare the reader for a war story, with armies fording the river and marching on in full battle array. Instead, the crossing unfolds in a manner that seems more liturgical than martial. Levitical priests bear the ark, Israel's central religious symbol, through the midst of miraculously parted waters, followed by the Israelites in formal procession. Joshua preaches (3:10–13), commands the people to establish a memorial (4:2–3), and establishes a catechism (4:6–7, 21–24). After the crossing, the Israelites camp at Gilgal, an important religious sanctuary. In the ancient Near East, war was considered a sacred event; nonetheless, the liturgical character of the narrative is unexpectedly strong. Except for one verse (4:13), religious elements completely eclipse military concerns.

Most commentators believe that the traditions found in chapters 3–4 had their roots in worship settings. Parallels between the Jordan crossing and the miracle at the Red Sea (or Sea of Reeds) (Exod. 14–15) lead many to suggest that Joshua 3–4 evolved as Israelites ritually celebrated their deliverance from Egypt and the gift of the land. Some recent scholars challenge this view of the origins of the crossing traditions, however, arguing that editors added the liturgical elements to an older literary composition. Perhaps creative editors made the additions in order to demonstrate

Joshua's faithfulness or to elevate the significance of the river crossing. In any case, the narrative has an unmistakable cultic quality that reinforces the sacred significance of the gift of the land.

The story of the Jordan crossing and its memorial does not flow smoothly. Repetition and tension disrupt the narrative. For example, twice the narrative reports that the people finished crossing the Jordan (3:17–4:1; 4:10–11). Twelve stones are set up as a memorial to the crossing in Gilgal (4:8; 4:20), but Joshua sets up twelve more stones in the middle of the Jordan (4:9). Twice Joshua instructs the Israelites what to teach their children about the memorial stones (4:6–7; 21–24). The disjointed nature of the narrative may stem partly from the difficulty the ancient writers had narrating simultaneous events. It also stems from the various layers of tradition that grew up as Israel reflected on the significance of the event, in and out of worship, over and over again.

THE CROSSING: GOD'S MIGHTY ACT
Joshua 3

3:1 **Early in the morning Joshua rose and set out from Shittim with all the Israelites, and they came to the Jordan. They camped there before crossing over.** [2] **At the end of three days the officers went through the camp** [3] **and commanded the people, "When you see the ark of the covenant of the LORD your God being carried by the levitical priests, then you shall set out from your place. Follow it,** [4] **so that you may know the way you should go, for you have not passed this way before. Yet there shall be a space between you and it, a distance of about two thousand cubits; do not come any nearer to it."** [5] **Then Joshua said to the people, "Sanctify yourselves; for tomorrow the LORD will do wonders among you."** [6] **To the priests Joshua said, "Take up the ark of the covenant, and pass on in front of the people." So they took up the ark of the covenant and went in front of the people.**

[7] **The LORD said to Joshua, "This day I will begin to exalt you in the sight of all Israel, so that they may know that I will be with you as I was with Moses.** [8] **You are the one who shall command the priests who bear the ark of the covenant, 'When you come to the edge of the waters of the Jordan, you shall stand still in the Jordan.'"** [9] **Joshua then said to the Israelites, "Draw near and hear the words of the LORD your God."** [10] **Joshua said, "By this you shall know that among you is the living God who without fail will drive out from before you the Canaanites, Hittites, Hivites, Perizzites, Girgashites, Amorites, and Jebusites:** [11] **the ark of the covenant of the LORD of all the earth is going to pass before you into the Jordan.** [12] **So now select twelve men from the tribes of Israel, one from each tribe.** [13] **When the soles of the feet of the priests who**

bear the ark of the LORD, the LORD of all the earth, rest in the waters of the Jordan, the waters of the Jordan flowing from above shall be cut off; they shall stand in a single heap."

[14] When the people set out from their tents to cross over the Jordan, the priests bearing the ark of the covenant were in front of the people. [15] Now the Jordan overflows all its banks throughout the time of harvest. So when those who bore the ark had come to the Jordan, and the feet of the priests bearing the ark were dipped in the edge of the water, [16] the waters flowing from above stood still, rising up in a single heap far off at Adam, the city that is beside Zarethan, while those flowing toward the sea of the Arabah, the Dead Sea, were wholly cut off. Then the people crossed over opposite Jericho. [17] While all Israel were crossing over on dry ground, the priests who bore the ark of the covenant of the LORD stood on dry ground in the middle of the Jordan, until the entire nation finished crossing over the Jordan.

Because of the disjointed nature of the passage, the following comments are organized around key themes of the two chapters, rather than the order of the narrative. Clearly, the overarching theme of the two chapters is that by God's power Israel is able to cross the Jordan, just as by God's gift they receive the land.

Despite the words of the familiar spiritual, the Jordan River is neither deep nor wide. It is two to ten feet deep and ninety to one hundred feet wide. It may be forded easily most times of the year. Only when the Jordan is in flood (3:15) is it possible to conceive that crossing it would be a miracle. The Jordan is less a physical barrier than a symbolic boundary.

As a symbol, the Jordan is indeed "deep and wide." The memory of crossing the Jordan was of utmost significance to Israel. Although persistently reminding readers that the eastern tribes are part of Israel, the book of Joshua presupposes that the Jordan serves as the eastern boundary of the promised land. Crossing that boundary, the people move from landless wandering to settlement in their own land.

The narrators depict the crossing as a miraculous event. God parts the waters and the people walk across dry-shod. The miracle is heightened by the reference to the spring floods, when the waters of the Jordan are impassable (3:15), and by the note that the waters piled up at some distance from Jericho, where the people cross. The riverbed was dry from Adam to Jericho, a distance of some twenty-seven kilometers.

Indeed, according to the storytellers the crossing is a mighty act of God, comparable to the Exodus from Egypt. The waters divide, forming a "heap," a rare Hebrew word found in Joshua 3:16, and in the Song of the Sea, Exodus 15:8. Joshua and his people walk across the Jordan on dry ground, just as their parents crossed the sea on dry ground (Josh. 3:17, 4:18; Exod. 14:22). Joshua's role, as he proclaims what God is about to do, resembles the role of Moses at the sea. The result of the crossing is that the Israelites "fear the LORD" (Josh. 4:24), just as they fear God in Exodus 14:31. The comparison between the crossing of the Jordan and the miracle at the sea is explicitly drawn in Joshua 4:23.

The miraculous nature of the crossing stresses its significance and emphasizes that Israel entered the promised land not by its own power but by a divine act. The parallels between the Jordan miracle and the miracle of the sea sets the crossing among God's "wonders" (3:5); it was one of the saving deeds that God did for Israel. The miracle also functions to strengthen Israel's self-understanding. The Israelites are God's people, for whom God has acted and will act. It undergirds Israel's claims to the land. "The LORD of all the earth" (3:13) miraculously gave it to them, driving out the various groups inhabiting Canaan.

The miracle also exalts Joshua, whoes leadership is one theme of the miraculous crossing. The account is framed by God's promise to exalt Joshua and by the narrator's assertion that God had exalted him, demonstrating that God is with Joshua (3:7; 4:14). As a result, the Israelites "stood in awe of" their leader. The Hebrew verb translated "stood in awe of" in 4:14 is the same verb translated "fear" when its object is God in 4:24.

Most important, the miraculous tale of the crossing extols Israel's God. The purpose of the crossing is that Israel shall "know" that "the living God" is among them (3:10). The meaning of the Hebrew word translated "know" extends beyond cognition, relating to experience and acknowledgment. Here, "knowing" God means acknowledging God's sovereignty and recognizing God's presence. "Knowing" that the living God is among them gives the narrative's characters confidence that God has the power and will to drive out the inhabitants of Canaan. For the later audiences, to "know" God is to acknowledge that the divine power that gave Israel its land in Joshua's day can restore the nation's independence and unity in Josiah's time. For Jews in exile, the knowledge offers hope that God will once again give them the land.

Like God's promise to exalt Joshua, the assertion that God's greatness will be made known frames the narrative. The passage just cited (3:10) is echoed at the end of the narrative (4:24): "All the peoples . . . may know that the hand of the LORD is mighty, and so that you may fear the LORD your God forever."

The circle of people who are to "know" God through this miraculous event extends forward in time from Joshua and his people to future generations of Israel. "You shall let your children know . . . the LORD your God dried up the waters of the Jordan . . ." (4:22–23). The event extends outward in space to "all the peoples of the earth" who shall know "that the hand (power) of the LORD is mighty" (4:24). The narrative goes on to assert that the effect of the knowledge on the kings of Canaan was that "their hearts melted" (5:1).

Yahweh's powerful presence is conveyed by the symbol of the ark, the most important of ancient Israel's religious symbols. Beyond the fact that it was a box, what the ark looked like is uncertain. Deuteronomy 10:1–3 envisions a box made of acacia wood. Long after the ark disappears, later writers remembered it as a lavish object plated with gold (Exod. 25:10–22).

Israel's understanding of the significance of the ark evolved over time. In the early period of its history, Israel viewed the ark as the seat or foot-stool of God, invisibly enthroned. Thus, it represented the Sovereign One's powerful presence. Later tradition (Deuteronomy) viewed the ark as a box in which the tablets of the Decalogue were kept and on top of which the Book of the Law was placed. In this view, the ark symbolizes God's covenant with God's people.

Both earlier and later views of the ark are found in the multilayered crossing narrative. The early view that the ark represents God's sovereign presence is seen in its miraculous effect on the river. The Jordan parts as soon as the feet of the bearers of the ark touch the waters. The waters flow again when the bearers of the ark reach the riverbank (4:18). The Deutero-nomic perspective that the ark symbolizes God's covenant with Israel is expressed in the use of titles. The Deuteronomic thinkers called the ark the "ark of covenant," a title found repeatedly in Joshua 3 and 4. The ark also points to God's holiness. The officers instruct the people to stay two thousand cubits (about one thousand yards) away from it because close contact with holiness was dangerous.

Joshua's instructions to the people to "sanctify" themselves (3:5) also stress God's holiness. Elsewhere in the scriptures, ritual sanctification involves prescribed washings and abstaining from sexual intercourse and from certain foods. The people sanctified themselves to prepare for un-usual manifestations of God's power (see Josh. 7:13). Israelite warriors also sanctified themselves in preparation for battle.

The human response to the manifestation of God's power at the Jordan is fear. "Fear" of God has to do with reverence and obedience, and with wholehearted allegiance. The Israelites "fear" the Lord; their opponents "dread" God. When the kings of Canaan hear what God has done, their "hearts melt." "They no longer [have] any spirit."

TO REMEMBER AND TO TEACH
Joshua 4

The story of the memorial stones lifts up two additional appropriate responses to God's mighty act—to remember and to teach.

4:1 **When the entire nation had finished crossing over the Jordan, the LORD said to Joshua:** [2] **"Select twelve men from the people, one from each tribe,** [3] **and command them, 'Take twelve stones from here out of the middle of the Jordan, from the place where the priests' feet stood, carry them over with you, and lay them down in the place where you camp tonight.'"** [4] **Then Joshua summoned the twelve men from the Israelites, whom he had appointed, one from each tribe.** [5] **Joshua said to them, "Pass on before the ark of the LORD your God into the middle of the Jordan, and each of you take up a stone on his shoulder, one for each of the tribes of the Israelites,** [6] **so that this may be a sign among you. When your children ask in time to come, 'What do those stones mean to you?'** [7] **then you shall tell them that the waters of the Jordan were cut off in front of the ark of the covenant of the LORD. When it crossed over the Jordan, the waters of the Jordan were cut off. So these stones shall be to the Israelites a memorial forever."**

[8] **The Israelites did as Joshua commanded. They took up twelve stones out of the middle of the Jordan, according to the number of the tribes of the Israelites, as the LORD told Joshua, carried them over with them to the place where they camped, and laid them down there.** [9] **(Joshua set up twelve stones in the middle of the Jordan, in the place where the feet of the priests bearing the ark of the covenant had stood; and they are there to this day.)**

[10] **The priests who bore the ark remained standing in the middle of the Jordan, until everything was finished that the LORD commanded Joshua to tell the people, according to all that Moses had commanded Joshua. The people crossed over in haste.** [11] **As soon as all the people had finished crossing over, the ark of the LORD, and the priests, crossed over in front of the people.** [12] **The Reubenites, the Gadites, and the half-tribe of Manasseh crossed over armed before the Israelites, as Moses had ordered them.** [13] **About forty thousand armed for war crossed over before the LORD to the plains of Jericho for battle.**

[14] **On that day the LORD exalted Joshua in the sight of all Israel; and they stood in awe of him, as they had stood in awe of Moses, all the days of his life.**

[15] **The LORD said to Joshua,** [16] **"Command the priests who bear the ark of the covenant, to come up out of the Jordan."** [17] **Joshua therefore commanded the priests, "Come up out of the Jordan."** [18] **When the priests bearing the ark of the covenant of the LORD came up from the middle of the Jordan, and the soles of the priests' feet touched dry ground, the waters of the Jordan returned to their place and overflowed all its banks, as before.**

¹⁹ **The people came up out of the Jordan on the tenth day of the first month, and they camped in Gilgal on the east border of Jericho.** ²⁰ **Those twelve stones, which they had taken out of the Jordan, Joshua set up in Gilgal,** ²¹ **saying to the Israelites, "When your children ask their parents in time to come, 'What do these stones mean?'** ²² **then you shall let your children know, 'Israel crossed over the Jordan here on dry ground.'** ²³ **For the LORD your God dried up the waters of the Jordan for you until you crossed over, as the LORD your God did to the Red Sea, which he dried up for us until we crossed over,** ²⁴ **so that all the peoples of the earth may know that the hand of the LORD is mighty, and so that you may fear the LORD your God forever."**

5:1 **When all the kings of the Amorites beyond the Jordan to the west, and all the kings of the Canaanites by the sea, heard that the LORD had dried up the waters of the Jordan for the Israelites until they had crossed over, their hearts melted, and there was no longer any spirit in them, because of the Israelites.**

The story of the miraculous crossing is interwoven with a story of stones set up as a memorial of the event. The stones may have been erected before Israel arose in the land, and may have inspired the story. The name "Gilgal," where the tribes camped, probably means "circle of stones." Within the biblical story, the stones serve as a symbol of Israelite unity. There are twelve, one for each tribe. Most importantly, the stones serve as a memorial to God's act of parting the waters at the Jordan.

The memorial points to the vital role memory plays in faith. What God has done in the past serves as a basis for hope that God will again act in the future. The memorial also serves as the basis of allegiance and obedience. Judges 2:10–15 suggests what happens when Israel does not remember what God has done for them.

Passing the memories on to future generations is an equally vital aspect of faith. The catechism in verses 6–7 and 21–24 underscores the importance of teaching the children the traditions. The catechism follows a form found in instructions for Passover (Exod. 12:26–27) and for the dedication of the firstborn (Exod. 13:14–15), and in explanation of the meaning of the law (Deut. 6:20–24). "When your children ask you . . . you shall say. . . ." The explanation is usually a story of what God has done for Israel. Joshua commands the adult Israelites to teach the stories of the faith explicitly and caringly.

The adults are to tell the children the meaning of the stones in such a way that the story becomes the children's own. It is just barely possible to understand 4:6–7 as action that happened in the past that has historical meaning only. That possibility is eliminated by 4:23. The adults are to draw the children into the story. Note the use of the pronouns "you" and "us." The miracle at the Jordan and the deliverance at the sea were not understood as events that happened long ago and that were therefore finished and forgotten. The deliverance at the sea happened to "us" (the adult generation); the Jordan crossing is something God has done for "you." The catechism functions like the lyrics from the Christian hymn, "Were you there when they crucified my Lord," assuming the answer "yes, I was," or, like the celebration of Eucharist, by which Christians participate again and again in the redeeming death and resurrection of Christ. Through ritual, the Israelites went back to their past and drew their past into the present. They laid claim on God's merciful, mighty acts, so that they and their children might once again encounter God and revere Yahweh their God forever.

4. Rites of Passage
Joshua 5

The journey across the Jordan is accomplished. Israel is encamped in the promised land for the first time. The wars of conquest are about to begin. Israel's encampment at Gilgal comes as a brief lull in the action; the tribes prepare for battle using ritual.

The liturgical character of the story, prominent in chapters 3 and 4, continues through chapter 5. Military themes are present in the opening and closing verses of the chapter. The notice in verse 1 that the indigenous kings' will to resist had melted and the appearance in verses 13–15 of the "commander of the armies of the LORD" remind the reader that the chapter is situated in the midst of conquest narratives; the rituals it narrates are preparation for the upcoming battles and the occupation of the land. The bulk of chapter 5, however, is comprised of accounts of Joshua circumcising the Israelites and their subsequent celebration of Passover. Nelson aptly calls these rituals "rites of passage" (Nelson, 1997, 74). The rituals mark the significance of this transitional moment, as Israel moves into its promised land for the first time, and highlight the sacred nature of Israel's upcoming battles and eventual occupation of Canaan.

Key themes voiced in chapters 1 through 4 continue to weave through chapter 5; Yahweh's agency, Israel's call to obedience, Joshua's leadership, and the identity of Israel as God's covenant people are again asserted. A less dominant voice, heard in Rahab's story, that the Lord who fights for Israel is nonetheless not owned by Israel, sounds in the chapter's closing vignette; the commander of the armies of Yahweh is neither Israelite nor Canaanite.

The narratives in chapter 5 appear to be multilayered. Language that is at times convoluted (especially in vv. 4–7) suggests that different editors have contributed their reflections to the text. Who these editors were and when they wrote is debated. Some scholars believe that the traditions found in the chapter have their roots in an annual festival celebrated at Gilgal. According to this view, the setting that gave rise to much of Joshua 3–6 consisted of liturgical reenactments of the crossing of the Jordan, circumcision of any uncircumcised males (a requirement for participation in Passover), Passover, and a celebration of the conquest of the land. More recently, some scholars argue that the accounts found in chapter 5 originated independently of each other and were brought together at a literary level to tell a story. If so, the liturgical character of the narratives must be understood not as a reflection of their origins but as an indication of the compilers' desire to communicate the sacred character of the crossing and the conquest.

The historical development of circumcision and of Passover is as debated as the question of how the text evolved. Circumcision, as practiced by many of the peoples surrounding Israel, may have been a rite of boys' passage into manhood or a marital rite. Passover and the Feast of Unleavened Bread seem to have been originally two distinct festivals that eventually were combined. Passover may have begun as a pastoral ritual aimed at warding off harm to the flocks, while the Feast of Unleavened Bread seems to be at home among farmers. By the time circumcision is referred to in the biblical texts, the rite is understood as a sign of the covenant and a mark of Israel's national identity. Biblical references to Passover and the Feast of Unleavened Bread view the festivals as celebrations of exodus, that is, of the deliverance from slavery in Egypt.

Gilgal appears to have been an important cult center up through the time of Saul, who was anointed king there, and became important again in the time of the eighth-century prophets. The location of Gilgal must have been somewhere close to Jericho, but its exact location is not known.

5:1 **When all the kings of the Amorites beyond the Jordan to the west, and all the kings of the Canaanites by the sea, heard that the LORD had dried up the waters of the Jordan for the Israelites until they had crossed over, their hearts melted, and there was no longer any spirit in them, because of the Israelites.** **² At that time the LORD said to Joshua, "Make flint knives and circumcise the Israelites a second time."** **³ So Joshua made flint knives, and circumcised the Israelites at Gibeath-haaraloth.** **⁴ This is the reason why Joshua circumcised them: all the males of the people who came out of Egypt, all the warriors, had died during the journey through the wilderness after they had come out of Egypt.** **⁵ Although all the people who came out had been circumcised, yet all the people born on the journey through the wilderness after they had come out of Egypt had not been circumcised.** **⁶ For the Israelites traveled forty years in the wilderness, until all the nation, the warriors who came out of Egypt, perished, not having listened to the voice of the LORD. To them the LORD swore that he would not let them see the land that he had sworn to their ancestors to give us, a land flowing with milk and honey.** **⁷ So** it was their children, whom he raised up in their place, that Joshua circumcised; for they were uncircumcised, because they had not been circumcised on the way.

[8] When the circumcising of all the nation was done, they remained in their places in the camp until they were healed. [9] The LORD said to Joshua, "Today I have rolled away from you the disgrace of Egypt." And so that place is called Gilgal to this day.

[10] While the Israelites were camped in Gilgal they kept the passover in the evening on the fourteenth day of the month in the plains of Jericho. [11] On the day after the passover, on that very day, they ate the produce of the land, unleavened cakes and parched grain. [12] The manna ceased on the day they ate the produce of the land, and the Israelites no longer had manna; they ate the crops of the land of Canaan that year.

[13] Once when Joshua was by Jericho, he looked up and saw a man standing before him with a drawn sword in his hand. Joshua went to him and said to him, "Are you one of us, or one of our adversaries?" [14] He replied, "Neither; but as commander of the army of the LORD I have now come." And Joshua fell on his face to the earth and worshiped, and he said to him, "What do you command your servant, my lord?" [15] The commander of the army of the LORD said to Joshua, "Remove the sandals from your feet, for the place where you stand is holy." And Joshua did so.

THE INDIGENOUS KINGS
Joshua 5:1

Rahab had assured the spies that "all the inhabitants of the land melt in fear before" Israel because of rumors of how Yahweh had delivered them at the sea and rumors of their conquest of kings east of the Jordan (Josh. 2:9–10). After the miraculous parting of the Jordan, the "hearts" (wills, minds) of even the kings of the land "melt" (5:1). The terms "Amorite" and "Canaanite" are used in varying ways in the Bible. Here the "Amorite" kings are in the hill country; the Canaanite kings rule in the coastal region. All of them lose their will to resist Israel when they hear what its God has done. The victory won for Israel will be won by Yahweh.

CIRCUMCISION AT GILGAL
Joshua 5:2–9

Circumcision was practiced by many of the peoples of the ancient Near East. Scholars speculate that originally the custom may have been a rite of passage for adolescent males or a fertility ritual. In Israel, circumcision became a central sign of the peoples' covenant with Yahweh. According to the stories handed down by Israel's priests, circumcision is integrally related to the divine gift of the land. God promises Abraham, "I will establish my covenant between me and you, and your offspring after you throughout their generation, for an everlasting covenant, to be God to you and to your offspring after you. And I will give to you, and to your offspring after you . . . all the land of Canaan . . ." (Gen. 17:7–8). Abraham and his descendents are to signify their embrace of the covenant by circumcising themselves and their sons. "You shall circumcise the flesh of your foreskins, and it shall be a sign of the covenant between me and you. Throughout your generations every male among you shall be circumcised when he is eight days old . . ." (Gen. 17:11–12). In Joshua 5:2–9, the Israelite warriors prepare for battle and for life as God's people in the land by undergoing circumcision, the mark of their relationship with the God who gives them that land.

The story line is found in verses 2–3 and 8–9. The vignette begins and ends with a divine utterance (vv. 2, 9), a reminder that God's word moves Israel's history. The people's response is obedience. In a now familiar pattern, God's command is directed to Joshua, who carries it out among Israel. That the rite is to be carried out with "flint knives" (v. 2) may indicate the antiquity of the practice or the inherently conservative nature of ritual. The circumcision is a "second time" because, according to the story, the people had let the practice lapse during their wilderness wanderings.

The narrative includes two etiologies, that is, folkloric explanations of a name, an unusual feature of the land, or some other circumstance. The story of Joshua circumcising the Israelite males is used to explain the name of a hill in verse 3. The hill "Gibeath-haaraloth"—"Hill of Foreskins"— may actually have received its name because circumcisions were customarily carried out there, or because at that place people ritually buried the circumcised foreskins.

A second etiology found in verse 9 uses the story to explain the name "Gilgal." God is supposed to have "rolled away the disgrace of Egypt" through the circumcision of Israel's males. A folk tradition derived "Gilgal" from *galal*, the Hebrew verb translated "rolled away."

Commentators debate the meaning of the phrase "disgrace of Egypt." Since God removes the disgrace by having Joshua circumcise the Israelite males, perhaps the storytellers viewed the Israelites' previously uncircumcised state as disgraceful disobedience of God's command (Lev. 12:3; Gen. 17:11–12). On the other hand, the word translated "disgrace" usually refers to insult, loss of social status, or shattering and even victimizing circumstances, rather than to guilty behavior. More likely, the "disgrace of Egypt" is the people's enslavement in Egypt. Divine deliverance of the Hebrews is not complete until the former slaves are settled on their own land as God's free, covenant people. Circumcision, the sign of covenant and promise, marks their new status. They are no longer slaves, no longer wilderness wanderers.

Later editors who felt the need to explain why the Israelite men had not been circumcised in infancy added verses 4–7. The repetitive nature of the explanation suggests that the verses represent the thoughts of more than one writer. Apparently circumcision was a focus of intense reflection for ancient Israelites.

According to verses 4–7, the male Israelites who escaped Egypt had indeed been circumcised, but because of their rebelliousness, they were not allowed to enter the promised land. (See Deut. 1:35). The next generation, though, was allowed to enter Canaan. They were born in the wilderness where, presumably, rigorous conditions prevented Israel from carrying out the command to circumcise its sons.

PASSOVER AND PASSAGE
Joshua 5:10–12

Passover is Israel's great central ritual celebrating God's deliverance of the people from slavery in Egypt. In Passover, Israel commemorates God's having "passed over," that is, spared, their firstborn sons while slaughtering the firstborn males of Egypt. According to Israel's traditions, this tenth plague finally drove Pharaoh to let the people go (Exod. 12). Through the Passover ritual, each new generation of Israel becomes part of God's saving act. When the child asks the parent why they celebrate the Passover feast, the parent answers, "God spared our houses" (Exod. 12:27). The Deuteronomic authors tell their late monarchical audience, "God brought you out of Egypt" (Deut. 16:1).

The celebration of Passover in Gilgal ties the conquest to the deliverance from Egypt while also signaling transition to a new era. The journey out of Egypt begins and ends with Passover (Exod. 12; Josh. 5:10–12). The Bible recounts the ancient Israelite celebration of six Passovers; each marks a pivotal moment in the people's story. The original Passover demarcates the end of slavery in Egypt (Exod. 12); the Passover at Sinai marks the end of their sojourn there (Num. 9); Joshua's Passover occurs as Israel enters its land (Josh. 5:10–12); the reforms of King Hezekiah and King Josiah culminate in Passover celebrations (2 Chr. 30; 2 Kings 23:21–23); finally, Ezra (6:19–22) depicts the Judeans celebrating the rebuilding of the temple with a Passover meal. Passover strengthens the identity of the people as a community whose roots go deep into history and commemorates the saving mercy of God. Such celebration is especially significant at points of transition. The Israelites begin life in the land with Passover.

The Passover meal is followed by the Festival of Unleavened Bread. For seven days, no leaven is allowed in any home in Israel (Exod. 12:15–20; Deut. 16:3). Within Israel's remembered history, the Festival of Unleavened Bread is integrally linked to Passover and commemorates the exodus, when those fleeing Egypt had no time to bake leavened bread.

The Deuteronomistic Historians give the festival a new level of meaning. They depict Joshua's Passover as the first time Israelites ate food harvested from the land. The shift from manna, the food God provides Israel in the wilderness, to Canaanite produce is another indication that entering the land of Canaan is a momentous transition. The wilderness period, the period of manna, is over. A new epoch has begun, in which God provides for God's people in new ways.

THE COMMANDER OF THE ARMY OF THE LORD
Joshua 5:13–15

Chapter 5 concludes with a strange, almost haunting tale. Joshua, meeting an armed man, reasonably assumes that he is a warrior and asks, "Friend or foe?" The man refuses to identify himself as either. Naming himself the "commander of the army of the LORD," he reveals his divine character to Joshua, who falls down in worship. As the story continues, the commander speaks to Joshua in words quoted nearly verbatim from the story of God's appearance to Moses in the burning bush: "Remove the sandals from your feet, for the place on which you are standing is holy ground" (Exod. 3:5).

The commander is a self-manifestation of God. A number of such theophanies occur in the Bible, often at critical junctures in the life of the individual or the life of the nation. God appears to Moses in the burning bush to give him his commission (Exod. 3); the angel of the Lord finds Gideon hovering in a winepress to call him to lead his people in a fight for freedom (Judg. 6:11–18). That a divine being appears to Joshua just before he leads Israel in their battle against Jericho, their first military action in

Canaan, is not unexpected. What is surprising is the enigmatic nature of what the divine figure says and does, or rather, does not say or do. There is no call, no oracle of victory, no command. Rather, immediately before the Israelite's first battle in the land, God appears to Joshua as a divine warrior, declaring God's self to be neither friend nor foe, neither "one of us" nor "one of the adversaries," and then insists that the place is holy.

Nearly all commentators interpret verses 13–15 as a positive oracle. Comparing the vignette with the story of Moses' call, they view the appearance of the commander of the army of Yahweh as a call and commissioning story. Alternatively, commentators understand the appearance of the divine warrior as an assurance that God will fight on Israel's side and thus ensure its victory.

The common interpretation of the story has difficulties, however. First, as a call narrative or an oracle of victory, the passage is highly redundant. There have already been three stories of the commissioning of Joshua (Deut. 31:7–8, 23; Josh. 1:2–9) and several promises that Israel will prevail (Josh. 1:2–9; 2:9–11; 3:10). Moreover, no words in this passage indicate that the commander is on Israel's side. Rather, the commander explicitly asserts that he is *neither* "one of us" nor "one of our adversaries," neither friend nor foe. Finally, elsewhere in the Bible, divine figures with drawn swords are hostile to the recipient of the vision. Such divine figures bring pestilence on David's people (1 Chr. 21:16) and threaten to kill Balaam (Num. 22:23).

Rather than convey assurance of victory, the story of the commander of the Lord's army seems to ward off triumphalistic assumptions that God takes sides permanently. The passage raises three themes. First, God appears as the warrior whose power will determine the outcome of the battle. In this case, Yahweh has already promised to give Israel the land. Israel's role is to dedicate itself to God (as it has, through circumcision and Passover) and to obey the Lord's commands (exemplified in Joshua's ready obedience [v. 2] and readiness to be commanded [v. 14]). Second, the divine warrior is not bound to any side; the commander of the army of the Lord maintains his freedom. Together with the stories of Rahab and the Gibeonites, Joshua 5:13–15 sets limits on what could otherwise be interpreted as unmitigated ethnocentrism in the book of Joshua. Third, the sketch asserts the awesomeness of God and the holiness of God's land. God's word and will are active in Israel's battles for the land. They are thus holy, as the land God gives Israel is holy. The words of the commander suggest that Joshua's vocation is a matter of awe, not of arrogance. God and God's gifts may not be taken for granted.

The second and third themes come down, finally, to the same thing. If Joshua—and we—keep hold of the awareness that we are creatures and servants of God, not God's owners, we will not be tempted to believe that we can domesticate the Lord, treating the Holy One of Israel as a creature whom we can control or possess. If we recognize that the place on which we stand is holy—if, that is, we take off our shoes—we will not mistake God's deep concern for us and our community as divine disregard for others.

5. And the Walls Came Tumblin' Down
Joshua 6

The story of the defeat of Jericho is the best known of the conquest narratives. People who know nothing else about Joshua know that he "fit the battle of Jericho and the walls came tumblin' down." The story has been an emblem of hope and inspiration for many—a witness to the miraculous power of God to overcome obstacles that, humanly speaking, are insurmountable. The miraculous victory at Jericho is supposed to have inspired the ancient freedom fighter Judas Maccabee (2 Macc. 12:15). African American captives found comfort in recalling the tumblin' walls of Jericho. For others, the story represents the worst of the Bible. A violent God commands and leads Israel to invade Canaan, exterminate its conquered population, and lay claim to its lands. The story has been used to legitimize genocide and oppression. European settlers identified themselves with the Israelites in their wars against American Indians. Afrikaaners drew on the conquest narratives as they developed the theological underpinnings of apartheid.

The fame, or notoriety, of the story accurately reflects its pivotal role in Joshua 1–12. For good or ill, many of the main themes of Joshua 1–12 are concentrated in the account of Jericho. Key threads of the book of Joshua weave through this paradigmatic story of Israel's invasion of Canaan, including the sovereign agency of Yahweh, who gives Israel the land; the obedience and the worship that constitute Israel's role in the conquest; the importance of Joshua as mediator and leader; the image of God as warrior and war as sacred; and the command to devote the enemy to destruction. Its liturgical shape provides a clue to its purpose. The genre is not historical or military reporting, but theological, even doxological, literature. Its purpose is not to recount "what really happened" but to extol the God who brought Israel into being and gave the nation its land. That characterization should not imply that the account is untrue. Rather, the truth of this liturgically shaped story has less to do with facts about something that happened long ago and more to do with the ongoing reality of divine sovereignty and divine generosity.

Given the purpose of the narrative, that archaeological evidence casts doubt on the historicity of the Jericho account should not come as a surprise. Because of its importance in the conquest narratives, numerous archaeological teams have investigated the site of Jericho, *tell es sultan*. They have found that the *tell* is extraordinarily ancient. It was first inhabited around 9000 B.C.E.; walls and a tower built in 8000–7000 B.C.E. make neolithic Jericho the oldest known walled city. Over the millennia since *tell es sultan* was first settled, periods when the site supported a flourishing population alternated with periods when it was abandoned or sparsely inhabited. According to the most recent and best archaeological study, few if any people lived in Jericho during the time Israel arose in Canaan (the latter part of the thirteenth century).

In the 1930s, an archaeologist thought he had uncovered evidence of Joshua's triumph: mud brick walls that had collapsed possibly as a result of an earthquake. In the 1950s, a more scientific investigation of the site demonstrated that the mud brick walls had actually fallen centuries before Israel came on the scene. Next to no evidence was found of occupation of the site during the thirteenth and twelfth centuries B.C.E. Even allowing for the effects of erosion, had there been a fortified town at that time, some signs of its existence would remain. At best, Jericho was a poor, small, unwalled village when Joshua was supposed to have conquered it. More likely, it was an uninhabited ruin.

The site, two kilometers northwest of modern Jericho, is strategically important. It controls the fords and thus movement from the Transjordan (the lands east of the Jordan) into the Judean hill country. It dominates the Jordan Valley. Moreover, the site possesses two springs, which in that hot, arid, low-lying land are vital. When the Deuteronomistic Historians compiled their work, Jericho was an important city, dominating its region and guarding the route to Jerusalem. These historians, reflecting on Israel's conquest of Canaan, would logically place its first battle at Jericho.

6:1 Now Jericho was shut up inside and out because of the Israelites; no one came out and no one went in. ² The LORD said to Joshua, "See, I have handed Jericho over to you, along with its king and soldiers. ³ You shall march around the city, all the warriors circling the city once. Thus you shall do for six days, ⁴ with seven priests bearing seven trumpets of rams' horns before the ark. On the seventh day you shall march around the city seven times, the priests blowing the trumpets. ⁵ When they make a long blast with the ram's horn, as soon as you hear the sound of the trumpet, then all the people shall shout with a

great shout; and the wall of the city will fall down flat, and all the people shall charge straight ahead." ⁶ So Joshua son of Nun summoned the priests and said to them, "Take up the ark of the covenant, and have seven priests carry seven trumpets of rams' horns in front of the ark of the Lord." ⁷ To the people he said, "Go forward and march around the city; have the armed men pass on before the ark of the Lord."

⁸ As Joshua had commanded the people, the seven priests carrying the seven trumpets of rams' horns before the Lord went forward, blowing the trumpets, with the ark of the covenant of the Lord following them. ⁹ And the armed men went before the priests who blew the trumpets; the rear guard came after the ark, while the trumpets blew continually. ¹⁰ To the people Joshua gave this command: "You shall not shout or let your voice be heard, nor shall you utter a word, until the day I tell you to shout. Then you shall shout." ¹¹ So the ark of the Lord went around the city, circling it once; and they came into the camp, and spent the night in the camp.

¹² Then Joshua rose early in the morning, and the priests took up the ark of the Lord. ¹³ The seven priests carrying the seven trumpets of rams' horns before the ark of the Lord passed on, blowing the trumpets continually. The armed men went before them, and the rear guard came after the ark of the Lord, while the trumpets blew continually. ¹⁴ On the second day they marched around the city once and then returned to the camp. They did this for six days.

¹⁵ On the seventh day they rose early, at dawn, and marched around the city in the same manner seven times. It was only on that day that they marched around the city seven times. ¹⁶ And at the seventh time, when the priests had blown the trumpets, Joshua said to the people, "Shout! For the Lord has given you the city. ¹⁷ The city and all that is in it shall be devoted to the Lord for destruction. Only Rahab the prostitute and all who are with her in her house shall live because she hid the messengers we sent. ¹⁸ As for you, keep away from the things devoted to destruction, so as not to covet and take any of the devoted things and make the camp of Israel an object for destruction, bringing trouble upon it. ¹⁹ But all silver and gold, and vessels of bronze and iron, are sacred to the Lord; they shall go into the treasury of the Lord." ²⁰ So the people shouted, and the trumpets were blown. As soon as the people heard the sound of the trumpets, they raised a great shout, and the wall fell down flat; so the people charged straight ahead into the city and captured it. ²¹ Then they devoted to destruction by the edge of the sword all in the city, both men and women, young and old, oxen, sheep, and donkeys.

²² Joshua said to the two men who had spied out the land, "Go into the prostitute's house, and bring the woman out of it and all who belong to her, as you swore to her." ²³ So the young men who had been spies went in and brought Rahab out, along with her father, her mother, her brothers, and all who belonged to her—they brought all her kindred out—and set them out-

side the camp of Israel. ^{24} They burned down the city, and everything in it; only the silver and gold, and the vessels of bronze and iron, they put into the treasury of the house of the LORD. ^{25} But Rahab the prostitute, with her family and all who belonged to her, Joshua spared. Her family has lived in Israel ever since. For she hid the messengers whom Joshua sent to spy out Jericho.
^{26} Joshua then pronounced this oath, saying,

> "Cursed before the LORD be anyone who tries
>   to build this city—this Jericho!
> At the cost of his firstborn he shall lay its foundation,
>   and at the cost of his youngest he shall set up its gates!"

^{27} So the LORD was with Joshua; and his fame was in all the land.

A LITURGICAL VICTORY
Joshua 6:1–20

The account of Israel's victory at Jericho is highly symbolic and ritualized. Ancient Israel, like its neighbors, did not separate war and religion. Wars were to be fought by consecrated warriors at the instigation of, or at least with the authorization of, the deity. Priests accompanied the troops into battle. Paraphernalia closely associated with the cult was also found in military settings. Trumpets, used liturgically to announce holy days and festivals, appear in battle scenes, mustering or dismissing the troops, raising an alarm, or signaling victory or retreat. In Gideon's battle against the Midianites, a story in many ways similar to the Jericho account, trumpets serve as a weapon of war (Judg. 7:16–23). The ark, the most holy of Israel's liturgical objects, was carried into battle as a manifestation of God's presence, offering protection and a rallying point (1 Sam. 4:5). Israel won battles because God fought with and for the people.

In Joshua 6, the religious dimension is so intensified that it eclipses the military aspect of the story. The opening verse of the account describes a state of siege, while the end of the narrative describes the carnage of battle (vv. 21, 24). The heart of the account, however, is liturgical. Rather than surrounding Jericho for battle, warriors, priests, and rearguard march around the city in formal procession. No human military action is involved in the destruction of the walls; only ceremonial trumpet blowing and shouts signal Israel's participation in the victory. The constant repetition of words associated with worship—trumpet or ram's horn, ark, and the sacred number "seven"—contribute to the liturgical flavor of the passage, as does its repetitive structure. The narrative has the kind of circularity found in ritual rather than the linear, fast-moving story line of a battle account.

The liturgical character of the story provides important clues to its message. First, liturgy is doxological; its primary purpose is to praise God. The liturgical shape of the Jericho account expresses the storytellers' conviction that Israel did not occupy Jericho (or Canaan) by its own efforts. Divine action, not human force or valor, brought the mighty walls down. The ark, the same symbol of divine presence that stopped the waters of the Jordan, now signals the collapse of Jericho's defenses.

The assertion that God is giving Jericho to the Israelites frames the account. The story begins with a word that is at once an oracle of assurance of victory and an assertion that the source of victory is God: "I have handed Jericho over to you" (literally, "have given Jericho into your hand") (v. 2). Joshua affirms the oracle in verse 16: "The LORD has given you the city" (literally, "given the city into your hand)." The action is carried out in such a way as to leave no doubt at all. The walls are breached and the city conquered by the action of God.

Second, the liturgical character of the text underscores the importance and the nature of human participation in the conquest. Israel has a significant role in the defeat of Jericho. Presumably, had the Israelites not marched and shouted, Jericho would have remained inviolable. The people's shout brings down the walls. But the way in which the Israelites participate in the battle shows that they do not achieve victory by their own strength or merit. The story does not speak of human strategizing or human feats of war. Rather, the role of Israel is twofold: obedience and praise. The now-familiar pattern reappears: God instructs Joshua (vv. 2–5) and Joshua communicates God's instructions to the people (vv. 6–7, 10), who execute the divine commands. Israel triumphs not because of its strength, but because of its obedience.

Joshua's and Israel's obedience is neither wooden nor unthinking, however. Joshua *interprets* the instructions that God gives him. God's command includes no details about the order of the procession; Joshua places the armed men before the ark and the rearguard afterwards. Joshua instructs the priests to blow the trumpets continually during the first six days they circle the city. Indeed, Joshua and Israel even set aside a divine law. The messengers whom Joshua sent to spy out Jericho had promised Rahab, the Canaanite woman who saved them from the king of Jericho, that they would spare her and her family. The promise directly violates the Deuteronomic law that no Canaanite should be spared (Deut. 20:16–18). Yet Joshua determines that upholding the spies' covenantal obligation to Rahab is more important than carrying out the law. The story offers no hint that Joshua's judgment was wrong. The first role of the people is thoughtful obedience.

The people are to obey and also to worship. In ritual, the participant acknowledges, and thus knows at a new level, the sovereign power of God. Whether or not the origins of the passage trace back to a religious festival, the liturgical shape draws the reader into a ritual celebration of Yahweh's mighty deeds.

Third, the liturgical character of the story underlines the archetypal nature of the conquest of Jericho. Ritual lifts its participants out of linear time. The liturgical celebration of the "walls tumblin' down" suggests that the account is concerned not with what happened at a particular moment in history, but with what God has regularly done, is doing, and can be trusted to do in the future. The passage is an archetypal story showing that God accomplished for Israel what it could not do on its own. The story-tellers use the language of liturgy and miracle to express their conviction that the land was Israel's by virtue of divine gift.

HOLY WAR AND *HEREM*
Joshua 6:21

The battle of Jericho brings together key issues and themes in the conquest narratives. Among them, presented with particular clarity, is the under-standing that God is a warrior who fights with and for Israel, that war is sacred, and that obedience to divine Torah requires Israel to "devote to destruction" the Canaanites whom it conquers (cf. Deut. 20:16–18).

Israel, like the nations surrounding it, saw no split between the spheres of religion and war. God was Israel's sovereign; as king, God waged war. The conduct of war, under divine command, involved seeking a divine word to initiate battle, consecrating the human warriors to the service of God, and attributing victory to Yahweh. Numerous biblical passages, early and late, picture God as a divine warrior who fought with and for Israel, spreading panic among its enemies.

Prior to Deuteronomy, Israel was familiar with the concept of *herem*, "devotion to destruction," as an occasional phenomenon, prompted by a vow or a prophetic oracle. The nations surrounding Israel appear to have had a similar concept and practice. A ninth-century-B.C.E. inscription by the Moabite king, Mesha, brags that he retook cities in the east of Jordan that Israel had conquered, and in the case of one, devoted (*hrm*) its seven thousand citizens to Moab's god, Chemosh, slaughtering them all.

The Deuteronomistic Historians systematized the Israelite under-standing of holy war. Devoting conquered peoples to destruction was no longer optional. Rather, all Canaanite people were subject to destruction by divine command. Joshua 10:40 reads, "So Joshua defeated the whole land, the hill country and the Negeb and the lowland and the slopes, and all their kings; he left no one remaining, but utterly destroyed all that breathed, *as the* LORD *God of Israel commanded*" (italics added). The Deuteronomistic thinkers provided a rationale for the slaughter: concern for the purity and exclusivity of worship of Yahweh. If allowed to live, the Canaanites would teach Israel to worship their deities, and so abandon the true God.

The notions that war is holy and that God's sovereign rule includes the exercise of violent force are problematic. The idea that the warrior God requires and participates in genocidal destruction of conquered peoples is among the most troublesome in the Bible. We cannot and should not try to eliminate the offensiveness of *herem*. As Patrick Miller writes, "It must be said from the beginning that there is no real way to make such reports palatable to the minds and hearts of contemporary readers and believers. There is certainly no way such reports instruct our lives in the matter of the conduct of war or in dealing with enemies. We have learned too much from the Scriptures about the humane treatment of other persons . . . and about another way of dealing with enemies: with the power of love rather than hatred, belligerence, or destruction" (Miller, 1990, 40).

We ought not try to whitewash problematic biblical texts or themes. Rather, we ought to attempt to understand them in the time periods out of which they emerged and in light of their literary contexts. Further, we ought to wrestle with them long enough to learn what questions or challenges they may pose for us.

Relatively powerful nations have used the Joshua narratives to legitimate invasion, exploitation, and slaughter of less powerful peoples. As Richard Nelson points out, for most of their history, Israel and Judah were relatively weak, indigenous peoples struggling to keep hold of their land against constant threats (Nelson, 1997, 18), particularly during the times that the Deuteronomistic History was compiled.

The compilers and editors of the book of Joshua gave it its decisive shape during two time periods: the reign of King Josiah in the late seventh century and the period of exile in the mid-sixth century B.C.E. The prominence of holy war themes, particularly the notion of *herem*, or "utter destruction," is best understood in relation to those two time periods.

Josiah reigned as centuries of Assyrian domination of Israel and Judah were coming to an end. Assyria had demolished Israel, the northern kingdom, in the late eighth century B.C.E. After Judah led an abortive revolt, Assyria reduced the southern kingdom to a fraction of its former territory and imposed onerous tribute on it. Besides its material losses, Judah suffered a loss of pride and identity.

In the latter part of the seventh century B.C.E., Assyria, weakened by internal conflict, released its grip over Judah. King Josiah, taking advantage of Assyrian weakness, embarked on a program of nationalistic expansion and religious reform. He attempted to expand Judah to its original borders and even to reincorporate the northern kingdom, which had been separate for some three hundred years.

The stories in Joshua, re-presenting Israel's past as one nation—with one central leader, under the rule of one God—supported Josiah's nationalistic program. Nelson and others suggest that the stories were not intended to function as historical reports, nor even as models for Josiah's own military campaign, but as a "myth of origins" to bolster Judah's national identity and pride. They may have also been saber rattling, designed to intimidate into submission Judahites and Israelites who resisted Josiah's program.

Renee Whiterabbit, a HoChunk tribeswoman, helped me understand how the stories may have functioned. Ms. Whiterabbit was a storyteller for her clan. She said that the Joshua narratives are the kinds of stories she might tell to convince young HoChunk men that they were warriors descended from warriors, in order to instill in them pride, courage, and tribal identity, and to help them resist assimilation into the dominant culture.

The mythical or metaphorical way in which the conquest narratives would have functioned is even clearer when one considers them in the context of exile. The Babylonians conquered Judah in 587 B.C.E., destroying its temple, ending its dynasty, razing much of the city, exiling the elite of Judah's citizens, and colonizing those that remained. The conquest was a disaster of overwhelming proportions. Survivors must have asked why such a tragedy befell them: *Was God powerless to protect them? Indifferent to their suffering? Unjust?* The Judeans, powerless and colonized or exiled, must have despaired of ever recovering their own land.

In such a setting, conquest narratives function to provide an explanation of the people's suffering that justifies God and yet offers hope. Judah suffered defeat because it had been unfaithful to Yahweh; the Canaanites seduced Judah to worship their gods. Hope lay in the mercy of God, who had the power to do for Israel what it could not do for itself: reestablish its land. God, not the people, acquired Israel's land for it in the first place, and God could restore the land once again.

Understanding the themes in historical context does not eliminate the ambiguity inherent in imaging God as a warrior, nor does it make palatable the notion of divinely authored ethnic cleansing. Understanding does, however, rule out naive and ahistorical uses of Joshua to support the exploitation of powerless people by powerful aggressors. The narrators apparently did not intend the stories to be treated literally, as patterns for conduct in war. Nor are they tales of a dominant people. The relationship between Europeans and American Indians, or between Afrikaaners and black South Africans, is not analogous to the relationship between Judeans and the Assyrians.

Consider also a second set of contexts: the interpreters' own. Where we stand socially and politically makes a difference in the message that a biblical text has for us. Communities struggling to free themselves from oppression have found comfort, strength, and courage in the belief that God fights with and for them. The story of Jericho serves as a metaphor for God's power to do the impossible on behalf of God's people. For relatively powerless people to embrace the conquest stories as metaphors is in line with how they functioned for their earliest audiences.

Communities of relative power and privilege may need to let the text confront them with questions rather than answers. For them, embracing the way God is present in Joshua—as a divine warrior ruling through violence—may not be possible. Attention to the claims of the text forces one to wrestle with the questions about the nature of war, and especially the role of God in war. The Deuteronomists insisted that no sphere was outside the realm of God's presence and rule. Contemporary people need to hear that word, even as we may need to rethink the relationship between God and war.

The third context helpful to understanding the stories is literary. The Deuteronomic war laws (Deut. 20) and the Deuteronomistic Historians' insistence that Joshua had carried out those laws, appear absolute and unambiguous. All Canaanites were to be killed; at the battle of Jericho, and in subsequent conquests, Joshua ordered the army to devote all of their enemies to destruction.

Within the larger literary context of the book of Joshua, the destruction is apparently neither as complete nor as absolute as it first appears. The story of Jericho is closely linked to three other stories in Joshua: the story of Rahab (Josh. 2); the story of Achan (Josh. 7); and the account of the Gibeonites (Josh. 9).

The Israelites enter into covenant with Rahab without censor. The Gibeonites, another group of indigenous people, trick Israel into believing that they have come from a far distant land, and thus persuade Israel to make a covenant with them. As with Rahab, Joshua ratifies the covenant; again, the editors offer no sign of disapproval.

The story of Achan offers a reverse image of Rahab, the outsider who, by faith in Yahweh and faithfulness towards God's people, becomes an insider. Achan *is* an insider, a member of the favored tribe of Judah. He resists Yahweh, stealing devoted objects. By his disobedience, the insider becomes an outsider and is put to death.

An examination of the larger literary context of the story of Jericho unveils that the belief that Israel should slaughter the Canaanites is not so absolute. At least three times, Joshua violates the command (Rahab, the Gibeonites, and in Joshua 24). He is not censured for these lapses. Additionally, the clearly drawn distinction between "them" and "us," between Canaanite and Israelite, begins to break down. Finally, membership in the people of God appears to be determined by faithfulness to Yahweh, not by ethnicity.

6. THE BATTLE OF AI: A CAUTIONARY TALE
Joshua 7–8:29

At Jericho, God gives victory. At Ai, God shows that the gift is not unconditional. The Israelites' initial assault results in a rout, a disaster that the narrator unequivocally ascribes to Israel's sin. Only after the Israelites identify the offender and purge themselves of guilt are they able to conquer Ai. Strikingly, the disobedience of a single person, Achan, is responsible for the guilt and defeat of the whole people. The account presupposes a view of community solidarity foreign to our more individualistic age.

If God's gift is conditional, dependent upon faithfulness, then it does *not* belong to Israel by virtue of ethnicity. Nationality is no guarantee of election. The fate of Achan, especially in contrast to the fate of Rahab, makes clear that faithfulness, not ethnicity alone, defines who belongs to the people of God.

Scholars concur that the account of the battle of Ai (Josh. 7:1–8:29) is comprised of two originally independent stories. The first narrates the Israelites' defeat, then their subsequent victory over the Canaanite city. Sometime before the Deuteronomistic History was compiled, an editor inserted the tale of Achan's sin and punishment into the battle account. Splicing the two traditions reframed the meaning of the defeat of Ai. Instead of ascribing Israel's failure to overconfidence, the combined story traced defeat to faithlessness. At the same time, the significance of Achan's execution is modified; rather than simply punishment, his death becomes understood as an act of purification.

As with the battle of Jericho, the writers who compiled Joshua 7 and 8 were not interested in providing a disinterested account of historical events. The story of Ai is a cautionary tale, urging obedience lest one suffer the fate of Achan. The narrative also makes a theological assertion: Disaster comes not because of divine powerlessness or divine capriciousness, but because of divine judgment. Israel sinned.

Given that the purpose of the story is to teach, not to report, readers should neither be shocked nor dismayed that archaeological evidence does not support its historical reliability. During the late Bronze Age, the time that Israel emerged in the land, Ai was uninhabited. By the time the narratives in Joshua 7–8 were told, Ai was an impressive ruin. Indeed, the name *ha-Ai* means "ruin," just as the modern Arabic name of the site, *et Tell*, refers to an artificial hill created as subsequent generations built over the remains of the site's previous occupants. In its current form, the purpose of the story goes beyond etiology, beyond explaining the existence of impressive ruins and stone cairns. The narrative preaches obedience and warns that faithlessness leads to disaster. The "happy ending" of chapter 8 urges the possibility of reversing loss by eliminating the community's offenses and obeying God once again.

THE SIN OF ACHAN
Joshua 7

7:1 But the Israelites broke faith in regard to the devoted things: Achan son of Carmi son of Zabdi son of Zerah, of the tribe of Judah, took some of the devoted things; and the anger of the LORD burned against the Israelites.

² Joshua sent men from Jericho to Ai, which is near Beth-aven, east of Bethel, and said to them, "Go up and spy out the land." And the men went up and spied out Ai. ³ Then they returned to Joshua and said to him, "Not all the people need go up; about two or three thousand men should go up and attack Ai. Since they are so few, do not make the whole people toil up there." ⁴ So about three thousand of the people went up there; and they fled before the men of Ai. ⁵ The men of Ai killed about thirty-six of them, chasing them from outside the gate as far as Shebarim and killing them on the slope. The hearts of the people melted and turned to water.

⁶ Then Joshua tore his clothes, and fell to the ground on his face before the ark of the LORD until the evening, he and the elders of Israel; and they put dust on their heads. ⁷ Joshua said, "Ah, Lord GOD! Why have you brought this people across the Jordan at all, to hand us over to the Amorites so as to destroy us? Would that we had been content to settle beyond the Jordan! ⁸ O Lord, what can I say, now that Israel has turned their backs to their enemies! ⁹ The Canaanites and all the inhabitants of the land will hear of it, and surround us, and cut off our name from the earth. Then what will you do for your great name?"

¹⁰ The LORD said to Joshua, "Stand up! Why have you fallen upon your face? ¹¹ Israel has sinned; they have transgressed my covenant that I imposed on them. They have taken some of the devoted things; they have stolen, they have acted deceitfully, and they have put them among their own belongings.

[12] Therefore the Israelites are unable to stand before their enemies; they turn their backs to their enemies, because they have become a thing devoted for destruction themselves. I will be with you no more, unless you destroy the devoted things from among you. [13] Proceed to sanctify the people, and say, 'Sanctify yourselves for tomorrow; for thus says the LORD, the God of Israel, "There are devoted things among you, O Israel; you will be unable to stand before your enemies until you take away the devoted things from among you." [14] In the morning therefore you shall come forward tribe by tribe. The tribe that the LORD takes shall come near by clans, the clan that the LORD takes shall come near by households, and the household that the LORD takes shall come near one by one. [15] And the one who is taken as having the devoted things shall be burned with fire, together with all that he has, for having transgressed the covenant of the LORD, and for having done an out-rageous thing in Israel.'"

[16] So Joshua rose early in the morning, and brought Israel near tribe by tribe, and the tribe of Judah was taken. [17] He brought near the clans of Judah, and the clan of the Zerahites was taken; and he brought near the clan of the Zerahites, family by family, and Zabdi was taken. [18] And he brought near his household one by one, and Achan son of Carmi son of Zabdi son of Zerah, of the tribe of Judah, was taken. [19] Then Joshua said to Achan, "My son, give glory to the LORD God of Israel and make confession to him. Tell me now what you have done; do not hide it from me." [20] And Achan answered Joshua, "It is true; I am the one who sinned against the LORD God of Israel. This is what I did: [21] when I saw among the spoil a beautiful mantle from Shinar, and two hundred shekels of silver, and a bar of gold weighing fifty shekels, then I cov-eted them and took them. They now lie hidden in the ground inside my tent, with the silver underneath."

[22] So Joshua sent messengers, and they ran to the tent; and there it was, hidden in his tent with the silver underneath. [23] They took them out of the tent and brought them to Joshua and all the Israelites; and they spread them out before the LORD. [24] Then Joshua and all Israel with him took Achan son of Zerah, with the silver, the mantle, and the bar of gold, with his sons and daughters, with his oxen, donkeys, and sheep, and his tent and all that he had; and they brought them up to the Valley of Achor. [25] Joshua said, "Why did you bring trouble on us? The LORD is bringing trouble on you today." And all Israel stoned him to death; they burned them with fire, cast stones on them, [26] and raised over him a great heap of stones that remains to this day. Then the LORD turned from his burning anger. Therefore that place to this day is called the Valley of Achor.

From the beginning of the account of Israel's defeat at Ai, Israel was clearly at fault. The people "broke faith." Moses (the story goes) had warned his people against taking Canaanite silver or gold lest they "be set apart for destruction" (Deut. 7:25–26). Joshua reiterated the warning as his warriors advanced on Jericho: "Keep away from the things devoted to destruction, so as not to covet and take any of the devoted things and make the camp of Israel an object for destruction, bringing trouble upon it" (Josh. 6:18). Achan disregards Moses' and Joshua's commands and takes devoted things, bringing God's wrath against the entire camp (7:1).

The solidarity of the community, assumed throughout the account, is already suggested by the first verse. Achan commits the offense, yet the narrator asserts that "the Israelites broke faith," that God's anger burned "against the Israelites."

Achan's genealogy, given in verse one, hints that the story will blur the distinction between insider and outsider. Achan is an insider par excellence, a Judahite man from a prominent family. Tradition held that his ancestor, Zerah, was one of the twins whom Tamar bore to Judah (Gen. 38). Yet this Judahite causes the Israelites to break faith.

The reader, knowing that Israel has incurred God's anger, expects things to go wrong. The characters within the story do not share that knowledge. The gap gives an ironic tone to the narrative as Joshua sends his spies to Ai, just as he sent them to Jericho, and acts on their optimistic report. Without divine instruction or assurance, Joshua sends a contingent of soldiers against the Canaanites. (Three thousand troops is an exaggeration, as indicated by the low number of casualties in verse 5.) Defeat is immediate: the people go up; they flee.

The defeat is a stunning reversal. Up until now, the Canaanites' "hearts" (resolve, will) "melted" because of Israel and Israel's God (2:11; 5:1). Now, defeat at Ai melts the Israelites' hearts (7:5). Previously, the Canaanites have "heard" about Israel's victories and responded with debilitating fear (2:11; 5:1). Now the inhabitants of the land will "hear" that Israel has turned tail and will be emboldened to destroy them.

Joshua and the elders respond to the rout with typical acts of mourning: tearing their garments, falling to the ground, and putting dust on their heads. The gestures recall Moses and Joshua's response to the people's rebellion in the wilderness, when they refused to go up and take the land (Num. 14). There, also, the story begins with spies who give a positive account of the land, though its inhabitants are frightening. The people, terrified, reject Yahweh's plan to give them Canaan, opting to return to Egypt. Joshua tears his garments; Moses falls on his face, interceding before God to forgive Israel's sin. Moses' prayer, like Joshua's before Ai, invokes the divine reputation ("great name") to motivate God to save the people.

The echoes of Moses' prayer in Joshua's lament (Josh. 7:7–9) sound ironic in light of his ignorance of Israel's sin. In the earlier story, Moses and the leaders knew that Israel was at fault, and they implore God's pardon (Num. 14:13–19). After the defeat at Ai, Joshua, assuming a posture of injured innocence, blames God for bringing the people across the Jordan. In the wilderness the frightened, rebellious people complained (Num. 14:2). Here, Joshua sounds more like the quarrelling people than like their leader Moses.

God will have none of it. Although lament is appropriate in many circumstances (it is the most common form of prayer in the Old Testament), in this instance, it is the wrong response. Israel is guilty. Joshua must identify and eradicate the guilt. The rhetoric of God's reply to Joshua (7:10–15) hammers home Israel's egregious fault. Yahweh's answer begins and ends with the charge "they have transgressed my/the covenant" (vv. 11, 15). God indicts the people at a rapid-fire pace: Israel has "sinned," "transgressed," "taken," "stolen," "acted deceitfully" (v. 11). Lest they miss the specific charge, Yahweh's speech repeats the word *herem*, "devote to destruction" or "devoted," six times in six verses. The terrible thrust of Yahweh's message is found in verse 12. Repeatedly, God has assured Joshua of the divine presence. "I will be with you" (1:5, 9; 3:7). Now, God rescinds that promise, declaring "I will be with you no more."

Yahweh instructs Joshua to identify the offender using lots, which in ancient Israel was a common way of discerning the divine will (1 Sam. 10:20–22, 14:41–42). God also instructs Joshua concerning the offender's fate; the punishment, death, is a purification ritual. Israel's guilt must be expurgated. Joshua carries out God's instructions. After the breach, the pattern of command-obedience is reestablished. The process of identifying the culprit proceeds with a sense of orderliness and inevitability. The lots lead to Achan, who since verse 1 the reader has known was guilty.

Achan's confession (vv. 20–21) uses the same verbs employed in the story of the first disobedience in Eden. He "saw," "coveted," and "took" the devoted things just as the woman "saw," "coveted," and "took" the fruit. The parallels underscore the primal significance of Achan's offense: the first Israelite sin in the promised land. Achan's confession and the discovery of the stolen items (v. 22) also confirms the trustworthiness of the oracular process and the reliability of God's word.

Joshua has warned the people at Jericho: the booty, which has been devoted to God, must be destroyed or, in the case of precious metals, given to the Deity at the temple. To steal what is devoted to God would "bring trouble (*achor*) on Israel" (6:18). Joshua demands of Achan, "Why did you bring trouble on us?" and takes him up to the Valley of Achor, "Trouble Valley."

The "troubler" is "troubled" in "Trouble Valley." Joshua warned that taking a "devoted thing" would make the entire camp of Israel *herem* (Josh. 6:18). *Herem* seems here to be contagious. Achan has made himself and all that is his *herem* by stealing *herem* things. He must be destroyed, lest he infect the whole of Israel. In an act of corporate condemnation and corporate defense, all Israel stones him.

The story concludes with the execution of Achan, his property, and his offspring. Some scholars propose that Achan's family were excommunicated rather than executed. In other versions of the story, Israel does not kill Achan's sons and daughters. The words, "they burned them with fire, cast stones on them," (v. 25) are redundant; moreover, the plural "them" is in tension with the singular "him" in the surrounding phrases. The Old Greek translation of verse 25 omits the phrase, which seems to have been added to the Hebrew text in order to harmonize Achan's fate with God's instructions in verse 15: "And the one who is taken . . . shall be burned with fire, together with all that he has." The action offends our sense of justice. Why should innocent people perish along with the guilty? The act violates Israelite legal philosophy as well. Deuteronomy explicitly prohibits putting children to death because of their parents (or vice versa): "only for their own crimes may persons be put to death" (24:16).

The inclusion of Achan's children in the stoning reflects the ancient Near Eastern assumption that a parent's children were in some sense his or her possessions. (Israel did not consider the wife her husband's property, so Achan's wife was spared.) Moreover, because *herem* was considered contagious, as his property, Achan's sons and daughters were seen as infected and had to be destroyed. Perhaps the later storytellers included the offspring in Achan's punishment to emphasize the gravity of his offense, and thus to warn their audiences against transgressing Yahweh's commands. In the time of Josiah's reforms, the story would be an effective, albeit horrifying deterrent to violating the covenant.

For us, the story is less a model than a mirror; it is descriptive rather than prescriptive. Our actions impact others in ways we do not know and may be horrified to discover. Ancient Israel was more aware of the inescapable interconnectedness of the human community than we modern Westerners, shaped by the individualistic ethos of our culture, can be. Even a cursory awareness of family systems makes it clear: The sins of the parents are all too often visited on the children to the third and fourth generation.

We ought not let the offensiveness of the story obscure the realism of its word about human sin. On some occasions, lament is appropriate, but other occasions call upon us to identify the human causes of suffering and work to eradicate them. Like Joshua, we do at times lament the wrongs and brokenness around us without acknowledging human responsibility for them. One benefit of prayer such as Joshua's is that it can create a space for the Spirit to correct our distorted perspectives, so that rather than blaming God we come to acknowledge human culpability, including our own.

The narrative also contributes a word to the "countervoice" challenging clear-cut distinctions between "insiders" and "outsiders," "them" and "us." Scholars widely recognize that Achan presents a reverse image of Rahab. Rahab, as Canaanite, female, and whore, is a paradigmatic outsider, subject as such to death. Declaring her faith and acting with covenantal loyalty, she saves her family and herself from destruction. Achan is the quintessential insider. He is a Judahite from a prominent family, possessed of substantial wealth (oxen, donkeys, sheep [v. 24]), the patriarch of a family. Achan, breaking faith, brings destruction on himself and his family. Faithfulness, not simply ethnicity, defines the people of God.

THE CONQUEST OF AI
Joshua 8:1–29

> 8:1 Then the LORD said to Joshua, "Do not fear or be dismayed; take all the fighting men with you, and go up now to Ai. See, I have handed over to you the king of Ai with his people, his city, and his land. ² You shall do to Ai and its king as you did to Jericho and its king; only its spoil and its livestock you may take as booty for yourselves. Set an ambush against the city, behind it."
> ³ So Joshua and all the fighting men set out to go up against Ai. Joshua chose thirty thousand warriors and sent them out by night ⁴ with the command, "You shall lie in ambush against the city, behind it; do not go very far from the city, but all of you stay alert. ⁵ I and all the people who are with me will approach the city. When they come out against us, as before, we shall flee from them. ⁶ They will come out after us until we have drawn them away from the city; for they will say, 'They are fleeing from us, as before.' While we flee from them, ⁷ you shall rise up from the ambush and seize the city; for the LORD your God will give it into your hand. ⁸ And when you have taken the city, you shall set the city on fire, doing as the LORD has ordered; see, I have commanded you." ⁹ So Joshua sent them out; and they went to the place of ambush, and lay between Bethel and Ai, to the west of Ai; but Joshua spent that night in the camp.

¹⁰ In the morning Joshua rose early and mustered the people, and went up, with the elders of Israel, before the people to Ai. ¹¹ All the fighting men who were with him went up, and drew near before the city, and camped on the north side of Ai, with a ravine between them and Ai. ¹² Taking about five thousand men, he set them in ambush between Bethel and Ai, to the west of the city. ¹³ So they stationed the forces, the main encampment that was north of the city and its rear guard west of the city. But Joshua spent that night in the valley. ¹⁴ When the king of Ai saw this, he and all his people, the inhabitants of the city, hurried out early in the morning to the meeting place facing the Arabah to meet Israel in battle; but he did not know that there was an ambush against him behind the city. ¹⁵ And Joshua and all Israel made a pretense of being beaten before them, and fled in the direction of the wilderness. ¹⁶ So all the people who were in the city were called together to pursue them, and as they pursued Joshua they were drawn away from the city. ¹⁷ There was not a man left in Ai or Bethel who did not go out after Israel; they left the city open, and pursued Israel.

¹⁸ Then the LORD said to Joshua, "Stretch out the sword that is in your hand toward Ai; for I will give it into your hand." And Joshua stretched out the sword that was in his hand toward the city. ¹⁹ As soon as he stretched out his hand, the troops in ambush rose quickly out of their place and rushed forward. They entered the city, took it, and at once set the city on fire. ²⁰ So when the men of Ai looked back, the smoke of the city was rising to the sky. They had no power to flee this way or that, for the people who fled to the wilderness turned back against the pursuers. ²¹ When Joshua and all Israel saw that the ambush had taken the city and that the smoke of the city was rising, then they turned back and struck down the men of Ai. ²² And the others came out from the city against them; so they were surrounded by Israelites, some on one side, and some on the other; and Israel struck them down until no one was left who survived or escaped. ²³ But the king of Ai was taken alive and brought to Joshua.

²⁴ When Israel had finished slaughtering all the inhabitants of Ai in the open wilderness where they pursued them, and when all of them to the very last had fallen by the edge of the sword, all Israel returned to Ai, and attacked it with the edge of the sword. ²⁵ The total of those who fell that day, both men and women, was twelve thousand—all the people of Ai. ²⁶ For Joshua did not draw back his hand, with which he stretched out the sword, until he had utterly destroyed all the inhabitants of Ai. ²⁷ Only the livestock and the spoil of that city Israel took as their booty, according to the word of the LORD that he had issued to Joshua. ²⁸ So Joshua burned Ai, and made it forever a heap of ruins, as it is to this day. ²⁹ And he hanged the king of Ai on a tree until evening; and at sunset Joshua commanded, and they took his body down from the tree, threw it down at the entrance of the gate of the city, and raised over it a great heap of stones, which stands there to this day.

The guilty party has been identified and the offense eliminated. Now the relationship between God and Israel can be restored. Israel's second attack against Ai, like the conquest of Jericho, is an exemplar of "holy war." The second battle of Ai begins with Yahweh's assurance and instruction. This approach is a sharp contrast to the initial, failed attempt, when Joshua sent warriors against the city without consulting God. Yahweh's first words, "Do not fear," are a typical element of holy war narratives. As at Jericho (6:2), Israel receives divine assurance that God has "handed over to" them the city and its king (8:1).

The conquest of Ai differs from that of Jericho. Ai is won by shrewd military tactics, rather than by a liturgical procession culminating in miraculous victory. God instructs Joshua to set an ambush against the city. The divine warrior is the principal actor in the story; nonetheless, human strategy plays a significant role.

The ruse, found also in Judges 20, is effective. In spite of duplications and tensions in the text, the plot line is sufficiently clear. Joshua sends a contingent to hide west of the city. The story gives conflicting descriptions of the contingent's size; both numbers—thirty thousand (Josh. 8:3) and five thousand (8:12)—are too large for a secret foray. In the meantime, Joshua and the main army approach from the north of the city in plain sight.

The king of Ai and his soldiers fall for the ruse. The main Israelite army draws them off, leaving the town vulnerable for the hidden warriors to take. The ambushers and the main body of Israelites then turn, catching the Canaanites in a pincers' motion.

As at Jericho, the slaughter is total. Unlike Jericho, however, the livestock and spoils of Ai are exempted from destruction. The victorious warriors are allowed to take booty, the act for which Achan was executed. The issue seems to be not whether the Israelites take spoil, but whether they obey God's commands.

The storyteller uses the battle of Ai to draw another parallel between Moses and Joshua. During Israel's fight against Amalek (Exod. 17:8–12), the tide of battle was controlled by Moses' outstretched arm. When he raised it, Israel prevailed; when he lowered it, Amalek gained power. In the assault against Ai, Joshua similarly extends his sword, not drawing back his hand until the conquest is complete.

Joshua executes the king of Ai, and later, in scrupulous obedience to Deuteronomic law (Deut. 21:22–23), removes his body before nightfall. Like Achan (Josh. 7:26), the king is buried under a cairn of stones visible "to this day" (8:29).

Explanatory motives have played a strong role in shaping the story of Ai's conquest. As in the Achan account, the narrative explains two phenomena. The story tells how an impressive "heap of ruins" near Bethel was formed. The account also explains the presence of a particular heap of stones at the gate of the destroyed city.

The larger purpose of the story is not simply to explain geographical phenomena, but to proclaim Yahweh's agency. God gives the victory. Israel's role is to obey. Sin leads to devastation; obedience leads to success assured by the divine warrior. The story differs from the Jericho account in that the warriors who fought at Ai had experienced defeat. Victory may no longer be taken for granted. Yet, with renewed obedience, Israel's restoration is possible. The story would have had a profound word for its exilic audience, who believed their guilt led to the loss of their land. Renewal is still possible, if Israel will turn and obey.

7. JOSHUA'S ALTAR
Joshua 8:30–35

The covenant violation, restoration, and conquest at Ai culminates in a covenant renewal ceremony at Mt. Ebal. Joshua calls upon the people to reaffirm and celebrate their relationship to Yahweh with sacrifice and obedience.

Like Joshua 1, Joshua 8:30–35 is a Deuteronomistic composition, based on a number of commands from the book of Deuteronomy (Deut. 4–8; 12–14; 11:29–30; 27; 29:10–11; and 31:10–13). The account of Joshua building an altar and reciting the law interrupts the conquest narratives.

The placement of the passage is difficult to explain in terms of geography, history, or plot line. Geographically, the text depicts Joshua and the Israelites moving from Ai to worship at Mt. Ebal, twenty miles north of Ai, then doubling back to Gilgal, which is south and east of Ai (Josh. 9:6). Historically, the passage has little claim to reliability. It was compiled at least six hundred years after the events it purports to describe. An archaeologist has uncovered an Iron Age installation that he believes is Joshua's altar, but his conclusions have not been widely accepted by other archaeologists or biblical scholars. In terms of plot, the passage interrupts the story line, which would more naturally lead from Israel's victory at Ai (8:1–29) to the Canaanite kings' fearful, belligerent response (9:1–2).

The passage's awkward placement serves as a clue to its significance; the composition and addition of the story of Joshua's altar were determined not by historical, geographical, or narrative concerns, but by theological convictions. The passage serves a threefold theological purpose. First, the covenant, broken by Achan's sin, is restored in a covenant renewal ceremony. Building an altar, copying the law, reading the law, and reciting blessings and curses are associated with covenant renewal. Placing such a ceremony after the story of Achan's covenant violation shows that restoring the breach that sin causes in the community's relationship with God is both possible and necessary.

Second, the passage urges its audience to obey Torah. The content of the passage emphasizes the centrality of obedience; verses 32–35 have to do with writing, proclaiming, and affirming the book of the law (probably an early form of Deuteronomy). The story also emphasizes faithfulness to Torah by providing a positive example of careful obedience. According to Deuteronomy, Moses had instructed the people to build an altar of unhewn stones (Deut. 27:5–7), to recite blessings on Mt. Gerezim (27:12) and curses on Mt. Ebal (27:13–26), and to recite the law aloud (31:10–11). In this passage, Joshua and the Israelites scrupulously fulfill Moses' commands.

Third, interrupting the story of Israel's conquests with a story of sacrifice and Torah reminds the audience that worship and obedience, not military victory, are the basis of the people's life in the land. Joshua 8:30–35 was composed by the same Deuteronomistic writers who compiled God's speech in the first chapter (Josh. 1:1–9) and Joshua's speech (23:2–16), which insist that the land will be won by careful observance of Moses' instructions. Placing these three passages at the beginning and end of the book and at the center of the conquest narratives creates a structure that subsumes all Joshua's battles and military stratagems to obeying God's laws. The passages establish the priority of faithfulness over military might.

8:30 Then Joshua built on Mount Ebal an altar to the LORD, the God of Israel, ³¹ just as Moses the servant of the LORD had commanded the Israelites, as it is written in the book of the law of Moses, "an altar of unhewn stones, on which no iron tool has been used"; and they offered on it burnt offerings to the LORD, and sacrificed offerings of well-being. ³² And there, in the presence of the Israelites, Joshua wrote on the stones a copy of the law of Moses, which he had written. ³³ All Israel, alien as well as citizen, with their elders and officers and their judges, stood on opposite sides of the ark in front of the levitical priests who carried the ark of the covenant of the LORD, half of them in front of Mount Gerizim and half of them in front of Mount Ebal, as Moses the servant of the LORD had commanded at the first, that they should bless the people of Israel. ³⁴ And afterward he read all the words of the law, blessings and curses, according to all that is written in the book of the law. ³⁵ There was not a word of all that Moses commanded that Joshua did not read before all the assembly of Israel, and the women, and the little ones, and the aliens who resided among them.

According to Deuteronomy 27:5–7, Moses commanded that on the day they crossed the Jordan River into the land, the Israelites were to go to Mount Ebal and build an altar of unhewn stones. The Israelite victory at Ai makes establishing an altar at Mount Ebal feasible; Joshua and the people carry out Moses' command as soon as possible. The Deuteronomic command and the account of its fulfillment is in some tension with the Deuteronomistic authors' efforts to centralize sacrificial worship of Yahweh at the temple in Jerusalem. Apparently Deuteronomy 27 and Joshua 8:30–35 represent an alternative tradition. That tradition appears to be quite ancient; a command to use only unhewn stones in constructing altars is found in a very old collection of laws (Exod. 20:25).

In accordance with Moses' instructions, Joshua and the Israelites offer up whole burnt offerings and sacrifices of well-being on the newly built altar (Josh. 8:31). "Sacrifice" has acquired a negative, even onerous tone for modern Christians. It was not so for ancient Israelites. Sacrifice in Israel was sacramental, understood as a means provided by God for restoring and celebrating the divine-human relationship. Whole burnt offerings were completely consumed by fire and represented the congregation's thanksgiving and total allegiance to God. In the case of sacrifices of well-being, certain portions of animals were burned; the rest were cooked and eaten by the worshipers. Sacrifices of well-being represented a meal shared by God and the faithful. Sacrifice was not seen as an attempt to propitiate an angry God, but as a way to "rejoice before the LORD" (Deut. 12:12, see also Deut. 12:7; 16:14).

Worship is inseparable from obedience. The offering of sacrifices is immediately followed by attention to the law. Joshua copies all the words of the law onto stones, monuments testifying to the authority of the laws. (The passage makes it appear as if Joshua wrote the laws on the stones of the altar itself. Presumably the audience would have assumed that he set up a second set of stones. Writing on rough, unhewn rock is not plausible; moreover, the Deuteronomic law instructs the people to write the laws on stele [monuments] prepared with plaster.)

If sacrifice was viewed as celebrative, law was understood as blessing (8:33). Ancient Israel believed that Torah was given for the sake of life. Deuteronomy 6:24 instructs parents to tell their children that "the LORD commanded us to observe all these statutes, to fear the LORD our God, for our lasting good, so as to keep us alive. . . ." The psalmist declares

The law of the LORD is perfect,
    reviving the soul;
the decrees of the LORD are sure,
    making wise the simple;
the precepts of the LORD are right,
    rejoicing the heart;

the commandment of the LORD is clear,
    enlightening the eyes;
the fear of the LORD is pure,
    enduring forever;
the ordinances of the LORD are true
    and righteous altogether.
More to be desired are they than gold,
    even much fine gold. . . .
                            (Ps. 19:7–10)

Yet the laws are to be taken seriously. The curses remind the audience that obedience is also a matter of urgency, even of life and death (Deut. 30:15–20).

The passage emphasizes the importance of the whole of the law. Three times it insists that the people are to hear and obey every word that Moses commanded (Josh. 8:34–35). Moreover, *all* of Israel is responsible for upholding the covenant, alien and citizen alike (8:32), all of the men who comprised the assembly of Israel, and women, little ones, and aliens (8:35).

8. The Gibeonite Ruse
Joshua 9

How Israel is to relate to other peoples is an issue that recurs throughout the book of Joshua (and the Bible). The dominant voice understands the "nations" as a threat to the purity of Israel's faith. Israel is to separate itself from them completely—a notion expressed in stories of annihilation of the peoples of Canaan (Josh. 6:21; 8:22–26). A countervoice is heard in the stories of Rahab (Josh. 2) and Achan (Josh. 7) as discussed previously.

The story of the Gibeonites speaks of "the nations" with yet another voice. The narrative depicts the indigenous Gibeonites as God-fearing people who escape destruction by entering into covenant with Israel. As such, the story explicitly counters the dominant view, that Israel is to have no dealings with the nations. Unlike Rahab, however, the Gibeonites are saved not by heroism but by trickery. By the end of the story, Joshua curses them, condemning them to menial labor. The narrative suggests that Israel must coexist with other peoples, to live and let live, but that sometimes the nations remain objects of distrust and even oppression.

It seems likely that historically the Gibeonites, a non-Israelite enclave in the midst of Israel, were protected by and subject to the ancient Israelites. According to 2 Samuel 21:1, Saul is supposed to have brought famine upon the people by putting Gibeonites to death. The report is Davidic propaganda; however, for such a report to have any usefulness as propaganda, its audience must have understood that Israel was obligated to protect Gibeon. The account of Joshua and his troops coming to Gibeon's aid (Josh. 10:6) suggests that the treaty between the Gibeonites and Israel involved mutual assistance and defense. The account of the origins and dating of the Gibeonite-Israelite treaty in Joshua 9 is not historically reliable, however. Both archaeological and textual evidence suggest that Joshua 9 is an idealogically shaped story, not a historical report.

Gibeon is identified with the modern site El Jib, eight miles northwest of Jerusalem, on the ancient route from Jericho to the coast. Archaeologists have found no evidence that the site was occupied in the Late Bronze period when Israel emerged in the land. That is, there were no "Gibeonites" to enter into covenant with Israel at the time Joshua was supposed to have lived. The site was reoccupied in the early Iron Age (1200–900 B.C.E.), presumably the period in which the Gibeonites allied with Israel.

As a number of commentators point out, the story told in Joshua 9 is inherently implausible. Why would a mighty city or coalition of cities (9:17) beg Joshua's ragtag army for peace? Why would the Israelites be so gullible as to accept the Gibeonites' ruse? Furthermore, tensions in the story and the Deuteronomic cadence in which the final form of the tale is couched suggest that the tale was transmitted and edited by a long line of storytellers. Its final form derives from a period hundreds of years after Israel arose in Canaan.

The Gibeonite account serves two purposes: to explain Israel's relationship with Gibeon (vv. 3–27), and as an occasion to wrestle with Israel's identity vis-à-vis the nations.

9:1 Now when all the kings who were beyond the Jordan in the hill country and in the lowland all along the coast of the Great Sea toward Lebanon—the Hittites, the Amorites, the Canaanites, the Perizzites, the Hivites, and the Jebusites—heard of this, ² they gathered together with one accord to fight Joshua and Israel.

³ But when the inhabitants of Gibeon heard what Joshua had done to Jericho and to Ai, ⁴ they on their part acted with cunning: they went and prepared provisions, and took worn-out sacks for their donkeys, and wineskins, worn-out and torn and mended, ⁵ with worn-out, patched sandals on their feet, and worn-out clothes; and all their provisions were dry and moldy. ⁶ They went to Joshua in the camp at Gilgal, and said to him and to the Israelites, "We have come from a far country; so now make a treaty with us." ⁷ But the Israelites said to the Hivites, "Perhaps you live among us; then how can we make a treaty with you?" ⁸ They said to Joshua, "We are your servants." And Joshua said to them, "Who are you? And where do you come from?" ⁹ They said to him, "Your servants have come from a very far country, because of the name of the LORD your God; for we have heard a report of him, of all that he did in Egypt, ¹⁰ and of all that he did to the two kings of the Amorites who were beyond the Jordan, King Sihon of Heshbon, and King Og of Bashan who lived in Ashtaroth. ¹¹ So our elders and all the inhabitants of our country said to us, 'Take provisions in your hand for the journey; go to meet them, and say to them, "We are your servants; come now, make a treaty with us."' ¹² Here is our bread; it was still warm when we took it from our houses as our food for the journey, on the day we set out to come to you, but now, see, it is dry and moldy; ¹³ these wineskins were new when we filled

them, and see, they are burst; and these garments and sandals of ours are worn out from the very long journey." [14] So the leaders partook of their provisions, and did not ask direction from the LORD. [15] And Joshua made peace with them, guaranteeing their lives by a treaty; and the leaders of the congregation swore an oath to them.

[16] But when three days had passed after they had made a treaty with them, they heard that they were their neighbors and were living among them. [17] So the Israelites set out and reached their cities on the third day. Now their cities were Gibeon, Chephirah, Beeroth, and Kiriath-jearim. [18] But the Israelites did not attack them, because the leaders of the congregation had sworn to them by the LORD, the God of Israel. Then all the congregation murmured against the leaders. [19] But all the leaders said to all the congregation, "We have sworn to them by the LORD, the God of Israel, and now we must not touch them. [20] This is what we will do to them: We will let them live, so that wrath may not come upon us, because of the oath that we swore to them." [21] The leaders said to them, "Let them live." So they became hewers of wood and drawers of water for all the congregation, as the leaders had decided concerning them.

[22] Joshua summoned them, and said to them, "Why did you deceive us, saying, 'We are very far from you,' while in fact you are living among us? [23] Now therefore you are cursed, and some of you shall always be slaves, hewers of wood and drawers of water for the house of my God." [24] They answered Joshua, "Because it was told to your servants for a certainty that the LORD your God had commanded his servant Moses to give you all the land, and to destroy all the inhabitants of the land before you; so we were in great fear for our lives because of you, and did this thing. [25] And now we are in your hand: do as it seems good and right in your sight to do to us." [26] This is what he did for them: he saved them from the Israelites; and they did not kill them. [27] But on that day Joshua made them hewers of wood and drawers of water for the congregation and for the altar of the LORD, to continue to this day, in the place that he should choose.

The focus of Joshua 9 is on the Gibeonites, a people who opt for alliance with Israel. It begins with a list of kings who opt for war (vv. 1–2). The list in 9:1 is comprised of six of the seven peoples traditionally cited as occupants of Canaan (3:10).

The kings of these peoples hear what has happened to Jericho and to Ai. "Hearing" what God has done for Israel, and what Israel has been empowered to do to the indigenous peoples, is a repeated motif in the conquest narratives. People of Canaan "hear" and respond in differing ways. Rahab accounts for her deliverance of the Israelite spies by asserting, "we heard ..." about Yahweh parting the sea. In 5:1, the kings of the land "hear" about the miraculous crossing of the Jordan and are panicked. The Gibeonites "hear" what Israel did to Jericho and to Ai and seek to trick Israel into making a treaty with them (9:3). In contrast, 9:1 reports that the kings of the land "hear" what has happened and join to fight against Israel. Lawson Stone convincingly argues that the compilers of the conquest narratives use the motif of "hearing" to suggest that the indigenous people's fate is determined by their varying responses to what they have heard (Stone, 1991, 33–34). The kings, opposing Joshua, serve as a foil to the Gibeonite citizens who seek peaceable cooperation.

The story has two main parts. The first, older section (vv. 3–15) tells how the Gibeonites trick Israel into establishing a treaty with them. It answers the question, "Why are there Gibeonites, non-Israelites, living in our midst?" The second part (vv. 16–27) narrates Joshua's discovery of the Gibeonites' ruse. It answers the questions, "Why are the Gibeonites pressed into menial labor?" and "Why do these non-Israelites serve (in however lowly a capacity) in the temple?"

THE GIBEONITE RUSE
Joshua 9:3–15

The Gibeonite citizens (there are no references to a Gibeonite king) fear that they will share the fate of the inhabitants of Jericho and Ai. They seek to save their lives by a trick, convincing the Israelites that they are from a distant land and so not subject to destruction like the people of Canaan.

The story may have roots that go back earlier than the Deuteronomic Historians. Perhaps in the ancient Near East, invaders often treated neighboring populations more leniently than they treated the inhabitants of the land they sought to conquer. Moreover, the notion of an underdog gaining power from trickery is a common folkloric motif. As it stands now, however, the story depends upon the laws of Deuteronomy. The distinction between Israelite treatment of distant nations and its policy toward indigenous peoples is codified in Deuteronomy 20:10–18:

> When you draw near to a town to fight against it, offer it terms of peace. If it accepts your terms of peace and surrenders to you, then all the people in it shall serve you at forced labor. If it does not submit to you peacefully, but makes war against you, then you shall besiege it; and when the LORD your God gives it into your hand, you shall put all its males to the sword. You may, however, take as your booty the women, the children, livestock, and everything else in the town, all its spoil. You may enjoy the spoil of your enemies, which the LORD your God has given you. Thus you shall treat all the towns

that are very far from you, which are not towns of the nations here. But as for the towns of these peoples that the LORD your God is giving you as an inheritance, you must not let anything that breathes remain alive. You shall annihilate them—the Hittites and the Amorites, the Canaanites and the Perizzites, the Hivites and the Jebusites—just as the LORD your God has commanded. . . .

The Gibeonites appear to have studied Deuteronomy with care!

The passage also alludes to the covenant-making ceremony in Deuteronomy 29. The Gibeonites' worn-out clothes and patched sandals contrast with the clothes and sandals of the Israelites, which did not wear out the forty years that Moses led them through the wilderness (Deut. 29:5). These verbal connections serve to remind the audience of the covenant renewal described in Deuteronomy 29, a ceremony that included all members of Israelite society, alien as well as citizen, lowly as well as leaders.

Like Rahab (Josh. 2:8–11), the Gibeonites are indigenous people who fear Israel's God and are aware of Yahweh's saving deeds (9:9–10). Like Rahab (2:12), their fear of Yahweh motivates them to exact from the Israelites a promise to spare their lives (9:15), an oath which the Israelites keep in explicit violation of Deuteronomic law. The Israelites keep their promise and spare the Gibeonites' lives, as they spared Rahab (6:22–23). Both stories undercut the belief that Israel was to separate itself from the nations, a belief the Deuteronomists expressed, represented by their revisionist history of its annihilation of the inhabitants of Canaan.

The author of verses 3–15 tells the story with a certain admiration for the Gibeonites' cunning. The assertion that the Israelites "did not ask" Yahweh raises a note of caution (9:14). The implication is that God would have said "no." Nonetheless, the account treats the Gibeonites positively. Perhaps it reflects underdog Israel's sympathy toward a powerless indigenous people who are able to outwit more powerful invaders.

CONDEMNATION
Joshua 9:16–27

The tone of the story shifts in the second part of the tale; verses 16–27 may have been added by later editors for whom the presence of Gibeonites serving as functionaries in the temple was an embarrassment. Alternatively, it may reflect a time when Israelite policy was to subject non-Israelite populations to forced labor. In any case, admiration (vv. 3–15) turns to condemnation (vv. 16–27). The Gibeonites are allowed to live, but such leniency requires explanation. Three times, the narrative explains that the binding oath that the Israelites were tricked into gave them no choice (vv. 18, 19, 20). They had to spare the Gibeonites to avoid God's punishing wrath. Three times, the narrative declares the Gibeonites' demotion; they will be reduced to slaves: "hewers of wood and drawers of water" (vv. 21, 23, 27). The survival of the Gibeonites is sufficiently embarrassing to these later editors that they take pains to shift the blame from Joshua to the leaders of the congregation (vv. 18–21). These later storytellers convey their belief that Israel might have to relate to other peoples, but that the relationship should not be one of mutuality or trust.

The narrative includes a number of verbal links to other texts that recall less harsh views of the "stranger." The phrase used to depict the Gibeonites' servile status, "hewers of wood and drawers of water," is found in only one other place in the Bible: the covenant-making ceremony on the plains of Moab (Deut. 29:11). The link is not accidental. As noted above, the Gibeonite tale includes other allusions to Deuteronomy 29, including the reference to sandals and clothes that do or do not wear out, and the recital of Yahweh's deeds against Sihon and Og (Deut. 29:7). The connections invite those hearing the Gibeonite story to recall Moses' insistence that all members of Israelite society were part of the covenant of Yahweh.

The Gibeonite story contains distinctive language that links it to the prayer with which Solomon dedicates the temple (1 Kgs. 8:41–43). The Gibeonites describe themselves as from a far land (Josh. 9:9) and declare that they have come because of the "name of the LORD." Solomon asks God to hear and answer the prayers of foreigners from "a far land," who come to the temple because of the Lord's "name."

Most immediately, the story of Joshua 9 leads directly to Joshua's coming to Gibeon's defense in Joshua 10:6. Joshua's defense of Gibeon suggests a more positive view of Israel's relationship to Gibeon. Israel's obligation to the subject population was not simply to spare their lives. Rather, it becomes clear that Israel was pledged to offer Gibeon aid and defense.

9. The Promise Fulfilled
Joshua 10–12

The book of Joshua begins with God's renewed promise to be with Israel so that "no one shall be able to stand against" it as it occupies Canaan (Josh. 1:5). That promise is at the same time a command. Joshua is to be strong and courageous, leading the Israelites to take the land they have been given. The first half of Joshua deals with the unfolding of that promise and command. Chapters 10–12 conclude the stories of the conquest. Joshua's assigned task and God's repeated promise are strikingly fulfilled.

Before looking at specific passages, we need to discuss two issues. First, we must ask whether the narratives in Joshua 10–12 are history or something else. Second, the three chapters pose again the ethical issue of "holy war," that is, divinely mandated violence.

THE CONQUEST: STORY OR HISTORY?

Joshua 10–12, along with Joshua 6–8, have long been important sources of the church's traditional understanding of the Israelite occupation of Canaan as a fast and total offensive, consisting of three campaigns: one in the center of the land (Josh. 6–8), one in the south (Josh. 10), and one in the north (Josh. 11). For several decades, however, biblical scholarship has challenged that traditional view. Both archaeology and the biblical texts suggest that the narratives in Joshua 10–12 are not "factual" and were never intended to be historical reports.

Archaeologists have found that at least two of the cities whose conquest Joshua 10–11 describes, Lachish (10:31–32) and Hazor (11:10–11) were destroyed during the early Iron Age, roughly the period when Israel arose in the land. But the timing of the overthrow of the two cities does not support the biblical account of a single general (Joshua) leading campaigns against both cities. Hazor was razed around 1250 B.C.E., a full century before the destruction of Lachish. Other cities that play key roles in the conquest narratives, Jericho, Ai, and Gibeon, were at most unwalled, sparsely populated villages when Israel arose in the land.

What archaeologists have uncovered from this period are hundreds of villages in the hill country of Israel, villages that arose in land that had been uninhabited for centuries. Scholars debate where the villagers came from; they may have been a motley population. Many specialists in premonarchical Israel believe that a large number of the early Israelites were Canaanite peasants who left Canaanite society for the hill country in order to escape crushing taxation and socially chaotic conditions in the cities. Perhaps they were joined by a group of ex-slaves from Egypt who brought with them memories of miraculous deliverance. From a variety of sources apart from the Bible, we know that the Canaanite city-states were under the dominion of the Egyptian Pharaoh, who forced them to pay heavy tribute. Refugees from these city-states may well have embraced as their own traditions that told of the oppressive power of the Pharaohs and celebrated freedom from Egyptian bondage, for the stories of Joshua do not seem to correspond in any direct way with what archaeologists have discovered about the rise of ancient Israel.

A close reading of Joshua and Judges also challenges the impression left by Joshua 10–12 that the conquest of Canaan was total, rapid, and accomplished by the whole of Israel. Joshua 11:19–23 insists that Joshua took "the whole land," killing all of its inhabitants except the Gibeonites. In contrast, subsequent chapters are punctuated by notices that Judah "could not drive out the Jebusites" (15:63), the Ephraimites did not "drive out the Canaanites who lived in Gezer" (16:10), the tribe of Manassah could not take possession of the towns Joshua allotted it (17:12), and so on. Moreover, the notion that Israel took the land quickly, "at one time" (10:42), is balanced by Joshua 11:18: "Joshua made war a long time with all those kings."

It is not necessary to ascribe discrepancies among various biblical accounts of the conquest to clumsy editing or to a desire not to tamper with venerable traditions. The Deuteronomistic Historians who edited and reedited Joshua (like the storytellers who compiled the materials before them) were quite capable of adapting their sources and ironing out tensions between inherited material and their own perspectives. Rather, the Deuteronomists and their predecessors seem to have had little interest in presenting a historical account. The accounts are theological (language about God) and doxological (praise of and to God). They attest that God's promises are good: what Yahweh determines to do will come to fruition.

The juxtaposition of accounts of Israel's swift, total conquest of the land with traditions of prolonged, arduous struggle may itself be theologically important. Chapter 1 declares both that God *will give* Joshua and his people the land, and that God *has given* it already. At that point in the story, Israel's full possession of Canaan lay in the future—yet, by God's determination, it was an accomplished fact. The juxtaposition of a confident account of total victory with glimpses of hard-fought, only partially successful battles may speak a similar word of hope to its audiences. However ambiguous things may appear, however uncertain the outcome, the future that God has promised is ultimately the only reality that will stand. That statement would have been powerful in Josiah's time, when the little vassal nation battled for its unlikely independence, or still more during the exile, when the conquered, colonized people despaired of reclaiming their land. The promise continues to be an important word for people engaged in the struggle for freedom. By God's word, the future is an accomplished fact. Living out of that reality is possible even in the midst of ambiguous experience, when victory seems far from assured.

"HOLY" WAR?

Readers of the book of Joshua cannot evade the issue of divinely mandated violence. The ideology of war that Israel shared with its neighbors thoroughly shapes chapters 10–12. The narratives are full of "holy war" motifs: divine sanction (10:8; 11:6); oracles offering assurance of victory (10:8; 11:6); and divine involvement in the battle, whether directly through supernatural intervention (chap. 10) or indirectly, by empowering and instructing leaders (chap. 11). As is typical of holy wars, victory is achieved against great, even insurmountable, odds, and the conquest is total. Joshua meticulously obeys the Deuteronomic command to devote the indigenous people of the land to destruction. In the book of Joshua a full half of the references to *herem* ("devotion to destruction") are in chapters 10–11. The language of the reports, that Joshua "destroyed all that breathed" (10:40), is a direct quotation of the Deuteronomic law calling for Israel to kill all the prior inhabitants of Canaan (Deut. 20:15–18).

Chapters 10–12 contribute an additional insight into the question of holy war. The structure of the chapters suggests that the issue of divinely mandated violence is not only a modern concern. Lawson Stone notes that the pre-Deuteronomistic compiler of Joshua 2–11 arranged the traditions in such a way that all of Israel's campaigns after Ai are defensive battles. In chapters 10 and 11, Israel's opponents are the aggressors. The Jerusalemite king and his allies attack Gibeon, forcing Joshua to honor a mutual defense pact. Similarly, the northern campaign is depicted as a preemptive strike, aimed at halting aggression against Israel by the coalition of northern Canaanite kings. The compiler's efforts to portray the Israelite campaigns as defensive measures indicate an uneasiness with the earlier holy war traditions. (Stone, 1991, 25–36; for additional discussion of holy war, see pp. 49–53.)

In an age of ethnic cleansing, acknowledging the danger of the ideology of the conquest narratives—that God fights for us and that we are commanded to fight for God—is important. The danger is exponentially multiplied when the literature of a minority or subordinate population like ancient Judah is appropriated by a dominant culture to justify domination rather than to stiffen resistance to it. As Stone notes, the dynamic of questioning and reinterpreting ancient traditions on ethical grounds appears to be built into the canon itself.

THE CONQUEST OF THE SOUTH
Joshua 10

10:1 When King Adoni-zedek of Jerusalem heard how Joshua had taken Ai, and had utterly destroyed it, doing to Ai and its king as he had done to Jericho and its king, and how the inhabitants of Gibeon had made peace with Israel and were among them, ² he became greatly frightened, because Gibeon was a large city, like one of the royal cities, and was larger than Ai, and all its men were warriors. ³ So King Adoni-zedek of Jerusalem sent a message to King Hoham of Hebron, to King Piram of Jarmuth, to King Japhia of Lachish, and to King Debir of Eglon, saying, ⁴ "Come up and help me, and let us attack Gibeon; for it has made peace with Joshua and with the Israelites." ⁵ Then the five kings of the Amorites—the king of Jerusalem, the king of Hebron, the king of Jarmuth, the king of Lachish, and the king of Eglon—gathered their forces, and went up with all their armies and camped against Gibeon, and made war against it.

⁶ And the Gibeonites sent to Joshua at the camp in Gilgal, saying, "Do not abandon your servants; come up to us quickly, and save us, and help us; for all the kings of the Amorites who live in the hill country are gathered against us." ⁷ So Joshua went up from Gilgal, he and all the fighting force with him, all the mighty warriors. ⁸ The LORD said to Joshua, "Do not fear them, for I have handed them over to you; not one of them shall stand before you." ⁹ So Joshua came upon them suddenly, having marched up all night from Gilgal. ¹⁰ And the LORD threw them into a panic before Israel, who inflicted a great slaughter on them at Gibeon, chased them by the way of the ascent of Beth-horon, and struck them down as far as Azekah and

Makkedah. [11] As they fled before Israel, while they were going down the slope of Beth-horon, the LORD threw down huge stones from heaven on them as far as Azekah, and they died; there were more who died because of the hailstones than the Israelites killed with the sword.

[12] On the day when the LORD gave the Amorites over to the Israelites, Joshua spoke to the LORD; and he said in the sight of Israel,

"Sun, stand still at Gibeon,
    and Moon, in the valley of Aijalon."

[13] And the sun stood still, and the moon stopped,
    until the nation took vengeance on their enemies.

Is this not written in the Book of Jashar? The sun stopped in mid-heaven, and did not hurry to set for about a whole day. [14] There has been no day like it before or since, when the LORD heeded a human voice; for the LORD fought for Israel.

[15] Then Joshua returned, and all Israel with him, to the camp at Gilgal.

[16] Meanwhile, these five kings fled and hid themselves in the cave at Makkedah. [17] And it was told Joshua, "The five kings have been found, hidden in the cave at Makkedah." [18] Joshua said, "Roll large stones against the mouth of the cave, and set men by it to guard them; [19] but do not stay there yourselves; pursue your enemies, and attack them from the rear. Do not let them enter their towns, for the LORD your God has given them into your hand." [20] When Joshua and the Israelites had finished inflicting a very great slaughter on them, until they were wiped out, and when the survivors had entered into the fortified towns, [21] all the people returned safe to Joshua in the camp at Makkedah; no one dared to speak against any of the Israelites.

[22] Then Joshua said, "Open the mouth of the cave, and bring those five kings out to me from the cave." [23] They did so, and brought the five kings out to him from the cave, the king of Jerusalem, the king of Hebron, the king of Jarmuth, the king of Lachish, and the king of Eglon. [24] When they brought the kings out to Joshua, Joshua summoned all the Israelites, and said to the chiefs of the warriors who had gone with him, "Come near, put your feet on the necks of these kings." Then they came near and put their feet on their necks. [25] And Joshua said to them, "Do not be afraid or dismayed; be strong and courageous; for thus the LORD will do to all the enemies against whom you fight." [26] Afterward Joshua struck them down and put them to death, and he hung them on five trees. And they hung on the trees until evening. [27] At sunset Joshua commanded, and they took them down from the trees and threw them into the cave where they had hidden themselves; they set large stones against the mouth of the cave, which remain to this very day.

[28] Joshua took Makkedah on that day, and struck it and its king with the edge of the sword; he utterly destroyed every person in it; he left no one remaining. And he did to the king of Makkedah as he had done to the king of Jericho.

²⁹ Then Joshua passed on from Makkedah, and all Israel with him, to Libnah, and fought against Libnah. ³⁰ The Lord gave it also and its king into the hand of Israel; and he struck it with the edge of the sword, and every person in it; he left no one remaining in it; and he did to its king as he had done to the king of Jericho.

³¹ Next Joshua passed on from Libnah, and all Israel with him, to Lachish, and laid siege to it, and assaulted it. ³² The Lord gave Lachish into the hand of Israel, and he took it on the second day, and struck it with the edge of the sword, and every person in it, as he had done to Libnah.

³³ Then King Horam of Gezer came up to help Lachish; and Joshua struck him and his people, leaving him no survivors.

³⁴ From Lachish Joshua passed on with all Israel to Eglon; and they laid siege to it, and assaulted it; ³⁵ and they took it that day, and struck it with the edge of the sword; and every person in it he utterly destroyed that day, as he had done to Lachish.

³⁶ Then Joshua went up with all Israel from Eglon to Hebron; they assaulted it, ³⁷ and took it, and struck it with the edge of the sword, and its king and its towns, and every person in it; he left no one remaining, just as he had done to Eglon, and utterly destroyed it with every person in it.

³⁸ Then Joshua, with all Israel, turned back to Debir and assaulted it, ³⁹ and he took it with its king and all its towns; they struck them with the edge of the sword, and utterly destroyed every person in it; he left no one remaining; just as he had done to Hebron, and, as he had done to Libnah and its king, so he did to Debir and its king.

⁴⁰ So Joshua defeated the whole land, the hill country and the Negeb and the lowland and the slopes, and all their kings; he left no one remaining, but utterly destroyed all that breathed, as the Lord God of Israel commanded. ⁴¹ And Joshua defeated them from Kadesh-barnea to Gaza, and all the country of Goshen, as far as Gibeon. ⁴² Joshua took all these kings and their land at one time, because the Lord God of Israel fought for Israel. ⁴³ Then Joshua returned, and all Israel with him, to the camp at Gilgal.

Three main movements make up the plot of chapter 10: the formation and defeat of the Amorite coalition (vv. 1–15), the fate of the allied Amorite kings (vv. 16–27), and the mopping up campaign in the south (vv. 28–43). The three sections are not entirely consistent; the list of conquered cities in verses 28–43 omits two of the cities named in verses 1–15 (Jerusalem and Jarmouth) and includes three others (Makkedah, Libnah, and Debir). Different memories of Israel's acquisition of the land seem to be woven together. As it stands, the chapter forms a coherent narrative, closely and logically linked to the story of the Gibeonite-Israelite alliance told in Joshua 9. Gibeon was located on an important route from the lowlands to the hill country. A treaty between Israel and Gibeon would allow Israel easy passageway to Jerusalem; the king of Jerusalem responds to the threat by organizing an alliance of kings from the hill country and lowlands of southern Judah.

Joshua 10:1 is the first time that Jerusalem is explicitly mentioned in the Bible. Ironically, the city destined to be Israel's spiritual center initially comes into view as an enemy determined to stop Israelite encroachment and punish Israel's allies. The Jerusalemite king, Adoni-zedek, is not known apart from biblical materials. With his power to draw together alliances, Adoni-zedek comes across as a power to be reckoned with.

Adoni-zedek's alliance appears to be a formidable obstacle to Israel's pursuit of land. The Canaanite kings ruled over city-states. Egyptian sources and other extrabiblical materials support the biblical view that pre-monarchical Israel was organized into petty kingdoms consisting of towns together with their dependent fields and villages. To be sure, the city-states are not much like modern urban centers. Pre-Israelite Jerusalem, for example, had a population of roughly one thousand and occupied about fifteen acres. Nonetheless, the sites named as Jerusalem's allies (Josh. 10) include some of the most important power centers in southern Canaan. The ancient audience would understand that this coalition of kings was formidable. The message comes across clearly: The power of God is able to overcome insurmountable odds.

The Divine Warrior's activity is portrayed three ways in verses 6–14. First, God works through human beings. In verses 7–10, the Lord fights in and through Joshua's troops with a human-divine synergism. The Israelites march all night from Gilgal to Gibeon to launch a surprise counteroffensive against the Amorites, who flee in terror. Divinely induced panic is a typical motif in biblical accounts of holy war. Second, God works directly through natural forces. Just as God plagued the Egyptians with hail (Exod. 9:22–26) or used torrential rainfalls to aid Deborah and Barak (Judg. 5:20–21), here God fights for Israel using hailstones for ammunition. Third, an ancient fragment of poetry has been inserted in verses 12–13 to assert that God can also intervene supernaturally on behalf of God's people. An editor has interpreted the poem to mean that God miraculously lengthened the day so that Israel could continue to fight until victory was complete.

The poetic fragment cannot originally have had to do with a lengthened day. The sun is over Gibeon to the east and the moon over the Aijalon Valley to the west only at daybreak; if the poet was asking time to stand still, he or she was asking that dawn be extended. Scholars debate the original meaning of the poetic plea. Perhaps the request was for an omen: for the sun and moon to be visible at once. Perhaps it was a fragment of a myth, in which the sun and moon were regarded as deities. Richard Nelson offers the most likely interpretation of the verse: The poet is using metaphorical language, calling out to the sun and moon to stand still in amazement at God's mighty deeds (Nelson, 1997, 144–45). As the text now stands, the brief poem affirms divine power and will to bend even nature to accomplish God's purpose.

All of these perspectives insist that Yahweh is powerfully active on behalf of Israel. The panic, the hailstones, and the supernatural behavior of the sun and moon are all God's doing. Verse 14 states the message explicitly: "The LORD fought for Israel."

The second section of the chapter (vv. 16–27) describes the subjugation and execution of the kings who fought against Gibeon, its ally Israel, and Israel's champion, God. The account fits rather oddly with the previous battle narrative. Some backtracking in the chronology of the chapter takes place. Moreover, the story of the five kings hiding in a cave is improbable. To be sure, many caves exist in the chalky rock of the lowlands, but the kings would not likely seek refuge in a cave when they had their own fortified cities.

Most commentators believe that the story grew up in order to explain the presence of a cave whose mouth had been blocked by a rockfall and a nearby cluster of trees. Within the context of chapter 10, the story serves a different purpose, attesting to the totality of Israel's victory over its enemies. Stepping on someone is an act of humiliation and subordination. God promises one of the kings of Judah to "make your enemies your footstool" (Ps. 110:1). According to the Apostle Paul, Christ will "put all his enemies under his feet"; the "last enemy . . . is death" (1 Cor. 15:25–26). The same idea is found in the slogan, "Don't tread on me." Joshua demonstrates Israel's full triumph over its enemies.

The execution of the five kings and Joshua's contemptuous treatment of their bodies, while grisly, conveys the Deuteronomists' message. When Israel is faithful, God is faithful, allowing Israel to triumph regardless of the odds. The heart of the message is found in verse 25: "Do not be afraid . . . for thus the LORD will do to all the enemies." This word would be powerful to an audience in Josiah's time, as Judah struggled to reassert its national identity. It would be even more vital for the battered communities of exiled and colonized Judeans who, humanly speaking, had no power at all to resist their enemies. Joshua's command to take the kings' bodies down from the trees (v. 27) is in fulfillment of Deuteronomic law (Deut. 21:22–23; Josh. 8:29).

The account of Israel's triumphant southern campaign concludes with a stereotyped list of cities that Joshua captured (vv. 28–39) and a final sweeping Deuteronomistic summary of Israel's conquests to date (vv. 40–43). Some scholars believe that the list preserves ancient traditions. Other, more recent commentators argue that the list is a literary composition that reflects territorial boundaries more relevant to the time of King Josiah than to the premonarchical period. The notes are couched in stereotypical, ideological language. Repeated terms like "all Israel," "the LORD gave," "struck with the edge of the sword," and "utterly destroyed" have more to do with the importance that the compilers placed on Israelite unity, the divine gift of the land, or the totality of the conquest than they have to do with details of military history. But Israel eventually did come to possess all of the cities listed. When and how they were given the land is perhaps less crucial theologically than the fact that Israel did arise in Canaan, and that it understood itself to possess its land by the gift and grace of God.

The list recounts the conquest of six cities and one additional king. The cities overlap but are not identical to the five cities whose monarchs attacked Gibeon in verses 1–15. Makkedah and Libnah are not among the allied towns named earlier; Jerusalem and Jarmuth, whose kings were part of the coalition, are not mentioned in verses 28–39. In the case of Jerusalem, the well-established tradition that it became Israelite only in the time of King David may explain the compiler's disregard. Why Jarmuth was not added is unclear.

Like the story of the Amorite coalition and the account of the death of the Amorite kings, the list of cities conquered by Joshua and his troops serves to emphasize the totality of the conquest and its seeming rapidity (v. 42). The compiler has telescoped events in order to magnify the achievement of Israel and particularly its God.

The Deuteronomists' claims concerning the amount of territory conquered are expansive. The "hill country," "Negeb," and "lowland" together comprise all of Judah. The location of Goshen is uncertain; it is not the region in Egypt called by the same name. Kadesh-barnea is on the extreme southern edge of Canaan. Gaza was a Philistine city well into the period of Israel's monarchy. Like the rest of the chapter, the summary serves a doxological purpose rather than a historical one: The whole of the land is Israel's by virtue of divine gift.

THE NORTHERN CAMPAIGN
Joshua 11

11:1 When King Jabin of Hazor heard of this, he sent to King Jobab of Madon, to the king of Shimron, to the king of Achshaph, [2] and to the kings who were in the northern hill country, and in the Arabah south of Chinneroth, and in the lowland, and in Naphoth-dor on the west, [3] to the Canaanites in the east and the west, the Amorites, the Hittites, the Perizzites, and the Jebusites in the hill country, and the Hivites under Hermon in the land of Mizpah. [4] They came out, with all their troops, a great army, in number like the sand on the seashore, with very many horses and chariots. [5] All these kings joined their forces, and came and camped together at the waters of Merom, to fight with Israel.

[6] And the LORD said to Joshua, "Do not be afraid of them, for tomorrow at this time I will hand over all of them, slain, to Israel; you shall hamstring their horses, and burn their chariots with fire." [7] So Joshua came suddenly upon them with all his fighting force, by the waters of Merom, and fell upon them. [8] And the LORD handed them over to Israel, who attacked them and chased them as far as Great Sidon and Misrephoth-maim, and eastward as far as the valley of Mizpeh. They struck them down, until they had left no one remaining. [9] And Joshua did to them as the LORD commanded him; he hamstrung their horses, and burned their chariots with fire.

[10] Joshua turned back at that time, and took Hazor, and struck its king down with the sword. Before that time Hazor was the head of all those kingdoms. [11] And they put to the sword all who were in it, utterly destroying them; there was no one left who breathed, and he burned Hazor with fire. [12] And all the towns of those kings, and all their kings, Joshua took, and struck them with the edge of the sword, utterly destroying them, as Moses the servant of the LORD had commanded. [13] But Israel burned none of the towns that stood on mounds except Hazor, which Joshua did burn. [14] All the spoil of these towns, and the livestock, the Israelites took for their booty; but all the people they struck down with the edge of the sword, until they had destroyed them, and they did not leave any who breathed. [15] As the LORD had commanded his servant Moses, so Moses commanded Joshua, and so Joshua did; he left nothing undone of all that the LORD had commanded Moses.

[16] So Joshua took all that land: the hill country and all the Negeb and all the land of Goshen and the lowland and the Arabah and the hill country of Israel and its lowland, [17] from Mount Halak, which rises toward Seir, as far as Baal-gad in the valley of Lebanon below Mount Hermon. He took all their kings, struck them down, and put them to death. [18] Joshua made war a long time with all those kings. [19] There was not a town that made peace with the Israelites, except the Hivites, the inhabitants of Gibeon; all were taken in battle. [20] For it was the LORD's doing to harden their hearts so that they would

come against Israel in battle, in order that they might be utterly destroyed, and might receive no mercy, but be exterminated, just as the LORD had commanded Moses.

[21] At that time Joshua came and wiped out the Anakim from the hill country, from Hebron, from Debir, from Anab, and from all the hill country of Judah, and from all the hill country of Israel; Joshua utterly destroyed them with their towns. [22] None of the Anakim was left in the land of the Israelites; some remained only in Gaza, in Gath, and in Ashdod. [23] So Joshua took the whole land, according to all that the LORD had spoken to Moses; and Joshua gave it for an inheritance to Israel according to their tribal allotments. And the land had rest from war.

Israel's victory over the south complete, attention turns to the conquest of northern Canaan. The central action, the battle at Merom, takes place in upper Galilee, an area assigned to Naphtali and Zebulun, the northernmost tribes of Israel. Some commentators believe that the story of the battle is based on the memories of those northern tribes, especially Napthali. Others argue that the story is a literary construction prompted by extensive ruins at Hazor.

The narrative has been patterned after the account of the southern campaign in chapter 10. Again, Israel's success threatens a king who organizes a coalition to stop Israelite incursion into the land. Again a proactive Joshua leads a night march to seize the initiative of the battle, overcoming his opponents in a surprise attack. As in chapter 10, Yahweh assures Joshua that Israel will win the battle (v. 6). Defeat of the allied kings and their forces on the battlefield is followed again by Israel's far-flung pursuit of fleeing enemies and by the destruction of their cities. Like chapter 10, chapter 11 ends with a summary of Joshua's victories, this time including the whole of Canaan.

The purpose of chapter 11 mirrors that of chapter 10. The battle accounts witness to the power of the Divine Warrior to prevail against seemingly insurmountable odds. They are meant to encourage their audiences not to fear Israel's opponents, but to have confidence in God and to obey.

While the account of the northern campaign significantly parallels the story of the southern campaign, significant differences are also present. First, while the enemy coalition in chapter 10 is described quite specifically, the description of the northern allies becomes increasingly general and vague.

The first site that the story names is historically recognizable. Hazor was the largest city in Canaan. The upper city occupied 25 acres; the lower city covered 170 acres, dwarfing any other town in Palestine in that period.

Jabin, the king named in 11:1, is associated with Hazor elsewhere in the Bible (Judg. 4:2).

The next three allies that King Jabin calls upon are Madon, Shimron, and Achshaph. Now unknown, these cities were probably located in the upper Galilee south of Hazor. After they are specified, the narrative presents a sweeping, generalized list of the foes arrayed against Israel from as far away as the region of Dor (a Mediterranean coastal city) and the Jordan Valley south of the Sea of Galilee (the Arabah south of Chinneroth). All of the inhabitants of Canaan, as the tradition named them (v. 3), came out to battle.

The aim of the list is not to provide military history, but to impress the audience with the vast numbers and superior weaponry arrayed against Joshua. Israel's enemies were like the sand on the seashore, too numerous to count. Their military technology—horses and chariots—greatly outstripped the Israelite foot soldiers. The pattern reappears: against insurmountable odds, Israel utterly devastates its foes. The story's embattled audience is to realize their God is able.

A second difference between chapter 11 and chapter 10 is the nature of divine participation in battle. In the story of the southern campaign, the "LORD fought for Israel" directly, using panic, hailstones, and celestial powers to defeat the Amorites. No such miraculous intervention takes place in the northern conquest stories. Rather, God acts indirectly through human beings, reassuring Joshua, instructing him in battle tactics, and issuing commands. Israel was convinced that God's power is at work behind the scenes of history as well as manifesting itself in more dramatic ways.

Third, the description of the northern campaign explicitly emphasizes the link between obedience and success. The summary of Israel's victories in the south already pointedly notes that Joshua acted "as the LORD God of Israel commanded" (10:40). "Commanded" is repeated six more times in the account of the northern conquest (vv. 9, 12, 15, 20). The first speech in the book of Joshua specifies the content of the command that Joshua is to obey: the law of Moses. The northern conquest stories stress both the chain of command—God, Moses, Joshua, Israel (11:12, 15)—and Joshua's complete fidelity ("he left nothing undone" [11:15]).

The fourth difference is the assertion that "the Lord hardened (the) hearts" of all of the towns except Gibeon so that in battling Israel "they might be utterly destroyed." The view that God is responsible when Israel's enemies resist them (and so, resist God) is best known from the stories of God hardening the heart of Pharaoh so that he would not let the Hebrews go (Exod. 7–14). The notion is a difficult one, whether we are dealing with the Exodus story or with Joshua, because of its incompatibility with what Scriptures elsewhere teach us about God's love for all creation.

In part, the view that God sets up people in order to punish them or to demonstrate divine glory reflects the authors' efforts to hold together their belief that nothing is outside God's power with their recognition that some people resist God's will. The problem of evil is real; ascribing responsibility for it to God as God moves towards some larger good purpose is a common human response.

The assertion that "God hardened their hearts" may have encouraged the ancient audiences of Joshua; the struggling, relatively powerless Judeans in the time of Josiah; or the defeated community in exile. For those audiences, the assertion that their enemies' violent actions were part of God's plan for Israel's welfare would have been a hopeful word. As Richard Nelson notes, the theological word behind the claim that God hardens hearts is that even apparent setbacks serve God's good goals (Nelson, 1997, 152).

The note in 11:21–22 that Joshua drove out the Anakim from the whole of the land does not fit well with other biblical references to them. Elsewhere, the Anakim are referred to as gigantic people living around Hebron. Moreover, in Joshua 14:12, Caleb asks to be given Hebron, in the hopes that he will be able to drive out the Anakim and take possession of the city. Like so much of the conquest narratives, the notice makes sense when one looks at it from a theological rather than a historical perspective. God has already empowered Joshua to drive out enemies vast in numbers. Now God empowers Joshua to drive out giants, vast in size. The whole functions to assert that nothing can thwart Israel, so long as Israel is obedient.

Like chapter 10, the account of victory in the north ends with a description of the extent of Joshua's conquests. The summary is as sweeping as the conclusion of the southern conquest stories (10:40–43). Israel controls the land from Mount Halak (a point comparable to, but probably even further south than, Beersheba) to Baal-gad, a site described as under Mount Hermon, the very northernmost point that tradition ascribed Israel's boundaries. The list of conquered cities in chapter 12 serves the same purpose. It lifts up God's awesome power and complete fidelity to the divine promise.

10. Possessing the Land
Joshua 13–19

In chapter 1, God lays on Joshua a twofold charge: first, to lead the Israelites in battle, and second, to "put this people in possession" of the newly conquered land. Joshua accomplishes the first task in chapters 2–12. In chapters 13–19, Joshua undertakes his second assignment, dividing the newly vanquished territory.

The kind of material in Joshua 13–19 differs from that of Joshua 2–12. Battle stories, spy narratives, and liturgically colored accounts give way to list after list of frontier points and towns with their hinterlands, interspersed with very brief, intriguing narratives. It would be tempting to set the lists aside as archival material, of interest to historians but without relevance for theology or the life of faith.

Such a dismissal would be a mistake. As noted earlier, chapters 2–12 are theological writings in the shape of history. Chapters 13–19 are theology in the guise of geography. Both assert God's gracious governance of Israel. In the first part of the book, the Divine Warrior fights for Israel to gain its land. In the second part of the book, God as landowner grants each of the remaining tribes their inheritances. The message is clear; God sets the boundaries of the nation as a whole and of each separate Israelite tribe. The importance of this God-given land to the ancient Israelites can hardly be overstated. Land represents a means of livelihood, a place of safety, a source of national identity. The ideal life is "rest" in the land. Land is freedom and salvation.

Other theological issues raised in the first half of the book are lifted up in the account of the division of the land. The *synergistic quality of divine/human action* is again apparent. That God determines Israel's borders does not negate Israel's role in allotting and possessing their territory. Joshua is commanded to divide the land (13:6). The northern tribes are chided for failing to take the inheritance God has given them (18:3). Divine agency and human action again combine to put Israel in possession of the land.

The *leadership of Joshua* is reasserted and nuanced. An editor working sometime after the Deuteronomistic Historians inserted a note that the priest Eleazar and the heads of the families also lead in the allotment.

The *unity of Israel* finds expression in an emphasis on the twelve land-holding tribes of Israel. There is widespread agreement that the idea that Israel was comprised of exactly twelve tribes descended from the twelve sons of Jacob was superimposed on a much more fluid tribal reality. The emphasis on Israel's twelve tribes has more to do with theology and politics than with sociology. The compilers and editors of Joshua agreed: *All* of the people of Israel occupied Canaan.

Four issues must be raised before comment on the individual chapters begins. The first concerns the nature of Israelite tribes. From a sociological perspective, the notion that the tribes were comprised of the descendants of Jacob's (Israel's) twelve sons oversimplifies the complexities of Israelite tribal society. The kinship ties upon which the tribes are supposed to be based are partly real in a biological sense, and partly expressions of social bonds. Renee Whiterabbit, a HoChunk clanswoman and Christian minister, finds similarity between ancient Israel's use of family trees to express social relationships and HoChunk customs. The HoChunk adjust their genealogies to incorporate new members brought into the clan through marriage by grafting their parents or grandparents onto the family tree. Such readjustments are not lies; they are ways of expressing social realities.

The idea of exactly twelve tribes is also a simplification. Some of the tribes in the list (Simeon, Reuben) seem to have disappeared or been assimilated into other groups by the monarchical period, while certain individuals (e.g., Caleb, Othniel) appear to represent tribes rather than persons. The complexity and fluidity of tribal reality can be glimpsed in the efforts that the editors had to make in order to arrive at a consistent total of twelve tribes. The repeated references to the Levites' lack of territory, the explanation that the House of Joseph is comprised of two tribes, and the recollection that two and a half tribes occupied land east of the Jordan are all part of an effort to make the arithmetic work.

The second issue addresses the kind of material found in chapters 13–19. The lists read like a bureaucrat's papers and may be just that. Most commentators believe that the town lists were compiled by administrators in the late monarchical period in order to gather taxes, conscript soldiers and forced laborers, or determine legal jurisdiction. The boundary descriptions may be administrative documents from an earlier day. Some scholars argue that they were compiled by officials during the time of King

David or of Solomon in order to adjudicate disputes between tribes over water or grazing rights. Others understand the boundary lists as academic exercises from much later in the monarchy.

Third, we must note that the boundary reports are far from clear. Even specialists in Palestinian topography acknowledge that many of the descriptions are obscured by the large percentage of sites not yet identified, the fragmentary nature of many of the lists, and the heavy and inconsistent editing that the texts have undergone. Because numerous towns have the same name and because different names are given to the same town, following the descriptions of the allotments is difficult. The comments below focus on the theological significance of the tribal allotments and present only general efforts to identify the borders of each tribe.

Fourth, the multiple editing that chapters 13–19 have undergone is itself an important issue for understanding these texts. The complex history of the composition of these chapters has not yet been untangled in a way on which scholars can agree. Cities or boundary points have been added or changed in individual lists, and materials from different periods and places have been woven together, giving rise to inconsistencies and contradictions.

UNFINISHED BUSINESS
Joshua 13

13:1 Now Joshua was old and advanced in years; and the LORD said to him, "You are old and advanced in years, and very much of the land still remains to be possessed. ² This is the land that still remains: all the regions of the Philistines, and all those of the Geshurites ³ (from the Shihor, which is east of Egypt, northward to the boundary of Ekron, it is reckoned as Canaanite; there are five rulers of the Philistines, those of Gaza, Ashdod, Ashkelon, Gath, and Ekron), and those of the Avvim, ⁴ in the south, all the land of the Canaanites, and Mearah that belongs to the Sidonians, to Aphek, to the boundary of the Amorites, ⁵ and the land of the Gebalites, and all Lebanon, toward the east, from Baal-gad below Mount Hermon to Lebo-hamath, ⁶ all the inhabitants of the hill country from Lebanon to Misrephoth-maim, even all the Sidonians. I will myself drive them out from before the Israelites; only allot the land to Israel for an inheritance, as I have commanded you. ⁷ Now therefore divide this land for an inheritance to the nine tribes and the half-tribe of Manasseh."

The chapter begins with a notice that Joshua has grown old. The audience is to assume that years have passed since Joshua led his troops into battle. There is still work to be done, and Joshua must do it before he dies. In Joshua 1:1–9, God's speech to Joshua launched the conquest of the land; now, divine speech sets in motion the division of their newly conquered territory among the tribes (13:1–7).

The content of the divine speech has to do with land yet to be possessed. In the first instance, the unpossessed land refers to territory already seized in battle that must be parceled out among the tribes and occupied (vv. 1, 7). The Israelites are to settle down, farm the land, and make it theirs.

A later editor added verses 2–6, reinterpreting the meaning of "land that still remains" to refer to territory that Israel had not conquered. The descriptions of the unconquered territories are not entirely clear. Apparently verses 3–6 lay claim to the southern coastal plain of the Philistines, the Aviim, and the Gershurites, and the northern coastal regions of Phoenicia.

The late editor's territorial claims are highly idealistic. Verses 2–6 describe territory that was never incorporated into Judah. The Philistines, Israel's main rivals for dominance of Canaan, fell under Israelite hegemony only briefly, during the time of David and Solomon. Israel never controlled the Phoenician territory. After the Babylonian conquest, such claims form a kind of outrageous promise. Israel would regain not only its historical land, but would expand to ideal boundaries. Although the exiled Israelites did eventually receive permission to return to their homeland, the boundaries of the restored Jewish community never reached such utopian dimensions. Nonetheless, the verses suggest the "already" and "not yet" inherent in the life of faith. Then and now, communities of faith always live toward a vision of what God has yet to do. (The clans that comprised Manasseh were settled both east and west of the Jordan. The "half tribe" of Manasseh refers to the eastern clans.)

The second section of the chapter (vv. 8–32) delineates the territories of the eastern tribes. The land yet to be distributed is west of the Jordan River. Moses had already given the eastern tribes their portions. Nonetheless, the borders of Reuben, Gad, and the half tribe of Manasseh are included here in order to remind the audience that "all Israel" includes each of the twelve tribes.

By the time the Deuteronomists compiled their work, the land east of the Jordan River had been lost to Israel for a long time. The boundary descriptions may reflect King Josiah's expansionist aspirations for his nationalist renewal movement. If they were compiled later, the descriptions would function like the utopian claims of verses 2–6.

Moses' conquest of the kings, Sihon and Og, must have been considered models of the Divine Warrior's saving deeds on Israel's behalf. The

Deuteronomists refer to Sihon and Og often. In this instance (13:21), triumph over the eastern kings is joined to traditions about Moses' victory over five Midianite princes (Num. 31:8). The reference to Moses' execution of Balaam, a Moabite diviner, also draws on Numbers 31:8; Balaam is remembered more positively in Numbers 22–24.

CALEB'S CLAIM
Joshua 14

14:1 These are the inheritances that the Israelites received in the land of Canaan, which the priest Eleazar, and Joshua son of Nun, and the heads of the families of the tribes of the Israelites distributed to them. ² Their inheritance was by lot, as the LORD had commanded Moses for the nine and one-half tribes. ³ For Moses had given an inheritance to the two and one-half tribes beyond the Jordan; but to the Levites he gave no inheritance among them. ⁴ For the people of Joseph were two tribes, Manasseh and Ephraim; and no portion was given to the Levites in the land, but only towns to live in, with their pasture lands for their flocks and herds. ⁵ The Israelites did as the LORD commanded Moses; they allotted the land.

⁶ Then the people of Judah came to Joshua at Gilgal; and Caleb son of Jephunneh the Kenizzite said to him, "You know what the LORD said to Moses the man of God in Kadesh-barnea concerning you and me. ⁷ I was forty years old when Moses the servant of the LORD sent me from Kadesh-barnea to spy out the land; and I brought him an honest report. ⁸ But my companions who went up with me made the heart of the people melt; yet I wholeheartedly followed the LORD my God. ⁹ And Moses swore on that day, saying, 'Surely the land on which your foot has trodden shall be an inheritance for you and your children forever, because you have wholeheartedly followed the LORD my God.' ¹⁰ And now, as you see, the LORD has kept me alive, as he said, these forty-five years since the time that the LORD spoke this word to Moses, while Israel was journeying through the wilderness; and here I am today, eighty-five years old. ¹¹ I am still as strong today as I was on the day that Moses sent me; my strength now is as my strength was then, for war, and for going and coming. ¹² So now give me this hill country of which the LORD spoke on that day; for you heard on that day how the Anakim were there, with great fortified cities; it may be that the LORD will be with me, and I shall drive them out, as the LORD said."

¹³ Then Joshua blessed him, and gave Hebron to Caleb son of Jephunneh for an inheritance. ¹⁴ So Hebron became the inheritance of Caleb son of Jephunneh the Kenizzite to this day, because he wholeheartedly followed the LORD, the God of Israel. ¹⁵ Now the name of Hebron formerly was Kiriath-arba; this Arba was the greatest man among the Anakim. And the land had rest from war.

Verses 1–5 present the cast of characters involved in the allotment of the newly acquired territory west of the Jordan: Eleazar, Joshua, and the heads of the families of Israel (v. 1). Eleazar, Joshua, and representatives of the tribes are responsible for land distribution in Numbers 34:17; in the book of Joshua, the presence of Eleazar and the heads of the families comes as a surprise. Most commentators assume that a late editor associated with priestly circles inserted references to the priest Eleazar into the text. Note that the priest, Eleazar, is given priority over Joshua each time the two characters are listed together.

The method by which tribal lands will be assigned is alluded to in verse 2; the inheritances are determined by lot. The use of some sort of lottery system to apportion land is common across cultures and throughout history. Ancient Israel used the lot not only to ensure fairness, but primarily as a means of ascertaining the will of God. The outcome of the lot, according to Israelite belief, was divinely determined.

Both the division of the land and the method by which it is carried out are by divine command. The introductory verses are bracketed by the assertion that the Israelites are doing just as the Lord had commanded Moses (vv. 2, 5). The theme of obedience to divine command as it is mediated through Moses, sounded often in the first twelve chapters of Joshua, receives no less emphasis in the second part of the book.

Verses 3 and 4 focus on the math by which one arrives at "twelve tribes," an assertion that is more theological than historical. King Josiah reigned over a land that consisted of Judah and a portion of Benjamin; the northern tribes had fallen to Assyria over a century before. For the Deuteronomists of Josiah's time to emphasize Israel's twelve tribes was a way of asserting Josiah's rights to the lost northern and eastern lands. For the exiles, the attention to the mathematics of the twelve-tribe scheme would serve as a reminder of how completely God had fulfilled the promises to their ancestors; all of Israel received its land. The presence of a dozen tribes also held out an impossibly grand vision; Israel was not to be just a restored Jerusalem and the battered lands around it. Rather, Israel would constitute the whole of the southern and northern kingdoms as they were in their most glorious days.

With the end of the introduction in verse 5, the reader expects an account of the distribution of land to the western tribes. Instead, the narrative detours; Caleb requests and is given his promised inheritance, as Joshua will receive his at the end of the distribution (19:49–50). The story of tribal allotments begins and ends with grants to individuals, while a grant to a group of sisters, the daughters of Zelophehad, is found at the center of the account (17:3–4).

The Caleb account is an etiology, that is, an explanatory tale. Most scholars understand Caleb as the legendary ancestor of the Calebites, a tribe or subtribe that was probably related to Edom. The Calebites eventually were absorbed into greater Judah. The story of the granting of Caleb's request would have explained why the important Judean town of Hebron was a Calebite possession.

The story also models faithfulness. The Israelites fulfill the promise that God made to Caleb through Moses (v. 9; see also Deut. 1:36). Caleb is an example as well as a recipient of faithful action. According to a tradition recorded in Numbers 13, Moses sent representatives from each of the twelve tribes to scout out their promised inheritance. The returning spies agreed that Canaan was rich and fertile, but ten of them reported that its inhabitants were too powerful to conquer. Only Caleb and Joshua urged the Israelites to trust God's promise and follow the divine command to enter and take the land. Hebron is the prize for this fealty, a point underscored by the threefold insistence that Caleb wholeheartedly followed the Lord (Josh. 14:8, 9, 14). The very name "Caleb" suggests obedience. Derived from the Hebrew word for "dog," the name serves as an image of self-abasement but also of loyalty. Caleb is a model in which Judah is to see itself. The message is clear; such faithfulness is rewarded with land, blessing (v. 13), and rest from war (v. 15). The story would call Josiah's subjects to covenantal loyalty and would have offered exiled and colonized Judah hope: Faithfulness might still be rewarded with the gift of land.

Moreover, the model of faithfulness is a non-Israelite. The text explicitly identifies Caleb as a Kenizzite, understood as an Edomite group. (According to Joshua 15:17, Caleb and his brother Othniel are descendents of Kenaz, who is identified in a genealogy in Genesis as a son of Esau, that is, Edom. Whether identifying the Kenizzites with the Edomites has any historical basis is not the point. The compilers of this text explicitly identify Caleb as a non-Israelite.) The conquest narratives began with the exemplary faithfulness of a Canaanite prostitute (Josh. 2). The accounts of the distribution of land likewise begin with the model loyalty of a non-Israelite. Once again the narrative declares that the true Israelite is defined by faithfulness, not ethnicity.

THE TERRITORY OF JUDAH
Joshua 15

At last, in chapter 15, one comes to an account of the allotment of land. The account begins with Judah. Joshua is written from a Judahite perspective.

Judah is not the first-born in the legends about Jacob and his children. He has no special standing in the ancestral tales. But the Deuteronomistic History, including Joshua, was compiled in the south after the northern tribes (all but Judah and parts of Benjamin) had become part of an Assyrian province. Naturally, the Deuteronomists dealt with the description of their own territory first and in the most detail.

The description of Judah's territory has three parts: first, the delineation of Judah's borders (vv. 1–12); then, additional Calebite traditions (vv. 13–19); and finally, lists of towns assigned to Judah (vv. 20–63).

Boundary Lists
Joshua 15:1–12

The description of Judah's territory begins with lists of frontier towns and landmarks that, connected together like a child's connect-the-dots picture, give a rough idea of the tribe's borders. The territory ascribed to Judah in the boundary lists of verses 1–12 is smaller than the Judah of the city lists (vv. 20–63). The boundary list does not, for example, include Jerusalem (contrary to verse 63). Nonetheless, Judah of the boundary descriptions is still idealized. The borders run to the Mediterranean Sea, taking in the coastal plain, a region that was never part of Judah proper. The Deuteronomists were less interested in accurate geography than in Israelite national identity and Israelite aspirations.

Another Calebite Tradition
Joshua 15:13–19

The previous chapter focuses on the story of Caleb's request for Hebron and its environs (14:6–15). Caleb's petition cites his resolve to drive out the Anakim, giants who inhabit fortified towns in the region: "It may be that the LORD will be with me, and I shall drive them out. . . ." Joshua 15:13–19 continues the Caleb narrative, showing that the Lord was indeed with Caleb, who succeeds in eliminating the Anakim. Once again, obedience is blessed by divine aid.

The story also explains why Debir, a Judahite city, belongs to the Othnielites, apparently another Kenizzite group related to the Edomites. According to legend, their ancestor, Othniel, won both the town and Caleb's daughter by military victory. Othniel appears again in Judges 3:7–11 as an ideal judge/deliverer.

The Achsah narrative (vv. 16–19) explains why two springs of water belong to the Othnielites. This passage is one of four accounts of land grants to individuals in the Joshua distribution narratives. The first grantee, Caleb, was a non-Israelite. The second, Achsah, is a non-Israelite *woman*. Achsah is hardly a passive or submissive character; her initiative is rewarded.

The picture of Achsah in this brief tale conforms to the little we know about the status of women in ancient Israel. She is under the authority first of her father, who gives her in marriage as a prize, then under the authority of her husband. Nonetheless, her gender does not make her chattel. Achsah's assertive and successful request for a gift illustrates the influence that a woman might have had, and demonstrates the difference between formal power and informal influence. Her influence is greater than the legal status of ancient Israelite women might suggest. The story of Achsah must have been significant for the ancient Judean storytellers, because it turns up again in Judges 1:11–15.

City Lists

Joshua 15:20–63

The chapter concludes with an extensive list of towns assigned to Judah, again reflecting the compilers' perspective. Over a third of the towns enumerated in Joshua belong to the southern tribe.

Though tedious and, to all but specialists in Israelite topography, obscure, the town list makes a significant theological point. God's gift to Israel has a this-worldly dimension that takes shape concretely, in the economic, political, and social spheres of life.

The chapter ends with a cautionary note. Judah was not able to drive the Jebusites out of Jerusalem. The note acknowledges a historical fact: Jerusalem became Israelite only during David's reign. It also puts the Josianic and exilic audiences on notice: the land is a gift, but the gift is not automatic. Receiving it can involve struggle; failure is possible, but does not cancel the promised gift.

THE HOUSE OF JOSEPH
Joshua 16 and 17

From the Deuteronomists' perspective, the most important tribes after Judah were Ephraim and Manasseh. Their significance lay in part in their proximity; Ephraim was immediately north of Benjamin, only a few miles from Judah. They were also the largest and most influential northern tribes. These Josephite tribes dominated tribes of the north—so much that the northern kingdom was frequently referred to as "Ephraim." Because of their importance, the Deuteronomists discuss the Josephite tribes immediately after describing Judah's territory.

The discussion of Ephraim and Manasseh shows the same concern for the twelve-tribe schema already noted. Some lists of Israel's twelve tribes count Joseph and Levi as separate tribes. In Joshua, we are repeatedly reminded that Levi had no inheritance; it is not included in the tally. Ephraim and Manasseh are counted separately to make up the twelve.

An ancestral saga found in Genesis 48 depicts Ephraim and Manasseh as Joseph's sons. The saga accounts for the allotment of two shares rather than one to the house of Joseph. Jacob adopted them as his own, bequeathing them each the portion of a son, rather than a grandson. The same story explains that Ephraim (who tradition held was the younger brother) outranked his elder brother Manasseh because the former received Jacob's special blessing.

The Deuteronomists recognized both the closeness and the distinctiveness of Ephraim and Manasseh. At the beginning (16:1–4) and end (17:14–18) of the discussion of their territories, the two tribes are treated as a single unit: "the Josephites." The middle of the account delineates Ephraim's (16:6–10) and Manasseh's (17:1–13) allotments separately. Whether because of the ancestral legend or because of its proximity to Judah, Ephraim is described first.

The number of sites that remain unidentified and the fragmentary condition of the boundary list render the descriptions of Ephraim and Manasseh notoriously obscure. In addition to the boundary lists, the editors included intriguing land grant accounts.

First is the story of the daughters of Zelophehad (17:3–4), found also in Numbers 27:1–11. There, the tale functions to explain and legitimize a rule permitting daughters to inherit if their fathers had no sons. Joshua 17 assumes the inheritance rights of such daughters. The emphasis here (17:3–4) is on the fulfillment of Moses' pledge to the daughters. Like the account of land granted to Caleb (14:6–15), the story models loyalty to the Mosaic word while also reinforcing the lines of authority found elsewhere in the book of Joshua: the Lord, to Moses, to Joshua, and to other designated leaders. Never in the book of Joshua does God speak directly to the Israelites.

The tale of Zelophehad's daughters provides insight into the status of ancient Israelite women as one of a few late texts that attest to Judean women's capacity to inherit land, at least in the postexilic period. The portrayal of Mahlah, Noah, Hoglah, Milcah, and Tirzah is also notable in that they, like Achsah, are women whose assertiveness is rewarded. The text is clearly patriarchally shaped. Inheritance by women is an exception rather than a rule; authority is held by men. Nonetheless, female passivity is not idealized.

In the final verses of chapter 17 (vv. 14–18), the Josephites approach Joshua with a request for land. Like Caleb, Achsah, and Zelophehad's daughters, they present their case: they are too numerous for the allotted territory. This time, however, the petition is denied. Instead, Joshua offers two strategies for dealing with their cramped condition. The first assumes that the problem stems from the densely wooded nature of the land given Ephraim and Manasseh; Joshua instructs the brother-tribes to clear the hills and settle them. The second identifies the problem as the two tribes' inability to conquer completely their assigned land. The enemy is too powerful. (The "Rephaim" of verse 15 were a legendary group of extraordinarily tall people.) Moreover, they possess superior technology (17:18). Joshua assures Ephraim and Manasseh that they will drive out the Canaanites, despite the enemy's numerical strength, military superiority, and physical stature. Implicit in Joshua's speech is the belief that God will continue to fight on Israel's behalf.

DISTRIBUTION AT SHILOH
Joshua 18–19

The accounts of the distribution of land to the remaining seven tribes form a single unit, distinguished from the previous chapters by a new introduction (18:1), and by a shift in setting from Gilgal (14:6) to Shiloh. References to Shiloh and the tent of meeting bracket chapters 18 and 19, further defining them as a unit.

The Joshua account of land distribution at Shiloh is politically realistic. Commentators point out that the account divides Israelite territory roughly into thirds. Judah receives the first third; Ephraim and Manasseh—large, dominant tribes—the second third; the remaining tribes receive the final third.

The narrative of the allotments to the seven remaining tribes raises themes that we have already encountered. Joshua's leadership is reasserted. He, not Eleazar, casts the lots that determine each tribe's share. The section concludes with a land grant to Joshua, rewarding his faithfulness (19:49–50).

That God has granted land to all Israel and that "all Israel" consists of twelve tribes is again stressed. The Galilean tribes (Zebulun, Issachar, Asher, and Naphtali) had lost their lands and their identities to Assyria over a hundred years before the time of King Josiah, when the book was first compiled. Simeon's towns had long been absorbed into Judah; by the time of the exile, when the book was revised, those towns had been taken by Edom. The compilers insisted that these regions were also part of Israel, laying claim to the land and fostering Israel's sense of national identity.

The synergistic relationship of God's action and human effort is again apparent. In Joshua 18–19, the human role is to survey the remaining territory, parceling it into equitable portions and casting lots to assign the parcels to the seven tribes.

Within this synergism, God's action and authorization has priority. Through the allotment, God gives concrete shape to the promise made to the ancestors and reiterated to Joshua and Israel.

In 18:1, the scene shifts from Gilgal to Shiloh. The compilers may have felt that Gilgal was too far from the territory being divided to set the final allotment there. Shiloh, a town in Ephraim some twenty miles north of Jerusalem, was a more logical setting. The Deuteronomists may also have been motivated by their conviction that Shiloh was the legitimate sanctuary city before Jerusalem became the tribes' religious center. Shiloh was the only town apart from Jerusalem where Deuteronomistic editors said that God's name had dwelt (Jer. 7:12).

With the new location comes a new process. Joshua instructs representatives from each of the tribes to survey the remaining land and divide it into seven portions. Not knowing which portions they would receive would encourage evenhandedness among those responsible for the survey. The description of the distribution at Shiloh gives particular emphasis to the fairness of Israel's division of the land. No backroom dealing occurs here. All the tribes are involved in surveying and dividing the territory. Joshua assigns the territories in the presence of all Israel. The division is equitable. The first lot falls to Benjamin (18:11–27); its territory is described in far more detail than that of the remaining tribes. From the Deuteronomists' Judahite perspective, Benjamin was especially important. Its territory was adjacent to Judah's; much of Benjamin remained part of the kingdom of Judah when the nation split in 922 B.C.E.

The next tribal territory described is that of Simeon. Like Benjamin, Simeon was important from a Judahite perspective. Simeon had no contiguous territory. Rather, its land consisted of towns that were located within Judah and are included in Judah's city lists. The Judahite Deuteronomists present their tribe's relationship to the Simeonite towns not as appropriation, but as an act of magnanimity.

Zebulun (19:10–16) is consistently associated in biblical texts with Issachar (19:17–23). Zebulun occupied poor land in a southern flank of the Galilean hills, as well as a wedge of arable land in the Jezreel Valley. Issachar's portion was in the Jezreel, a fertile valley, the breadbasket of both ancient and modern Israel. Jezreel was strategically crucial, containing the most important crossroads in all Canaan. Because of its fertility and its strategic importance, the Jezreel Valley was disputed territory long after Israel arose in the land.

The land assigned to Asher (19:24–31) includes lush coastal plains reaching from Carmel in the south to Sidon in the north (that is, land north and south of modern-day Haifa) as well as western reaches of the Galilean hills. Much of the rich coastal territory was under Phoenician control. Commentators suggest that Asher was probably settled in the hill country rather than on the plain.

Naphtali (19:32–39) received as its land the heart of the Galilee, the region between the Sea of Galilee and Lake Hulah. Like Issachar, Naphtali was both blessed and cursed by major trade routes that traversed its territory.

The last tribal territory described is that of Dan. According to tradition, Dan, pressured by the Canaanites and Philistines, was unable to occupy its assigned lands. Joshua 19:47–48 describes Dan's migration to the far north of Israel, a story elaborated in Judges 18. It may be that the tribe was split, with some Danites living in the south and a majority in the north.

The division of the land ends with Joshua receiving his inheritance (19:49–50), Timnath-serah, an Ephraimite city. As in the case of the Caleb story, the grant to Joshua shows Israel fulfilling its obligations and models Israelite obedience. Israel gives Joshua the town "by command of the LORD." Like Caleb, Joshua is a model Israelite; one message of the story is that God rewards such loyalty.

With Joshua 19:51, Joshua's second task, putting the western tribes in possession of their land, is accomplished. God's promise that Israel will possess the land of Canaan is concretely fulfilled.

11. For the Sake of Justice
Joshua 20

Eleazar, Joshua, and the heads of the families have allotted the tribes their land. The discussion of territory is not yet finished, however. Two matters of land use remain. The tribal assignments in Joshua 13–19 determined the shape of Israel's land. The assignments in Joshua 20–21 suggest *how* Israel is to live on that land. Israel is to show care for its vulnerable members. It is, moreover, to be a land where justice prevails over vengeance, and where the Levitical priesthood maintains a sacral presence. In chapter 20, Joshua designates cities of refuge where people who commit unintentional homicide will be protected from blood vengeance and assured of a fair trial.

The designation of cities of refuge presupposes the practice of blood vengeance, a practice found in many cultures throughout history. Ancient Israel believed that a murder victim's closest male relative had both the responsibility and the right to avenge the death. Israel did distinguish between intentional and unintentional homicide, but rage or honor might well blind the "avenger of blood," the victim's kinsman, to the distinction.

Several biblical passages address the need to protect the accidental manslayer. A very ancient law allows unintentional homicides to claim asylum, presumably in the sanctuary, while denying asylum to deliberate murderers (Exod. 21:12–14). The practice of granting asylum to fugitives who grasp an altar is attested both in the Bible (1 Kgs. 1:50) and in a wide range of cultures.

Whether cities of refuge ever actually existed is a matter of much debate among biblical scholars. In addition to Joshua 20, Numbers 35:9–34 and Deuteronomy 19:1–13 speak of a command to establish such cities. The three interdependent passages may be expressions of a vision rather than a practice. Granted, the detailed list of cities (20:7–8) appears convincing. Nonetheless, the absence of any reference to cities of asylum in the biblical stories and the artificially schematic character of the list raise doubts about its historicity. The best approach may be to take the passage as a witness to the Israelite ideals of justice and protecting the vulnerable, rather than as historical evidence.

20:1 **Then the L**ORD **spoke to Joshua, saying,** [2] **"Say to the Israelites, 'Appoint the cities of refuge, of which I spoke to you through Moses,** [3] **so that anyone who kills a person without intent or by mistake may flee there; they shall be for you a refuge from the avenger of blood.** [4] **The slayer shall flee to one of these cities and shall stand at the entrance of the gate of the city, and explain the case to the elders of that city; then the fugitive shall be taken into the city, and given a place, and shall remain with them.** [5] **And if the avenger of blood is in pursuit, they shall not give up the slayer, because the neighbor was killed by mistake, there having been no enmity between them before.** [6] **The slayer shall remain in that city until there is a trial before the congregation, until the death of the one who is high priest at the time: then the slayer may return home, to the town in which the deed was done.'"**

Throughout the book of Joshua, God's word drives the action. Divine speech initiates the two main movements of the book: the conquest (chapters 1–12) and the distribution of the land (chapters 13–19). In an ongoing way, God commands and instructs Joshua when and how to cross the Jordan, prepare ritually for battle, and enter into battle. Now divine speech impels Joshua and the people to establish cities of refuge. This passage is the last direct speech of God in the book, though the divine will mediated by lot, by the remembered words of Moses, and by Joshua's prophetic voice continue to move Israel's story forward.

As always in the book, God speaks to Joshua, who sees that the Israelites carry out the command, a pattern that the compilers set forth in order to undergird the legitimacy of centralized leadership. As is typical, God's speech points back to Moses, highlighting the authority of Mosaic Torah.

The divine instructions assume that Joshua is already aware of the need to establish cities of asylum. In Numbers 35:9–34, God commands Moses to designate cities of refuge; in Deuteronomy 19:1–13, Moses conveys God's command to the people. In Joshua 20, the command is fulfilled.

The process for granting asylum is given in verses 2–6. Presumably, the fugitive must convince the elders of the city of refuge that enough evidence exists that his or her action was an accident rather than deliberate murder to warrant sheltering him or her. A city's elders were responsible for legal decisions, which they made at the gate, a large public area containing several rooms (see pp. 296–97).

The town is to give the fugitive "a place"; the ancient Rabbis interpreted the requirement as provision of shelter and a profession. The town is also to protect the manslayer from blood vengeance until he or she has had a fair trial. Verse 6 appears to set two different limits on how long the fugitive is to stay in the city of refuge: until the trial, and until the death of the high priest. The latter phrase seems to be taken from Numbers 35, which establishes cities of refuge both to protect the fugitive from lynching before the trial and to serve as places of exile afterward. The passage prohibits the fugitive from leaving the city of refuge before the death of the high priest (Num. 35:32). Apparently even accidental killing required expiation. Perhaps, as many scholars believe, the death of the high priest served as vicarious atonement.

Joshua and Israel carry out God's instructions in verses 7–8, designating three cities to the west of the Jordan and three on the east. (But see Deut. 4:41–43.) The parallel texts in Numbers and Deuteronomy explain that a number of towns were chosen so that they might be accessible to the fugitive, lest he or she be caught and lynched.

The purpose of the system of refuge is clearly stated in Joshua 20:9; the system exists so that persons who do not deserve death may be protected from blood vengeance. The cities are to protect both Israelites and aliens. The Hebrew word translated "aliens" refers to displaced and landless persons dependent upon landowning citizens for work and protection, persons like Rahab or the Gibeonites. Aliens were among those responsible to Mosaic law (Josh. 8:35). This passage states that they are also to benefit from it.

In the parallel passages in Deuteronomy and Numbers, desire to protect the fugitive and ensure due process is set alongside concern to protect the community from bloodguilt and pollution. These parallel texts explicitly prohibit granting asylum to deliberate murderers. Joshua 20 does not rule out these concerns, but the selection is more tightly focused. The tribes are to use some of their God-given land for the sake of justice, to protect a group of particularly vulnerable persons and to ensure due process for Israelite and alien alike.

12. Priestly Presence
Joshua 21

The land allotted to the tribes is theirs by divine gift, but it is not theirs to use heedless of God's commands or others' needs. In the previous chapter, Joshua and his people designate certain towns as cities of refuge for accidental homicides. In Joshua 21, Israel sets aside forty-eight towns for a different group of vulnerable people: the Levites. The reader is told repeatedly in Joshua 13–19 that the tribe of Levites received no allotment (13:14; 18:7). Without a contiguous territory of their own, the Levites need places to live and pasture for their herds and flocks.

If the designation of cities of refuge affirms that justice is to characterize Israel's life on the land, the allocation of Levitical cities affirms the sacral character of Israel. In addition to their landlessness, references to the Levites in the book of Joshua stress their priesthood. The Levitical priests carry the ark, emblem of the presence of the Lord (3:3; 8:33). The same notices that recall the Levites' lack of territory insist that they receive a sacred inheritance. "The LORD God of Israel is their inheritance" (13:33); "the priesthood of the LORD is their heritage" (18:7). The authors of Joshua 21 envision the Levites spread throughout Israelite territory, a visible emblem of the invisible presence of God.

The list of the cities of refuge and the catalogue of Levitical cities are integrally related, so it is not surprising that many of the scholarly issues raised about Joshua 21 echo those of Joshua 20. The historicity of the Levitical cities catalogue, like that of the cities of refuge, has been a focus of scholarly debate. As it appears in Joshua 21, the catalogue is clearly idealized. At no time in Israel's history were all forty-eight towns listed occupied by Israel. Some scholars believe that an early list of Levitical cities has been schematized and enlarged. Others argue that, by and large, the schema was a literary construct. Whether or not a network of Levitical cities existed in the tenth century, the incorporation of such a list into the seventh-century book of Joshua serves political and theological aims, affirming Levitical claims to towns and pasturelands. Within the Levites, the list emphasizes the priority of the Aaronite branch. Furthermore, the extent of the territory in which the Levitical towns are found asserts Israel's claim to the whole of Canaan, including lands east of the Jordan River that had been lost to Israel long before the book of Joshua was compiled. Most important, the catalogue of Levitical cities affirms the sacral character of Israel.

> 21:1 **Then the heads of the families of the Levites came to the priest Eleazar and to Joshua son of Nun and to the heads of the families of the tribes of the Israelites;** [2] **they said to them at Shiloh in the land of Canaan, "The LORD commanded through Moses that we be given towns to live in, along with their pasture lands for our livestock."** [3] **So by command of the LORD the Israelites gave to the Levites the following towns and pasture lands out of their inheritance. . . .** [43] **Thus the LORD gave to Israel all the land that he swore to their ancestors that he would give them; and having taken possession of it, they settled there.** [44] **And the LORD gave them rest on every side just as he had sworn to their ancestors; not one of all their enemies had withstood them, for the LORD had given all their enemies into their hands.** [45] **Not one of all the good promises that the LORD had made to the house of Israel had failed; all came to pass.**

The Levites bring their request for land to Joshua, Eleazar, and the heads of families at Shiloh. The form of the Levites' request is similar to Caleb's and the daughters of Zelophehad's requests for land. Like them, the Levites appeal to God's word as it is mediated through Moses (Num. 35:1–8). Their request is granted. The passage legitimates Levitical claims to the towns while contributing to the authors' portrayal of Joshua and his people as an obedient generation.

The history of the Levites is a topic of great debate among biblical scholars. Biblical tradition, as reflected in the genealogies, held that the tribe of Levi consisted of three major clans: the Kohathites, the Gershonites, and the Merarites (Gen. 46:11; Exod. 6:16; Num. 3:17). The "clans" seem to be the main Levitical groups in the postexilic period. A subgroup of the Kohathites that claimed descendance from Aaron eventually gained control of the priesthood and was able to subordinate the rest of the Levites. The schema laid out in Joshua 21 reflects this complex political situation. The verses accord the Aaronites the stature of an entire clan; the cities are divided among the Aaronites, the remaining Kohathites, and the other two Levitical clans. Of the four, the Aaronites are given priority. Their towns are listed first and are the cities closest to the temple in

Jerusalem. (The Holy City itself is not listed among the Levitical towns, perhaps because doing so would be anachronistic.)

With the assignment of cities to the Levitical clans, allotment of the land is complete. The chapter ends with a summary that once again declares that the God of Israel has fulfilled the promise (vv. 43–45). The assertion is sweeping. The Hebrew word translated "every" or "all" is repeated no less than six times in the three verses. Every dimension of the promise has been kept; God has given the Israelites the land, defeated all of their enemies, and granted them rest, that is, secure peace.

13. Tension and Unity
Joshua 22

At various points in the book of Joshua, special attention is given to the tribes that were allotted land east of the Jordan: Gad, Reuben, and the half-tribe of Manasseh. The repeated focus on the eastern tribes reflects a certain tension in the perspective of the book. The Deuteronomistic Historians define the promised land, the land that Yahweh gives Israel to possess, as the land west of the Jordan River (1:11). Yet they also want to assert the unity of Israel. The compilers emphasize the role of the eastern tribes in order to stress that they, too, are part of Israel. *All* Israel, fighting together, conquered Canaan.

Chapter 22 takes up the issue of the tribes settled "across the Jordan" one last time. The chapter has two parts. In verses 1–8, the Deuteronomistic Historians address a number of themes introduced in Joshua's first speech to the eastern tribes (Josh. 1:12–18). Joshua praises Gad, Reuben, and the half-tribe of Manasseh for exemplary loyalty. The unity of Israel is unquestioned.

The second part of the chapter seems to have been heavily edited by priestly writers in the postexilic period, a time when the beginning of the Jewish Diaspora made the unity of Israel both important and problematic. In verses 9–34, confrontation between the tribes comes perilously close to civil war. At issue are two questions: "Where may Israel worship?" and "Who belongs to the worshiping community?" The conflict is resolved in shared understanding that there is to be one central altar. More important, the resolution affirms that people living outside Israel's heartland are nonetheless part of Israel.

TASK FULFILLED; A BLESSING GIVEN
Joshua 22:1–8

22:1 **Then Joshua summoned the Reubenites, the Gadites, and the half-tribe of Manasseh,** [2] **and said to them, "You have observed all that Moses the ser-**

vant of the LORD commanded you, and have obeyed me in all that I have commanded you; [3] you have not forsaken your kindred these many days, down to this day, but have been careful to keep the charge of the LORD your God. [4] And now the LORD your God has given rest to your kindred, as he promised them; therefore turn and go to your tents in the land where your possession lies, which Moses the servant of the LORD gave you on the other side of the Jordan. [5] Take good care to observe the commandment and instruction that Moses the servant of the LORD commanded you, to love the LORD your God, to walk in all his ways, to keep his commandments, and to hold fast to him, and to serve him with all your heart and with all your soul." [6] So Joshua blessed them and sent them away, and they went to their tents.

[7] Now to the one half of the tribe of Manasseh Moses had given a possession in Bashan; but to the other half Joshua had given a possession beside their fellow Israelites in the land west of the Jordan. And when Joshua sent them away to their tents and blessed them, [8] he said to them, "Go back to your tents with much wealth, and with very much livestock, with silver, gold, bronze, and iron, and with a great quantity of clothing; divide the spoil of your enemies with your kindred."

Joshua's speech to the eastern tribes (22:1–8) forms part of the framework that the Deuteronomistic Historians constructed around the book. In his initial speech (1:12–18) Joshua addresses Gad, Reuben, and the half-tribe of Manasseh, to whom Moses had already allotted territory east of the Jordan. He reminds the easterners of their obligation to cross the Jordan and fight until the conquest of Canaan is complete and their kindred also have rest on their land. In chapter 22, Joshua addresses the same tribes with language that echoes his introductory speech. Joshua's blessing and dismissal of the eastern tribes take up a number of themes introduced in chapter 1.

The first theme is the unity of Israel. In the opening chapter, the eastern tribes, those with the least at stake in the conquest of Canaan, agree to lead the battle. Now, Joshua commends the easterners for carrying out their obligations with exemplary faithfulness. Gad, Reuben, and the half-tribe of Manasseh have obeyed Moses and Joshua, loyally stood by their kindred, and carefully heeded Yahweh's charge. They are indeed part of Israel.

Second, when Israel is obedient, Yahweh is faithful. The land that God promised the remaining tribes has been won. The western tribes have "rest"; that is, they dwell in their own land in security (1:13; 21:44; 22:4). Joshua dismisses the eastern tribes with his blessing. The rich plunder that accompanies the blessing underlines how lavishly God has fulfilled every promise (22:8).

The authority of Moses' commands, emphasized in chapter 1, is reiter-ated in Joshua's final remarks to the eastern tribes. The phrase "Moses, ser-vant of the LORD" recurs three times in four verses (vv. 2–5).

The dismissal and blessing serve as an occasion for further exhortation. The language of the command "love the LORD your God" (v. 5) occurs for the first time in the book of Joshua. The phrase encapsulates the theology that undergirds the book of Joshua, however. The command is repeated throughout Deuteronomy. Love of God, in the Deuteronomic sense, is a matter of behavior as well as emotion, involving obedience, discipleship (walking in God's ways), and serving God. To love God is to manifest wholehearted allegiance concretely in all areas of life. To the ancient Israelite, the "heart" is the seat of will and thought as well as emotion. One is to love God with all one's mind, indeed, with one's entire being. (The word translated "soul" is better understood as "self.")

Joshua's concluding speech to the eastern tribes provides a satisfying sense of completion. It rounds out themes introduced in the beginning of the book and offers the Deuteronomists' theology in a nutshell. There is no tension here, no question as to the unity of Israel or the place of the eastern tribes within the larger community.

WAR AVERTED; UNITY AFFIRMED
Joshua 22:9–34

22:9 So the Reubenites and the Gadites and the half-tribe of Manasseh returned home, parting from the Israelites at Shiloh, which is in the land of Canaan, to go to the land of Gilead, their own land of which they had taken possession by command of the LORD through Moses.
 ^{10} When they came to the region near the Jordan that lies in the land of Canaan, the Reubenites and the Gadites and the half-tribe of Manasseh built there an altar by the Jordan, an altar of great size. ^{11} The Israelites heard that the Reubenites and the Gadites and the half-tribe of Manasseh had built an altar at the frontier of the land of Canaan, in the region near the Jordan, on the side that belongs to the Israelites. ^{12} And when the people of Israel heard of it, the whole assembly of the Israelites gathered at Shiloh, to make war against them.
 ^{13} Then the Israelites sent the priest Phinehas son of Eleazar to the Reuben-ites and the Gadites and the half-tribe of Manasseh, in the land of Gilead, ^{14} and with him ten chiefs, one from each of the tribal families of Israel, every one of them the head of a family among the clans of Israel. ^{15} They came to the Reubenites, the Gadites, and the half-tribe of Manasseh, in the land of Gilead, and they said to them, ^{16} "Thus says the whole congregation of the LORD, 'What is this treachery that you have committed against the God of

Israel in turning away today from following the Lord, by building yourselves an altar today in rebellion against the Lord? [17] Have we not had enough of the sin at Peor from which even yet we have not cleansed ourselves, and for which a plague came upon the congregation of the Lord, [18] that you must turn away today from following the Lord! If you rebel against the Lord today, he will be angry with the whole congregation of Israel tomorrow. [19] But now, if your land is unclean, cross over into the Lord's land where the Lord's tabernacle now stands, and take for yourselves a possession among us; only do not rebel against the Lord, or rebel against us by building yourselves an altar other than the altar of the Lord our God. [20] Did not Achan son of Zerah break faith in the matter of the devoted things, and wrath fell upon all the congregation of Israel? And he did not perish alone for his iniquity!'"

[21] Then the Reubenites, the Gadites, and the half-tribe of Manasseh said in answer to the heads of the families of Israel, [22] "The Lord, God of gods! The Lord, God of gods! He knows; and let Israel itself know! If it was in rebellion or in breach of faith toward the Lord, do not spare us today [23] for building an altar to turn away from following the Lord; or if we did so to offer burnt offerings or grain offerings or offerings of well-being on it, may the Lord himself take vengeance. [24] No! We did it from fear that in time to come your children might say to our children, 'What have you to do with the Lord, the God of Israel? [25] For the Lord has made the Jordan a boundary between us and you, you Reubenites and Gadites; you have no portion in the Lord.' So your children might make our children cease to worship the Lord. [26] Therefore we said, 'Let us now build an altar, not for burnt offering, nor for sacrifice, [27] but to be a witness between us and you, and between the generations after us, that we do perform the service of the Lord in his presence with our burnt offerings and sacrifices and offerings of well-being; so that your children may never say to our children in time to come, "You have no portion in the Lord."' [28] And we thought, If this should be said to us or to our descendants in time to come, we could say, 'Look at this copy of the altar of the Lord, which our ancestors made, not for burnt offerings, nor for sacrifice, but to be a witness between us and you.' [29] Far be it from us that we should rebel against the Lord, and turn away this day from following the Lord by building an altar for burnt offering, grain offering, or sacrifice, other than the altar of the Lord our God that stands before his tabernacle!"

[30] When the priest Phinehas and the chiefs of the congregation, the heads of the families of Israel who were with him, heard the words that the Reubenites and the Gadites and the Manassites spoke, they were satisfied. [31] The priest Phinehas son of Eleazar said to the Reubenites and the Gadites and the Manassites, "Today we know that the Lord is among us, because you have not committed this treachery against the Lord; now you have saved the Israelites from the hand of the Lord."

[32] Then the priest Phinehas son of Eleazar and the chiefs returned from the Reubenites and the Gadites in the land of Gilead to the land of Canaan,

to the Israelites, and brought back word to them. [33] The report pleased the
Israelites; and the Israelites blessed God and spoke no more of making war
against them, to destroy the land where the Reubenites and the Gadites were
settled. [34] The Reubenites and the Gadites called the altar Witness; "For," said
they, "it is a witness between us that the LORD is God."

The tone shifts in verse 9; conflict between the eastern and western
tribes over an altar built by the easterners brings Israel to the brink of civil
war. Scholars debate how early to date the traditions of an "altar of great
size" underlying verses 9–34. Most agree that priestly writers have heavily
edited the story as it is found in Joshua. Phinehas, rather than Joshua,
serves as Israel's spokesperson. Tradition held that Phinehas was the grandson of Aaron, and thus among the first of the ancient line of Israelite priests
(see commentary on Judg. 20:28). The priestly editors, at work during the
postexilic period, shaped the tale to extol one of their own.

The conflict reflects tensions within postexilic Israel when the relationship of Jews dwelling in Israel's heartland to those living in other lands was
particularly acute. Some fifty years after Babylon destroyed Jerusalem and
exiled its leaders, Persia conquered Babylon. They allowed any exiled
Judeans who chose to do so to return to Judah. Some did, rejoining Judeans
who had never left their homeland. The majority of the Jews (as Judeans
came to be called) who were exiled to Babylon or who fled to Egypt opted
to remain where they were. For the postexilic editors, a tradition about a
crisis between the tribes living in Canaan and those living east of the Jordan served as an excellent vehicle for exploring the relationship of Jews in
Diaspora and Jews in Judah. The resolution of the east-west crisis served
to affirm the unity of the scattered community.

The story presupposes that only one legitimate altar can exist in Israel.
Both the Deuteronomistic Historians and the priestly writers believed that
sacrificial worship must take place in the temple in Jerusalem. The issue
was not hypothetical; Jews in the Diaspora would have been tempted to
offer sacrifices wherever they lived. Consequently, a Jewish community in
Egypt built its own temple. However, the Jerusalemite leaders of the postexilic community were concerned for the purity of Jewish worship. They
believed that allowing people to offer sacrifices outside of the Jerusalemite
temple would lead to the adoption of foreign worship practices, and to
blending Yahweh worship with worship of foreign gods.

It would have been anachronistic to refer to the temple in Jerusalem in
a story in Joshua; the temple was not built until the tenth century B.C.E. But
(according to the narrative), Moses had already commanded Israel to wor-

ship only at the one place that God would choose (Deut. 12). Before Solomon built the temple, that place would be wherever the ark was located.

The eastern tribes' altar appears to the rest of Israel as a rival to the sole legitimate sanctuary, and thus a grave offense against the law of Moses, one that could destroy all of Israel. Israel had a strong understanding of the solidarity of the community. The sins of one person or one tribe could bring God's wrath against the whole people. The westerners recall how God sent a plague to punish the Israelites' idolatrous worship of Baal at Peor (22:17, see Num. 25:1–9) and how Achan's sin provoked Yahweh to punish the nation by military defeat (22:20; see Josh. 7). The seriousness of the offense is attested by the tribes' readiness to go to war to stop it (22:12).

Civil war is averted when the eastern tribes declare that their monument is not a real altar intended for sacrifice. Their purpose is not to engage in foreign worship practices. Quite the opposite, the memorial is to witness to their faith in, and worship of, Yahweh.

The story seems to have three aims. First, it affirms that only one legitimate site can exist for sacrificial worship. The eastern and western tribes agree: sacrificing elsewhere is blasphemy. The narrative may reflect the existence of a large altar on the banks of the Jordan River. If so, the storytellers have cleverly explained and reinterpreted its existence as testimony to the sole legitimacy of the one altar. Their postexilic audience was to understand that the only legitimate altar was the one in the Jerusalemite temple.

Second, the story resolves the even more important question of who may participate in the worshiping community. Were the exiles' descendents, living in Babylon or Egypt, still faithful Jews? Verse 19 raises the possibility that the lands outside Canaan were unclean, which would make the people living in those lands unclean. "Cleanness" and "uncleanness" were ritual categories. Unclean people could not participate in worship. The story firmly rejects the notion that Jews living outside of the borders of the promised land were unclean. The eastern tribes indeed have a "portion in the LORD" (22:27). Membership in the worshiping community is determined not by geography but by loyalty to Yahweh, by belief that "the LORD is God" (22:34).

Third, as Nelson suggests, the story serves as a model for resolving disputes in the worshiping community (Nelson, 1997, 249). To be sure, the western tribes jump rather hastily to the conclusion that their eastern kinfolk have committed sacrilege. After years of obedient solidarity, the eastern tribes might justly complain that they deserved more trust. Still, in contrast to stories of intertribal antagonism leading to battle and to all-out civil war (Judg. 12; 20–21), this tale demonstrates the tribes resolving a crisis with words, not arms.

14. Joshua's Farewell
Joshua 23

Guided by the Divine Warrior, Joshua has led Israel to take the land and has allotted the conquered territory to the tribes. Joshua's mission is accomplished; he is approaching death. According to the Deuteronomistic Historians, this is the end of the era of conquest, an era of faithfulness to the covenant.

The Deuteronomistic Historians frequently use a leader's parting words in their narrative to guide their audience's interpretation at critical junctions. The emergence of kingship is introduced by Samuel's final speech (1 Sam. 12). Later, in words that echo Joshua 23, David declares he is "about to go the way of all the earth" and exhorts Solomon to "keep the charge of the LORD . . . as it is written in the law of Moses" (1 Kgs. 2:2–9). The whole of the book of Deuteronomy, especially chapters 29–31, are Moses' valedictory address. Similarly, the Deuteronomists conclude their account of the conquest with the aged Joshua admonishing the summoned people.

Casting Joshua 23 as a farewell speech gives the chapter the authority and importance of a last will and testament. It also passes responsibility for observing Torah to the tribes. Joshua enjoins on all Israel what God had commanded him in the opening chapter of the book, that is, to "to act in accordance with all the law" of Moses (Josh. 1:7; 23:6). The direct address is aimed at moving the audience of the book to exclusive and obedient service of Yahweh.

> 23:1 **A long time afterward, when the LORD had given rest to Israel from all their enemies all around, and Joshua was old and well advanced in years,** [2] **Joshua summoned all Israel, their elders and heads, their judges and officers, and said to them, "I am now old and well advanced in years;** [3] **and you have seen all that the LORD your God has done to all these nations for your sake, for it is the LORD your God who has fought for you.** [4] **I have allotted to you as an inheritance for your tribes those nations that remain, along with all**

the nations that I have already cut off, from the Jordan to the Great Sea in the west. [5] The LORD your God will push them back before you, and drive them out of your sight; and you shall possess their land, as the LORD your God promised you. [6] Therefore be very steadfast to observe and do all that is written in the book of the law of Moses, turning aside from it neither to the right nor to the left, [7] so that you may not be mixed with these nations left here among you, or make mention of the names of their gods, or swear by them, or serve them, or bow yourselves down to them, [8] but hold fast to the LORD your God, as you have done to this day. [9] For the LORD has driven out before you great and strong nations; and as for you, no one has been able to withstand you to this day. [10] One of you puts to flight a thousand, since it is the LORD your God who fights for you, as he promised you. [11] Be very careful, therefore, to love the LORD your God. [12] For if you turn back, and join the survivors of these nations left here among you, and intermarry with them, so that you marry their women and they yours, [13] know assuredly that the LORD your God will not continue to drive out these nations before you; but they shall be a snare and a trap for you, a scourge on your sides, and thorns in your eyes, until you perish from this good land that the LORD your God has given you.

[14] "And now I am about to go the way of all the earth, and you know in your hearts and souls, all of you, that not one thing has failed of all the good things that the LORD your God promised concerning you; all have come to pass for you, not one of them has failed. [15] But just as all the good things that the LORD your God promised concerning you have been fulfilled for you, so the LORD will bring upon you all the bad things, until he has destroyed you from this good land that the LORD your God has given you. [16] If you transgress the covenant of the LORD your God, which he enjoined on you, and go and serve other gods and bow down to them, then the anger of the LORD will be kindled against you, and you shall perish quickly from the good land that he has given to you."

Joshua's farewell address drives home the message reinforced throughout the book: Be loyal to Yahweh, who has fought for Israel and given it the land. The themes and language of the chapter echo the divine speech in Joshua 1. There, Yahweh recalls and renews the promise to give Israel the land of Canaan (1:3) and assures Joshua that no one will be able to stand against him (1:5). In chapter 23, the aging Joshua declares that all of God's promises have come to pass (23:14); Yahweh has fought for Israel (vv. 3, 10), so that no one has withstood them (23:9). The tribes have been allotted all the land from the Jordan to the "Great Sea in the west" (a phrase found only in Josh. 1:4 and 23:4). Chapter 1 also introduces the concept of "rest," that is, a time when Israel dwells in its own land in security (1:13, 15). Joshua 23:1 begins by declaring that God has given Israel rest.

The book of Joshua is thus framed with assertions of God's gracious actions on Israel's behalf. The land is Israel's by divine gift, not by Israel's merit. God's agency is highlighted; the action of human warriors recedes.

The gift of land is unmerited; it is not unconditional. Israel has a vital role to play—obedience—in conquering and keeping the land. In the first chapter, God tells Joshua to "be strong and very courageous, being careful to act in accordance with all" Moses' law, turning from it neither "to the right hand or to the left" (1:7). Now, Joshua repeats the command to the people. The Hebrew word translated "be steadfast" in Joshua 23:6 is the same verb rendered "be strong" in Joshua 1:7. Joshua exhorts the people to be strong and observe "the law of Moses, turning aside from it neither to the right nor to the left."

The heart of that law is the first commandment: "I am the LORD your God, who brought you out of the land of Egypt, out of the house of slavery; you shall have no other gods before me" (Deut. 5:6–7). Joshua commands the people to show exclusive loyalty to Yahweh, their God. Serving any other deity is utterly forbidden. This is the essence of the covenant and the message of the book of Joshua: Yahweh, and only Yahweh, is Israel's God; that is what it means to be God's people. This covenantal command is not made in a vacuum, but is based on the "good things" God has done for Israel (Josh. 23:14; the word "good" is repeated five times in the last four verses of the chapter). Because of God's gracious, unmerited gift of the land, "therefore" Israel is called to obey God, hold fast to God, love God.

The prohibition against intermarriage (v. 12) should be understood within the context of the command to serve Yahweh alone. At the time the Deuteronomists composed their narrative, Judah was a small, struggling community. Assimilating to the religions and cultures of the more powerful, more cosmopolitan empires that dominated them must have been a temptation to Israelites throughout their history. Especially after the exile, the possibility that the conquerors would absorb the deportees or the colonized Jerusalemites into their own culture must have been a very real threat. The Deuteronomists believed that intermarriage would lead Judeans to worship their foreign wives' gods (1 Kgs. 11; Deut. 7:3–4). They sought to preserve Israel's identity and its faith.

The sense of urgent warning that Israel must not turn away from its God is stronger in Joshua 23 than elsewhere in the book. Throughout most of Joshua, the covenant between God and the people is working as it should. Joshua and Israel are faithful to their gracious, faithful God. Israel's obedience, and thus its continued life on the land, is not to be taken for granted, however. Joshua 23 emphasizes that transgressing the covenant by worshiping other gods will result in disaster.

The language of Joshua 23:15 echoes that of 21:45; none of God's good promises have failed. As a number of commentators note, however, the two passages have very different moods. Joshua 21:45 is victorious. Joshua 23:15 is somber, even menacing. The God who brings about "good things" (the phrase could be translated "good words") is equally able to bring about "bad things" (v. 15) if Israel fails to serve Yahweh alone. The sense of threat anticipates the downward spiral of disobedience and judgment that characterizes the book of Judges.

The Deuteronomistic Historians may have written this passage towards the end of the monarchy, as an urgent call to repentance in the face of the looming threat of war, conquest, and exile. More likely, they composed it after the conquest of Jerusalem was a fact and its citizens were colonized or scattered. In that case, the chapter explains why the kingdom of Judah "perished" from its good land. Within that context, threats and judgments served to help their audience hold on to the belief that their God was powerful and just. They also held out hope that the covenant was still possible. The people could still return to serve Yahweh with undivided loyalty; God might yet give them rest in their land.

15. Covenant and Final Note
Joshua 24

The church where I was raised marked each new year with the Wesleyan Covenant service. In language both grand and familiar, we recited the sweeping story of God's mighty acts of deliverance and pledged unconditional loyalty in grateful response. I recall the seriousness and seeming impossibility of the covenantal oath that promised complete, unreserved obedience.

The covenant service celebrated by that little Midwestern church has deep and ancient roots. "Covenant" was at the center of Israel's understanding of its relationship to Yahweh and its identity as a people. Accounts of covenant-making ceremonies between God and the people punctuate Israel's story at pivotal points. God made covenant with Noah, beginning again after the flood; with Abraham, Israel's ancestor; with Moses and Israel at Sinai, where the delivered slaves became a people; and again at Moab, on the brink of entering the promised land. In Joshua 24, the period of the conquest and the era of Joshua's leadership conclude with a solemn celebration of covenant.

The book's conclusion is highly effective. The rhetoric of the chapter brings the reader to the point toward which the whole of Joshua aims: the need to decide to worship Yahweh exclusively.

As both an important text and, from the standpoint of composition history, a very complex one, Joshua 24 has been the focus of an enormous amount of study. Many scholars hold that the chapter reflects very ancient Shechemite traditions. Others believe that the narrative is a literary work written (like a good sermon) to meet the needs of a later Judean audience.

A second set of issues regards the relationship of the chapter to Joshua 23. The transition from chapter 23 to chapter 24 does not flow smoothly. In Joshua 23, an aged Joshua summons the people and preaches his parting sermon. The site of the assembly, presumably Shiloh, is not mentioned. In Joshua 24, without having dismissed the people, Joshua summons them again, this time to Shechem, and again gives a farewell address. Many scholars argue that chapter 24 was the earlier conclusion of Joshua and that chapter 23 was written later, to round out key themes of the book. Others believe that Joshua originally ended with chapter 23. Much study has yielded little scholarly agreement; the origins of Joshua 24 and its relationship to the preceding chapter remain open questions.

The following comments assume an exilic context for the chapter. The account may or may not have existed in the late monarchy; one may be relatively confident that the Deuteronomists' exilic audience read it. Considering the narrative in relationship to the exile brings it into sharp focus. It addresses issues of immediate concern for the deportees and for the colonized Judeans remaining in Palestine. For the conquered Judeans, worshiping the gods of their captors, that is, the gods "beyond the River" (24:15), would have been a serious temptation. The decision to serve Yahweh would have been a daily, existential choice. The text continues to issue a challenge to the church of the twenty-first century. The command to have no other gods besides Yahweh may be as difficult and as urgent for modern folk as it was for the exiles.

CHOOSE THIS DAY WHOM YOU WILL SERVE
Joshua 24:1–28

24:1 **Then Joshua gathered all the tribes of Israel to Shechem, and summoned the elders, the heads, the judges, and the officers of Israel; and they presented themselves before God.** [2] **And Joshua said to all the people, "Thus says the LORD, the God of Israel: Long ago your ancestors—Terah and his sons Abraham and Nahor—lived beyond the Euphrates and served other gods.** [3] **Then I took your father Abraham from beyond the River and led him through all the land of Canaan and made his offspring many. I gave him Isaac;** [4] **and to Isaac I gave Jacob and Esau. I gave Esau the hill country of Seir to possess, but Jacob and his children went down to Egypt.** [5] **Then I sent Moses and Aaron, and I plagued Egypt with what I did in its midst; and afterwards I brought you out.** [6] **When I brought your ancestors out of Egypt, you came to the sea; and the Egyptians pursued your ancestors with chariots and horsemen to the Red Sea.** [7] **When they cried out to the LORD, he put darkness between you and the Egyptians, and made the sea come upon them and cover them; and your eyes saw what I did to Egypt. Afterwards you lived in the wilderness a long time.** [8] **Then I brought you to the land of the Amorites, who lived on the other side of the Jordan; they fought with you, and I handed them over to you, and you took possession of their land, and I destroyed them before you.** [9] **Then King Balak son of Zippor of Moab, set out to fight against**

Israel. He sent and invited Balaam son of Beor to curse you, [10] but I would not listen to Balaam; therefore he blessed you; so I rescued you out of his hand. [11] When you went over the Jordan and came to Jericho, the citizens of Jericho fought against you, and also the Amorites, the Perizzites, the Canaanites, the Hittites, the Girgashites, the Hivites, and the Jebusites; and I handed them over to you. [12] I sent the hornet ahead of you, which drove out before you the two kings of the Amorites; it was not by your sword or by your bow. [13] I gave you a land on which you had not labored, and towns that you had not built, and you live in them; you eat the fruit of vineyards and oliveyards that you did not plant.

[14] "Now therefore revere the LORD, and serve him in sincerity and in faithfulness; put away the gods that your ancestors served beyond the River and in Egypt, and serve the LORD. [15] Now if you are unwilling to serve the LORD, choose this day whom you will serve, whether the gods your ancestors served in the region beyond the River or the gods of the Amorites in whose land you are living; but as for me and my household, we will serve the LORD."

[16] Then the people answered, "Far be it from us that we should forsake the LORD to serve other gods; [17] for it is the LORD our God who brought us and our ancestors up from the land of Egypt, out of the house of slavery, and who did those great signs in our sight. He protected us along all the way that we went, and among all the peoples through whom we passed; [18] and the LORD drove out before us all the peoples, the Amorites who lived in the land. Therefore we also will serve the LORD, for he is our God."

[19] But Joshua said to the people, "You cannot serve the LORD, for he is a holy God. He is a jealous God; he will not forgive your transgressions or your sins. [20] If you forsake the LORD and serve foreign gods, then he will turn and do you harm, and consume you, after having done you good." [21] And the people said to Joshua, "No, we will serve the LORD!" [22] Then Joshua said to the people, "You are witnesses against yourselves that you have chosen the LORD, to serve him." And they said, "We are witnesses." [23] He said, "Then put away the foreign gods that are among you, and incline your hearts to the LORD, the God of Israel." [24] The people said to Joshua, "The LORD our God we will serve, and him we will obey." [25] So Joshua made a covenant with the people that day, and made statutes and ordinances for them at Shechem. [26] Joshua wrote these words in the book of the law of God; and he took a large stone, and set it up there under the oak in the sanctuary of the LORD. [27] Joshua said to all the people, "See, this stone shall be a witness against us; for it has heard all the words of the LORD that he spoke to us; therefore it shall be a witness against you, if you deal falsely with your God." [28] So Joshua sent the people away to their inheritances.

The first verse of chapter 24 sets the stage. At Joshua's command, Israel again gathers, this time at Shechem, an ancient Canaanite and Israelite religious site near the modern-day Palestinian city of Nablus. The shift in locale is unexpected. Shechem figures in the covenant-like ceremony in Joshua 8:30–35, a passage closely related to Joshua 24. The rest of the book is geographically centered in Gilgal or Shiloh. The narrative envisions a liturgical setting. Israel's leaders (the list in v. 1 echoes Josh. 23:2) "present themselves before God," that is, in a sanctuary, presumably before the ark.

Joshua instructs Israel one (very) last time. His instructions have a three-part structure: recital of God's gracious acts (vv. 2–13), dialogue leading to covenant (vv. 14–24), and acts solemnizing the covenant (vv. 25–28).

In verses 2–13, Joshua speaks as a prophet, addressing the people in the name of God in the first person. The phrase "Thus says the LORD, the God of Israel" is formulaic, the classic introduction to prophetic speech. The genre is significant, serving to elevate Joshua. Moses was a prophet. Now, for the first time, Joshua is cast in that role.

Moreover, the prophetic genre of Joshua's address recites God's gracious deeds in the first person, giving them a heightened authority. These words are not human; this is divine speech. The words exert a powerful claim on the reader.

Presenting the recital of God's gracious deeds in the first person also emphasizes God's agency in all that Israel has been given. The divine "I" rings out again and again (some eighteen times). "I took, I gave, I sent, I plagued, I brought, I destroyed, I rescued, I handed, I gave. . . ." Yahweh, not the people themselves, and certainly not any other deity, brought Israel into being, delivered Israel from slavery in Egypt, and brought the tribes into the land.

The divine "I" addresses the people directly. The word "you" is repeated even more frequently than the word "I." Israel—and, thereby the reader—is placed in direct relationship with God. That relationship precedes the command.

Divine speech, then, frames the book of Joshua. The book begins with God's speech to Joshua, a speech centered on God's promises. Then the book ends with Joshua, speaking in God's name, reciting all that God has done for Israel. God has done much. The promises are fulfilled.

The content of the prophetic speech goes beyond the gift of the land presented in Joshua, to recite God's mighty acts from Abraham through the conquest. The recital takes up and summarizes events recounted in the Pentateuch (the first five books of the Bible): the call of Abraham (Gen. 12, 15), the birth of Isaac to Sarah and Abraham (Gen. 21), the gift of Esau and Jacob to Isaac and Rebecca (Gen. 25:19–26), deliverance from Egypt (Exod. 1–15), wilderness wanderings (Exod. 16–18; Num. 10ff.), victory over the Amorite kings Og and Sihon (Num. 21:21–35), the incident of Balak and Balaam (Num. 22–24), and the conquest of Jericho (Josh. 6).

Recitals similar to 24:2–13 are found at numerous points in the Bible. The form of the biblical recitals of God's saving deeds is not rigid. Joshua 24:2–13 recounts familiar events, but also includes unique elements. Nowhere else in the Bible is it said that Israel's ancestors worshiped other gods. Moreover the reference to the conquest of Jericho in verse 11 differs from the earlier account of Jericho's fall. In Joshua 6, Jericho falls into Israel's hand by a miracle, not a battle. Joshua 24:11 presupposes that not only the citizens of Jericho, but all the armies of the Canaanites, fought Israel there. Terence Fretheim notes that the dynamic freedom with which Israel told and retold its sacred story, as it urged utter fidelity to its God, provides an appropriate model for the church today (Fretheim, 1983, 81).

Like Jews reciting the sacred story at the Seder meal, or Christians recounting God's mighty acts in Eucharistic prayers, these biblical recitals evoke gratitude, confess faith, and assert the basis of God's claim to Israel and the church's wholehearted loyalty. God's saving deeds are prior; the people's covenantal obligation is a response to what God has already done.

The second part of the narrative consists of a dialogue between Joshua and the people (vv. 14–24). At issue is whom Israel will serve (that is, worship). The word "serve" is found no fewer than fifteen times in these eleven verses. Repeatedly, Joshua presses the people to choose whom they will serve, and drives home the seriousness of their decision. Repeatedly, the people affirm that they will serve Yahweh alone.

Israel's decision is free and deliberate. Joshua begins the dialogue by offering the gathered people a striking choice: serve Yahweh, serve the gods "beyond the river," or serve the deities of the earlier inhabitants of Israel's new land. The exilic audience lived among people who worshiped a pantheon of deities. Serving Marduk and Yahweh and Baal must have been plausible, even prudent. Why choose?

The God of Israel will not settle for fractured allegiance. Joshua confronts Israel, the editors confront the exiles, and the text confronts us with the necessity of choice.

The passage does not present the choice as open-ended. The recital of Yahweh's saving deeds urges the people toward one conclusion. Yahweh alone brought Israel into being. Yahweh alone delivered it from Egypt. Yahweh alone defeated Israel's enemies and gave it the land. Israel lives by the gift of its Lord. To choose any other god, in the words of Deuteronomy 30:19, is to choose death. Joshua's famous confession models the only viable response: "As for me and my household we will serve the LORD."

The people recognize Yahweh's gift and claim. They affirm loyalty to Yahweh with a shortened recital of God's gracious acts on their behalf.

Joshua's response to the people's decision comes as a surprise. Having exhorted Israel to revere and serve Yahweh, he now turns and insists that they cannot do so. The point is not the impossibility of serving the God of Israel. The point is, rather, the seriousness of the choice. The text is akin to the passage in Luke's Gospel where Jesus admonishes his followers that discipleship is costly: "Whoever does not carry the cross and follow me cannot be my disciple. For which of you, intending to build a tower, does not first sit down and estimate the cost, to see whether he has enough to complete it? Otherwise, when he has laid a foundation and is not able to finish, all who see it will begin to ridicule him" (Luke 14:27–29). One cannot serve Yahweh lightly.

The biblical concepts of divine holiness and jealousy are troublesome or foreign to many modern Christians. Israel understood that one may not trifle with, nor try to tame, God's holiness, God's utter otherness from all creatures. Paul expresses a similar awareness of the danger of hypocritical worship: "Examine yourselves, and only then eat of the bread and drink of the cup. For all who eat and drink without discerning the body, eat and drink judgment against themselves" (1 Cor. 11:28–29).

Divine "jealousy" is not about intolerance of others' religious beliefs or about fanaticism. Rather, it is about the wholehearted commitment to which God lays claim. As Patrick Miller writes, "The jealousy of God . . . is that dimension within the divine encounter with the Lord's people that brooks no other final loyalty and ensures no other recipient of such unbounding love and grace. It is God's way of saying, I will have nothing less than your full devotion, and you will have nothing less than all my love" (Miller, 1990, 76).

When in verse 21 the people again affirm their decision to serve the Lord, they do so at a deeper level, with greater awareness of the costliness of their choice. That the people are witnesses against themselves relates to that fuller awareness. They know the consequences of their actions and cannot plead ignorance.

Many scholars suggest that the command to "put away foreign gods" reflects a ritual associated with Shechem, entailing hiding or burying images of foreign deities. A passage in Genesis where Jacob, having issued the same command to his household, hides their idols at Shechem is said to reflect the same ritual.

Joshua's recurring challenges and the people's insistent response that they will indeed serve Yahweh is effective rhetoric. Like Jesus' repeated question and command to Peter—"Do you love me" . . . "Feed my lambs" (John 21:15–17)—the dialogue pushes its ancient audience, and its contemporary readers, to assert their commitment more deeply and more deliberately.

The third part of the passage, verses 25–28, consists of Joshua's actions, which solemnize and attest the binding oath that he has led the people to make. The Hebrew words translated "statutes and ordinances" are actually singular rather than plural. One "statute and ordinance" stands at the heart of Israel's covenant with God: the commandment to offer God exclusive, wholehearted loyalty and love. "I am the LORD your God, who brought you out of the land of Egypt, out of the house of slavery; you shall have no other gods before me" (Deut. 5:6–7).

The stone witness in verse 27 echoes the altar named "Witness" that the eastern tribes erected to attest that "the LORD is God" (Josh. 22:34). It also recalls the standing stones that Israel set up to serve as testimony that God had led them across the Jordan on dry ground (Josh. 4:5–8).

For the exilic audience literally living "beyond the River" (24:14), this chapter must have had urgent and existential significance. They were confronted daily with the possibility of serving foreign gods. Assimilation, abandoning Israelite religion and customs in favor of Babylonian practices, probably brought economic and social benefits. Moreover, the exile itself was a faith-shaking experience. Had Yahweh abandoned the people? Was Israel's God perhaps powerless to help? In that context, Joshua 24 asserts the necessity of a choice. Like Elijah, who chastises the people for "limping with two different opinions" (1 Kgs. 18:21), the Deuteronomists challenge their audience, "If Yahweh is God, follow Yahweh." In the context of exile, the chapter also offers a word of hope. Choice is not only necessary; it is also possible. The people are reminded that their God had called, delivered, guided, and given them the land. They are assured that covenant is still offered. The choice to worship Yahweh is still open.

The choice is still possible and necessary today. For a twenty-first-century audience, the temptation to worship other gods alongside the God of Israel and of Jesus may not be the primary threat to the covenant. Walter Harrelson brilliantly argues that contemporary Christians' issue with the first commandment may be whether we acknowledge and worship God at all. Do we recognize God as a vivid reality who claims our wholehearted allegiance (Harrelson, 1980, 54–61)? Perhaps we do not limp between Yahweh and other deities so much as we limp between God and apathy or autonomy. The choice is nonetheless serious, even a matter of life and death. Joshua 24 calls not for fanaticism nor rigidity, but for free, dynamic faithfulness: the orientation of one's whole life towards the God who has acted mightily and mercifully on our behalf.

THREE BURIAL NOTICES
Joshua 24:29–33

24:29 **After these things Joshua son of Nun, the servant of the LORD, died, being one hundred ten years old.** [30] **They buried him in his own inheritance at Timnath-serah, which is in the hill country of Ephraim, north of Mount Gaash.**

[31] **Israel served the LORD all the days of Joshua, and all the days of the elders who outlived Joshua and had known all the work that the LORD did for Israel.**

[32] **The bones of Joseph, which the Israelites had brought up from Egypt, were buried at Shechem, in the portion of ground that Jacob had bought from the children of Hamor, the father of Shechem, for one hundred pieces of money; it became an inheritance of the descendants of Joseph.**

[33] **Eleazar son of Aaron died; and they buried him at Gibeah, the town of his son Phinehas, which had been given him in the hill country of Ephraim.**

The book of Joshua began with the death of Moses and ends with the death of Joshua (24:29–30). Joshua's leadership defines an era. The notice of his death and burial marks the end of that era and also honors Joshua. For the first time, he, like Moses, is called "the servant of the LORD." His age, 110 years, recalls the life span of other major Israelite heroes, such as Joseph. The notice also points toward the book of Judges, which adds to the report of Joshua's death (Judg. 2:6–9) the ominous note that the generation following Joshua's "did not know the LORD or the work" that God had done (Judg. 2:10).

Later editors have appended two additional burial notices to the book. Genesis 50:25 narrates Joseph's death in Egypt. He is said to have elicited a promise from the Israelites that they would take his bones back to the land promised to his ancestors for burial. Here, that promise is fulfilled (24:32).

The priest Eleazar plays a role in the allotment of territory to the tribes. It may be that priestly editors were responsible both for Eleazar's presence in the allotment accounts and for the notice of his death and burial in chapter 24.

Judges

16. Introduction
Judges 1:1–3:6

SETTING THE STAGE
Judges 1

The first chapter of Judges sets the stage for the stories of oppression and deliverance that make up the body of the book, establishing the period in which the stories are set as a time of transition and uncertainty. Joshua, the great religious and military leader, is dead; he has no obvious successor. The Israelites' effort to possess the land has been a prolonged and difficult struggle.

Implicit in Judges 1 is a theme of disobedience and judgment. The northern tribes fail to conquer major parts of their territories. While the list of their failures appears to be presented factually, hints arise of a theological explanation of the failures—that is, that military defeat is linked to disobedience. The description of the northern tribes' failure to take various cities says that they "did not" conquer them—not "*could* not," but "*did* not." The wording implies that the tribes could have obeyed God's order to drive out the native inhabitants of the cities, had they chosen to obey. Moreover, as Judges 1 describes the conquests or defeats of each of the tribes, the situation grows progressively worse; the lists of unconquered cities grow longer. The last tribe, Dan, is unable to hold onto its land at all and is pushed away into the hills. The increasing failure of the tribes to hold their land foreshadows the social and religious disintegration of premonarchical Israel as a consequence of accumulated sin.

The stories of Judges have historical as well as theological implications. The first half of Joshua depicts all twelve tribes acting together to take the land of Canaan in lightning-strike campaigns. An alternative view is offered in Judges 1. This view understands Israel's occupation of Canaan as a long, piecemeal struggle to subdue the indigenous peoples of the land, a struggle completed only in the time of King David. The alternative view presented in Judges is the more realistic of the two. Archaeological and anthropological studies suggest that Israel arose gradually in the land.

While Judges 1 is more realistic than Joshua 1–12, the former account is not an objective report of what actually happened. Judges' compilers seem to have utilized annals recording military victories or defeats as well as more folksy anecdotes, but they selected, organized, and edited their sources to serve their own purposes. The compilers elevate Judah at the expense of the northern tribes and introduce the tribes' failure to obey God's command to possess the land.

Most commentators believe that chapter 1 at one time existed as an independent account, and that an editor added it to Judges after the core of the book had been compiled. That same editor is thought to have composed Judges 2:1–5 as an explicitly theological key by which to interpret chapter 1 as a history of the tribes' failures to obey God's command to drive out the pre-Israelite inhabitants of Canaan.

1:1 **After the death of Joshua, the Israelites inquired of the LORD, "Who shall go up first for us against the Canaanites, to fight against them?"** [2] **The LORD said, "Judah shall go up. I hereby give the land into his hand."** [3] **Judah said to his brother Simeon, "Come up with me into the territory allotted to me, that we may fight against the Canaanites; then I too will go with you into the territory allotted to you." So Simeon went with him.** [4] **Then Judah went up and the LORD gave the Canaanites and the Perizzites into their hand; and they defeated ten thousand of them at Bezek.** [5] **They came upon Adoni-bezek at Bezek, and fought against him, and defeated the Canaanites and the Perizzites.** [6] **Adoni-bezek fled; but they pursued him, and caught him, and cut off his thumbs and big toes.** [7] **Adoni-bezek said, "Seventy kings with their thumbs and big toes cut off used to pick up scraps under my table; as I have done, so God has paid me back." They brought him to Jerusalem, and he died there.**

[8] **Then the people of Judah fought against Jerusalem and took it. They put it to the sword and set the city on fire.** [9] **Afterward the people of Judah went down to fight against the Canaanites who lived in the hill country, in the Negeb, and in the lowland.** [10] **Judah went against the Canaanites who lived in Hebron (the name of Hebron was formerly Kiriath-arba); and they defeated Sheshai and Ahiman and Talmai.**

[11] **From there they went against the inhabitants of Debir (the name of Debir was formerly Kiriath-sepher).** [12] **Then Caleb said, "Whoever attacks Kiriath-sepher and takes it, I will give him my daughter Achsah as wife."** [13] **And Othniel son of Kenaz, Caleb's younger brother, took it; and he gave him his daughter Achsah as wife.** [14] **When she came to him, she urged him to ask her father for a field. As she dismounted from her donkey, Caleb said**

to her, "What do you wish?" [15] She said to him, "Give me a present; since you have set me in the land of the Negeb, give me also Gulloth-mayim." So Caleb gave her Upper Gulloth and Lower Gulloth.

[16] The descendants of Hobab the Kenite, Moses' father-in-law, went up with the people of Judah from the city of palms into the wilderness of Judah, which lies in the Negeb near Arad. Then they went and settled with the Amalekites. [17] Judah went with his brother Simeon, and they defeated the Canaanites who inhabited Zephath, and devoted it to destruction. So the city was called Hormah. [18] Judah took Gaza with its territory, Ashkelon with its territory, and Ekron with its territory. [19] The LORD was with Judah, and he took possession of the hill country, but could not drive out the inhabitants of the plain, because they had chariots of iron. [20] Hebron was given to Caleb, as Moses had said; and he drove out from it the three sons of Anak. [21] But the Benjaminites did not drive out the Jebusites who lived in Jerusalem; so the Jebusites have lived in Jerusalem among the Benjaminites to this day.

[22] The house of Joseph also went up against Bethel; and the LORD was with them. [23] The house of Joseph sent out spies to Bethel (the name of the city was formerly Luz). [24] When the spies saw a man coming out of the city, they said to him, "Show us the way into the city, and we will deal kindly with you." [25] So he showed them the way into the city; and they put the city to the sword, but they let the man and all his family go. [26] So the man went to the land of the Hittites and built a city, and named it Luz; that is its name to this day.

[27] Manasseh did not drive out the inhabitants of Beth-shean and its villages, or Taanach and its villages, or the inhabitants of Dor and its villages, or the inhabitants of Ibleam and its villages, or the inhabitants of Megiddo and its villages; but the Canaanites continued to live in that land. [28] When Israel grew strong, they put the Canaanites to forced labor, but did not in fact drive them out.

[29] And Ephraim did not drive out the Canaanites who lived in Gezer; but the Canaanites lived among them in Gezer.

[30] Zebulun did not drive out the inhabitants of Kitron, or the inhabitants of Nahalol; but the Canaanites lived among them, and became subject to forced labor.

[31] Asher did not drive out the inhabitants of Acco, or the inhabitants of Sidon, or of Ahlab, or of Achzib, or of Helbah, or of Aphik, or of Rehob; [32] but the Asherites lived among the Canaanites, the inhabitants of the land; for they did not drive them out.

[33] Naphtali did not drive out the inhabitants of Beth-shemesh, or the inhabitants of Beth-anath, but lived among the Canaanites, the inhabitants of the land; nevertheless the inhabitants of Beth-shemesh and of Beth-anath became subject to forced labor for them.

[34] The Amorites pressed the Danites back into the hill country; they did not allow them to come down to the plain. [35] The Amorites continued to live

in Har-heres, in Aijalon, and in Shaalbim, but the hand of the house of Joseph rested heavily on them, and they became subject to forced labor. [36] **The border of the Amorites ran from the ascent of Akrabbim, from Sela and upward.**

The opening words of the book, "After the death of Joshua," suggest that we have entered a time of transition. Continuity is present with what has gone before; the first words echo Joshua 1:1: "After the death of Moses . . ." But there is also marked discontinuity. The report of the death of Moses is quickly followed by God's announcement that Joshua will be his successor. In Judges, no one is named to succeed Joshua. Indeed, the era of the great leaders—Moses and Joshua, servants of the Lord (Josh. 1:1; Judg. 2:8)—has ended. In Judges, God raises up powerful deliverers, but they are not of the stature of Moses and Joshua. None of them are called "servant of the LORD."

Being without an established leader is risky for the Israelites at this time. They have been assigned their allotted inheritances but have yet to possess the land fully. The first verse of Judges creates a sense of uncertainty. How will the tribes fare, struggling to establish themselves in the land without Moses or Joshua to lead them?

Judah's Success

The chapter begins optimistically. The Israelite tribes, functioning as a unit, "inquired of the LORD" as to who should go into battle first. Their inquiry, conducted by lot or by some other oracular means, was proper and faithful behavior in ancient Israel. The answer to the people's inquiry comes back: "Judah." The answer establishes the southern tribe's preeminence, a theme repeated throughout the chapter.

In verses 3–18, Judah and allied tribal groups rack up success after success. Judah first allies itself with Simeon, a closely related tribe that seems to have lost its independent identity and to have been absorbed by Judah very early. (Joshua 19 describes the territory allotted to Simeon as located within Judah's boundaries.) Together Judah and Simeon defeat the Canaanites and Perizzites, two of the seven populations cited by tradition as inhabiting Canaan. The location of the battle, Bezek, is uncertain. In any case, the southern tribes take Bezek and subdue its king.

The narratives go on to report Judah's rapid victories over Jerusalem, the future capital of Judah; over the hill country between Jerusalem and Hebron; over the Negeb, an arid land in southernmost Palestine; over the lowlands; and finally, over Hebron. The southerners' string of successes mounts further when Caleb and Othniel, who represent two tribal groups closely associated with Judah, capture Debir.

The narrative then pauses to explain how the Kenites, a group friendly toward Israel, moved from the city of palms (Jericho) to territory further south. (The note that the Kenites are descendants of Moses' father-in-law Hobab is confusing. Elsewhere, Moses' father-in-law is called "Jethro" or "Reuel," and Hobab is identified as Moses' brother-in-law.)

The narrative resumes its description of Judah and Simeon's triumphs in verse 17. They are said to conquer Zephath and to place it under the ban, that is, to kill all of its inhabitants. The Hebrew word for "ban" is *herem*, so Judah and Simeon rename the town "Hormah," which we can translate as "Bantown" (Boling, 1975, 58). The report of Judah's military successes culminates in the triumphant assertion that the tribe conquered Gaza, Ashkelon, and Ekron, mighty city-states on the coastal plain belonging to the Philistines. The Philistines were sea peoples who arrived in Canaan shortly after Israel began to emerge in the land and quickly became the Israelites' most powerful rivals. The list of Judah's successes concludes with a victorious note: "The LORD was with Judah" (v. 19a).

The fast-paced account of Judah's preeminence and victories slows to recount two anecdotes that underscore its success. Verses 5–7 report that the Judahites capture Adoni-bezek, the Lord of Bezek, and cut off his thumbs and big toes. This is not wanton mutilation; the purpose is to ensure that Adoni-bezek will not be able to bear arms or to serve priestly functions, and so can never again rule as king. The captive himself acknowledges that his fate is just recompense for his treatment of peoples whom he had conquered. Modern scholars often identify Adoni-bezek with Adonizedek, the Jerusalemite king who led a coalition of Canaanite rulers against Gibeon and Israel (Joshua 10). If so, he was a major threat to the Israelites. In any case, the narrator of this brutal little story appears to relish recounting his defeat. Judah has conquered. Moreover, according to the storyteller, Judah's conquest is just.

The second anecdote, the story of Caleb, Othniel, and Achsah, is taken almost word for word from Joshua 15:15–19 (see commentary there). In the context of Judges 1, the story flags the role of women characters in Judges: women serve as a mirror to the situation of Israel as a whole. The relationship of Achsah, her father, and her husband is presented as a model of how family relationships ought to be. To be sure, the story reflects the patriarchal character of early Israelite culture. In true patriarchal fairy-tale manner, Caleb promises the hand of his daughter to the man who conquers Kiriath-sepher, "Town of the Book." Achsah is the prize awarded the conquering hero. Within the confines of patriarchy, however, Achsah and Othniel are an ideal match. Caleb, the father, is a proven hero—one of two from his generation whom God allowed to enter the promised land (see Josh. 14:6–13). Othniel is of impeccable lineage, a tested warrior who is about to be a judge/savior of Israel (Judg. 3:7–11). Achsah, an object of her marriage, is nonetheless the real subject of the tale. Wise and determined, she sees to it that she receives a useable dowry, not waterless land. Achsah is the first of many women who play leading roles in Judges: Deborah, Jael, the woman at Thebez, and the wife of Manoah all overshadow their male counterparts. Assuming women mirror the health of Israel as a whole, as the book begins, the nation is well.

The highly positive account of Judah's victories begins to falter in the second half of verse 19: "The LORD was with Judah, and he took possession of the hill country, but could not drive out the inhabitants of the plain." In fact, verses 19–21 contradict what has just been reported. The narrator has asserted that Judah defeated three of the strongest cities of the plain (v. 18); now we read that he could not conquer them. Similarly, verse 8 claims that Judah took Jerusalem, an assertion contradicted by verse 21, which acknowledges that the Benjaminites were unable to drive the Jebusites from Jerusalem. (In Josh. 15:63, it is Judah that fails to eliminate the Jebusites.) The more sober reports of verses 19–21 are in fact historically accurate. The Israelites were unable to subdue the cities of the plains or Jerusalem until the time of David. The reports in verses 3–18 were selected and edited to exalt Judah. Perhaps a later editor concerned with historical accuracy added verses 19–21.

Trouble in the North

The second half of the chapter (vv. 22–36) concerns the efforts of the central and northern tribes to secure their allotted territories. The account of the northern tribes begins with a highly ambiguous victory. The house of Joseph takes Bethel. "House of Joseph" can be used to refer to all of the northern tribes; here the name probably refers in its more technical sense to Ephraim and Manasseh. In a story reminiscent of the tale of Rahab and the spies told in Joshua 2, Israelite agents on a spying mission make a deal with a citizen of Bethel. They offer to treat him kindly if he will help them gain access to the city. (The phrase "treat kindly," also found in the Rahab story, deals with covenantal faithfulness.) The Israelites capture the city and spare the Bethelite collaborator. As one commentator notes, the story is a model of covenantal loyalty. The ambiguity lies in the fact that God has commanded Israel not to "make a covenant with the inhabitants of [the] land" (Judg. 2:2). Is the northern tribes' failure to occupy their lands a result of their disobedience in making this treaty? Or should we understand the story as a challenge to rigid doctrines of ethnic purity? Like the Rahab account, the story of the Bethelite spy undercuts the Deuteronomistic insistence that Israel remain utterly separate from the populace of Canaan. The story may also serve to challenge a strictly retributive view that disobedience necessarily leads to failure. Remarkably the story depicts the Israelites as conquering Bethel despite their treaty with a citizen of that town.

The capture of Bethel is the last victory narrated in chapter 1. What follows is a catalogue of towns that Manasseh, Ephraim, Asher, Naphtali, and Dan failed to take. The situation deteriorates. Manasseh and Ephraim did not drive out the Canaanites, and so the Canaanites continued to live among them. Asher, on the other hand, lived among the Canaanites. Dan was not even able to live among the indigenous population in its allotted territory. The Amorites ("westerners") pressed the Danites back into the hills. The towns that remained outside Israelite control were strategically important. Possession of the fertile coastal plain and Jezreel Valley eluded the tribes. Key mountain passes and a corridor between Jerusalem and the sea also remained outside Israelite control.

Significantly, the text does not say that the northern tribes *could not* conquer the inhabitants of the land, rather that they *did not* do so. Four references to subjecting the inhabitants of the land to forced labor (vv. 28, 30, 33, 35) suggest that the tribes eventually became strong enough to drive them out, but chose instead to exploit their labor. The theme of disobedience, prominent in the rest of Judges, is introduced here.

The tribes' inability (v. 19) or failure (vv. 27–35) to drive out the inhabitants of the land sets the stage for the rest of the book. The tribes will have to struggle against the pre-Israelite populations of Canaan as well as against neighboring populations as they attempt to possess their inheritances. Their hold on the promised land is precarious. Moreover, the reports of Israelite occupation are increasingly negative as the chapter progresses, introducing a downward spiral that will be played out in the book as a whole.

The northern tribes' failure to obey God's command to take possession of the land sounds an ominous note that will crescendo in subsequent chapters, leading to social disintegration. Yet chapter 1 also reminds the reader that God acts (vv. 19 and 22) and human beings live out their obedience or disobedience in the mundane, concrete, political affairs of life.

THEOLOGICAL KEY
Judges 2:1–5

> 2:1 **Now the angel of the LORD went up from Gilgal to Bochim, and said, "I brought you up from Egypt, and brought you into the land that I had promised to your ancestors. I said, 'I will never break my covenant with you.** [2] **For your part, do not make a covenant with the inhabitants of this land; tear down their altars.' But you have not obeyed my command. See what you have done!** [3] **So now I say, I will not drive them out before you; but they shall become adversaries to you, and their gods shall be a snare to you."** [4] **When the angel of the LORD spoke these words to all the Israelites, the people lifted up their voices and wept.** [5] **So they named that place Bochim, and there they sacrificed to the LORD.**

The ominous note implicit in the failures of the Israelite tribes to obey God's command to possess the land is made explicit in this passage. The editors who inserted chapter 1 into the book of Judges provided a theological interpretation of the events it described in Judges 2:1–5.

The "angel of the LORD" goes up from Gilgal to Bochim ("Weepers"). Gilgal is Joshua's military base (see commentary on Josh. 4:19). "Bochim" is not referred to outside this passage. The Septuagint identifies Bochim with Bethel, which may be correct. If so, the passage is linked to the epilogue, in which the Israelite tribes gather in Bethel, weeping before God. The "angel of the LORD" is an earthly manifestation of God, not an entity separate from Yahweh. God's angel or envoy appears in Judges 5:23; 6:11–12, 13–20; 13:3, 13–21 and frequently throughout the Bible (especially the Pentateuch) to admonish, command, deliver, and curse.

The angel of the Lord admonishes the Israelites in covenantal terms, reciting God's saving acts on Israel's behalf: delivering the people from Egypt, giving them the land, keeping the promise to the ancestors. The recital underlines the people's obligations and reiterates God's unswerving faithfulness to the covenant. Israel's covenantal obligations are restated: to avoid making treaties with the inhabitants of the land, and especially to avoid religious compromises. They are to tear down the altars of the inhabitants' gods. The angel's insistence that Israel has not kept its command suggests that Israel's accommodation of the Canaanites and the Philistine inhabitants of the plains is considered a form of treaty making and a violation of covenant. Joshua had warned the Israelites that they must not mix with the nations in the land, for then God would no longer drive out its inhabitants; the inhabitants' gods would become a snare for Israel, and Israel would perish from the land (Josh. 23:7, 13). The Lord's angel declares that judgment is imminent (Judg. 2:3). Israel has indeed accommodated the nations. Yahweh will no longer drive the nations out of Canaan; their gods will be a snare to the Israelites.

Two points must be made about the angel's indictment. First, the vehemence with which the authors of Judges condemn any mingling between Israel and the pre-Israelite inhabitants of the land is not simply a matter of ethnocentrism. The phrase "and their gods shall be a snare to you" makes it clear that the Deuteronomistic Historians were more concerned with religious purity than ethnic purity.

Second, the view of judgment found in the passage is less rigid than it might appear to be. At first glance, the passages seem to suggest that obedience leads to blessing and disobedience to cursing in a quite mechanistic way. A mechanistic view of God's action is challenged by the phrase "I will never break my covenant with you" (Judg. 2:1b), a phrase in some tension with the assertion that God will no longer drive out the nations. The tension could be resolved by interpreting the former phrase to mean that God promised not to be the first to abandon the treaty with Israel. Elsewhere in Judges, divine judgment and divine mercy are held in tension in the very heart of God. Allowing the tension to remain unresolved in Judges 2:1–5 is a better approach. Actions do have consequences and God does judge, yet the divine promise *never* to break covenant remains even beyond judgment.

THEOLOGICAL INTRODUCTION
Judges 2:6–3:6

2:6 **When Joshua dismissed the people, the Israelites all went to their own inheritances to take possession of the land.** [7] **The people worshiped the LORD all the days of Joshua, and all the days of the elders who outlived Joshua, who had seen all the great work that the LORD had done for Israel.** [8] **Joshua son of Nun, the servant of the LORD, died at the age of one hundred ten years.** [9] **So they buried him within the bounds of his inheritance in Timnath-heres, in the hill country of Ephraim, north of Mount Gaash.** [10] **Moreover, that whole generation was gathered to their ancestors, and another generation grew up after them, who did not know the LORD or the work that he had done for Israel.**

[11] **Then the Israelites did what was evil in the sight of the LORD and worshiped the Baals;** [12] **and they abandoned the LORD, the God of their ancestors, who had brought them out of the land of Egypt; they followed other gods, from among the gods of the peoples who were all around them, and**

bowed down to them; and they provoked the LORD to anger. [13] They abandoned the LORD, and worshiped Baal and the Astartes. [14] So the anger of the LORD was kindled against Israel, and he gave them over to plunderers who plundered them, and he sold them into the power of their enemies all around, so that they could no longer withstand their enemies. [15] Whenever they marched out, the hand of the LORD was against them to bring misfortune, as the LORD had warned them and sworn to them; and they were in great distress.

[16] Then the LORD raised up judges, who delivered them out of the power of those who plundered them. [17] Yet they did not listen even to their judges; for they lusted after other gods and bowed down to them. They soon turned aside from the way in which their ancestors had walked, who had obeyed the commandments of the LORD; they did not follow their example. [18] Whenever the LORD raised up judges for them, the LORD was with the judge, and he delivered them from the hand of their enemies all the days of the judge; for the LORD would be moved to pity by their groaning because of those who persecuted and oppressed them. [19] But whenever the judge died, they would relapse and behave worse than their ancestors, following other gods, worshiping them and bowing down to them. They would not drop any of their practices or their stubborn ways. [20] So the anger of the LORD was kindled against Israel; and he said, "Because this people have transgressed my covenant that I commanded their ancestors, and have not obeyed my voice, [21] I will no longer drive out before them any of the nations that Joshua left when he died." [22] In order to test Israel, whether or not they would take care to walk in the way of the LORD as their ancestors did, [23] the LORD had left those nations, not driving them out at once, and had not handed them over to Joshua.

3:1 Now these are the nations that the LORD left to test all those in Israel who had no experience of any war in Canaan [2] (it was only that successive generations of Israelites might know war, to teach those who had no experience of it before): [3] the five lords of the Philistines, and all the Canaanites, and the Sidonians, and the Hivites who lived on Mount Lebanon, from Mount Baal-hermon as far as Lebo-hamath. [4] They were for the testing of Israel, to know whether Israel would obey the commandments of the LORD, which he commanded their ancestors by Moses. [5] So the Israelites lived among the Canaanites, the Hittites, the Amorites, the Perizzites, the Hivites, and the Jebusites; [6] and they took their daughters as wives for themselves, and their own daughters they gave to their sons; and they worshiped their gods.

The first chapter of Judges is concrete and specific, reminding us that God's word moves in and through messy, mundane events. Judges 2:6–3:6 serves as a second introduction, reflecting in an abstract way on the theological significance of the events.

Faithful Generation, Faithless Generation

Judges 2:6–10

The theological introduction seems to begin with a time warp. Joshua 24:29–30 announced that Joshua had died and was buried, and Judges 1 narrated events "after the death of Joshua." Now, suddenly, we find a notice that "Joshua dismissed the people" and then died. Most modern commentators agree that Judges 1:1–2:5, which interrupts the story narrated in Joshua/Judges, was inserted late in the books' composition, and the notification of Joshua's death added in order to signal that the story told in the book of Joshua now continues. As the text stands, 2:6–10 must be interpreted as a flashback and translated in past perfect: "When Joshua *had* dismissed the people. . . ."

The passage explains how, in spite of God's saving acts on its behalf, Israel came to worship other gods. Verses 6–9 and the first half of verse 10 repeat phrases of Joshua 24:28–31, but in a different order. A description of the faithfulness of Joshua and his generation precedes a notice of their deaths, which leads to the plaint that the next generation did not know Yahweh. The second half of verse 10 echoes an ominous note in Exodus 1:8: "a new king arose over Egypt, who did not know Joseph." "To know" is not simply a matter of conceptual knowledge. "Knowing" God, like knowing a person, is experiential and relational. In the case of both the Egyptian king and the Israelites, such knowledge involves obligation arising out of gratitude for what the one known had done for them. Knowledge of God is part of covenantal relationship. Not to know God is to abandon that relationship. The heart of the prophet Hosea's indictment against his people is that they "do not know the LORD" (Hos. 5:4). The generation following Joshua and his cohorts did not know God.

Sin, Wrath, and Mercy

2:11–23

Scholars have long recognized that Judges is made up of a series of ancient tales about military heroes who arose to rescue the beleaguered tribes from their oppressors. The stories have been set in a framework that interprets the distress in which the subdued tribes find themselves as divine judgment for their sin, and the heroes as deliverers whom God raised up in response to their distress. The framework is made up of stereotypical elements:

Sin: "The Israelites did what was evil in the sight of the LORD.
Punishment: "The LORD sold them into the hand of . . ." their enemies.
Distress and outcry: "Israel cried to the LORD."
Deliverance: God raises up a savior who rescues Israel and the enemy is
    subdued.
A period of peace: "The land had rest."

This pattern of sin, punishment, distress, and deliverance is elaborated on
in 2:11–23 to make it very clear that Israel's suffering is the result of its own
faithlessness; God is both just and merciful.

Verses 11–13 emphasize Israel's sin, its failure to know Yahweh. Indict-
ments pile up: The Israelites "did what was evil," "worshipped the Baals,"
"abandoned the LORD," "followed other gods," "provoked the LORD to
anger," "worshiped Baal and the Astartes." Clearly the people, not God,
betrayed the covenant. The egregiousness of their sin is underlined by
God's claims on Israel. Yahweh is not just any god but the God of their
ancestors, the one who delivered them from bondage in Egypt. The people's sin is highly personal; like a lover betraying his partner, Israel has
abandoned its God. And their sin is unrelieved. In verse 17, we read that
even during the times that God raises up a judge to deliver the people, they
continue to lust after other deities. Indeed, throughout this section, the
only action in which Israel engages is the act of abandoning Yahweh.
Although the framework regularly includes the phrase "Israel cried to the
LORD," that element is omitted from our passage; Israel does not turn to
its God even to cry in distress.

Israel's apostasy provokes divine wrath. Verses 14–15 depict military
defeat and political oppression as God's angry judgment. Four times Yahweh grows angry and gives Israel into the power of its enemies. The passage
is very clear that divine judgment is justified; Israel has provoked the wrath.
Israel could not say that they were not warned (v. 15); indeed, God had
sworn to punish them, and the punishment fits the crime. Yahweh's action
is essentially passive. Israel has abandoned God, and God lets them go, with-
drawing the divine protection that had rescued them from their enemies.

The Israelites are conquered and in great distress. No textual evidence
indicates that their distress includes repentance, however. In only one
instance in the book of Judges does Israel repent of its sin (10:10). As many
modern commentators point out, the dynamic in the book of Judges is less
"repentance/forgiveness" than "judgment/mercy." Israel's attitude towards
God is consistently faithless. God's response is the one that changes. The
tension in the book is a tension in the very heart of God between anger and

pity, judgment and mercy. In language reminiscent of Exodus 2:24, God raises up judges and delivers the people because God was "moved to pity by their groaning" (v. 18). The number of judges whom God sends to deliver Israel is a measure of God's mercy.

Yet God's mercy does not evoke faithfulness in response. Verse 19 indicates that after each judge died, the people's behavior was even worse than that of the previous generation. Israel's pattern of apostasy is not just a vicious cycle; it is a downward spiral. According to verses 20–21, God finally has enough. Echoing the words of verse 3, God declares that the covenant is broken; God will no longer drive out the nations from the land.

The Nations

Judges 2:22–3:6

The compilers who gave Judges its final shape were convinced that Israel and Judah suffered conquest and exile because they had been lured away from following Yahweh by the false gods of other peoples. Why God permitted those peoples to remain as a snare must have troubled the compilers deeply. Different editors answered the question in different ways. Judges 2:3 and 20–21 understand the presence of foreign peoples and gods as punishment for Israel. Because Joshua and his generation were remembered as faithful, however, the notion of punishment does not adequately explain God's failure to drive out the nations during Joshua's lifetime. Judges 2:22–3:6 offers alternate explanations. In one, the nations were left as a test, to see if subsequent Israelite generations would be faithful (2:22–23; 3:4). Judges 3:1–2 suggests that the nations were left to provide Israelite warriors with combat practice. Such differing explanations for God's failure to rid the land of non-Israelites indicates how worrying the issue was for the ancient authors and their inability to come to any final resolution.

The theological introduction ends with two traditional lists of the peoples who remained in Canaan (3:3, 5).

17. Othniel, Ehud, and Eglon
Judges 3:7–31

OTHNIEL: THE PATTERN OF LEADERSHIP

Judges 3:7–11

The account of Othniel is the first of a series of stories about military heroes ("judges") that make up the core of Judges. The Deuteronomistic Historians appear to have presented Othniel's story as a pattern for understanding the theological significance of the remaining deliverers. The Deuteronomistic Historians were interested not in simply reporting events of Israel's history for history's sake, but in drawing out lessons from God's past actions for their own time. To do so, they framed ancient traditions with theological interpretations. In the Othniel account, the ancient tradition has been reduced to an absolute minimum: the names of the hero and his enemy, and where his enemy came from. Neither dialogue nor action is reported. Apart from these scant details, the account consists of phrases from the framework found around the various judges' stories. The editor of this passage avoided any narrative detail that would clutter up the theological lessons he wished to convey. The result is a paradigm that helps shape the reader's understanding of the remaining narratives in the main section of Judges.

3:7 **The Israelites did what was evil in the sight of the LORD, forgetting the LORD their God, and worshiping the Baals and the Asherahs.** [8] **Therefore the anger of the LORD was kindled against Israel, and he sold them into the hand of King Cushan-rishathaim of Aram-naharaim; and the Israelites served Cushan-rishathaim eight years.** [9] **But when the Israelites cried out to the LORD, the LORD raised up a deliverer for the Israelites, who delivered them, Othniel son of Kenaz, Caleb's younger brother.** [10] **The spirit of the LORD came upon him, and he judged Israel; he went out to war, and the LORD gave King Cushan-rishathaim of Aram into his hand; and his hand prevailed over**

Cushan-rishathaim. [11] **So the land had rest forty years. Then Othniel son of Kenaz died.**

Othniel, son of Kenaz, has already made an appearance in Joshua 15:17 and Judges 1:13. Othniel is a Southern hero who, like a prince in a fairy tale, wins the hand of Achsah, the daughter of his Uncle Caleb, for capturing the Canaanite city of Debir. Othniel's name is found in two other places in the Hebrew Bible. First Chronicles 4:13 lists him as the son of Kenaz and the nephew of Caleb, while 1 Chronicles 27:15 remembers him as a clan or tribe rather than an individual. Othniel is probably the traditional ancestor of a clan belonging to the Kenizzite tribe. Many stories may have once been told about Othniel. Whatever legends clustered about this Southern hero are reduced to the barest bones in the story as it appears in the Bible. Othniel went to war; he prevailed.

The text does provide the name of his enemy: King Cushan-rishathaim, and the place where his enemy was from, Aram-naharaim. But neither name seems historically likely. "Cushan-rishathaim" means "Cushan of the two evils," which sounds much more like a taunt or caricature than a name parents would give their child. "Aram-naharaim," "Aram of the Two Rivers," is the name of an actual place, northern Mesopotamia (modern-day eastern Syria and northern Iraq). Othniel would not likely have led Israelites in a battle against a Mesopotamian king. Othniel's base of operations was near Hebron, in the far south of Judah, and Mesopotamia lies at a distance north and east of Israel. Moreover, no evidence is available to show that northern Mesopotamia attempted to expand into Judah's territory during the premonarchical era. The name "Aram-naharaim" was probably chosen as a symbol of oppression. During the centuries just before and during the time that the Deuteronomistic Historians were working on their interpretation of Israel's history, two northern Mesopotamian empires, Assyria and Babylon, were great and oppressive powers. The historians probably constructed the opponent king's name and region to suggest the archetypal enemy; "Cushan Double-Trouble of the Evil Empire" was defeated by the exemplary judge!

The Theological Framework

Many of the stock phrases comprising this passage have been encountered in the theological introduction (Judg. 2:6–3:6) and will recur over and over in subsequent passages. The editors seem to have shaped the Othniel story as a model for instructing the reader on the meaning of the remaining stories of the judges. We will take the opportunity they provided to reflect theologically on various elements of the editorial framework.

The Israelites Did Evil

The story begins with the Israelites doing what was "evil in the sight of the LORD" (see 3:11), breaking covenant with their own God to worship the Baals and Asherahs. "Baal" was a prominent Canaanite god of the storm. Given the dependence of the land upon rain, Baal also controlled fertility. Surrounded by Canaanite Baal-worshipers and living precariously as farmers in a very dry land, Israelites were strongly tempted to worship Baal before and during the monarchical period. Asherah is the name of both the Canaanite goddess who was the mother of the gods and the wooden object that represented the goddess in the cult. (Gideon cuts down an Asherah in 6:25–27.) The Baals and Asherahs represent all of the foreign deities Israel was tempted to worship.

The Deuteronomistic Historians abhorred idolatrous worship as the worst possible sin. They used Israel's obedience to God's command, and especially obedience to the first commandment, "You shall have no other gods before me," as the yardstick by which to assess Israel's history. To serve other deities, or to confuse the one God of Israel with Canaanite gods fundamentally violated the relationship between Israel and its Lord.

In our day, we may rarely be tempted to worship other deities actively. Moreover, we value respect for other religious traditions. The Deuteronomistic Historian's abhorrence of other gods can seem troubling or foreign. Perhaps for us the question is less *Will we worship other gods?* and more *Will we recognize and follow the one God? Can we really believe in and open ourselves to the Holy One as a vivid reality at the core of our lives?* At issue is God's right to our unrivaled and existential loyalty. At stake also is our capacity as human beings to live with integrity of purpose. Ultimately, God's exclusive claim upon our allegiance makes human life possible, by ordering out the competing claims of the world, which would otherwise pull us apart (Miller, 1990, 103–4).

Divine Judgment

Israel's faithlessness provokes God's anger; God sells Israel into the hand of its enemy. The motif of divine wrath and punishment occurs in 2:14–15 and will crop up again, in various forms, in the introductions to each judge's story. As in chapter 2, the Historians are careful to indicate that the punishment fits the crime. The verb translated "worshiping" in verse 7 is the same verb translated "serve" in verse 8. Israel "served" foreign gods; now it must "serve" foreign masters (v. 8).

Divine judgment and wrath are difficult concepts for many of us to accept. Isn't God a God of love and mercy? Students tend to recoil at the harsh words of the prophets announcing the coming doom, or of the Deuteronomistic Historians blaming the suffering of a defeated and exploited people on their own sin.

Divine judgment is a concept we may invoke only with some care. A readiness to blame the victim weaves its way through our culture, and we must be careful to avoid it. Significantly the prophets and the Deuteronomistic Historians name as judgment the plight of themselves and their own people, not the sufferings of others. Moreover, judgment is far from the only explanation of suffering found in the Scriptures. The central story of the exodus portrays the suffering of victims whose pain is caused by the sins of others. The many psalms of lament presuppose that suffering is a brokenness in creation that God should and will put right. The pathos of Jeremiah, the suffering servant of Isaiah (52:13–53:12), and the cry of Jesus on the cross attest to a form of suffering that is borne for others.

Nonetheless, the biblical assertion that God judges persons and nations is one that we must take seriously. Divine love cannot be indifferent to sin and evil. Israel, according to the book of Judges, had sundered its relationship with God, violating the heart of its vocation, its identity, and its very being. Actions do have consequences. When we sin against God or against one another, God must act to stop the evil and redress the situation. Judgment is the divine "no" to forces of death.

Finally, we must note that where the Bible depicts suffering as a just consequence of sin, judgment does not have the final word. The people's distress evokes God's pity; God raises up a deliverer to save them. The final word in Scripture is God's determination to restore the world God loves, God's life-giving "yes."

They Cried to the Lord: Distress and Mercy

The third formulaic element in the Othniel account is the Israelites in distress crying "out to the LORD." The cry is not found in chapter 2 but is present in the stories of all of the judges except Samson. The texts give no indication that the cry is a sign of repentance. Rather, the cry is one of suffering—a cry for help. God's response is not a reward for Israel's repentance. Rather, God responds in pity for its pain.

The outcry is a motif that runs through both testaments of the Bible. From Abel's blood crying out from the ground (Gen. 4:10) to Jesus crying out from the cross (Matt. 27:46), those suffering violence or oppression cry out to Yahweh, and Yahweh responds. God "does not forget the cry of the afflicted" (Ps. 9:12). Even here, where affliction is the result of God's own judgment, God hears the people's cry and raises up a deliverer. Judgment and mercy battle in the heart of God, but mercy has the final word.

God raises up Othniel, a deliverer. The compilers are quite clear. The heroes who rescue Israel do not act on their own power. God delivers, using human agents. In the case of Othniel (3:10), Gideon (6:34), Jephthah (11:29), and Samson (13:25, 14:6, 19; 15:14), deliverance is expressed by the statement that the "Spirit of the LORD" came upon the leaders, empowering them to do what they otherwise could not do. The Lord's spirit is a power that imbues Othniel, Gideon, and Jephthah with the courage and magnetism to muster Israel for battle; the spirit gives Samson superhuman physical strength. The spirit does not eclipse the leaders' personalities, nor eliminate their personal faults. Jephthah, filled with the spirit, nonetheless rashly utters a vow that will cost his daughter her life. Samson, stirred by the spirit, pursues a brutal personal vendetta. The spirit does enable the leaders to accomplish tasks that ultimately serve God's purpose in spite of their very human failings.

In Judges, salvation, or deliverance, has to do with the material as well as the spiritual dimensions of life. In modern Christian usage, "salvation" tends to be understood in spiritual and individualistic ways. The biblical concept of salvation is consistently religious—the ultimate agent of salvation is God—but salvation is political and social as well. In fact, the Bible does not separate "spiritual" from political, economic, and even military spheres of life. Salvation has to do with God's intervening in Israel's history to bring needed help. In Judges, the deliverers God raises up are military heroes who rescue Israel from oppression.

Othniel is a deliverer or savior who delivers Israel from "Double Trouble." One aspect of his saving mission is to judge Israel. The meaning of the verb "judge" in this context has to do with leadership in a general sense, rather than rendering legal decisions. Like the other "judges" in the book, Othniel leads Israel into battle.

He is victorious. Israel had been sold into the hand of its enemy, but now Othniel's hand prevails (v. 10), and the "land had rest forty years." All of the leaders except Samson will triumph. All except Samson and Jephthah will bring rest—that is, peace—to the land.

EHUD AND EGLON: AN ANCIENT ADVENTURE TALE
Judges 3:12–30

3:12 **The Israelites again did what was evil in the sight of the LORD; and the LORD strengthened King Eglon of Moab against Israel, because they had done what was evil in the sight of the LORD.** [13] **In alliance with the Ammonites and the Amalekites, he went and defeated Israel; and they took possession of the city of palms.** [14] **So the Israelites served King Eglon of Moab eighteen years.**

[15] **But when the Israelites cried out to the LORD, the LORD raised up for them a deliverer, Ehud son of Gera, the Benjaminite, a left-handed man. The Israelites sent tribute by him to King Eglon of Moab.** [16] **Ehud made for himself a sword with two edges, a cubit in length; and he fastened it on his right thigh under his clothes.** [17] **Then he presented the tribute to King Eglon of Moab. Now Eglon was a very fat man.** [18] **When Ehud had finished presenting the tribute, he sent the people who carried the tribute on their way.** [19] **But he himself turned back at the sculptured stones near Gilgal, and said, "I have a secret message for you, O king." So the king said, "Silence!" and all his attendants went out from his presence.** [20] **Ehud came to him, while he was sitting alone in his cool roof chamber, and said, "I have a message from God for you." So he rose from his seat.** [21] **Then Ehud reached with his left hand, took the sword from his right thigh, and thrust it into Eglon's belly;** [22] **the hilt also went in after the blade, and the fat closed over the blade, for he did not draw the sword out of his belly; and the dirt came out.** [23] **Then Ehud went out into the vestibule, and closed the doors of the roof chamber on him, and locked them.**

[24] **After he had gone, the servants came. When they saw that the doors of the roof chamber were locked, they thought, "He must be relieving himself in the cool chamber."** [25] **So they waited until they were embarrassed. When he still did not open the doors of the roof chamber, they took the key and opened them. There was their lord lying dead on the floor.**

[26] **Ehud escaped while they delayed, and passed beyond the sculptured stones, and escaped to Seirah.** [27] **When he arrived, he sounded the trumpet in the hill country of Ephraim; and the Israelites went down with him from the hill country, having him at their head.** [28] **He said to them, "Follow after me; for the LORD has given your enemies the Moabites into your hand." So they went down after him, and seized the fords of the Jordan against the Moabites, and allowed no one to cross over.** [29] **At that time they killed about ten thousand of the Moabites, all strong, able-bodied men; no one escaped.**

[30] **So Moab was subdued that day under the hand of Israel. And the land had rest eighty years.**

If ancient traditions had been incorporated into the Othniel account, they have been stripped of narrative action and reduced to a few names. In contrast, the Ehud-Eglon narrative (3:12–30) displays the rich colorful detail of a popular tale that has been told and retold over generations. Later editors set the earlier story within their theological framework (vv. 12–15, 30) but left the traditional account intact.

The Theological Framework
Judges 3:12–15, 30

The passage includes all the standard elements of the framework. The Israelites do evil in the sight of the Lord (v. 12). The Israelites' responsibility for their oppression is stressed by the double declaration that they did what is evil (v. 12). By stating that they did evil "again," the editors both connect the Ehud story to the prior passage and underline the stubborn consistency of Israel's sin.

God punishes Israel by subjecting it to oppression for eighteen years (vv. 14–15). The oppressor in this passage is a Moabite king, Eglon, who either forms a coalition with the Ammonites and the Amalekites, or hires them as mercenaries. Moab was a near neighbor of Israel located to the east of the Dead Sea (in the southern part of what is now Jordan). Relations between Israel and Moab were most often hostile, largely because of territorial disputes. The Ammonites were a people located north and east of Moab; the Amalekites, a nomadic or seminomadic people who moved across a wide expanse of land on the southern fringes of Israel, were a bitter and ancient enemy of Israel. Moab, Ammon, and Israel all vied for possession of a section of land east of the Jordan and north of the Arnon River (opposite Jericho). Our story presupposes that Moab controls the disputed territory and from there crosses the Jordan into Israel's heartland, capturing Jericho, "the city of palms" (v. 13). Such a conquest would have been strategically important, because possession of Jericho meant control of the southern Jordan River valley.

The introductory framework ends with a note that the suffering Israelites "cried out to the LORD" (v. 15), and God raised up a deliverer to rescue them. The framework at the conclusion of the story (v. 30) observes that the enemy was subdued and the land had rest for eighty years, an unusually long period of peace.

The Adventure Tale
Judges 3:15–29

The beginning of the older saga is woven into the framework at verse 15. The story is adventuresome and satirical; we can imagine that the Israelites relished telling this tale that ridicules their enemy and vaunts a shrewd Israelite hero. Secular and even crude, the story is characterized by ribald humor: puns, insults, scatological jokes. Like many folktales told by under-dogs, its plot turns on trickery and deceit.

The enemy king, Eglon, is a ridiculous figure, obese and gullible. His name means "calf." Given his girth, the name suggests "fat calf," which would have much the same meaning as the English phrase "fat cat." The name may also allude to Eglon's fate; Eglon will be slain like a fatted calf.

The hero, Ehud, is a kind of ancient James Bond who single-handedly upsets Moabite rule by successful political assassination. The name "Ehud" may be derived from the word for "one," playing off of the fact that our champion acts as a loner; alternatively, the name may derive from a word meaning "majesty," in which case it serves to applaud him. Ehud is a Ben-jaminite, a tribal name that means "son of the right hand." In a delightful play on words, the story tells us that this "right-hand son" is "left-handed" (v. 15). The narrator's play on the word "hand" is more obvious in the Hebrew than in the NRSV. Verse 15 states that the Israelites send Eglon tribute (a heavy tax imposed on subjected peoples) by Ehud's hand.

The Hebrew words translated "left-handed" literally mean "restricted as to the right hand." Bible scholars debate the precise meaning of the phrase. Some think that it has to do with a disability, which would account for the Moabites' lack of suspicion about this Israelite. A reference to a group of Benjaminites "restricted in their right hands" who were excep-tionally skilled warriors (Judg. 20:16) makes it unlikely that the phrase refers to a physical impediment. Possibly the phrase simply means "left-handed." Left-handed fighters would have had an advantage in combat. They would be used to fighting sword to sword and shield to shield with right-handed opponents, while right-handed men, used to fighting sword to shield, would have had much less practice with left-handed foes. The most likely explanation, however, is that Ehud belonged to an elite group of commandos trained to wield a sword with either hand, possibly by binding their dominant hand. Benjaminite warriors were known for being ambidextrous (1 Chr. 12:2).

In any case, the success of Ehud's plot depends on the skill of his left hand. He makes himself a short sword, which he hides under his clothing on his right leg. The guards, assuming that he was right-handed, would have been on the lookout for weapons hidden on his left side. He heads up a party bringing tribute to Eglon, a role that would allow him access to the king without raising Moabite suspicions, and sneaks his weapon in past the guards.

The story moves briskly until Ehud is about to deliver the tribute, then pauses to tell the audience that Eglon was a "very fat man." This seemingly irrelevant detail is in part an insult, a way of ridiculing the Moabite foe. It also characterizes the king as a "fat cat," an oppressor who gorges on food extorted from the oppressed. The Hebrew word translated "fat," when used to describe people, often has to do with those who grow fat eating the food of the poor. The tribute Israel paid Moab was probably agricultural products; Eglon quite literally grew corpulent at his vassal's expense. The storyteller takes some vengeful glee in recounting the role Eglon's girth plays in his death (v. 22); the "fat cat" got his comeuppance.

After the Israelites finish delivering their taxes to the king, the party sets off for home. Ehud accompanies them as far as the "sculptured stones" near Gilgal, then returns to the king.

The geography is not entirely clear; presumably the king resides in Jericho, but the story possibly takes place in Moab, on the east side of the Jordan. The meaning of the term translated "sculptured stones" is also debated. Some take it to refer to the twelve stones that the Israelite tribes set up to commemorate God's having parted the Jordan to let Israel cross (Josh. 4:1–9). Elsewhere, however, the term consistently means "graven images." Most likely that meaning applies to this passage, too. The graven image may be a depiction of the Moabite king or of the Moabite god, set up to mark the boundaries of Moab's control. The stones bracket the main episode of the story. In verse 19, Ehud turns back from the stones; in verse 26, he passes beyond them. If the stones are graven images, they serve a symbolic function. Ehud turns away from such ensnaring idols (cf. 2:3). By the end of the story, he has moved far beyond them.

The plot thickens in verse 19. Ehud gains a private audience with King Eglon by engaging in another bit of deceit based on another pun. He claims he has a "secret message" for Eglon. The words translated "secret message" are as double-edged as Ehud's sword; they can also mean "hidden thing." Eglon, as Ehud intends, expects to hear a political secret or a divine oracle. Ehud is actually referring to his hidden thing, his sword.

The duped king sends his attendants away and invites the assassin into his private room. In another double entendre, Ehud says he has a message from the gods, or from God. Eglon expects an oracle, but God's word for Eglon is death.

The sword thrust by which Ehud slays Eglon is described in great detail. The narrator tells the story with a spirit of vengeance, a spirit of glee that a hated tyrant is defeated.

When he completes his mission, Ehud makes good his escape. The details of that escape are cloudy because two Hebrew words in the verses describing the escape (vv. 22–23), which the NRSV translates "dirt" and "vestibule," are obscure. Ehud locks the doors of the king's chamber from the inside and slips away, presumably over the side or out some sort of passageway. It is unlikely that he could leave by the front doors, stopping to bolt them, without arousing suspicion.

Locked doors lead Eglon's attendants to assume that the king is relieving himself so that they refrain from opening the doors for a considerable period of time. The bathroom humor of verses 24–25, as coarse as it is, serves an important function in the story's plot. Ehud has only partly accomplished his mission. He must still deal with the Moabite army, and he needs time to rally the Israelite troops. The attendants' delay in opening the doors gives him the necessary time. Eventually the embarrassed guards do fetch a key to let themselves into the king's private room and discover him lying dead.

In the meantime, Ehud escapes to Seirah, an unknown site in Ephraim where he rallies the troops with a blast of the ram's horn. The ram's horn, or shofar, was used for both ritual and war. The Moabite soldiers are all stout men (the Hebrew term translated "able-bodied" has the same double meaning: corpulent and brave, as the English word "stout"). They are nonetheless thrown into confusion at the death of their king. The Israelites are able to annihilate them at the fords of the Jordan. The fords also play a significant role later in Judges; Jephthah and his Gileadite followers seize the fords against their Ephraimite opponents, slaughtering any fugitive who tries to pass (Judg. 12). The similarity between the two episodes is one of several motifs that hold together the various separate stories that comprise the book of Judges. Differences between the episodes—Ehud slaughters Moabite oppressors, while Jephthah kills his own Israelite kin —contribute to the downward spiral that characterizes the book. The numbers killed at the fords are, in both cases, exaggerated. In the Ehud story, the phrase translated "ten thousand" is perhaps better translated "ten contingents." Either way, the number is inflated to extol the Israelite victory.

As noted above, the period of rest (v. 30) is of exceptionally long duration. Perhaps the editors wanted to leave room for a downward spiral; the periods of rest grow shorter later in the book.

Reflections on Ehud

The story of Ehud is humorous and adventuresome, as well as violent and crude. The assassination, while understandable as the trickery of an underdog, is hardly morally uplifting. What is this story doing in the Bible?

The early storytellers no doubt told the tale of Ehud in part to vent their frustration at a powerful enemy. Satirizing the Moabites and extolling the Israelites would give storyteller and audience a delightful sense of superiority, as well as help define "insiders" and "outsiders." Seeing why the story was first passed down is easy. But why was the story included in the cycle of tales that early compilers put together to illustrate Israel's early beginnings? Apparently, editors living centuries after the story was first told saw God at work in the rough-and-tumble of everyday life. In the daring but violent action of this Israelite commando, they believed that God had set about to deliver God's people. That God delivers Israel is no surprise. We learn that in the first two chapters of Judges. *How* God does that comes as a surprise, one that does not necessarily fit into our moral codes. The Ehud story is the first of many accounts in Judges that show God working in unexpected ways, through surprising deliverers.

SHAMGAR BEN ANATH: A VERY SHORT TALE
Judges 3:31

> 3:31 **After him came Shamgar son of Anath, who killed six hundred of the Philistines with an oxgoad. He too delivered Israel.**

The story that follows Ehud's tale is very brief indeed. Shamgar, son of Anath appears to have been a well-known figure in ancient Israelite legend. The Song of Deborah refers to him to establish a chronological benchmark (Judg. 5:6). Nonetheless, the traditions about Shamgar have been almost entirely lost.

His story is, moreover, a kind of afterthought (Auld, 1984, 149). The introduction to Deborah's story (Judg. 4:1) refers back to Ehud, suggesting that the reference to Shamgar was added after the stories of Israel's deliverers had already been compiled. In form, Judges 3:31 more closely resembles the roster of King David's mighty warriors (2 Sam. 23:8–12) than it resembles any of the narratives found in the book of Judges.

Nonetheless, the editor who added this short story did so for good reasons. Shamgar is at home in the context of the book of Judges. Like the Ehud account, the brief description of Shamgar boasts of a hero who single-handedly bests, and thus ridicules, Israel's enemies. The verse points to the story of Deborah, where Shamgar is mentioned along with Jael (Judg. 5:6). Shamgar's exaggerated exploits with an ox-goad recall Samson's slaying Philistines with the jaw of an ass, an equally unconventional weapon (Judg. 15:14–17).

The brief story of Shamgar contributes to the message of Joshua and Judges. Here again, we find a non-Israelite delivering Israel. The name "Shamgar" is not Hebrew. Shamgar is the "son of Anath," a Canaanite goddess. The phrase "son of Anath" may refer to Shamgar's town; he may be a resident of Beth Anath, a city in Galilee. Given that Anath is a war deity, the phrase may refer to Shamgar's profession; he is a soldier. In either case, the phrase indicates he is Canaanite. Shamgar joins a group of non-Israelites who deliver Israel: the Canaanite prostitute Rahab, who saves Israelite spies from capture (Josh. 2); the citizen of Bethel who helps Israelite spies take his city (Judg. 1:23–26); and the Kenite Jael, who assassinates Israel's enemy, Sisera (Judg. 4:17–22; 5:24–27). The stories of non-Israelite heroes serve to challenge ethnocentrism. God can use anyone to deliver God's people.

Like several other accounts in Judges, the story of Shamgar suggests that God's chosen do not always work in predictable ways. Jael uses a tent peg to slay Sisera. Samson seizes the jaw of an ass for a weapon. Shamgar slaughters Israel's enemies with an ox-goad, an iron-tipped stick ordinarily used to prod cattle. God's unexpected deliverers act unconventionally.

18. Deborah and Barak
Judges 4–5

The story of Deborah and Barak is among the best-known, most-studied texts in the book of Judges. It has generated interest in part because of its complexity. Deborah and Barak's victory is told twice, in prose (chapter 4) and in poetry (chapter 5); each account is the work of more than one storyteller or songwriter. The poetic version, in particular, has been the subject of enormous scholarly discussion because of its antiquity. Although some interpreters debate the relative chronology of the two accounts, a majority believe that the poetic version is not only older than the narrative but among the most ancient traditions in the Bible.

Moreover, both are told with artistry and power. The story in chapter 4 displays sharply etched characters, lively dialogue, and an adventurous plot. While it never loses sight of the Divine Warrior's decisive activity on Israel's behalf, its focus is on the people and their interactions. The prophet, Deborah, declares God's word, and that word comes about. But it does so through very human players: a resistant general and a deceptive assassin. God's word is certain, but its fulfillment is not without surprises.

The poetic account of chapter 5 conveys the events of the battle via allusion rather than description. Its tone is elevated, epic; its use of language, magnificent. The focus of the poem is praise of divine and human participants in the war. God is front and center, bending natural and even cosmic forces to fight directly against Israel's enemies. The poem does celebrate human actors, but recognizes their deeds as finally the work of Yahweh, for which Yahweh is blessed.

The accounts relate a battle between Israelite tribes and a Canaanite king (or kings) for control of the Jezreel Valley, a fertile plain that opens out into otherwise rugged hill country in Israel. Such a contest would have been critically important for Israel. The Jezreel played a key role in agriculture, trade, and communications between the central and northern tribes. Whether there actually was such a battle, and if so, just what happened, is unclear. Poetry is notoriously difficult to use as a historical source. The singers who composed chapter 5 shaped it to extol Israel and its God, or for the sake of their artistry, or to convey an emotion or image, rather than for the sake of historical reporting. The prose account appears to depend upon the poem. Like the other stories in Judges, the tale of Deborah and Barak is more story and theology than history.

THE ADVENTURE STORY
Judges 4

4:1 **The Israelites again did what was evil in the sight of the LORD, after Ehud died.** [2] **So the LORD sold them into the hand of King Jabin of Canaan, who reigned in Hazor; the commander of his army was Sisera, who lived in Harosheth-ha-goiim.** [3] **Then the Israelites cried out to the LORD for help; for he had nine hundred chariots of iron, and had oppressed the Israelites cruelly twenty years.**

[4] **At that time Deborah, a prophetess, wife of Lappidoth, was judging Israel.** [5] **She used to sit under the palm of Deborah between Ramah and Bethel in the hill country of Ephraim; and the Israelites came up to her for judgment.** [6] **She sent and summoned Barak son of Abinoam from Kedesh in Naphtali, and said to him, "The LORD, the God of Israel, commands you, 'Go, take position at Mount Tabor, bringing ten thousand from the tribe of Naphtali and the tribe of Zebulun.** [7] **I will draw out Sisera, the general of Jabin's army, to meet you by the Wadi Kishon with his chariots and his troops; and I will give him into your hand.'"** [8] **Barak said to her, "If you will go with me, I will go; but if you will not go with me, I will not go."** [9] **And she said, "I will surely go with you; nevertheless, the road on which you are going will not lead to your glory, for the LORD will sell Sisera into the hand of a woman."** **Then Deborah got up and went with Barak to Kedesh.** [10] **Barak summoned Zebulun and Naphtali to Kedesh; and ten thousand warriors went up behind him; and Deborah went up with him.**

[11] **Now Heber the Kenite had separated from the other Kenites, that is, the descendants of Hobab the father-in-law of Moses, and had encamped as far away as Elon-bezaanannim, which is near Kedesh.**

[12] **When Sisera was told that Barak son of Abinoam had gone up to Mount Tabor,** [13] **Sisera called out all his chariots, nine hundred chariots of iron, and all the troops who were with him, from Harosheth-ha-goiim to the Wadi Kishon.** [14] **Then Deborah said to Barak, "Up! For this is the day on which the LORD has given Sisera into your hand. The LORD is indeed going out before you." So Barak went down from Mount Tabor with ten thousand warriors following him.** [15] **And the LORD threw Sisera and all his chariots and all his army into a panic before Barak; Sisera got down from his chariot and fled away on**

foot, [16] while Barak pursued the chariots and the army to Harosheth-ha-goiim. All the army of Sisera fell by the sword; no one was left.

[17] Now Sisera had fled away on foot to the tent of Jael wife of Heber the Kenite; for there was peace between King Jabin of Hazor and the clan of Heber the Kenite. [18] Jael came out to meet Sisera, and said to him, "Turn aside, my lord, turn aside to me; have no fear." So he turned aside to her into the tent, and she covered him with a rug. [19] Then he said to her, "Please give me a little water to drink; for I am thirsty." So she opened a skin of milk and gave him a drink and covered him. [20] He said to her, "Stand at the entrance of the tent, and if anybody comes and asks you, 'Is anyone here?' say, 'No.' " [21] But Jael wife of Heber took a tent peg, and took a hammer in her hand, and went softly to him and drove the peg into his temple, until it went down into the ground—he was lying fast asleep from weariness—and he died. [22] Then, as Barak came in pursuit of Sisera, Jael went out to meet him, and said to him, "Come, and I will show you the man whom you are seeking." So he went into her tent; and there was Sisera lying dead, with the tent peg in his temple.

[23] So on that day God subdued King Jabin of Canaan before the Israelites. [24] Then the hand of the Israelites bore harder and harder on King Jabin of Canaan, until they destroyed King Jabin of Canaan.

The prose account of Deborah and Barak is likely the product of many storytellers over a long period of time. Its final form, however, is a well-crafted story centered on Deborah's prophecies, Barak's reluctance, and Jael's deceptive heroism. The word of God comes to pass, but with twists and turns along the way.

The now-familiar elements of the editorial framework are found in verses 1–3. After the death of Ehud (the framework does not mention Shagmar), Israel again does evil in the sight of the Lord. God again responds by giving the people into the hands of an enemy. This time, the oppressors are Jabin, king of Canaan, and his general, Sisera. The references to Jabin were probably added after the story was largely complete. Jabin was Israel's foe in a different military campaign, narrated in Joshua 11. A storyteller recounting the tale somewhat late in its history may have added Jabin to make sure the audience knew Israel's opponents were formidable. They were up against no less than the king of Canaan! Moreover, adding Jabin creates a nice symmetry, as Jabin and his general, Sisera, are countered by Deborah and her general, Barak.

The active enemy in the story is Sisera. The narrative tells us three things about him. First, he is from Harosheth-ha-goiim, "Harosheth of the nations," which was probably located near Mount Carmel, on the western edge of the Jezreel Valley. Second, Sisera commanded nine hundred iron chariots—that is, wooden chariots equipped with iron plates and weapons. The Israelite warriors, an army of amateur foot soldiers with no access to iron, are up against a vast professional cavalry that possesses technologically advanced weapons. Third, Jabin and Sisera's army has subjugated Israel for twenty years, the longest period of oppression thus far.

The distressed Israelites again cry out to the Lord, who again delivers them. The next section of the story, verses 4–10, introduces the Israelite leaders, Deborah and Barak. In this case, the assertion that God raised up a deliverer is omitted; the curtain rises on Deborah in an ongoing position of leadership. We learn three things about Deborah in verses 4–5. She is a prophet, she is "the wife of Lappidoth," and she judges Israel.

Biblical scholars used to think that prophecy first arose in Israel with the emergence of kingship, and that the term "prophet" applied to Deborah was an honorific. The discovery of records from surrounding cultures show that women and men were prophesying in the ancient Near East centuries before Israel emerged in Canaan. These discoveries make it more likely that there were prophets in premonarchical Israel.

Israelite prophets served a highly political function, declaring God's word for a specific time and place. They appear to have had defined functions in premonarchical Israel's wars, declaring whether or not God would give the tribes victory. Deborah functions as a prophet as she tells Barak that he is to begin to resist the Canaanites, and assures him that Yahweh is with him. The presence of a woman prophet is not surprising. Prophets in the surrounding cultures could be male or female. In the biblical accounts, Miriam is called a prophet; the prophet Huldah, wife of Shallum, is in King Josiah's inner circle; and the woman Noadiah is the head of a group of prophets.

Married Israelite women were normally identified by the name of their husbands. Deborah is the "wife of Lappidoth." The word translated "wife" also means "woman"; "Lappidoth" literally means "torches." The phrase translated "wife of Lappidoth" could thus also be translated "fiery woman." (The New English Bible translates it "woman of spirit.") The storyteller's audience would have heard both meanings and would have enjoyed the play on words identifying independent, spirit-filled Deborah.

The verses also tell us that the prophetic, fiery woman is a judge. Judging is closely associated with deliverance. Deborah thus is identified as the deliverer through whom God will end Israel's oppression.

Unlike other leaders in the book, however, Deborah seems to "judge" Israel in the technical sense of rendering legal decisions (v. 5). For a woman to "judge" in this forensic sense is unexpected. The biblical or ancient Near

Eastern legal materials do not indicate that women could preside over court cases. The story gives no indication, however, that Deborah was doing something unusual.

In her role as prophet, Deborah summons Barak and conveys to him the word of Yahweh. This word includes command, strategy, and assurance (vv. 6–7).

The command is to begin the battle. Barak is to muster his troops and station them at Mount Tabor. The choice of Mount Tabor is strategically shrewd, as it is located at a boundary point between Naphtali and Zebulun (the two tribes that will fight in the battle). A thirteen-hundred-foot peak that stands alone in the flat valley, Mount Tabor commands the northwest section of the Jezreel plain. Stationing troops there would give Barak a military advantage over Sisera's army below. The instructions about strategy are followed by an assurance; God will give the Canaanite army into Barak's hand.

Up to this point, the story has unfolded in an orthodox, expected manner. As anticipated, the people sin, are judged, and cry out. As we have come to expect, God answers their cry not with the judgment that justice might suggest, but with the mercy that love inspires. God uses Deborah, the fiery woman and prophetic leader, to deliver the people by calling upon the general, Barak.

Barak's response to Deborah in verse 8 is the first unexpected twist in the story. Barak resists. He will go only if Deborah also goes. Perhaps he seeks her charismatic presence to help mobilize the troops. Perhaps he is testing her commitment and certainty about the outcome by requiring her to put her own life on the line. Perhaps he is dependent upon her oracular power for guidance in battle. In any case, Barak will not act without Deborah.

While Judges gives no indication that a woman judge or prophet was socially unexpected, Deborah's presence as the general goes to muster his troops is a surprise. The book clearly portrays battle as a male sphere. The account of Abimelech's death (9:53–54) depicts being one-upped by a woman in combat as an inglorious, even shameful fate. When a woman crushes Abimelech's head with a millstone, he orders his squire to slay him lest people say he was killed by a woman. Deborah accepts Barak's condition but, again speaking prophetically, declares the consequences of his reluctance. He will gain no glory. Yahweh will sell Sisera into the hand of a woman. At this point in the story, the reader assumes that the woman is Deborah; Barak's reputation will be tarnished by his dependence on her. In any case, Deborah goes with Barak to muster the troops. Barak obeys her command and follows her strategy.

The story line is interrupted in verse 11 with a seemingly extraneous piece of information. A group of Kenites is living near Kedesh. Actually, the notice does fit into the plot. A Kenite woman, Jael, plays a critical role in Sisera's defeat (vv. 17–22). The Kenites' homeland is in the southern reaches of the Judean wilderness. Verse 11 explains why some Kenites have traveled so far north.

After an unexpected plot development and brief detour, the story again unfolds in an orthodox manner. The prophetic promise in verse 7, that God will draw out Sisera's troops, is fulfilled in verses 12 and 13. Sisera moves his chariots and infantry to the Kishon.

The battle scene (vv. 14–16) is brief and stylized, told in language and categories that emphasize the role of the Divine Warrior. Deborah gives the command to begin fighting and reiterates God's promise to fight for Israel against their enemy. One of the motifs characteristic of Israel's holy war traditions is that Yahweh spreads panic among the enemy; victory over the Canaanites is ascribed to divinely induced terror in verse 15. Barak's troops engage the enemy, as made clear by the assertion that all of Sisera's army fell to the sword. The storyteller downplays the role of the Israelite soldiers in this part of the story, in order to emphasize the role of God. The decisiveness of Israel's victory over a militarily and numerically superior force seemed nothing short of miraculous. God won the victory.

The attention of the narrative shifts in verse 17 from God to human actors, and from expected events, described in the language of deep-rooted traditions, to another unexpected twist in the plot. As his army is routed, Sisera ignobly abandons the troops and flees on foot. (The storyteller must have enjoyed disparaging the enemy commander!) The battle-weary, defeated general seeks refuge in the tent of a Kenite woman, Jael. Jael's husband, Heber, is allied to Sisera's overlord, Jabin. Surely he will be safe with her.

Sisera's hopes for succor at first appear well grounded. Jael invites him in and treats him with almost maternal solicitude: covering him and giving him milk to drink. Like Ehud's words, Jael's are deceptive. In a move expected by neither the enemy general nor the story's audience, Jael, having lulled Sisera into complacency, takes up a tent peg and mallet and kills the sleeping man. Not Deborah, but Jael, a non-Israelite, is the woman to whom Yahweh sells Sisera. The prophecy of verse 9 is fulfilled in an unexpected way.

Modern commentators are greatly troubled by Jael's act. She ignores both ancient Near Eastern rules of hospitality and our own deeply rooted expectations about the behavior of maternal women. The commentators are far more disturbed by Jael than by Ehud, although he also is deceptive and violates strict cultural norms (the rules of diplomacy). The violation of motherly norms, therefore, is likely the act that most distresses biblical interpreters.

Jael can be understood as a woman trying to negotiate conflicting inter-ests. Her husband has entered into a treaty with Sisera's overlord and, so, indirectly with Sisera. Yet the Kenites' long-standing relationship with Israel also entails obligations. Moreover, Sisera lost. Israel decisively defeated the Canaanite army, and their leaders may be along any time. Harboring the enemy could be dangerous. Jael is a survivor who does what she must. The biblical authors have no such qualms about Jael's action. She fulfills God's word, spoken through Deborah in verse 9. The poetic ver-sion of the story declares, "Most blessed of women be Jael" (5:24).

The prose account ends with one last bit of deception. Jael, again tak-ing initiative with a powerful man, invites Barak into her tent to "show [him] the man [he is] seeking" (v. 22). Barak enters the tent, expecting to capture his enemy. He is thwarted; he gains no glory (v. 9), for Yahweh had already sold Sisera into the hands of a woman.

This adventurous story, with all its twists and turns, would have held the audience's attention. Its portrayal of the enemy's defeat would have evoked their glee. The story also scores a theological point. God does indeed ful-fill God's word, but how God does so comes as a surprise. Elements of orthodox belief—that oracles come to pass, that the Divine Warrior fights for Israel, and the like—are worked out in unorthodox, unexpected ways. God takes what is at hand to move the story of Israel forward. The nitty-gritty details of divine deliverance challenge human expectations.

ALL GLORY, LAUD, AND HONOR
Judges 5

The prose account of divine deliverance in chapter 4 works itself out in very earthy and unexpected ways. The prophetic word is fulfilled; God's decision to save is decisive. But the storyteller gives the most vivid, detailed attention to human actors and their encounters: Deborah's spirited instructions to Barak, Barak's hesitant obedience and subsequent loss of glory, Jael's treacherous heroism, and Sisera's ignoble death. The tone of the poetic account in chapter 5 is quite different. A lofty celebration of divine victory, its focus is Yahweh, who comes in terrible might to aid God's people (vv. 4–5). The song lauds human participants in the battle: warriors, peasantry, the leaders Deborah and Barak, those tribes who heeded the summons, and Jael. Their actions are not seen as distinct from those of the Divine Warrior, however, but as the actions of God. Focus is maintained on the Divine Warrior by the hymnic praise (vv. 1–9), the cosmic forces that God sets loose in battle (vv. 20–21), and the final petition that all God's foes might be defeated (v. 31).

"The Song of Deborah" (as the poem is commonly called) is among the oldest passages in the Bible. Scholars debate its exact date; a majority believe that the oldest parts of the poem were composed in the premonarchical period, perhaps as early as the late twelfth or early eleventh centuries B.C.E. The verse is highly valued for glimpses into Israel's earliest social and religious life. In particular, the "roll call of the tribes" in verses 14–18 has been the focus of scholarly debate. Unfortunately, the historical significance of the poem as a whole, and its treatment of the tribes in particular, is very difficult to assess. Translation problems, questions about the date of the poem, the possibility that the section concerning the tribes was added well after the rest of the victory song was written, and the fact that poetry is rarely intended to report historical data make it difficult to derive historical evidence from the song.

Not only is the song among the oldest passages in the Bible, its language is among the most obscure, but the obscurity of its language and syntax cannot hide the fact that the Song of Deborah is magnificent poetry. Vivid imagery, the abrupt juxtaposition of scenes, a striking use of repetition, and its use of allusion rather than explicit description all contribute to the enormous power of the poem.

As the work of more than one singer, the poem has no single genre or form. Nonetheless, the song is unified in celebration and praise, rejoicing in Israel's victory, and lauding the Divine Warrior and the human leaders through whom Yahweh works for the defeat of their oppressors.

5:1 **Then Deborah and Barak son of Abinoam sang on that day, saying:**
² **"When locks are long in Israel,**
    when the people offer themselves willingly—
    bless the LORD!
³ **"Hear, O kings; give ear, O princes;**
    to the LORD I will sing,
    I will make melody to the LORD, the God of Israel.
⁴ **"LORD, when you went out from Seir,**
    when you marched from the region of Edom,
  the earth trembled,
    and the heavens poured,
    the clouds indeed poured water.

⁵ The mountains quaked before the LORD, the One of Sinai,
    before the LORD, the God of Israel.
⁶ "In the days of Shamgar son of Anath,
    in the days of Jael, caravans ceased
    and travelers kept to the byways.
⁷ The peasantry prospered in Israel,
    they grew fat on plunder,
    because you arose, Deborah,
    arose as a mother in Israel.
⁸ When new gods were chosen,
    then war was in the gates.
  Was shield or spear to be seen
    among forty thousand in Israel?
⁹ My heart goes out to the commanders of Israel
    who offered themselves willingly among the people.
  Bless the LORD.
¹⁰ "Tell of it, you who ride on white donkeys,
    you who sit on rich carpets
    and you who walk by the way.
¹¹ To the sound of musicians at the watering places,
    there they repeat the triumphs of the LORD,
    the triumphs of his peasantry in Israel.
  "Then down to the gates marched the people of the LORD.
¹² "Awake, awake, Deborah!
    Awake, awake, utter a song!
  Arise, Barak, lead away your captives,
    O son of Abinoam.
¹³ Then down marched the remnant of the noble;
    the people of the LORD marched down for him against the mighty.
¹⁴ From Ephraim they set out into the valley,
    following you, Benjamin, with your kin;
  from Machir marched down the commanders,
    and from Zebulun those who bear the marshal's staff;
¹⁵ the chiefs of Issachar came with Deborah,
    and Issachar faithful to Barak;
  into the valley they rushed out at his heels.
  Among the clans of Reuben
    there were great searchings of heart.
¹⁶ Why did you tarry among the sheepfolds,
    to hear the piping for the flocks?
  Among the clans of Reuben
    there were great searchings of heart.
¹⁷ Gilead stayed beyond the Jordan;
    and Dan, why did he abide with the ships?

Asher sat still at the coast of the sea,
   settling down by his landings.
¹⁸ Zebulun is a people that scorned death;
   Naphtali too, on the heights of the field.
¹⁹ "The kings came, they fought;
   then fought the kings of Canaan,
at Taanach, by the waters of Megiddo;
   they got no spoils of silver.
²⁰ The stars fought from heaven,
   from their courses they fought against Sisera.
²¹ The torrent Kishon swept them away,
   the onrushing torrent, the torrent Kishon.
   March on, my soul, with might!
²² "Then loud beat the horses' hoofs
   with the galloping, galloping of his steeds.
²³ "Curse Meroz, says the angel of the LORD,
   curse bitterly its inhabitants,
because they did not come to the help of the LORD,
   to the help of the LORD against the mighty.
²⁴ "Most blessed of women be Jael,
   the wife of Heber the Kenite,
   of tent-dwelling women most blessed.
²⁵ He asked water and she gave him milk,
   she brought him curds in a lordly bowl.
²⁶ She put her hand to the tent peg
   and her right hand to the workmen's mallet;
she struck Sisera a blow,
   she crushed his head,
   she shattered and pierced his temple.
²⁷ He sank, he fell,
   he lay still at her feet;
at her feet he sank, he fell;
   where he sank, there he fell dead.
²⁸ "Out of the window she peered,
   the mother of Sisera gazed through the lattice:
'Why is his chariot so long in coming?
   Why tarry the hoofbeats of his chariots?'
²⁹ Her wisest ladies make answer,
   indeed, she answers the question herself:
³⁰ 'Are they not finding and dividing the spoil?—
   A girl or two for every man;
spoil of dyed stuffs for Sisera,
   spoil of dyed stuffs embroidered,
   two pieces of dyed work embroidered for my neck as spoil?'

³¹ "So perish all your enemies, O LORD!
   But may your friends be like the sun as it rises in its might."
   And the land had rest forty years.

A prose introduction presents Deborah and Barak as the singers of the song; they will also be among its subjects. In Hebrew, the verb "sang" requires a feminine subject; of the two leaders, Deborah is dominant.

The form of the first section of the poem (vv. 2–9) resembles other biblical hymns of praise. The singers invoke praise and declare that they will sing to the Lord (v. 3). The reason for the praise begins to emerge in verse 2. Volunteers have stepped forward to fight for Israel. "Long locks" refers to a vow neither to cut one's hair nor drink alcohol (Num. 6:2–21). Among others, the vow was apparently taken by men who consecrated themselves as warriors for Yahweh. The warriors' dedication is ascribed to God; "LORD" or "God" is named as the one to be praised four times in the first two verses of the song.

The poem moves from invoking praise to the subject of praise. Storms and earthquakes (vv. 4–5) are typical signs of theophany, that is, the coming of Yahweh with power. Some scholars see the verses as an allusion to Sinai, where God's presence was signaled by thunder, lightning, and the shaking of the mountain (Exod. 19:16–18). Others understand the passage as a reference to the conquest, when the Divine Warrior marched before the people from territory east of the Jordan (where Seir and Edom are located) across the river to take the promised land. In any case, the verses celebrate the awesome presence of God.

The theophany is followed by a passage centered on Deborah's leadership (vv. 6–8). The juxtaposition implicitly equates divine deliverance of Israel through Deborah with God's earlier awesome deeds.

The translation, and so the meaning, of verses 6–8 is a matter of debate. As the NRSV translates it, the passage contrasts the people's distress before Deborah arose with the prosperity that followed upon her leadership. Judges 4 referred to Israel's situation before the battle in brief, stereotypical language: Jabin and Sisera "oppressed" them for twenty years. The poem gives more content to that oppression. Either enemy control of the main routes or social chaos has made the roads through the Jezreel Valley too dangerous to use. Trade has ceased and travelers must take circuitous back routes. Access to routes through the Jezreel Valley, vital to the Israelites, was cut off. Deborah's prophetic leadership reverses the situation: "the peasantry prospered" (v. 7).

Alternatively, verse 7 can be translated "peasantry ceased in Israel . . . until you arose, O Deborah. . . ." In that case, verses 6–8 describe the people's miserable condition prior to Deborah's leadership. Their distress includes a lack of arms with which to resist the oppressors ("Was shield or spear to be seen?").

In either case, the rise of Deborah is pivotal. The poem implicitly depicts her as a prophet. "Mother in Israel" is the equivalent of the title "father" given to the prophets Elijah (2 Kgs. 2:12) and Elisha (2 Kgs. 6:21). That Deborah's leadership is God's doing is implied by the juxtaposition of verses 6–8 with the theophany in verses 4–5. God, in Deborah, has come in might.

The poem circles around to its opening in verse 9. Once again, it lauds those who voluntarily fought for Israel and commands the audience to "bless the Lord."

The singers continue to invoke praise in verses 10–11. Those who ride, those who sit, those who walk—*everyone* is instructed to declare God's deeds in all of their activities. Praise is not to be limited to settings of worship; the victory God wrought is to be told in the settings of daily life ("the watering places"). The close relationship between God's actions and the actions of God's people is seen in verse 11, where the "triumphs of the LORD" and the "triumphs of his peasantry in Israel" are presented as parallels.

The next section (vv. 12–18) is a flashback that recalls the mustering of Israel's troops. Some interpreters believe Deborah is asked to sing a victory song (v. 12). Others more plausibly argue that her song is intended to stir up the Israelites, calling them to battle. The closest parallel to the imperative "Awake, awake" is found in Isaiah 51:9, where God is implored to "awake, awake" and throw off the oppressor. The song then calls on Barak to "lead away your captives," summoning him, also, to war.

Recollection of the muster continues with the roll call of the tribes. Up until verse 14, the poem refers to the people collectively as "Israel," or as "the people of the LORD." Verses 14–18 name the tribes individually, praising them for their participation or chiding them for failing to join in the battle. The translation of these verses is problematic; whether a tribe is honored for fighting or rebuked for staying away is not always clear. Some read verse 14 as censuring Ephraim for remaining rooted in his land, unheeding of the call to arms. In contrast, at least one scholar argues that the verses applaud all of the tribes named for their participation (Miller, 1973, 96–97). A majority, including the translators of the NRSV, interpret the verses as commending six tribes for responding to the summons: Ephraim, Benjamin, Machir (that is, Manasseh), Zebulun, Issachar, and

Naphtali. Four are chastised for staying away: Reuben, Gilead (that is, Gad), Dan, and Asher. The southern tribes, Judah and Simeon, are not mentioned. Perhaps they were not considered part of Israel when this part of the poem was composed.

The roll call of the tribes is widely valued as an important resource for reconstructing the organization of the tribes in premonarchical Israel. Certainly the roll call involves the largest number of tribes mentioned together in any story in Judges. As noted above, difficulties in translating the verses and uncertainty about their dating make assessing their value as historical evidence difficult. The difficulty is accentuated by a discrepancy between chapter 5 and chapter 4 as to which tribes were involved (chapter 4 names only Zebulun and Naphtali).

Our primary interest is the contribution of verses 14–18 to the overall meaning of the poem. At least three such contributions are apparent. First, the roll call clarifies that ascribing victory to the Lord does not diminish the human role in the battle. The poem praises the valor of the soldiers who fought. Second, the song reflects the traditional, somewhat idealistic picture of premonarchical Israel as a confederacy of tribes who came to each others' aid when needed. This ideal complements the traditional view of God as a faithful, victorious warrior. Finally, the participation of six tribes establishes the scale of the battle as large, even epic.

The six tribes assemble against a coalition of Canaanite kings (v. 19). Again the poem depicts the battle as larger than the version given in the prose account, where two tribes meet just one Canaanite king. The poem continues to move back and forth from human participants to divine agency. God, who works through the warriors and their leaders, also acts directly on Israel's behalf, using the stars in the heavens and the River Kishon to undo the Canaanite kings. According to the mythology of Ugarit (Israel's near neighbor), stars cause rain. In this instance, the stars, God's heavenly host, fight for Israel by causing rain, which in turn makes the Kishon flood. The Wadi Kishon is a seasonal watercourse, little more than a trickle in dry periods and a torrent when it rains. Verses 20–21 seem to envision the Canaanite troops traveling near the Kishon when it was dry. Unseasonable rains cause a flash flood that overtakes and drowns the unsuspecting army.

The description of the battle does not refer to God explicitly. Nonetheless, within the context of a poem that begins and ends with praise of Yahweh (v. 31) and extols God's triumphs (v. 11), one must understand the stars and Kishon as weapons that God uses against the Canaanites, just as God used the Red Sea against Pharaoh and his army (Exodus 14–15).

The alternation between divine and human players continues in verse 23. The angel of the Lord (see commentary on 2:1–5) curses Meroz for failing to fight. Meroz is not mentioned elsewhere in the Bible; saying what or where Meroz was is not possible, although clearly the curse against Meroz is a foil for the blessing of Jael that follows.

The song extols Jael (vv. 24–27) for deceiving and killing Sisera. With unabashed delight, the singers declare, "Most blessed of women be Jael" (v. 24). Details of the poetic account of Jael's deed differ from the prose version. In Judges 4, Jael appears maternal. In contrast, many interpreters find sexual innuendo in the poetic depiction: "He sank, he fell, he lay still at [Hebrew, 'between'] her feet." Some, pointing to verse 30, where Sisera's mother speculates that he is dividing up the spoil—"a girl or two [Hebrew, 'womb or two'] for every man," read the poetic account of Jael's action as vengeance against Sisera's brutality toward women. In any case, the authors of both accounts certainly approve of Jael's deed. Both storyteller and singer are concerned with Israel's deliverance, not with abstract compliance to laws of hospitality. Jael's assassination of Israel's hated oppressor is the climax of the story of God's deliverance of the people.

In the final section of the poem (vv. 28–30), praise of divine and human warriors gives way to a scene at once mocking and poignant. Sisera's mother, anxious when her son does not return, desperately tries to explain his delay. The singers and their audience found satisfaction in the oppressor's fate: "so perish all your enemies, O Lord!" (v. 31). Yet the scene strikes a note of pathos. We cannot help but feel for this mother, who waits for the son who will never again come home.

We have looked at the two accounts of the story of Deborah and Barak separately in order to avoid blurring the insights that each offers. Finally, however, they are not presented as two distinct stories, but as a single unit. In the text as we have it, Judges 4 is presented as the basic story of the battle into which Judges 5 is incorporated as a victory song. Although it was composed first, the poem is thus presented as praise of the events related in the prose account. That approach in itself is grist for theological reflection.

As noted above, Judges 4 describes God working through mundane and even questionable human acts. The song nonetheless extols God's work as unambiguously praiseworthy. Moreover, the deeds of the Israelite actors through whom the Lord accomplishes Israel's deliverance are wholeheartedly praised. The triumphs of the peasantry are equated to the triumphs of the Lord. The rise of Deborah is implicitly viewed as an event through which God comes in power; her leadership is presented as parallel to the theophany of vv. 4–5. Jael is the "most blessed of women." The song does not allude to Barak's hesitation or failure to achieve glory, but presents him as a leader whom the tribes follow to victory. Consideration of the song as presented in the text that has come down to us serves as an important reminder. The Holy One acts within the messy contingencies of human history. And in those messy contingencies, God's deliverance may still be discerned and celebrated with wholehearted praise.

19. Gideon
Judges 6–8

The introduction and conclusion of the story of Gideon continue and develop the themes of divine judgment and mercy found in the previous chapters. The people again do what is evil in the sight of God; their punishment and distress are spelled out in some detail. God yet again raises up a deliverer to free them from oppression. The central portion of the Gideon account emphasizes the sovereignty of Yahweh and urges Israel to trust the power and reliability of its liberating God.

But Israel does not trust God. The Gideon narrative expands on the familiar theme of the fickleness of God's people. Not only does the story begin with Israel suffering the consequences of its sin of worshiping other gods, but the report ends with all Israel prostituting itself first to one idol, then another. Moreover, for the first time in Judges, the leader whom God raises up to deliver Israel is himself flawed. Initially vulnerable and frightened, Gideon ends by being overly confident in his own initiatives and creating an idolatrous image that ultimately "snares" both Israel and himself. The downward spiral of Israel's behavior is seen also in the discord between Gideon and his fellow Israelites (Ephraim, Succoth, Penuel). For the first time in Judges, the Israelites experience internal conflict.

The account of Gideon is among the largest and most complex stories in Judges. Readers may notice rough patches in the narrative where just what is happening is not clear, or where parts of the story don't seem to fit together very smoothly. For example, the hero has two names: Gideon and Jerubbaal. This Gideon/Jerubbaal summons four tribes to war, sends all but a very few warriors home, then calls them all out yet again to go running after the enemy after the main battle is over. Furthermore, the description of the battle itself pictures the soldiers with their hands full of torches, jars, trumpets, and swords—a load that would challenge a juggler. We need not worry too much about such inconsistencies; various people or groups of people remembered Gideon differently. Some legends originally told about other heroes possibly ascribed to him. The stories were collected by compilers who were not primarily interested in consistency or accuracy, or in reporting historical or military data. Rather, they were interested in proclaiming the reliability and rule of Israel's God. The details of the Gideon story are often somewhat cloudy; its theological message, that God is sovereign and to be relied upon, is clear.

The various memories about Gideon have been woven into a plot with two distinct movements. After the introduction, which includes the elements framing all of the stories of the judges, the narrative depicts Gideon as fearful yet faithful. The real hero of the first movement is God, who fights for Israel and alone gives them the victory. The second movement portrays a considerably more confident Gideon, yet his confidence appears to be in himself rather than in his God. Gideon is now the central actor; Yahweh neither speaks nor acts. Though Gideon is no less successful in the second part of the story than in the first, he is less faithful. Ultimately God's champion makes an idol that ensnares him and his family. At the end of the story, Israel's sin is even worse than when the story starts.

THE THEOLOGICAL FRAMEWORK
Judges 6:1–10; 8:28

6:1 The Israelites did what was evil in the sight of the LORD, and the LORD gave them into the hand of Midian seven years. ² The hand of Midian prevailed over Israel; and because of Midian the Israelites provided for themselves hiding places in the mountains, caves and strongholds. ³ For whenever the Israelites put in seed, the Midianites and the Amalekites and the people of the east would come up against them. ⁴ They would encamp against them and destroy the produce of the land, as far as the neighborhood of Gaza, and leave no sustenance in Israel, and no sheep or ox or donkey. ⁵ For they and their livestock would come up, and they would even bring their tents, as thick as locusts; neither they nor their camels could be counted; so they wasted the land as they came in. ⁶ Thus Israel was greatly impoverished because of Midian; and the Israelites cried out to the LORD for help.

⁷ When the Israelites cried to the LORD on account of the Midianites, ⁸ the LORD sent a prophet to the Israelites; and he said to them, "Thus says the LORD, the God of Israel: I led you up from Egypt, and brought you out of the house of slavery; ⁹ and I delivered you from the hand of the Egyptians, and from the hand of all who oppressed you, and drove them out before you, and gave you their land; ¹⁰ and I said to you, 'I am the LORD your God; you shall not pay reverence to the gods of the Amorites, in whose land you live.' But you have not given heed to my voice."

Gideon's story is framed by the elements that introduce and conclude each of the stories of early Israel's leaders. Sin, punishment, distress, and the people's cry are found in the initial verses (6:1–10); the last verse reports that the "land had rest" (8:28). The editors who framed Gideon's story with their theological interpretations did not do so woodenly. Some of the stock elements are more fully developed in the beginning and ending of Gideon's tale than they are elsewhere. Moreover, unexpected twists and turns appear.

As in earlier stories, the people "did what was evil in the sight of the LORD," and the Lord sold them into the hand of their enemies. This time, the oppressors are the Midianites. According to biblical traditions, the Midianites were descendants of Abraham by his wife Keturah, and thus kinfolk of the Israelites. Their relationship to Israel was mixed; Moses, fleeing Egypt, found hospitality among the Midianites and married a Midianite woman. On the other hand, several passages portray them as Israel's enemies (Num. 22:4–7; 25:6–18). In our passage, the Midianites are the chosen agents of divine judgment. They are allied to the Amalekites, an ancient people traditionally hostile toward Israel (see commentary on 3:13) and the "people of the east," a generic term that can refer to any of the various inhabitants of the tableland east of the Jordan River. The text depicts in unusual detail Israel's distress under Midianite oppression. The vast enemy devours Israel's livestock and produce, leaving the people famished.

As before, the distressed Israelites cry out to Yahweh for deliverance. God's response to the cry is unexpected. By now, the pattern has been established; the people cry and God raises up a deliverer to rescue them. This time the people cry and God sends a prophet. But unlike Judges 4—where the prophet, Deborah, delivers her people—here the prophet indicts the people. The text is very clear: Israel's troubles are its own fault. In language echoing Judges 2:1–5, God's spokesperson reminds Israel of God's saving acts, which are the basis of divine claims to Israel's allegiance. Israel's chief obligation, given in Judges 6:10, is to recognize God as "the LORD your God," and to refrain from worshiping any other deities. This obligation is a paraphrase of the first commandment and is the very heart of Yahweh's covenant with Israel. But, the prophet charges, Israel has broken the covenant. What is at stake here is a matter of single-minded commitment to Yahweh, not simply ethnic intolerance. Israel has betrayed its God.

Given the prophet's indictment, we might expect God to heap yet more punishment upon the people, or at least to withhold any further aid from them. God has, after all, repeatedly warned the Israelites. The text takes another unexpected twist. Instead of indictment being followed by judgment, God raises up yet another deliverer for Israel. The shift is as unexpected as it is gracious.

CALL AND COMMISSIONING OF GIDEON
Judges 6:11–24

6:11 Now the angel of the LORD came and sat under the oak at Ophrah, which belonged to Joash the Abiezrite, as his son Gideon was beating out wheat in the wine press, to hide it from the Midianites. 12 The angel of the LORD appeared to him and said to him, "The LORD is with you, you mighty warrior." 13 Gideon answered him, "But sir, if the LORD is with us, why then has all this happened to us? And where are all his wonderful deeds that our ancestors recounted to us, saying, 'Did not the LORD bring us up from Egypt?' But now the LORD has cast us off, and given us into the hand of Midian." 14 Then the LORD turned to him and said, "Go in this might of yours and deliver Israel from the hand of Midian; I hereby commission you." 15 He responded, "But sir, how can I deliver Israel? My clan is the weakest in Manasseh, and I am the least in my family." 16 The LORD said to him, "But I will be with you, and you shall strike down the Midianites, every one of them." 17 Then he said to him, "If now I have found favor with you, then show me a sign that it is you who speak with me. 18 Do not depart from here until I come to you, and bring out my present, and set it before you." And he said, "I will stay until you return."

19 So Gideon went into his house and prepared a kid, and unleavened cakes from an ephah of flour; the meat he put in a basket, and the broth he put in a pot, and brought them to him under the oak and presented them. 20 The angel of God said to him, "Take the meat and the unleavened cakes, and put them on this rock, and pour out the broth." And he did so. 21 Then the angel of the LORD reached out the tip of the staff that was in his hand, and touched the meat and the unleavened cakes; and fire sprang up from the rock and consumed the meat and the unleavened cakes; and the angel of the LORD vanished from his sight. 22 Then Gideon perceived that it was the angel of the LORD; and Gideon said, "Help me, Lord GOD! For I have seen the angel of the LORD face to face." 23 But the LORD said to him, "Peace be to you; do not fear, you shall not die." 24 Then Gideon built an altar there to the LORD, and called it, The LORD is peace. To this day it still stands at Ophrah, which belongs to the Abiezrites.

As the story opens, an angel of the Lord (see commentary on Judges 2:1), unrecognized as such, appears to Gideon in Ophrah, an unknown site somewhere in the Jezreel Valley. Threshing wheat normally takes place in a large, open space. The thresher tosses the grain into the air, letting the wind blow away the chaff. The picture of Gideon beating out the wheat in a small, enclosed winepress conveys his fear of the Midianites.

The angel's address to this frightened, cowering lad—"mighty warrior"—is more than a little ironic. So is Gideon's response. The angel extends a common greeting: "The LORD is with you." Gideon basically answers, "Oh yeah? If the LORD is with us, why then has all this happened to us?" The angel has said, "Good morning," and Gideon has replied, "What's so good about it?"

Ironic humor continues to mark the unfolding dialogue. In verses 8–9, the prophet had cited God's delivering Israel at the sea as the basis of Israel's covenantal obligation. Gideon cites the same event as the basis of his complaint. *Where are all God's wonderful and saving deeds now?* Complaining that something needs to be done can be quite risky. The person complaining is likely to be given the assignment. So it is with the angel and Gideon. Gideon rues Yahweh's failure to deliver Israel from Midian. Yahweh replies, "Go in this might of yours"—and do it!

The rest of the conversation (vv. 14–18) follows a pattern reminiscent of the call of Moses. God commissions Gideon; the commissioning is not general but for a specific task. Like Moses, Gideon is to deliver his people (see Exod. 3:10). Gideon's response to the commission is a protest. He is from the weakest clan of Manasseh, and he is the youngest member of that clan; how can he possibly deliver the people? Moses' protests are similar: "Who am I that I should go to Pharaoh?" (Exod. 3:11). In fact, Gideon's father appears to be a man of substance. The protest is a matter of humility and serves to make it clear that Gideon does not assume a leadership role out of his own initiative. God called him.

God responds to Gideon's protest not with anger but with words of assurance: "I will be with you." The phrase is an exact quotation of God's words to Moses when he protested that he could not deliver his people (Exod. 3:12).

The nature of the command and the assurance lead Gideon to suspect the divine identity of his guest. Like Moses, to whom God gave a sign (Exod. 3:12), Gideon requests a sign, the first of many that he will request or God will offer. Some commentators believe that Gideon's repeated requests for a sign betray a lack of trust. But Scripture is not critical of asking for such assurance. Isaiah tells King Ahab to ask for a sign. God gives Moses signs. Indeed, seeking God's word either through oracular devices or from a prophet before going to war was considered both faithful and prudent. Here, God accepts Gideon's questions and waits patiently while Gideon prepares a rather elaborate meal, then provides him with the sign that he needs.

Gideon's dependence on signs reflects his readiness to rely on God. While timid and testing, Gideon still trusts Yahweh to show him what to do.

Gideon prepares a meal, offered as a sacrifice. The presence of unleavened cakes and a large quantity of flour underlines the sacrificial character of the meal. The sign is the fire that consumes the offering (Judg. 6:21). Gideon's guest is indeed God. Gideon's dread at recognizing his visitor's divine nature reflects a common motif in biblical stories. Israel believed that a human being cannot see God face-to-face and live. The motif expresses awe in the presence of the Holy. Gideon builds an altar to commemorate his encounter with God—another common biblical motif. Yahweh's reassuring words to Gideon—"Peace . . . do not fear . . ."—are given as an explanation of the name of the altar: "The LORD is peace."

At one level, the story explains how an altar came to be at Ophrah and the reason for its name. At a deeper level, the story presents Gideon as a leader, not on his own initiative, but by the call of God. Gideon's authority stems from Yahweh. Moreover, Gideon's stature is suggested by the similarities between his call and that of Moses. The story implicitly compares Gideon to that great leader. Most importantly, the story emphasizes that the real actor in what is to come is not Gideon, but God. God calls Gideon. Gideon will succeed because God is with him.

"BREAK DOWN THEIR ALTARS AND . . . BURN THEIR SACRED POLES"
Judges 6:25–32

6:25 That night the LORD said to him, "Take your father's bull, the second bull seven years old, and pull down the altar of Baal that belongs to your father, and cut down the sacred pole that is beside it; [26] and build an altar to the LORD your God on the top of the stronghold here, in proper order; then take the second bull, and offer it as a burnt offering with the wood of the sacred pole that you shall cut down." [27] So Gideon took ten of his servants, and did as the LORD had told him; but because he was too afraid of his family and the townspeople to do it by day, he did it by night.

[28] When the townspeople rose early in the morning, the altar of Baal was broken down, and the sacred pole beside it was cut down, and the second bull was offered on the altar that had been built. [29] So they said to one another, "Who has done this?" After searching and inquiring, they were told, "Gideon son of Joash did it." [30] Then the townspeople said to Joash, "Bring out your son, so that he may die, for he has pulled down the altar of Baal and cut down the sacred pole beside it." [31] But Joash said to all who were arrayed

against him, "Will you contend for Baal? Or will you defend his cause? Whoever contends for him shall be put to death by morning. If he is a god, let him contend for himself, because his altar has been pulled down." [32] **Therefore on that day Gideon was called Jerubbaal, that is to say, "Let Baal contend against him," because he pulled down his altar.**

The next scene also finds Gideon erecting an altar for Yahweh at Ophrah, and also concludes with an explanation of a name. Its theme is quite different from that of the previous passage, however. Verses 11–24 deal with the call of Gideon, answering the question, "Who will lead Israel against Midian?" Verses 25–32 have to do with the destruction of an altar to Baal and the erection of one to Yahweh, and thus answer the question, "Who will be Israel's God?" Yahweh, who has demonstrated great patience with fear, doubt, and tests, has no tolerance at all for the worship of other deities.

Joash, Gideon's father, has an altar to Baal and an Asherah, a sacred pole representing the Canaanite goddess by that name. Immediately after commissioning him ("that same night"), God commands Gideon, whose name means "hewer" or "hacker," to hack down the idolatrous altar and pole and replace them with an altar for Yahweh (see Deut. 12:3). Gideon is instructed to sacrifice a bull on the newly built altar. The meaning of "your father's second bull" is not certain. What is certain is that the sacrifice is to be made to Yahweh.

Gideon is obedient, but also fearful. To go against his father and all of the people of his village would be very difficult for him. The call to act out of values contrary to those of one's family or friends can be one of the hardest challenges that faith poses. Gideon goes in the middle of the night to follow God's instructions. His fears prove justified. Apparently the Baal altar and the Asherah were important for the villagers, and not just for Joash's private use. The townspeople, discovering what Gideon has done, are up in arms. Gideon's father, Joash, is trapped between a rock and a hard place, between the loss of his son and the enmity of the townspeople. He shrewdly argues that if Baal is a real god, then he can take care of himself against his opponents. "Let Baal contend against [Gideon/Jerubbal]."

The last part of the story is a popular explanation of Gideon's second name, Jerubbaal: "Let Baal contend." (The actual meaning of "Jerubbaal" is probably "Baal is great," or "May Baal make great.") The story also explains why Gideon is known by a second name, and why his second name refers to Baal rather than Yahweh. Possibly a hero once lived who was named both "Gideon" and "Jerubbaal." An Israelite can have two names. However, Gideon is found primarily in chapters 6–8; Jerubbaal occurs most often in chapter 9. The distribution of the names in chapters 6–9 suggests that two streams of tradition, one having to do with Jerubbaal, and one with Gideon, have been merged.

TESTS AND OMENS
Judges 6:33–7:15

6:33 Then all the Midianites and the Amalekites and the people of the east came together, and crossing the Jordan they encamped in the Valley of Jezreel. [34] But the spirit of the LORD took possession of Gideon; and he sounded the trumpet, and the Abiezrites were called out to follow him. [35] He sent messengers throughout all Manasseh, and they too were called out to follow him. He also sent messengers to Asher, Zebulun, and Naphtali, and they went up to meet them.

[36] Then Gideon said to God, "In order to see whether you will deliver Israel by my hand, as you have said, [37] I am going to lay a fleece of wool on the threshing floor; if there is dew on the fleece alone, and it is dry on all the ground, then I shall know that you will deliver Israel by my hand, as you have said." [38] And it was so. When he rose early next morning and squeezed the fleece, he wrung enough dew from the fleece to fill a bowl with water. [39] Then Gideon said to God, "Do not let your anger burn against me, let me speak one more time; let me, please, make trial with the fleece just once more; let it be dry only on the fleece, and on all the ground let there be dew." [40] And God did so that night. It was dry on the fleece only, and on all the ground there was dew.

7:1 Then Jerubbaal (that is, Gideon) and all the troops that were with him rose early and encamped beside the spring of Harod; and the camp of Midian was north of them, below the hill of Moreh, in the valley.

[2] The LORD said to Gideon, "The troops with you are too many for me to give the Midianites into their hand. Israel would only take the credit away from me, saying, 'My own hand has delivered me.' [3] Now therefore proclaim this in the hearing of the troops, 'Whoever is fearful and trembling, let him return home.' " Thus Gideon sifted them out; twenty-two thousand returned, and ten thousand remained.

[4] Then the LORD said to Gideon, "The troops are still too many; take them down to the water and I will sift them out for you there. When I say, 'This one shall go with you,' he shall go with you; and when I say, 'This one shall not go with you,' he shall not go." [5] So he brought the troops down to the water; and the LORD said to Gideon, "All those who lap the water with their tongues, as a dog laps, you shall put to one side; all those who kneel down to drink, putting their hands to their mouths, you shall put to the other side." [6] The number of those that lapped was three hundred; but all the rest of the

troops knelt down to drink water. [7] Then the LORD said to Gideon, "With the three hundred that lapped I will deliver you, and give the Midianites into your hand. Let all the others go to their homes." [8] So he took the jars of the troops from their hands, and their trumpets; and he sent all the rest of Israel back to their own tents, but retained the three hundred. The camp of Midian was below him in the valley.

[9] That same night the LORD said to him, "Get up, attack the camp; for I have given it into your hand. [10] But if you fear to attack, go down to the camp with your servant Purah; [11] and you shall hear what they say, and afterward your hands shall be strengthened to attack the camp." Then he went down with his servant Purah to the outposts of the armed men that were in the camp. [12] The Midianites and the Amalekites and all the people of the east lay along the valley as thick as locusts; and their camels were without number, countless as the sand on the seashore. [13] When Gideon arrived, there was a man telling a dream to his comrade; and he said, "I had a dream, and in it a cake of barley bread tumbled into the camp of Midian, and came to the tent, and struck it so that it fell; it turned upside down, and the tent collapsed." [14] And his comrade answered, "This is no other than the sword of Gideon son of Joash, a man of Israel; into his hand God has given Midian and all the army."

[15] When Gideon heard the telling of the dream and its interpretation, he worshiped; and he returned to the camp of Israel, and said, "Get up; for the LORD has given the army of Midian into your hand."

With the elimination of the altar to Baal, the stage is set for Israel's battle against Midian. In verses 33–35, the troops are mustered and the battle lines drawn. The story of Gideon's victory over the Midianites was no doubt told and retold, and would have been embellished with each telling, as good tales are. Probably the battle originally involved Gideon's clan, the Abiezerites, and a small group of invaders. By the time generations enjoyed and embroidered upon the saga, the battle reached epic proportions, and four Israelite tribes confront a massive enemy army of 135,000 troops (8:10)!

In Judges 6:35, both Israel and Midian are arrayed for battle. They— and the reader—are prepared for action. Gideon is not. Gideon is still frightened, a natural reaction, given the odds. In the next episode (Judg. 6:36–40), our hesitant hero sets yet more tests to confirm that he has heard Yahweh correctly; he really is to lead 32,000 foot soldiers against an enemy mounted on camels and more than four times his army's size. In one of the most famous stories in the book of Judges, Gideon lays fleeces before God. His initial test—that the fleece be wet with dew while the surrounding soil is dry—could be explained by natural phenomena (sheep's wool would retain moisture while dry earth would not). Perhaps recognizing that, Gideon sets another test, reversing the conditions.

Judges 7:1 again describes the position of the opposing armies. The Israelites are encamped on a hill near Mount Gilboa, by the spring of "Harod," which means "trembling." Again, all is ready for battle, but this time God delays. Gideon had wanted to be sure that Yahweh would indeed give Israel victory. God wants to be sure that Israel knows that the one who gives them the victory is Yahweh. The Israelite army, numbering 32,000 troops, is too large to send against 135,000 enemy soldiers, and the Israelites might believe that they had won by their own strength. Therefore, God instructs Gideon to reduce his force. In words reminiscent of a Deuteronomic law exempting frightened people from fighting (Deut. 20:8), Gideon is told to send home all those who are "fearful and trembling."

But God says the 10,000 remaining troops are still too many, and gives Gideon a test to sift out the troops. He is to take them to the spring. The manner in which the soldiers drink will determine which are sent away and which kept for battle. Scholars debate the details and rationale of the selection process. What is abundantly clear is that the purpose of culling the troops is to ensure that victory will be credited to God and God alone. Gideon is left with 300 men to fight a force nearly five hundred times larger!

The details of Gideon's and God's "tests" are not allowed to distract the reader from the danger that the Israelite warriors face. For a third time, the reader is reminded that the camp of Midian and its allies lies below (7:8). Gideon and his men face impossible odds. In this situation, God does not wait for his frightened champion to set another test. God takes initiative and offers Gideon an oracle. Gideon is to go down to the Midianite camp, where he overhears soldiers discussing a dream about a cake of barley bread. Apparently as an agricultural product, barley bread symbolized the Israelite farmers. The Midianite listening to the dream immediately recognizes the image as an omen that God has given Midian and its allies into Gideon's hand. This oracle, spoken by the enemy itself, satisfies Gideon. Finally, he is ready to go to war.

THE "BATTLE"
Judges 7:16–25

7:16 **After he divided the three hundred men into three companies, and put trumpets into the hands of all of them, and empty jars, with torches inside the jars,** [17] **he said to them, "Look at me, and do the same; when I come to the outskirts of the camp, do as I do.** [18] **When I blow the trumpet, I and all who are with me, then you also blow the trumpets around the whole camp, and shout, 'For the LORD and for Gideon!'"**

[19] So Gideon and the hundred who were with him came to the outskirts of the camp at the beginning of the middle watch, when they had just set the watch; and they blew the trumpets and smashed the jars that were in their hands. [20] So the three companies blew the trumpets and broke the jars, holding in their left hands the torches, and in their right hands the trumpets to blow; and they cried, "A sword for the LORD and for Gideon!" [21] Every man stood in his place all around the camp, and all the men in camp ran; they cried out and fled. [22] When they blew the three hundred trumpets, the LORD set every man's sword against his fellow and against all the army; and the army fled as far as Beth-shittah toward Zererah, as far as the border of Abel-meholah, by Tabbath. [23] And the men of Israel were called out from Naphtali and from Asher and from all Manasseh, and they pursued after the Midianites.

[24] Then Gideon sent messengers throughout all the hill country of Ephraim, saying, "Come down against the Midianites and seize the waters against them, as far as Beth-barah, and also the Jordan." So all the men of Ephraim were called out, and they seized the waters as far as Beth-barah, and also the Jordan. [25] They captured the two captains of Midian, Oreb and Zeeb; they killed Oreb at the rock of Oreb, and Zeeb they killed at the wine press of Zeeb, as they pursued the Midianites. They brought the heads of Oreb and Zeeb to Gideon beyond the Jordan.

The storytellers make sure their audience understands: God and God alone gives the victory. The radically reduced group of Israelite warriors does not lift a weapon in the initial assault against the enemy camp. The logistics of Gideon's strategy are not entirely clear; his instructions seem to require the soldiers to possess more than two hands! They break jars to expose burning torches, blast trumpets, and shout war cries, then stand fast. The sudden noise and light confuse the enemy and send them into a panic.

The trumpets and shouts of Gideon's troops recall the battle of Jericho (Joshua 6). As at Jericho, the initial assault succeeds without any military activity on Israel's part. According to holy-war traditions, Yahweh fights for Israel by spreading panic among its enemies. Here, God so confounds and frightens the Midianites that they blindly turn and fight each other, then flee, while the Israelite warriors stand in place around the outskirts of the camp. The story sends a strong message: Trust in the Divine Warrior, who is able to give victory regardless of how impossible it might seem. Such a message would give hope to the exiles, the ancient audience of Judges. They had no power to resist the Babylonians, no army to reclaim their land. But they did have their God, who is able to make a way out of no way.

Routed, the Midianites and their allies flee. The locations of the towns mentioned in verses 22 are uncertain. Apparently the disarrayed army fled in two different directions, some nearby and some across the Jordan. As at Jericho, after God breaks their opponents' resistance, the human soldiers have a role. Gideon summons Naphtali, Asher, and Manasseh (7:23), three of the tribes first mustered and then sent away before the battle, to pursue the scattered enemy. He also belatedly calls on Ephraim, the most powerful of the central and northern tribes, to capture "the waters" and the Jordan. The phrase "the waters . . . and also the Jordan" is problematic. Some scholars have interpreted it to refer to watering places a few miles from the Jordan River as well as the river itself; others translate the phrase "the fords of the Jordan." In any case, Gideon's strategy is to cut off the Midianites' retreat. Ephraim does capture the waters and seizes two Midianite princes, Oreb ("raven") and Zeeb ("wolf"), as well. The story of the princes' execution is used to explain names given to particular places.

At the end of verse 25, we learn that Gideon, in hot pursuit of the enemy, has already crossed to the east side of the Jordan River. The Ephraimites bring the enemies' heads, grisly war trophies, to him there.

GIDEON'S DIPLOMACY AND GIDEON'S VIOLENCE
Judges 8:1–21

8:1 Then the Ephraimites said to him, "What have you done to us, not to call us when you went to fight against the Midianites?" And they upbraided him violently. [2] So he said to them, "What have I done now in comparison with you? Is not the gleaning of the grapes of Ephraim better than the vintage of Abiezer? [3] God has given into your hands the captains of Midian, Oreb and Zeeb; what have I been able to do in comparison with you?" When he said this, their anger against him subsided.

[4] Then Gideon came to the Jordan and crossed over, he and the three hundred who were with him, exhausted and famished. [5] So he said to the people of Succoth, "Please give some loaves of bread to my followers, for they are exhausted, and I am pursuing Zebah and Zalmunna, the kings of Midian." [6] But the officials of Succoth said, "Do you already have in your possession the hands of Zebah and Zalmunna, that we should give bread to your army?" [7] Gideon replied, "Well then, when the LORD has given Zebah and Zalmunna into my hand, I will trample your flesh on the thorns of the wilderness and on briers." [8] From there he went up to Penuel, and made the same request of them; and the people of Penuel answered him as the people of Succoth had answered. [9] So he said to the people of Penuel, "When I come back victorious, I will break down this tower."

[10] Now Zebah and Zalmunna were in Karkor with their army, about fifteen thousand men, all who were left of all the army of the people of the east;

for one hundred twenty thousand men bearing arms had fallen. ¹¹ So Gideon went up by the caravan route east of Nobah and Jogbehah, and attacked the army; for the army was off its guard. ¹² Zebah and Zalmunna fled; and he pursued them and took the two kings of Midian, Zebah and Zalmunna, and threw all the army into a panic.

¹³ When Gideon son of Joash returned from the battle by the ascent of Heres, ¹⁴ he caught a young man, one of the people of Succoth, and questioned him; and he listed for him the officials and elders of Succoth, seventy-seven people. ¹⁵ Then he came to the people of Succoth, and said, "Here are Zebah and Zalmunna, about whom you taunted me, saying, 'Do you already have in your possession the hands of Zebah and Zalmunna, that we should give bread to your troops who are exhausted?' " ¹⁶ So he took the elders of the city and he took thorns of the wilderness and briers and with them he trampled the people of Succoth. ¹⁷ He also broke down the tower of Penuel, and killed the men of the city.

¹⁸ Then he said to Zebah and Zalmunna, "What about the men whom you killed at Tabor?" They answered, "As you are, so were they, every one of them; they resembled the sons of a king." ¹⁹ And he replied, "They were my brothers, the sons of my mother; as the LORD lives, if you had saved them alive, I would not kill you." ²⁰ So he said to Jether his firstborn, "Go kill them!" But the boy did not draw his sword, for he was afraid, because he was still a boy. ²¹ Then Zebah and Zalmunna said, "You come and kill us; for as the man is, so is his strength." So Gideon proceeded to kill Zebah and Zalmunna; and he took the crescents that were on the necks of their camels.

The next episode (8:1–3) introduces the first note of discord among Israelite tribes in Judges—a note that will crescendo throughout the remainder of the book. The Ephraimites are furious, perhaps as a matter of honor, that Gideon did not initially summon them along with the other tribes (6:35). Perhaps the upstart Gideon's newfound power and prestige threaten Ephraim, which has held a position of dominance among the tribes. In any case, the Ephraimites' anger is calmed and violence averted by Gideon's masterful diplomacy. He soothes their pride by assuring them of their superiority. Ephraim is mollified, and the crisis is diffused.

So far, the story of Gideon is upbeat. During the first narrative movement of the story, Gideon is vulnerable and fearful, but ultimately faithful. He tests Yahweh and then obeys the divine command. In turn, Yahweh accepts Gideon's doubts and responds to his tests. God proves God's self to be utterly trustworthy. The impossible victory is won without human participation. A disquieting note is introduced in the confrontation between Ephraim and Abiezer. But Gideon's conciliatory words quickly resolve the conflict, and the story continues.

Judges 8:4 represents a shift in the direction of the story. Judges 8:4–21 narrates a second mopping-up campaign that contains many parallels to the earlier parts of Gideon's story. Again tensions arise between Gideon and fellow Israelites. For a second time, the successful pursuit of fleeing Midianites leads to the capture and execution of two of their leaders.

Marked differences are apparent between Judges 8:4–21 and the previous passages. Gideon's conflict in Judges 8:1–3 is with the largest, strongest Israelite tribe. His conflict in Judges 8:5–9 and 13–17 is with two unwalled villages. In the first case, Gideon resolves the tension with conciliatory words. Against the leaders of Succoth and Penuel, he uses brute force. Though the meaning of trampling the people with thorns and briars is uncertain, we must assume that Gideon's revenge against Succoth was brutal, and, given Penuel's fate, deadly. Diplomacy evaporates. An Israelite kills other Israelites.

Gideon's final battle with the Midianites (8:10–12) also both resembles and markedly differs from the initial assault against them (7:19–23). Again Gideon and three hundred men surprise the Midianites, or what is left of them, and throw them into a panic. Israel is able to capture two more Midianite kings, Zebah and Zalmunna (8:12). The kings share the fate of their compatriots Oreb and Zeeb: they are slain.

The contrast between the mopping-up campaign of Judges 8 with the previous battle and pursuit is stark. In the previous account, Gideon fought in order to deliver Israel from oppression. Gideon's pursuit of Zebah and Zalmunna is a personal vendetta. He seeks revenge for the death of his brothers, presumably killed in an earlier battle. Most important, in the previous episodes Gideon and his followers relied on God. God commands and Gideon, however hesitantly or fearfully, obeys. Gideon acts here on his own initiative. He sets no tests and receives no divine instructions. He captures and kills the Midianite kings for his own reasons. God's voice is not heard, nor does God take any part in the hostilities.

The difference can be explained partly in terms of the way the various stories about Gideon were brought together. Judges 6–8 is a kind of patchwork quilt. The patches in chapter 8 appear to be from a different source than those in chapter 6 and 7, reflecting different storytellers' emphases. Nonetheless, we must assume that those who put the material together in a certain order did so deliberately, and we must look for the purpose behind the final shape of the stories. Gideon's failure to rely on God in the second part of the narrative serves as a reminder of the fickleness of God's people and anticipates the downward spiral that marks the rest of the book of Judges.

KINGSHIP OFFERED AND REJECTED
Judges 8:22–35

8:22 Then the Israelites said to Gideon, "Rule over us, you and your son and your grandson also; for you have delivered us out of the hand of Midian." [23] Gideon said to them, "I will not rule over you, and my son will not rule over you; the LORD will rule over you." [24] Then Gideon said to them, "Let me make a request of you; each of you give me an earring he has taken as booty." (For the enemy had golden earrings, because they were Ishmaelites.) [25] "We will willingly give them," they answered. So they spread a garment, and each threw into it an earring he had taken as booty. [26] The weight of the golden earrings that he requested was one thousand seven hundred shekels of gold (apart from the crescents and the pendants and the purple garments worn by the kings of Midian, and the collars that were on the necks of their camels). [27] Gideon made an ephod of it and put it in his town, in Ophrah; and all Israel prostituted themselves to it there, and it became a snare to Gideon and to his family. [28] So Midian was subdued before the Israelites, and they lifted up their heads no more. So the land had rest forty years in the days of Gideon.

[29] Jerubbaal son of Joash went to live in his own house. [30] Now Gideon had seventy sons, his own offspring, for he had many wives. [31] His concubine who was in Shechem also bore him a son, and he named him Abimelech. [32] Then Gideon son of Joash died at a good old age, and was buried in the tomb of his father Joash at Ophrah of the Abiezrites.

[33] As soon as Gideon died, the Israelites relapsed and prostituted themselves with the Baals, making Baal-berith their god. [34] The Israelites did not remember the LORD their God, who had rescued them from the hand of all their enemies on every side; [35] and they did not exhibit loyalty to the house of Jerubbaal (that is, Gideon) in return for all the good that he had done to Israel.

At one moment in the midst of Gideon's shift away from reliance upon God, Gideon is faithful: the moment when he refuses to be king. The storytellers give the people's offer to make Gideon king an ironic cast. The people want Gideon to rule because he had "delivered (them) out of the hand of Midian." Their speech echoes the words of God who says that the Israelites "would only take the credit away from me, saying 'My own hand has delivered me.'" The tribes do take the credit away from God, ascribing victory not to themselves, but to Gideon.

Gideon rejects the offer. If the right to rule rests in having delivered the people, then God, who alone won the battle for Israel, alone has authority to govern Israel. God, not Gideon, nor Gideon's son, will be Israel's king. Scholars debate whether Gideon's rejection of dynastic rule was genuine.

Some scholars believe that it was only a polite demur, after which he indeed became king. They note that Gideon's large family, consisting of many wives and seventy sons, is more like that of a king than a commoner. Moreover, he names one of his sons "Abimelech," which means "my father is king," and that son does attempt to rule over Israel. Gideon seemingly does accept some of the trappings of kingship. Nonetheless, his refusal to rule over the tribes was not likely a polite sham. The storytellers would not narrate an event as significant as the establishment of the first king in Israel's history in such an oblique way. Moreover, Gideon's response, "Yahweh will rule," is too forceful an argument to use if he had intended to accept the people's offer. After that response, agreeing to rule would put Gideon in the position of appearing to reject God. Gideon's rejection of kingship seems to be a sincerely pious response.

While Gideon rejects kingship, he does accept oracular authority. In a scene reminiscent of Aaron collecting the people's golden earrings in order to mold an idolatrous calf (Exodus 32), Gideon asks the Israelites to give him the gold earrings from their booty. With the gold, he makes an ephod (Judg. 8:24–27). Elsewhere in the Bible, "ephod" refers to a garment worn by priests. The "Urim" and "Thurim," lots used to ascertain God's will, were worn on the breastplate of the high priest's ephod. In Judges, however, the ephod is connected with idolatry. Judges 17 and 18 speak of an ephod in connection with two idols, a "teraphim" and an "idol of cast metal" (18:14). Gideon's ephod becomes an idol, an object of worship rather than a tool of worship. The Israelites "prostitute" themselves before it. In Judges 2:3, the angel of the Lord warned that the gods of the nations will become a "snare" to Israel. Judges 8:27 pointedly states that the ephod was a "snare" to Gideon and his family.

The story of Gideon ends where it begins, at Ophrah. Gideon's life there after the conquest of Midian is a picture of affluence that offers a sharp contrast to the picture of frightful misery with which the story began. Gideon prospers. The seventeen hundred gold shekels that he collected to make the ephod represent a huge amount of wealth. He is blessed with progeny—seventy sons! And he lives to a "good old age." When he finally dies, Gideon is buried in his father's tomb, as every Israelite wants to be. The picture of Gideon in his old age appears to be of a man with a rich and blessed life.

In the early stages of the telling and retelling of these stories, the picture of the aging Gideon probably was seen as a happy ending. The deliverer was blessed by God for his faithfulness. The story as it finally comes down to us is more ambiguous. Reconciling an interpretation of Gideon's prosperity as divinely granted blessing with his creation of an idol is difficult. Gideon is not unambiguously obedient. His long, prosperous life is not unambiguously a reward. Once again, the narrative undercuts any mechanistic view that God inevitably punishes sin and rewards goodness. The perspective of these stories is more complicated than that.

The editors' theological framework is found in verses 33–35. Despite Israel's idolatrous worship of the ephod, the land has rest during Gideon's lifetime. After his death, Israel relapses completely, worshiping Baal once again (8:33). The more things change, the more they stay the same. After all God's mercy, commissioning a leader to deliver the Israelites and winning an impossible victory for them, the story ends where it began, with the people's faithlessness.

20. Abimelech: A(nother) Cautionary Tale
Judges 9

If Gideon/Jerubbaal is a flawed judge, Abimelech, his son, is no judge at all. The story of Abimelech's treacherous bid for kingship breaks from the established pattern of Israelite sin divinely punished by foreign oppression, leading to Israelite outcry and divine mercy. In Judges 9, an Israelite leader is the oppressor. Abimelech's brutal, illegitimate rule is the very opposite of the kind of leadership that the book of Judges applauds. The narrative condemns self-serving, violent power. The story of Abimelech is a cautionary tale. He and the Shechemite lords who abet him reap the violence that they sow.

Within its larger literary context, Judges 9 illustrates the "evil" that Israel "did in Yahweh's eyes." Judges 8:33–35 connect betrayal of Jerubbaal's household with rebellion against God. Forgetting Yahweh leads to disloyalty to the leader whom God has raised. The verses, together with 9:22 and 9:55, implicate all of "the Israelites" in Abimelech's treachery.

The setting of the story, Shechem, draws an implicit contrast between the evil that Abimelech and Israel commit in the generation of the judges with Israel's faithfulness in Joshua's generation. The last biblical reference to Shechem is found in Joshua 24, as Israel enters into covenant (*berith*) with Yahweh. Judges 8:33 notes that the Israelites embrace not their covenant lord, Yahweh, but the Canaanite god Baal-berith, Baal of the Covenant.

Seams or tensions in the account raise a number of unresolved questions. Most commentators hold that the chapter is comprised of several traditions that were originally separate, and that the account was reshaped to communicate differing messages at different times. No consensus exists, however, on when or why the story was told and retold. What is clear is that the editors responsible for its final shape crafted it artfully.

The number of circumstantial details in the chapter, the absence of a clear theological agenda shaping the story, and archaeological evidence that Shechem was destroyed about the time of the Judges suggest that the story may have some historical bases. Uncertainty about the dating of different parts of the story makes it difficult to access their reliability, however. A better approach is to read the account as a story, rather than to attempt to mine it for historical information.

ABIMELECH SEIZES KINGSHIP
Judges 9:1–6

9:1 **Now Abimelech son of Jerubbaal went to Shechem to his mother's kinsfolk and said to them and to the whole clan of his mother's family, ² "Say in the hearing of all the lords of Shechem, 'Which is better for you, that all seventy of the sons of Jerubbaal rule over you, or that one rule over you?' Remember also that I am your bone and your flesh." ³ So his mother's kinsfolk spoke all these words on his behalf in the hearing of all the lords of Shechem; and their hearts inclined to follow Abimelech, for they said, "He is our brother." ⁴ They gave him seventy pieces of silver out of the temple of Baal-berith with which Abimelech hired worthless and reckless fellows, who followed him. ⁵ He went to his father's house at Ophrah, and killed his brothers the sons of Jerubbaal, seventy men, on one stone; but Jotham, the youngest son of Jerubbaal, survived, for he hid himself. ⁶ Then all the lords of Shechem and all Beth-millo came together, and they went and made Abimelech king, by the oak of the pillar at Shechem.**

For the first time, an Israelite is crowned king, but he is hardly the kind of king of which the authors of Judges and of the Deuteronomistic History approve. According to Deuteronomy 17:14–20 (a late, Deuteronomistic law), the king must be a man Yahweh chooses, who does not lift himself above his brothers and whose primary role is to read and obey the law. Abimelech, whose name, ironically, means "my Father (God) is king," seizes power on his own initiative, slaughters his brothers, and utterly disregards Yahweh and Yahweh's Torah.

Drawing on kinship ties, Abimelech is able to garner Shechemite support for his coup. The Shechemite lords' reasoning is ironic; they agree to support Abimelech because he is their "brother." Abimelech will eventually treat them just as he treats his brothers—slaughtering them all. The elimination of rival claimants to the throne is not unusual in biblical accounts (see the stories of Jehu and of Ataliah). The violence is clearly condemned, however.

The significance of the "one stone" on which Abimelech killed his half-brothers is not clear. Perhaps the detail underlines the egregiousness of the offense; Abimelech kills all of his brothers, all at once! The "stone" motif connects Abimelech's actions with his fate; he kills his brothers on one "stone," and he is slain by a millstone.

JOTHAM'S CURSE
Judges 9:7–21

9:7 When it was told to Jotham, he went and stood on the top of Mount Ger-izim, and cried aloud and said to them, "Listen to me, you lords of Shechem, so that God may listen to you.

> ⁸ The trees once went out
> to anoint a king over themselves.
> So they said to the olive tree,
> 'Reign over us.'
> ⁹ The olive tree answered them,
> 'Shall I stop producing my rich oil
> by which gods and mortals are honored,
> and go to sway over the trees?'
> ¹⁰ Then the trees said to the fig tree,
> 'You come and reign over us.'
> ¹¹ But the fig tree answered them,
> 'Shall I stop producing my sweetness
> and my delicious fruit,
> and go to sway over the trees?'
> ¹² Then the trees said to the vine,
> 'You come and reign over us.'
> ¹³ But the vine said to them,
> 'Shall I stop producing my wine
> that cheers gods and mortals,
> and go to sway over the trees?'
> ¹⁴ So all the trees said to the bramble,
> 'You come and reign over us.'
> ¹⁵ And the bramble said to the trees,
> 'If in good faith you are anointing me king over you,
> then come and take refuge in my shade;
> but if not, let fire come out of the bramble
> and devour the cedars of Lebanon.'

¹⁶ "Now therefore, if you acted in good faith and honor when you made Abimelech king, and if you have dealt well with Jerubbaal and his house, and have done to him as his actions deserved—¹⁷ for my father fought for you, and risked his life, and rescued you from the hand of Midian; ¹⁸ but you have risen up against my father's house this day, and have killed his sons, seventy

men on one stone, and have made Abimelech, the son of his slave woman, king over the lords of Shechem, because he is your kinsman—[19] **if, I say, you have acted in good faith and honor with Jerubbaal and with his house this day, then rejoice in Abimelech, and let him also rejoice in you;** [20] **but if not, let fire come out from Abimelech, and devour the lords of Shechem, and Beth-millo; and let fire come out from the lords of Shechem, and from Beth-millo, and devour Abimelech."** [21] **Then Jotham ran away and fled, going to Beer, where he remained for fear of his brother Abimelech.**

Like Joash, the lone survivor of Ataliah's slaughter of Judah's royal household, one young lad, Jotham, escapes Abimelech's massacre. Joash goes to Mount Gerizim, the mountain of blessing (Deut. 11:29; 27:12–13) and delivers a curse against the man who killed his brothers. The curse begins with a fable (Judg. 9:8–15) typical of ancient Near Eastern plant or animal allegories (see 2 Kgs. 14:9).

Many scholars believe that before it was incorporated into the Abimelech narrative, the fable circulated independently as a critique of the monarchy or even as a critique of responsible citizens who refuse to accept kingship. In the final form of the text, the fable functions to condemn Abimelech as a worthless bramble; its concluding verse curses Abimelech and the Shechemites who aided him in the onslaught.

The fable suggests that people who are productive and fruitful are too busy with their work to desire power. The olive, the fig, and the vine (along with the almond tree) were among the most valued of all plants in ancient Israel. Besides giving light, olive oil was used for sacrifices, for anointing kings and other leaders, and for honoring guests. The fig and vine, of course, produce edible fruit. The bramble, though its role in preventing soil erosion is now recognized, in ancient times was seen as good for nothing except choking other plants and fueling wildfires. Only the worthless are willing to rule.

The final verse of the fable (v. 15) turns the passage into a curse. "Shade" in the ancient Near East was often used metaphorically to refer to protection. The bramble has no shade to offer; the worthless king Abimelech offers no protection. Both the bramble and Abimelech will prove dangerous to those who seek their "shade."

The meaning of Jotham's fable is explicated in verses 16–20. Jotham's speech further links disloyalty to Jerubbaal with infidelity to Yahweh. The Hebrew words underlying the phrase "good faith and honor" are found together only one other time in the Deuteronomistic History: in the covenant-making scene at Shechem, where the words describe how the Israelites are to treat Yahweh (Josh. 24:14).

THE CURSE UNFOLDS
Judges 9:22–57

9:22 Abimelech ruled over Israel three years. [23] But God sent an evil spirit between Abimelech and the lords of Shechem; and the lords of Shechem dealt treacherously with Abimelech. [24] This happened so that the violence done to the seventy sons of Jerubbaal might be avenged and their blood be laid on their brother Abimelech, who killed them, and on the lords of Shechem, who strengthened his hands to kill his brothers. [25] So, out of hostility to him, the lords of Shechem set ambushes on the mountain tops. They robbed all who passed by them along that way; and it was reported to Abimelech.

[26] When Gaal son of Ebed moved into Shechem with his kinsfolk, the lords of Shechem put confidence in him. [27] They went out into the field and gathered the grapes from their vineyards, trod them, and celebrated. Then they went into the temple of their god, ate and drank, and ridiculed Abimelech. [28] Gaal son of Ebed said, "Who is Abimelech, and who are we of Shechem, that we should serve him? Did not the son of Jerubbaal and Zebul his officer serve the men of Hamor father of Shechem? Why then should we serve him? [29] If only this people were under my command! Then I would remove Abimelech; I would say to him, 'Increase your army, and come out.'"

[30] When Zebul the ruler of the city heard the words of Gaal son of Ebed, his anger was kindled. [31] He sent messengers to Abimelech at Arumah, saying, "Look, Gaal son of Ebed and his kinsfolk have come to Shechem, and they are stirring up the city against you. [32] Now therefore, go by night, you and the troops that are with you, and lie in wait in the fields. [33] Then early in the morning, as soon as the sun rises, get up and rush on the city; and when he and the troops that are with him come out against you, you may deal with them as best you can."

[34] So Abimelech and all the troops with him got up by night and lay in wait against Shechem in four companies. [35] When Gaal son of Ebed went out and stood in the entrance of the gate of the city, Abimelech and the troops with him rose from the ambush. [36] And when Gaal saw them, he said to Zebul, "Look, people are coming down from the mountain tops!" And Zebul said to him, "The shadows on the mountains look like people to you." [37] Gaal spoke again and said, "Look, people are coming down from Tabbur-erez, and one company is coming from the direction of Elon-meonenim." [38] Then Zebul said to him, "Where is your boast now, you who said, 'Who is Abimelech, that we should serve him?' Are not these the troops you made light of? Go out now and fight with them." [39] So Gaal went out at the head of the lords of Shechem, and fought with Abimelech. [40] Abimelech chased him, and he fled before him. Many fell wounded, up to the entrance of the gate. [41] So Abimelech resided at Arumah; and Zebul drove out Gaal and his kinsfolk, so that they could not live on at Shechem.

⁴² On the following day the people went out into the fields. When Abimelech was told, ⁴³ he took his troops and divided them into three companies, and lay in wait in the fields. When he looked and saw the people coming out of the city, he rose against them and killed them. ⁴⁴ Abimelech and the company that was with him rushed forward and stood at the entrance of the gate of the city, while the two companies rushed on all who were in the fields and killed them. ⁴⁵ Abimelech fought against the city all that day; he took the city, and killed the people that were in it; and he razed the city and sowed it with salt.

⁴⁶ When all the lords of the Tower of Shechem heard of it, they entered the stronghold of the temple of El-berith. ⁴⁷ Abimelech was told that all the lords of the Tower of Shechem were gathered together. ⁴⁸ So Abimelech went up to Mount Zalmon, he and all the troops that were with him. Abimelech took an ax in his hand, cut down a bundle of brushwood, and took it up and laid it on his shoulder. Then he said to the troops with him, "What you have seen me do, do quickly, as I have done." ⁴⁹ So every one of the troops cut down a bundle and following Abimelech put it against the stronghold, and they set the stronghold on fire over them, so that all the people of the Tower of Shechem also died, about a thousand men and women.

⁵⁰ Then Abimelech went to Thebez, and encamped against Thebez, and took it. ⁵¹ But there was a strong tower within the city, and all the men and women and all the lords of the city fled to it and shut themselves in; and they went to the roof of the tower. ⁵² Abimelech came to the tower, and fought against it, and came near to the entrance of the tower to burn it with fire. ⁵³ But a certain woman threw an upper millstone on Abimelech's head, and crushed his skull. ⁵⁴ Immediately he called to the young man who carried his armor and said to him, "Draw your sword and kill me, so people will not say about me, 'A woman killed him.'" So the young man thrust him through, and he died. ⁵⁵ When the Israelites saw that Abimelech was dead, they all went home. ⁵⁶ Thus God repaid Abimelech for the crime he committed against his father in killing his seventy brothers; ⁵⁷ and God also made all the wickedness of the people of Shechem fall back on their heads, and on them came the curse of Jotham son of Jerubbaal.

The rest of Judges 9 narrates the fulfillment of Jotham's curse. Explanatory statements in verses 23–24 and 56–57 underline the message of the chapter: retribution befalls the evildoer. Moreover, the retribution is from God. Indeed, God's only action in this story is to send an evil spirit between Abimelech and Shechem (v. 23) in order to bring about their destruction to avenge the murder of Abimelech's brothers (vv. 56–57).

A similar claim, that God has sent an evil spirit on the king, is found in the story of Saul (1 Sam. 16:14–17). According to 1 Kings 22:21–23, God sends a "lying spirit" to entice Ahab to his death. In each of these three narratives, the "evil" or "lying" spirit brings down a disobedient or oppressive king. The stories assert that God destroys destructive powers.

The first rift between Abimelech and his Shechemite backers appears when the lords of Shechem plunder passing caravans (v. 25). Commentators differ on why such brigandage would be seen as revolt. Some argue that the marauders deprive Abimelech of tolls that he would otherwise have charged the caravans. Others more plausibly suggest that since a king's role is to ensure order, the bandits undermine Abimelech's authority by showing that he is unable to maintain the peace.

Gaal and his cohorts rebel against Abimelech more directly (vv. 26–41). Many commentators believe that the story of Gaal's rabble-rousing is an old tradition that once circulated independently of the rest of the Abimelech narrative. The tale may originally have been told to deter insurrection. The names suggest that the earliest version of the tale cast Abimelech ("My Father is king") and Zebul ("prince") as the story's heroes, and Gaal, son of Ebed ("Abhorrent, son of a slave"), as the villain of the piece. As it stands now, the story of Gaal underlines the message of divine retribution. Just as Abimelech evoked kinship ties with the Shechemites to incite rebellion against the legitimate rulers, so Gaal claims to be Shechemite, to incite rebellion against the upstart, Abimelech. That rebellion is unsuccessful.

Verses 42–45 probably originated as an alternative tradition about Abimelech's attack against Shechem. Placing the two battle narratives alongside each other makes the second assault appear brutal and unnecessary. Abimelech is in control; his agent, Zebul, has successfully banished the rebel Gaal. There is no need for further warfare. Yet Abimelech attacks the people, presumably farmers, as they go out in the fields, slaughtering them and all the city. As Olson notes, Abimelech's actions look like violence run amok (Olson, 1998, 817).

Whether "the Tower of Shechem" is part of the city or a distinct village dependent on Shechem (v. 46) is not clear. The temple of "El Berith" ("God of the Covenant") is probably the same as the temple of Baal-berith ("Lord of the Covenant"). Abimelech's assault of the elite seeking refuge in the fortress/temple quite literally fulfills the first half of Jotham's curse: "Let fire come out from Abimelech, and devour the lords of Shechem, and Beth-millo" (v. 20a).

No explanation is given for Abimelech's assault against Thebez. Perhaps Thebez had belonged to Shechem. Perhaps Abimelech, having destroyed his own city-state, seeks to conquer a town to rule. Perhaps Abimelech's violence is out of control. In any case, Abimelech attempts to use against the citizens of Thebez the strategy that was successful against the She-chemite elite. His assault is foiled when a woman throws or drops a mill-stone on his head, killing him. The king who slew his brothers on one stone is killed by a stone. The woman who kills him joins other women who bring down their country's enemy: Jael, Delilah, and (in a later story) Judith. Ironically, despite Abimelech's attempt to avoid being slain by a woman, precisely that tradition is remembered about him (2 Sam. 11:21). The Hebrew word for woman, *ishah*, sounds like the Hebrew word for fire, *esh*. In a nonmechanistic way, Abimelech's death fulfills the second part of Jotham's curse: "Let fire come out from the Lords of Shechem and Beth-millo, and devour Abimelech" (v. 20). The usurper's evil falls upon his own head. Government founded on violence will not stand.

21. The "Minor" Judges
Judges 10:1–5; 12:7–15

The stories of Gideon/Abimelech that precede the minor judges, and Jephthah, whose account follows, signal a downward spiral in Israel. Not only is the community increasingly chaotic; the leaders, even those hailed as deliverers, are increasingly flawed. In the middle of these narratives, two passages report the rule of five judges whose reigns were apparently characterized by peace, order, and prosperity. Judges 10:1–5 and 12:8–15 serve as respites from chaos. While the stories of the great military judges depict Yahweh powerfully intervening to judge and to deliver, the orderly lists of "minor" judges suggest the ongoing work of God behind the scenes, working in and through families and political institutions to promote stability and prosperity.

10:1 **After Abimelech, Tola son of Puah son of Dodo, a man of Issachar, who lived at Shamir in the hill country of Ephraim, rose to deliver Israel.** [2] **He judged Israel twenty-three years. Then he died, and was buried at Shamir.**

[3] **After him came Jair the Gileadite, who judged Israel twenty-two years.** [4] **He had thirty sons who rode on thirty donkeys; and they had thirty towns, which are in the land of Gilead, and are called Havvoth-jair to this day.** [5] **Jair died, and was buried in Kamon. . . .**

. . . .

12:8 **After him Ibzan of Bethlehem judged Israel.** [9] **He had thirty sons. He gave his thirty daughters in marriage outside his clan and brought in thirty young women from outside for his sons. He judged Israel seven years.** [10] **Then Ibzan died, and was buried at Bethlehem.**

[11] **After him Elon the Zebulunite judged Israel; and he judged Israel ten years.** [12] **Then Elon the Zebulunite died, and was buried at Aijalon in the land of Zebulun.**

[13] **After him Abdon son of Hillel the Pirathonite judged Israel.** [14] **He had forty sons and thirty grandsons, who rode on seventy donkeys; he judged Israel eight years.** [15] **Then Abdon son of Hillel the Pirathonite died, and was buried at Pirathon in the land of Ephraim, in the hill country of the Amalekites.**

The "minor judges" have received a great deal of scholarly attention. The biblical texts that note their role are distinct from the stories of the major judges. The theological framework (sin, judgment, outcry, deliverance) and developed stories that characterize figures like Ehud and Deborah are absent. Instead, one finds brief, formulaic notices consisting of the judge's name; the name of his father, tribe, or town; the number of years that he ruled; and a statement that he died and was buried. In contrast to the major deliverers, the length of the minor judges' reigns is not stereotyped. In the case of Jair, Ibzan, and Abdon, notices of their rules are followed by colorful information about the size and prestige of their families.

The formulaic quality of the two lists, together with the nonstereotypical length of their rules, has led scholars to assume that the lists stem from some sort of annals. Much of the scholarship concerning these judges has focused on asking who these officials were and how they functioned. Because Tola and Puah are found as the names of clans elsewhere in the Bible, early critical biblical scholars interpreted the "minor judges" as personifications of clans and tribal groupings. Later biblical historians, pointing to the difference between the deliverers like Gideon and the "minor judges," argued that the two kinds of narratives derived from completely different sources and represented very different offices. The minor judges were supposed to be the officials in premonarchical Israel responsible for passing on and interpreting the law for the allied Israelite tribes.

Recent scholarship has seriously challenged the view of premonarchical Israel as a league of twelve tribes who met for worship and for the adjudication of law. These challenges have undermined the basis for understanding the minor judges as league officials. For the most part, commentators now agree that simply not enough evidence is available to determine how the minor judges functioned, or even whether they differed from the leaders whose stories have come down in more fully developed forms.

During the past decade, several commentators have looked at the lists of the minor judges from a literary perspective, asking how they contribute to the overall meaning of the book of Judges. The literary approach has proved fruitful.

The two lists of minor judges convey a sense of stability. The opening words of each note, "after him," suggests orderly succession. That sense of order is reinforced by the identification of each leader's burial site. To be buried with one's ancestors was a sign of peace, a much-desired state in ancient Israel.

The families of Gideon and Jephthah, the deliverers whose stories precede the two lists, are decimated by the slaughter of their children.

Abimelech kills all but one of his seventy brothers, then is himself slain. Jephthah kills his only child to fulfill a foolish, faithless vow. In contrast, brief notes about the minor judges depict their families as flourishing. Jair has thirty sons; Ibzan, thirty sons and thirty daughters. Abdon's seventy sons and grandsons are particularly significant, as their number corresponds to the number of Gideon's murdered offspring.

The size of the judges' families also suggests their wealth and prestige. Jair, Ibzan, and Abdon were able to afford large harems. The thirty towns possessed by Jair's sons, and the asses that his sons and the sons and grandsons of Abdon rode, also paint a picture of financial success and social prestige. Ancient Near Easterners regarded the ass as a royal mount, the Cadillac of the time.

In the midst of escalating social chaos, the notices of the minor judges serve as refreshing interludes of order, family growth, and prosperity. The passages suggest God quietly at work for Israel's good.

Nonetheless, warning signals appear even in the midst of these orderly lists. The first two judges, Tola and Jair, reign for twenty-two and twenty-three years, respectively. The last three judges, Ibzan, Elon, and Abdon, have much briefer careers—ruling seven years, ten years, and eight years, respectively. The decline in their rule points to the decline in leadership seen in Jephthah and Samson. That decline is further suggested by the diminishing number of Abdon's descendants; his forty sons provide him with only thirty grandsons. Disobedient Israel is on a downward trajectory.

22. Jephthah
Judges 10:6–11:40; 12:1–7

The downward spiral of sin and chaos that began with Gideon in the previous chapters intensifies in the Jephthah account. To be sure, the themes of divine justice and divine mercy continue; God again punishes Israel, then relents. Again, a deliverer defeats Israel's oppressors. But God recedes into the background in the main part of the Jephthah story. Unlike Deborah, God's spokeswoman, or Gideon, who frequently inquires of the Lord, Jephthah speaks about God but neither consults God nor seeks to obey the divine will. Perhaps because of this distance, Jephthah's triumph quickly turns to tragedy. The account of Jephthah's victory is subordinated to the story of his disastrous vow that leads to his daughter's death. The final scene of the story depicts Jephthah engaged in a massive slaughter of fellow Israelites.

The Jephthah account has played a key role in scholarly discussion about how the book of Judges acquired its present shape. Jephthah is the only leader in the book of Judges who appears both as a "minor judge" (see pp. 192–94) and as a charismatic military leader. Some scholars see him as the link that allowed the compilers of the book to join the legends of the military deliverers and the list of judicial officeholders. Others believe that the portrayal of Jephthah as a military deliverer is secondary; that an editor took up the reference to Jephthah in the list of minor judges and greatly elaborated his role. Either is possible. What is clear is that the Jephthah narrative is a complex compilation of old traditions on the one hand and compositions written by the Deuteronomistic Historians on the other. In particular, the introduction (10:6–16) appears to be written by the same editor who composed Judges 2:6–3:6. Jephthah's message to the Ammonite king (11:15–28) also seems to have been added to the narrative by an editor who conflated two sets of traditions, one concerning Moab and one concerning Ammon. The argument, although addressed to the Ammonite king, has to do with matters of concern to Moab, not Ammon, referring to the land of Moab (11:18); the chief god of Moab, Chemosh (11:24); and citing as precedent Balak, an early Moabite king (11:25).

However composed, the final form of the Jephthah account has been carefully edited. The narrative follows a trajectory familiar to us from the story of Gideon. The first episodes about Gideon portray him quite positively, while in the second half of the narrative, he appears more flawed. Similarly, the first stories of the Jephthah cycle are sympathetic toward him. Jephthah is a wronged man who nonetheless rescues those who wronged him; he is also a statesman who diplomatically and justly presents his case to the enemy king. As in the Gideon story, Jephthah's initial faithfulness and success deteriorate in the later episodes of the story. In the case of Jephthah, the shift is lethal and results in the deaths of Jephthah's daughter and tens of thousands of Ephraimites.

THEOLOGICAL INTRODUCTION
Judges 10:6–18

10:6 The Israelites again did what was evil in the sight of the LORD, worshiping the Baals and the Astartes, the gods of Aram, the gods of Sidon, the gods of Moab, the gods of the Ammonites, and the gods of the Philistines. Thus they abandoned the LORD, and did not worship him. [7] So the anger of the LORD was kindled against Israel, and he sold them into the hand of the Philistines and into the hand of the Ammonites, [8] and they crushed and oppressed the Israelites that year. For eighteen years they oppressed all the Israelites that were beyond the Jordan in the land of the Amorites, which is in Gilead. [9] The Ammonites also crossed the Jordan to fight against Judah and against Benjamin and against the house of Ephraim; so that Israel was greatly distressed.

[10] So the Israelites cried to the LORD, saying, "We have sinned against you, because we have abandoned our God and have worshiped the Baals." [11] And the LORD said to the Israelites, "Did I not deliver you from the Egyptians and from the Amorites, from the Ammonites and from the Philistines? [12] The Sidonians also, and the Amalekites, and the Maonites, oppressed you; and you cried to me, and I delivered you out of their hand. [13] Yet you have abandoned me and worshiped other gods; therefore I will deliver you no more. [14] Go and cry to the gods whom you have chosen; let them deliver you in the time of your distress." [15] And the Israelites said to the LORD, "We have sinned; do to us whatever seems good to you; but deliver us this day!" [16] So they put away the foreign gods from among them and worshiped the LORD; and he could no longer bear to see Israel suffer.

[17] Then the Ammonites were called to arms, and they encamped in Gilead; and the Israelites came together, and they encamped at Mizpah. [18] The com-

**manders of the people of Gilead said to one another, "Who will begin the
fight against the Ammonites? He shall be head over all the inhabitants of
Gilead."**

The Jephthah narrative is introduced with the stock phrases that frame
the various stories of deliverance in Judges. The phrases are expanded in
language reminiscent of Judges 2:6–3:6, and they stress Israel's repeated
apostasy.

As in the other episodes, the theological introduction begins with the
assertion that the "Israelites again did what was evil in the sight of the
LORD." Israel has committed apostasy, worshiping all manner of foreign
gods. The specific identity of the gods listed is less important than the
sheer number of deities with whom Israel has betrayed Yahweh. Enumerating the gods whom Israel has worshiped underlines the massiveness of
its sin. The Israelites serve not one but many idols, and they fail to worship their own God (10:6). Their apostasy is personal betrayal, a violation
of the covenant relationship. They "abandoned the LORD."

The introduction reports in stereotypical language that God, abandoned, grows angry and once again sells Israel into the hands of its enemies.
As elsewhere, this phrase serves to define the specific situation of oppression in which Israel finds itself. Judges 10:7 identifies two enemies: the
Philistines and the Ammonites. The reference to the Philistines looks ahead
to the story of Samson. The Ammonites are the enemy in Jephthah's day.

The story of Jephthah is located primarily in Gilead, land east of the
Jordan ascribed to Reuben, Gad, and the eastern branch of Manasseh. In
its most expansive period, Gilead defined its borders as the Jordan River
in the west, the desert in the east, Bashan in the north, and the Arnon River
to the south. The southern portion of Gilead, from the Jabbok River to the
Arnon, was disputed territory, controlled at different times by Israel,
Moab, Ammon, Aram, and according to biblical traditions of conquest, the
Amorites. The authors of the Jephthah story did not envision Israel as one
of many nations with claims to this land, however. From their perspective,
all of Gilead belonged to Israel; the Ammonites were oppressors occupy-
ing Israelite land.

The third stock element of the framework—that Israel, distressed,
"cried unto the LORD"—is also expanded. In verse 10, the Israelites cry out
to the Lord in confession, acknowledging their sinful idolatry. This confession and the similar outcry in verse 15 are the only instances in the entire
book of Judges in which Israel explicitly repents. That deliverance does not
mechanically follow confession is made abundantly clear in verse 11. For

the first time, Israel confesses its sins; for the first time, God refuses to respond to the people's distress by delivering them: "I will deliver you no more" (v. 13).

The exchange between God and the Israelites in verses 11–16 closely resembles the indictment of Israel in Judges 2:1–5 and the prophetic speech against Israel in Judges 6:7–10. All three passages are lawsuits in which God or God's agent accuses Israel of breaking covenant. Each of the three passages recounts the saving acts of Yahweh, which serve as the basis of Israel's obligation to keep covenant. Each then indicts Israel for failing to keep its covenantal obligation to worship God alone. The indictment in Judges 10:10–16 is the most strongly worded of the three, enumerating all the oppressors from whom God delivered Israel. The specific identity of the nations from whom God has rescued Israel is less important than the sheer number listed. Yahweh has delivered Israel over and over and over again, and still Israel abandons its savior God! The indictment makes very clear that Israel, not God, has broken the covenant. God's judgment—withholding aid, letting Israel rely on the gods it has chosen—is just.

God's indictment of Israel also clarifies the nature of Israel's sin. The angel of Yahweh's accusation that Israel has made covenants with the people of Canaan could be read as sheer xenophobia (2:2). God's complaint (10:13–14) shows that the problem is not simply that Israel is coexisting with other peoples, but that the Israelites are worshiping foreign gods.

The divine speech shows that judgment is not the coldhearted decision of a distant dispassionate God. Rather, the speech is the passionate, pained response of a lover whose love is betrayed one too many times. God will not again rescue the people who have repeatedly violated their relationship.

Israel's response to God's refusal is to put away the idols it has been worshiping and to implore divine help once again. Some commentators believe that the people's first confession was hypocritical and its second genuine, so that God rightly rejected the first appeal for help but responds to the second. The second outcry appears as self-serving and utilitarian as the first, however. Israel's quick return to apostasy after the crisis is past (13:1) suggests that in both instances its "repentance" was superficial. In fact, the text does not say that God saves Israel because it was now properly penitent and thus merits deliverance. Rather, God "could no longer bear to see Israel suffer" (10:16). God's heart is torn by the competing demands of judgment and mercy, but mercy finally prevails.

Two elements that typically frame the deliverers' stories are missing in the case of Jephthah. First, each of the previous accounts carefully establish that God takes the initiative in raising up leaders to save Israel. In contrast, Jephthah is chosen by the elders of Gilead to lead the resistance against Ammon (11:6). The statement that God "could no longer bear to see Israel suffer" implies that divine desire to save the people undergirds the elders' plan; divine confirmation of the elders' choice is found in the assertion that "the spirit of the LORD came upon Jephthah" (11:29). Still, the narrative depicts God as less directly involved in the selection and initial actions of Jephthah than in the rise of Israel's other champions; this passage provides the first hint that God has a less active role in the Jephthah account than in prior stories.

The second element missing from the theological framework of Jephthah is the concluding statement that "the land had rest x years" (3:11, 30; 5:31b; 8:28). The omission appears deliberate. Jephthah's story ends with one Israelite group, the Gileadites, slaughtering tens of thousands of men from another Israelite group, the Ephraimites. Israelite social ties are disintegrating in violence and chaos; the land has no rest.

RECRUITMENT OF JEPHTHAH
Judges 11:1–11

11:1 Now Jephthah the Gileadite, the son of a prostitute, was a mighty warrior. Gilead was the father of Jephthah. [2] Gilead's wife also bore him sons; and when his wife's sons grew up, they drove Jephthah away, saying to him, "You shall not inherit anything in our father's house; for you are the son of another woman." [3] Then Jephthah fled from his brothers and lived in the land of Tob. Outlaws collected around Jephthah and went raiding with him.

[4] After a time the Ammonites made war against Israel. [5] And when the Ammonites made war against Israel, the elders of Gilead went to bring Jephthah from the land of Tob. [6] They said to Jephthah, "Come and be our commander, so that we may fight with the Ammonites." [7] But Jephthah said to the elders of Gilead, "Are you not the very ones who rejected me and drove me out of my father's house? So why do you come to me now when you are in trouble?" [8] The elders of Gilead said to Jephthah, "Nevertheless, we have now turned back to you, so that you may go with us and fight with the Ammonites, and become head over us, over all the inhabitants of Gilead." [9] Jephthah said to the elders of Gilead, "If you bring me home again to fight with the Ammonites, and the LORD gives them over to me, I will be your head." [10] And the elders of Gilead said to Jephthah, "The LORD will be witness between us; we will surely do as you say." [11] So Jephthah went with the elders of Gilead, and the people made him head and commander over them; and Jephthah spoke all his words before the LORD at Mizpah.

The initial presentation of Jephthah is sympathetic. Like Gideon (6:12), Jephthah is a "mighty warrior" (11:1). He is also an outsider. The motif of the "outsider who saves Israel" weaves its way through the books of Joshua, Judges, and Ruth. We have already met unlikely heroes: Rahab, the Canaanite prostitute; Ehud, the assassin; Jael, the non-Israelite seductress; Gideon, the cowering young "warrior." Jephthah is the son of a prostitute and Gilead (here personified). As such, he has no legal or social standing in Israelite society. Expelled from his father's household by his legitimate half-brothers, Jephthah makes his living as a brigand chief in "Tob," an area in Syria. He is an outsider and an outlaw, a most unexpected deliverer of those who had rejected him.

The sympathy with which Jephthah is initially portrayed stands out when one compares Jephthah to Abimelech. Both are illegitimate sons: Abimelech's mother is a concubine; Jephthah's, a harlot. Both come into conflict with their legitimate half-brothers. Both gather around themselves a band of "outlaws," a term that probably refers to landless, destitute men unable to find a place for themselves within society. Like David in the Judean wilderness (1 Sam. 22:1–2; 27:8–12), Abimelech, Jephthah, and their men survive by raiding surrounding peoples.

In contrast to Abimelech, however, Jephthah is the one wronged, rather than the wrongdoer. Abimelech slays his brothers. Jephthah's brothers drive him out. The brothers' act is legal. According to ancient Near Eastern law, the son of a prostitute is his father's heir only if his father's legal wife has no sons. But the text makes it clear that the expulsion is unfair, both by its wording (Jephthah is "driven out"; he "fled") and by Jephthah's accusation that the Gileadites had rejected him (v. 7).

Forced to survive as an outlaw, Jephthah becomes a skilled and experienced warrior with his own personal band of fighting men. When the Ammonites make war against Gilead, the Gileadite elders seek out Jephthah precisely because of his military prowess and because of the trained, experienced raiders at his command.

Jephthah holds his own against the elders. In Judges 10:18, the Gileadite commanders had agreed that whoever begins the fight against the Ammonites will be their "head," a term that most likely refers to a permanent civil leader. When the elders first approach Jephthah, they offer instead to make him "commander," presumably a temporary military commander, if he is willing to begin the fight against Ammon. Jephthah is a shrewd and skillful negotiator. He accepts the command only after the elders agree to make him head. The agreement is ratified before Yahweh in the sanctuary at Mizpah (a town east of the Jordan).

NEGOTIATIONS WITH THE AMMONITES
Judges 11:12–28

11:12 Then Jephthah sent messengers to the king of the Ammonites and said, "What is there between you and me, that you have come to me to fight against my land?" [13] The king of the Ammonites answered the messengers of Jephthah, "Because Israel, on coming from Egypt, took away my land from the Arnon to the Jabbok and to the Jordan; now therefore restore it peaceably." [14] Once again Jephthah sent messengers to the king of the Ammonites [15] and said to him: "Thus says Jephthah: Israel did not take away the land of Moab or the land of the Ammonites, [16] but when they came up from Egypt, Israel went through the wilderness to the Red Sea and came to Kadesh. [17] Israel then sent messengers to the king of Edom, saying, 'Let us pass through your land'; but the king of Edom would not listen. They also sent to the king of Moab, but he would not consent. So Israel remained at Kadesh. [18] Then they journeyed through the wilderness, went around the land of Edom and the land of Moab, arrived on the east side of the land of Moab, and camped on the other side of the Arnon. They did not enter the territory of Moab, for the Arnon was the boundary of Moab. [19] Israel then sent messengers to King Sihon of the Amorites, king of Heshbon; and Israel said to him, 'Let us pass through your land to our country.' [20] But Sihon did not trust Israel to pass through his territory; so Sihon gathered all his people together, and encamped at Jahaz, and fought with Israel. [21] Then the LORD, the God of Israel, gave Sihon and all his people into the hand of Israel, and they defeated them; so Israel occupied all the land of the Amorites, who inhabited that country. [22] They occupied all the territory of the Amorites from the Arnon to the Jabbok and from the wilderness to the Jordan. [23] So now the LORD, the God of Israel, has conquered the Amorites for the benefit of his people Israel. Do you intend to take their place? [24] Should you not possess what your god Chemosh gives you to possess? And should we not be the ones to possess everything that the LORD our God has conquered for our benefit? [25] Now are you any better than King Balak son of Zippor of Moab? Did he ever enter into conflict with Israel, or did he ever go to war with them? [26] While Israel lived in Heshbon and its villages, and in Aroer and its villages, and in all the towns that are along the Arnon, three hundred years, why did you not recover them within that time? [27] It is not I who have sinned against you, but you are the one who does me wrong by making war on me. Let the LORD, who is judge, decide today for the Israelites or for the Ammonites." [28] But the king of the Ammonites did not heed the message that Jephthah sent him.

The next scene (11:12–28) shows the Gileadite outlaw transformed into an Israelite statesman, negotiating with the Ammonite king. These verses appear to have been added to the Jephthah story after it was substantially complete (see p. 276). As it stands, the passage serves to present Jephthah as a diplomatic leader who has justice on his side.

Jephthah's argument against the Ammonite king has four points. First, Jephthah rejects the Ammonite king's complaint that Israel took away *his* land by arguing that Israel took the land not from the Ammonites but from the Amorites. Second, Jephthah stakes his claim to the disputed territory on religious grounds. Yahweh gave the land to Israel; the Ammonites should be satisfied with whatever land their god gave them. The reference here to Chemosh does not necessarily imply that the author (or character) is polytheistic. The argument may simply be pragmatic. Alternatively, it may reflect a belief that Israel's God ruled as king over a divine council who assigned its members to be the "gods" of other lands. Third, Jephthah cites a precedent. The great King Balak refused to fight Israel. The Ammonite king should follow Balak's example. Fourth, Israelites had lived in the region for over three hundred years, and now was too late to dispute their claims to the land. Jephthah's diplomacy does not sway the Ammonite king. Indeed, no response is given. If Jephthah's intent was to avoid war, he has failed. Based on his literary analysis of the story, Barry Webb convincingly argues that the character Jephthah never intended to sue for peace. Rather, his purpose was to demonstrate the justice of Israel's position and the injustice of Ammonite claims. The argument is aimed at persuading not the Ammonite king but Yahweh, whose favor or disfavor will determine the outcome of the ensuing battle. In any case, the Ammonites do not concede their claim to the territory (Webb, 1987, 58). The scene is set for battle.

TRIUMPH AND TRAGEDY
Judges 11:29–40

11:29 **Then the spirit of the** LORD **came upon Jephthah, and he passed through Gilead and Manasseh. He passed on to Mizpah of Gilead, and from Mizpah of Gilead he passed on to the Ammonites.** [30] **And Jephthah made a vow to the** LORD**, and said, "If you will give the Ammonites into my hand,** [31] **then whoever comes out of the doors of my house to meet me, when I return victorious from the Ammonites, shall be the** LORD**'s, to be offered up by me as a burnt offering."** [32] **So Jephthah crossed over to the Ammonites to fight against them; and the** LORD **gave them into his hand.** [33] **He inflicted a massive defeat on them from Aroer to the neighborhood of Minnith, twenty towns, and as far as Abel-keramim. So the Ammonites were subdued before the people of Israel.**

³⁴ **Then Jephthah came to his home at Mizpah; and there was his daughter coming out to meet him with timbrels and with dancing. She was his only child; he had no son or daughter except her.** ³⁵ **When he saw her, he tore his clothes, and said, "Alas, my daughter! You have brought me very low; you have become the cause of great trouble to me. For I have opened my mouth to the LORD, and I cannot take back my vow."** ³⁶ **She said to him, "My father, if you have opened your mouth to the LORD, do to me according to what has gone out of your mouth, now that the LORD has given you vengeance against your enemies, the Ammonites."** ³⁷ **And she said to her father, "Let this thing be done for me: Grant me two months, so that I may go and wander on the mountains, and bewail my virginity, my companions and I."** ³⁸ **"Go," he said and sent her away for two months. So she departed, she and her companions, and bewailed her virginity on the mountains.** ³⁹ **At the end of two months, she returned to her father, who did with her according to the vow he had made. She had never slept with a man. So there arose an Israelite custom that** ⁴⁰ **for four days every year the daughters of Israel would go out to lament the daughter of Jephthah the Gileadite.**

Yahweh finally acts directly as Gilead moves towards battle. God's spirit comes upon Jephthah, confirming the elders' choice and empowering Jephthah to muster troops from Israelite lands east of the Jordan (v. 29). Eventually, Jephthah deals Ammon a "massive defeat" (v. 33), a victory that the story ascribes to God (v. 32).

The outcome of the battle is highly ambiguous. Empowered by God's spirit, Jephthah subdues the Ammonite oppressors and delivers Israel. But the victory leads to domestic and civil violence. The report of the battle is subsumed under the story of Jephthah's vow and its tragic execution. Before the battle begins, Jephthah, apparently unable to trust the Spirit, tries to bargain with Yahweh. If God gives him victory, he will offer up as a burnt offering the first one to come out and greet him when he returns home. Jephthah, an outcast, needs this victory to reinstate him in Gilead, to secure his status and vindication. He is ready to sacrifice a human being to achieve it. Some commentators argue that Jephthah expected an animal to be the first to come out and meet him. The Hebrew phrase translated "whoever comes out" could possibly refer to an animal. Nonetheless, the gravity of the crisis and the solemnity of the vow suggest that Jephthah has human sacrifice in mind.

Jephthah clearly does not envision sacrificing his daughter. On his return, the first one to emerge to greet him is his only child, a virgin girl. That the daughter is Jephthah's only child increases, if possible, the pathos of the situation. Extirpation—dying without offspring—was among the worst possible fates for an ancient Israelite. Jephthah and his daughter will have no heir.

Jephthah responds to his innocently rejoicing daughter with a cry of genuine, though self-focused grief. In a typical Israelite act of mourning, he rends his clothes. In a classic case of blaming the victim, he tells his daughter that she has brought him "very low."

Both Jephthah and his daughter accept that the vow is irrevocable. The daughter submits to her fate without protest, though also without accepting the blame that her father tries to deflect onto her. "You have opened your mouth to the LORD," she says. The girl merely requests time in which to "bewail her virginity" in the company of female friends. (Except in certain legal texts, the Hebrew word translated "virginity" refers to an age category.) At the end of two months of mourning, she returns to her home and is sacrificed as a burnt offering in fulfillment of her father's terrible vow.

The story of Jephthah's daughter is one of several biblical passages having to do with human sacrifice. Prophetic and legal texts refer to the practice of immolating children in a desperate attempt to obtain God's favor in times of distress (2 Kgs. 16:3; 17:17; Ezek. 20:25–26). Abraham's willingness to sacrifice his son in response to God's command is seen as a demonstration of his utter obedience (Gen. 22). First Samuel 14:24–45 narrates Saul's vow that whoever had broken his command to fast should be put to death and his discovery that the culprit was his heir, Jonathan. But the prophetic and legal texts adamantly and consistently condemn human sacrifice, while God stays Abraham's hand from killing Isaac and the people intervene to rescue Jonathan. Only Jephthah's daughter is sacrificed without intervention or explicit condemnation.

An appendix to the story (vv. 39–40) links it to an annual mourning ritual. Peggy Day convincingly argues that the ritual originally had to do with a rite of passage in which adolescent girls commemorated the end of a life stage (their "maidenhood") (Day, 1989, 58–74). In the context of the story, the ritual is a lament for a girl whose life is cut short by her father's faithless vow and an act of solidarity among young women, who are all too likely to be sacrificed to male ambitions.

Ancient interpreters' evaluations of Jephthah's vow and its execution are mixed. Biblical references to Jephthah acclaim his faithfulness (1 Sam. 12:11; Heb. 11:32), but other traditions condemn Jephthah's cruelty. One early Jewish midrash recounts that Jephthah's prideful, ignorant immolation of his daughter was punished by dismemberment.

Modern scholarly assessment of Jephthah is also mixed. Some commentators have deemed him an "exemplary judge" or praised his willingness to fulfill his vow regardless of the cost. Many interpreters follow the midrash, condemning Jephthah for offering what was not his to sacrifice: another's life. Others have criticized the patriarchal values of unquestioning submission and female self-sacrifice encoded in the text. Some of the interpreters view the story as a mirror of the kind of violence and sacrifice too often inflicted on adolescent girls. The story may serve to raise consciousness, and to mourn not only Jephthah's nameless daughter but also all her violated sisters. Thus, the account can be used to resist the sacrifice of children in whatever form that may take. Viewing the story as a mirror of social and familial brokenness is not inconsistent with the biblical texts. In the overall narrative of Judges, Jephthah's vow and its terrible execution is part of a pattern of faithlessness and social disintegration that the book implicitly condemns.

INTERTRIBAL WAR
Judges 12:1–7

12:1 **The men of Ephraim were called to arms, and they crossed to Zaphon and said to Jephthah, "Why did you cross over to fight against the Ammonites, and did not call us to go with you? We will burn your house down over you!"** ^2 **Jephthah said to them, "My people and I were engaged in conflict with the Ammonites who oppressed us severely. But when I called you, you did not deliver me from their hand.** ^3 **When I saw that you would not deliver me, I took my life in my hand, and crossed over against the Ammonites, and the LORD gave them into my hand. Why then have you come up to me this day, to fight against me?"** ^4 **Then Jephthah gathered all the men of Gilead and fought with Ephraim; and the men of Gilead defeated Ephraim, because they said, "You are fugitives from Ephraim, you Gileadites—in the heart of Ephraim and Manasseh."** ^5 **Then the Gileadites took the fords of the Jordan against the Ephraimites. Whenever one of the fugitives of Ephraim said, "Let me go over," the men of Gilead would say to him, "Are you an Ephraimite?" When he said, "No,"** ^6 **they said to him, "Then say Shibboleth," and he said, "Sibboleth," for he could not pronounce it right. Then they seized him and killed him at the fords of the Jordan. Forty-two thousand of the Ephraimites fell at that time.**

^7 **Jephthah judged Israel six years. Then Jephthah the Gileadite died, and was buried in his town in Gilead.**

The final episode of the Jephthah account further demonstrates the faithlessness and social disintegration overtaking Israel. In a scene reminiscent of their conflict with Gideon (Judg. 8:1–3), the Ephraimites confront Jephthah over his failure to enlist their aid (12:1–6). The Ephraimites' anger appears to be a matter of wounded honor. As in the case of Gideon, the response is also an effort to restore the balance of power and prestige in their favor. The tribes west of the Jordan apparently held sway over the tribes to the east. Ephraim was the most powerful western tribe. The easterners' victory over the Ammonites would be seen as a threat to Ephraim's hegemony.

As in the case of the Gideon-Ephraim dispute, the confrontation between the Ephraimites and Jephthah takes place at the fords of the Jordan. The outcome of the conflict is radically different from the outcome of the parallel episode in the Gideon account. Gideon diplomatically averts intertribal war with conciliatory praise of the Ephraimites' accomplishments. Jephthah responds to the Ephraimites with a self-righteous and accusatory speech hardly likely to mollify the Ephraimites' pride or to appease their anger. Apparently the westerners have also wounded the Gileadites' pride, calling them "refugees from Ephraim." The conflict escalates into full-scale battle in which Jephthah's troops rout the Ephraimites.

Jephthah is unwilling to allow the surviving Ephraimites to flee home. In a famous scene, the Gileadites use regional differences in dialect to identify the westerners. The ethnicity of the defeated warriors is disclosed by their inability to pronounce the "sh" sound in "Shibboleth" ("stream"), and they are slaughtered. The cycle ends with the notice whose form is familiar from the list of "minor judges": Jephthah judged Israel six years, died, and was buried in Gilead. As discussed above, significantly, no concluding statement is offered that the land had rest.

CONCLUSIONS

The pattern of disintegration discernable in the story of Gideon is clear in the Jephthah account. Under the accumulated weight of years of rebellion and sin, both Israel's relationship with its God and its life as a society have begun to fall apart.

The downward spiral can be traced in the breakdown in social bonds. The Song of Deborah offers a picture of six tribes fighting a common enemy. The only sign of lack of cohesion is the failure of certain tribes to join their kinfolk in battle. Israelite fights Israelite for the first time in the story of Gideon. Gideon avenges himself against Succoth and Penuel,

Israelite towns east of the Jordan that had failed to offer Gideon and his men succor. The violence escalates with Jephthah as he slaughters forty-two thousand Israelites from Ephraim.

The worsening treatment of women in the text is another indicator of social and moral decay. The first woman mentioned in Judges is Achsah, Caleb's daughter. The story of Achsah is a patriarchal tale. She is given in marriage to Othniel for capturing Debir. Nonetheless, from the perspective of a thoroughly patriarchal society, Achsah's marriage is ideal. She is given a substantial dowry; her husband is a hero; she herself takes initiative to secure her own welfare. In the Jephthah account, we encounter another daughter, who is nameless. She, too, is given as the price of victory. But this nameless daughter is given up to death, not to marriage, and she has almost no say over her fate.

The breakdowns in social bonds and in the fate of the female characters correspond to and are perhaps rooted in the breakdown in Israel's relationship to God, which can be traced not only in the theological framework of the stories ("And the Israelites again did what was evil in the eyes of the LORD"), but also in the relationship of the leaders to their God. Deborah was a prophet, a woman so aligned with God that she can serve as God's mouthpiece. Gideon is a timorous warrior who is ultimately led astray by an ephod. In the first half of his career, however, Gideon regularly spoke and listened to Yahweh. The story depicts lively exchanges between Gideon and God.

In the Jephthah account, God remains strangely distant, acting directly only halfway into the story (11:29). Jephthah and other characters in his story speak *about* God. Jephthah ratifies his negotiations in the sanctuary and makes an unsolicited—and unholy—vow to the Lord. But he does not consult God; he does not seek to listen to God's word nor to obey God's will.

God's spirit comes on Jephthah and gives his troops victory. But comparatively little interaction occurs between God and Jephthah, and when Jephthah sacrifices his daughter and then slaughters the Ephraimites, God remains silent. In the Jephthah story, God is not known through the prophet's word, nor through oracular guidance, nor through prayer or listening. For the most part, God acts indirectly or from a distance, as if the accumulated weight of Israel's sin—of human failure to rely on God—has limited how God can act.

23. Samson
Judges 13–16

The previous stories in Judges depict God raising up unlikely champions to deliver an increasingly sinful Israel. The themes noted in the earlier tales—the unlikeliness of the heroes, the growing apostasy of the people, and the ongoing mercy of God, who rescues Israel in spite of its sin—are intensified in the Samson account (Judg. 13–16).

In the preceding narratives, God chose implausible people to lead Israel. There was a James Bond–like assassin, Ehud; an early Mata Hari, Jael; a female military advisor, Deborah; the "least" member of the weakest clan of Manasseh, Gideon; and an illegitimate, outcast brigand, Jephthah. The last deliverer, Samson, is an anomaly even among this unlikely group. Samson is no military leader and hardly a willing deliverer. Rather, he is a brawny, bawdy, amoral adventurer. Samson's attacks against the Philistines stem not from a desire to resist his people's enemies, but from his passions for women and for revenge. He engages in a personal vendetta that escalates, seemingly without his awareness or intent, and results in his death.

The downward spiral traced in the character of the leaders and the sin of the people in earlier stories continues in the story of Samson. Gideon ended his career by creating an idolatrous ephod that ensnared him and all Israel. Jephthah talked about but never consults God; his rash, unnecessary vow resulted in his daughter's death. Now, Samson, consecrated to God from the womb, disregards his consecrated status and attends to God only in two moments of acute distress. Desperately thirsty, he cries to God for water and life; blinded, enslaved, and humiliated, he prays for vengeance and death. For the remainder of the account, Samson ignores Yahweh.

The opening verses of the Samson cycle suggest that Israel's apostasy has escalated. God subjects the people to forty years of foreign domination, a period twice as long as the longest previous punishment (13:1).

Moreover, the introduction to the Samson stories omits the notice that the people cried out to the Lord. The people take no initiative in their relationship to God, not even the act of crying out. The downward spiral is also suggested by the conclusion of the story. Of all of the "major judges," only Samson fails to restore the tribes' independence. As in the case of Jephthah, the stereotypical assertion that "the land had rest" is missing.

Divine mercy continues in the face of the mounting apostasy. Although the people do not cry out, God, unbidden, initiates their deliverance, using Samson's amoral escapades to harass and contain the Philistines, Israel's oppressors. In the preceding stories of Judges, God acts with unexpected compassion, in unlikely ways. In Samson, the "hiddenness" of God's saving action becomes a major theme. God's role in events is not only unlikely, but unrecognized, yet all that happens serves divine deliverance of Israel.

The Samson account comprises a number of adventurous tales that circulated among the people and grew with each retelling. As we shall see, the stories bear the marks of folklore: humor, outrageous antics, hyperbole.

Many scholars have sought to explain the origins of the Samson stories in solar myths. Samson's name is derived from the Hebrew word for "sun"; his stories are set in the region around Beth Shemesh, "Temple of the Sun." But the essential nature of the tales seems clear. They are hero legends: ribald, adventurous, even absurd yarns told by an underdog population to vaunt their superiority over their conquerors. They would have been told gleefully, to entertain as well as to vent the frustration of a subjugated people.

The editors who brought the folktales together crafted their final product with great artistry. As J. Cheryl Exum has demonstrated (Exum, 1981, 3–29), the core of the Samson cycle is comprised of two well-balanced sets of stories, chapters 14–15 and chapter 16. Each begins when Samson sees and desires a Philistine woman. In each, the Philistine leaders persuade a woman to coax Samson to disclose a secret and the woman does so by pressuring Samson to prove his love for her. In each case, Samson's disclosure appears to be to his enemies' advantage, yet each action ultimately leads to the destruction of great numbers of Philistines. Throughout the cycle, the compilers have woven a rich tapestry of interconnected themes and motifs: knowing and not knowing, telling and keeping secrets, riddles, and the like. The narrative of Samson's birth (Judg. 13) has been prefaced to the exploits of the adult Samson, so that his divinely enabled death is balanced by his miraculous birth. God's explicit involvement in Samson's birth and death suggests God's hidden agency throughout the hero's life.

THE BIRTH OF SAMSON
Judges 13

13:1 The Israelites again did what was evil in the sight of the LORD, and the LORD gave them into the hand of the Philistines forty years.

^{2} There was a certain man of Zorah, of the tribe of the Danites, whose name was Manoah. His wife was barren, having borne no children. ^{3} And the angel of the LORD appeared to the woman and said to her, "Although you are barren, having borne no children, you shall conceive and bear a son. ^{4} Now be careful not to drink wine or strong drink, or to eat anything unclean, ^{5} for you shall conceive and bear a son. No razor is to come on his head, for the boy shall be a nazirite to God from birth. It is he who shall begin to deliver Israel from the hand of the Philistines." ^{6} Then the woman came and told her husband, "A man of God came to me, and his appearance was like that of an angel of God, most awe-inspiring; I did not ask him where he came from, and he did not tell me his name; ^{7} but he said to me, 'You shall conceive and bear a son. So then drink no wine or strong drink, and eat nothing unclean, for the boy shall be a nazirite to God from birth to the day of his death.'"

^{8} Then Manoah entreated the LORD, and said, "O, LORD, I pray, let the man of God whom you sent come to us again and teach us what we are to do concerning the boy who will be born." ^{9} God listened to Manoah, and the angel of God came again to the woman as she sat in the field; but her husband Manoah was not with her. ^{10} So the woman ran quickly and told her husband, "The man who came to me the other day has appeared to me." ^{11} Manoah got up and followed his wife, and came to the man and said to him, "Are you the man who spoke to this woman?" And he said, "I am." ^{12} Then Manoah said, "Now when your words come true, what is to be the boy's rule of life; what is he to do?" ^{13} The angel of the LORD said to Manoah, "Let the woman give heed to all that I said to her. ^{14} She may not eat of anything that comes from the vine. She is not to drink wine or strong drink, or eat any unclean thing. She is to observe everything that I commanded her."

^{15} Manoah said to the angel of the LORD, "Allow us to detain you, and prepare a kid for you." ^{16} The angel of the LORD said to Manoah, "If you detain me, I will not eat your food; but if you want to prepare a burnt offering, then offer it to the LORD." (For Manoah did not know that he was the angel of the LORD.) ^{17} Then Manoah said to the angel of the LORD, "What is your name, so that we may honor you when your words come true?" ^{18} But the angel of the LORD said to him, "Why do you ask my name? It is too wonderful."

^{19} So Manoah took the kid with the grain offering, and offered it on the rock to the LORD, to him who works wonders. ^{20} When the flame went up toward heaven from the altar, the angel of the LORD ascended in the flame of the altar while Manoah and his wife looked on; and they fell on their faces to the ground. ^{21} The angel of the LORD did not appear again to Manoah and

his wife. Then Manoah realized that it was the angel of the LORD. ²² And Manoah said to his wife, "We shall surely die, for we have seen God." ²³ But his wife said to him, "If the LORD had meant to kill us, he would not have accepted a burnt offering and a grain offering at our hands, or shown us all these things, or now announced to us such things as these."

²⁴ The woman bore a son, and named him Samson. The boy grew, and the LORD blessed him.

The stock theological phrases that frame the accounts of the other deliverers in Judges are found in the Samson narrative, but in abbreviated form. Once again the people sin against God, who allows them to be conquered as punishment. As noted above, the phrase "they cried out" is missing here. The weight of Israel's apostasy is such that they no longer turn to their God.

The conquerors in this case are the Philistines, historically the most serious, persistent threat that premonarchical Israel faced. The Philistines, a "Sea People" probably from the Aegean area originally, settled on the Mediterranean coast of what is now Israel at about the same time that the Israelite tribes began to emerge in the hill country. They bequeathed their name to the region: "Palestine" derives from "Philistine." The Philistines, the Israelites, and the indigenous Canaanites vied for control of the land. Philistines dominated until the early years of David's kingship.

The cycle begins with the story of Samson's birth. Our hero is set apart, consecrated to God in the womb. The birth narrative consists of three scenes. In scene one (Judg. 13:1–7), the angel of Yahweh, whom we have already encountered judging Israel (2:1) and commissioning Gideon (6:11), appears to an unnamed woman to announce that she will bear a son. The scene draws on common biblical motifs: the birth of a son to a barren woman (Sarah, Rebekah, Rachel, Hannah, Elizabeth), an angelic announcement of the coming birth (Sarah, Hagar, Hannah, Elizabeth, Mary), and divine election before birth (Jeremiah, the suffering servant of Isaiah). The motifs combine to emphasize that God has chosen Samson; from the womb, Samson is destined to be God's agent.

Annunciations typically culminate in the name to be given to the child. Here, the announcement focuses not on the baby's name, but on the fact that he is to be a Nazirite. According to Numbers 6:1–21, a Nazirite was a man or woman who consecrated himself or herself to Yahweh. The consecration was marked by three prohibitions: the consecrated person must avoid alcoholic drinks, corpse contamination, and cutting his or her hair. Numbers 6 speaks of Nazirite consecration as a temporary status, the result of a vow (the word "Nazirite" is derived from the Hebrew word for vow).

Samson, however, is consecrated to God for life. Samson's mother's observance of Nazirite prohibitions during her pregnancy is without parallel in the Bible.

Nazirites were set apart for specific purposes. Here, the purpose is to begin to liberate Israel from the Philistines (Judg. 13:5). The verse shows the storyteller's awareness that Philistine hegemony was not completely ended until the time of David.

The woman recognizes the numinous character of her visitor. Awed, she does not question the stranger, but seeks out her husband to tell him what this visitor who looked like an angel of God had said.

Manoah, the woman's husband, is the central character in scene two (vv. 8–14). Although his wife has told him about the rule enjoined on her and her son, Manoah prays that the man of God will return with instructions concerning the boy. Perhaps he found it difficult to accept the authority of a revelation communicated by a woman. Perhaps he wanted to participate in the revelation directly. In any case, Manoah's prayer is answered. The angel of Yahweh does come again, but refuses to undermine the woman's authority. Once more, the angel appears to the woman when she is alone. After she fetches her husband, the angel instructs Manoah that the woman is to carry out the commands already given to her.

This scene reinforces the theme that Samson is to be a Nazirite, one whose birth and consecrated status were miraculously foretold. The account also highlights another thread running throughout the Samson cycle: Women will play a key role in the story of Samson's life. Manoah's wife, a strong and pious Israelite woman, serves as a foil not only to her less perceptive husband but also to the foreign women who will later be Samson's nemeses.

The third scene (vv. 15–23) portrays Manoah and his wife's recognition of the angel's identity. As the scene opens, Manoah still does not recognize the visitor as a divine emissary. In a gesture of hospitality, he presses the stranger to stay and share a meal. The angel refuses, telling Manoah instead to offer the meal as a sacrifice.

In a narrative reminiscent of Gideon's sacrifice to the angel of Yahweh (6:19–24), Manoah recognizes the divinity of his guest when he offers a sacrifice of meat and grain to the Lord. In the story of Gideon, the angel set the offering aflame; here, the angel ascends in the flames. As Gideon had before him, Manoah recognizes the emissary's divinity by the miraculous flame and because the angel vanishes, to be seen no more. Like Gideon, Manoah reacts to the disclosure of the angel's identity with terror. The common biblical motif that no mortal may see God and live serves to acknowledge God's awesome holiness and might. Manoah, in the presence of the Holy One, is sure that he and his wife will die.

In Judges 6, God reassures the frightened Gideon that he will survive his encounter with the divine. In Judges 13, Manoah's wife offers such reassurance. She responds to Manoah's fears with common sense: God would not announce the birth of their child, instruct them as to his care, and accept their sacrifice, only to turn around and kill them.

Like the story of Gideon's sacrifice, the story of Manoah and his wife's offering may have been told in part to explain a name. Manoah's request for the angel's name, and the angel's reply that it is "too wonderful" for mortals to know, may have been associated with an altar called "worker of wonders." In addition, the story highlights the issue of how, where, and whether God is recognized, a thread that weaves its way throughout the Samson stories. The story also reinforces the expectations established by the annunciation (vv. 2–5): The child to be born receives life and destiny by the word of one who works wonders; surely the child will grow into someone wondrous.

The promise made to the woman is fulfilled. In verse 24, she gives birth to a son. The name of the child is given: Samson, which in Hebrew means "sunny."

THE ADVENTURES OF SAMSON

Samson's Marriage

Judges 14:1–20

14:1 **Once Samson went down to Timnah, and at Timnah he saw a Philistine woman.** [2] **Then he came up, and told his father and mother, "I saw a Philistine woman at Timnah; now get her for me as my wife."** [3] **But his father and mother said to him, "Is there not a woman among your kin, or among all our people, that you must go to take a wife from the uncircumcised Philistines?" But Samson said to his father, "Get her for me, because she pleases me."** [4] **His father and mother did not know that this was from the LORD; for he was seeking a pretext to act against the Philistines. At that time the Philistines had dominion over Israel.**

[5] **Then Samson went down with his father and mother to Timnah. When he came to the vineyards of Timnah, suddenly a young lion roared at him.** [6] **The spirit of the LORD rushed on him, and he tore the lion apart barehanded as one might tear apart a kid. But he did not tell his father or his mother what he had done.** [7] **Then he went down and talked with the woman, and she**

pleased Samson. [8] After a while he returned to marry her, and he turned aside to see the carcass of the lion, and there was a swarm of bees in the body of the lion, and honey. [9] He scraped it out into his hands, and went on, eating as he went. When he came to his father and mother, he gave some to them, and they ate it. But he did not tell them that he had taken the honey from the carcass of the lion.

[10] His father went down to the woman, and Samson made a feast there as the young men were accustomed to do. [11] When the people saw him, they brought thirty companions to be with him. [12] Samson said to them, "Let me now put a riddle to you. If you can explain it to me within the seven days of the feast, and find it out, then I will give you thirty linen garments and thirty festal garments. [13] But if you cannot explain it to me, then you shall give me thirty linen garments and thirty festal garments." So they said to him, "Ask your riddle; let us hear it." [14] He said to them,

"Out of the eater came something to eat.
Out of the strong came something sweet."
But for three days they could not explain the riddle.

[15] On the fourth day they said to Samson's wife, "Coax your husband to explain the riddle to us, or we will burn you and your father's house with fire. Have you invited us here to impoverish us?" [16] So Samson's wife wept before him, saying, "You hate me; you do not really love me. You have asked a riddle of my people, but you have not explained it to me." He said to her, "Look, I have not told my father or my mother. Why should I tell you?" [17] She wept before him the seven days that their feast lasted; and because she nagged him, on the seventh day he told her. Then she explained the riddle to her people. [18] The men of the town said to him on the seventh day before the sun went down,

"What is sweeter than honey?
What is stronger than a lion?"
And he said to them,

"If you had not plowed with my heifer,
you would not have found out my riddle."
[19] Then the spirit of the LORD rushed on him, and he went down to Ashkelon. He killed thirty men of the town, took their spoil, and gave the festal garments to those who had explained the riddle. In hot anger he went back to his father's house. [20] And Samson's wife was given to his companion, who had been his best man.

The birth narrative creates high expectations about Samson's destiny. After a series of unlikely deliverers, here at last is a leader with impeccable credentials. Samson is born to pious Israelite parents; his birth itself is miraculous. Moreover, he is consecrated to God, a Nazirite from the womb. And God *blesses* Samson (13:24). He is the only leader in Judges whom God is said to bless. We expect a military hero, an exemplary leader, a model of faith.

We get a womanizing adventurer. Samson shows no interest in resisting the Philistines and very little interest in Yahweh. His agenda is set by his passions, which first lead him to seek to live with the Philistines. Later, when his marriage goes awry, his passions lead him to seek revenge. Being God's agent for delivering Israel has no part in Samson's conscious plans.

Yahweh is the one who determines to deliver Israel by means of Samson's strength and cunning. Skillful editors compiled the adventure tales to show God secretly working in and through Samson's escapades. Unbeknownst to Samson's family, his enemies, or even Samson himself, God is using Samson to erode the Philistines' power.

The earthy character of Samson's motives is apparent in the first verses of the adventure tales. Samson sees and desires a woman from Timnah, a Philistine village near Beth Shemesh. Early Israelite audiences would suspect that Samson's passion for a Philistine bodes ill. Marriages between Israelites and non-Israelites happened, but in at least some circles they were considered highly undesirable. Deuteronomic instruction prohibits marriage between Israelites and the other peoples living in Canaan (Deut. 7:3). Joshua's last speech to the Israelites included a warning not to intermarry, lest God refuse to drive Israel's opponents out of the land.

Samson's parents are appalled by his choice of a wife. The Timnite is not only a foreign woman; she is a *Philistine*, one of Israel's oppressors. Samson is determined to marry her nonetheless.

Marriage in the ancient Near East was negotiated between the groom's parents, if they were still living (or the groom himself, if they were not), and the parents or guardian of the bride. When, despite their opposition, Samson continues to insist that he wants the Timnite woman, his father and mother travel with him to Timnah to make the necessary arrangements with the young woman's family.

Samson's determination to marry the Timnite woman sets in motion a series of events. The journey to Timnah to begin the negotiations becomes the occasion for Samson's first superhuman feat. En route, he encounters a lion. The spirit of the Lord, which has enabled other judges to muster their troops, gives Samson the strength to rip the animal apart bare-handed.

The wedding celebration and the exploit with the lion occasion Samson's first conflict with the Philistines. On his way back to Timnah for the marriage festivities, Samson finds a honeycomb in the lion's desiccated carcass. This discovery prompts Samson to pose his famous riddle. Especially in the context of marriage festivities, the most obvious answer to the riddle is sexual, even lewd. The true answer, however, depends upon knowing where Samson found the honey; a circumstance, the narrator stresses, that Samson has not told anyone, not even his parents. Samson's fury when the Philistine men are able to solve the riddle stems not only from chagrin at being bested, although in a shame-based culture, that would be very real. Nor was it simply a matter of the cost of losing the wager, although the garments would represent a serious expense. Samson is enraged because of the relationship with his wife implied by the men's knowledge. The riddle with which Samson responds essentially accuses the attendants of sleeping with his wife. Elsewhere, the spirit of the Lord had enabled leaders to muster the troops. Here the spirit endows Samson with superhuman strength to murder thirty men.

Ashkelon, whose citizens Samson kills for booty to pay his wager, is a major Philistine city. Samson's motivation for the slaughter has nothing to do with desire to free his people from the Philistine yoke. He needs money; he is outraged. Incidentally, as far as Samson is concerned, his action harasses Israel's opponents.

God's different agenda for Samson is apparent from the beginning of the cycle when the angel of Yahweh promises Manoah's wife that her child will "begin to deliver Israel from the hand of the Philistines" (Judg. 13:5). That God is behind Samson's desire for the Timnite woman and all the ensuing events is explicated in Judges 13:25: "The spirit of the LORD began to stir him. . . ." The Hebrew verb translated "stir," meaning "trouble" or "drive," is actually stronger than the English word would suggest. The spirit of Yahweh drove Samson.

God's agency in the story is hidden. Who would suspect that God would push Samson into a liaison that violated Mosaic law? An editorial comment (14:4) explains that Samson's parents did not know that his desire for the Timnite was from Yahweh, working behind the scenes to cause Samson to strike out against the Philistines. From all appearances, Samson himself was unaware of God's role in the events.

The theme of "knowing" and "not knowing," of hidden or unrecognized realities, present in chapter 13, increases in significance in chapter 14. The motif is reinforced by the role of the riddle—riddles having to do with knowing or not knowing secret realities. The theme is also conveyed by the motif of telling or not telling, making known or not making known, that runs through the chapter. God, whose angel openly appears to Samson's mother in the annunciation scene, is secretly at work in Samson's escapades.

Escalating Vendetta

Judges 15:1–20

15:1 After a while, at the time of the wheat harvest, Samson went to visit his wife, bringing along a kid. He said, "I want to go into my wife's room." But her father would not allow him to go in. ² Her father said, "I was sure that you had rejected her; so I gave her to your companion. Is not her younger sister prettier than she? Why not take her instead?" ³ Samson said to them, "This time, when I do mischief to the Philistines, I will be without blame." ⁴ So Samson went and caught three hundred foxes, and took some torches; and he turned the foxes tail to tail, and put a torch between each pair of tails. ⁵ When he had set fire to the torches, he let the foxes go into the standing grain of the Philistines, and burned up the shocks and the standing grain, as well as the vineyards and olive groves. ⁶ Then the Philistines asked, "Who has done this?" And they said, "Samson, the son-in-law of the Timnite, because he has taken Samson's wife and given her to his companion." So the Philistines came up, and burned her and her father. ⁷ Samson said to them, "If this is what you do, I swear I will not stop until I have taken revenge on you." ⁸ He struck them down hip and thigh with great slaughter; and he went down and stayed in the cleft of the rock of Etam.

⁹ Then the Philistines came up and encamped in Judah, and made a raid on Lehi. ¹⁰ The men of Judah said, "Why have you come up against us?" They said, "We have come up to bind Samson, to do to him as he did to us." ¹¹ Then three thousand men of Judah went down to the cleft of the rock of Etam, and they said to Samson, "Do you not know that the Philistines are rulers over us? What then have you done to us?" He replied, "As they did to me, so I have done to them." ¹² They said to him, "We have come down to bind you, so that we may give you into the hands of the Philistines." Samson answered them, "Swear to me that you yourselves will not attack me." ¹³ They said to him, "No, we will only bind you and give you into their hands; we will not kill you." So they bound him with two new ropes, and brought him up from the rock.

¹⁴ When he came to Lehi, the Philistines came shouting to meet him; and the spirit of the LORD rushed on him, and the ropes that were on his arms became like flax that has caught fire, and his bonds melted off his hands. ¹⁵ Then he found a fresh jawbone of a donkey, reached down and took it, and with it he killed a thousand men. ¹⁶ And Samson said,

"With the jawbone of a donkey,
   heaps upon heaps,
with the jawbone of a donkey
   I have slain a thousand men."

¹⁷ When he had finished speaking, he threw away the jawbone; and that place was called Ramath-lehi.

¹⁸ By then he was very thirsty, and he called on the LORD, saying, "You have granted this great victory by the hand of your servant. Am I now to die of thirst, and fall into the hands of the uncircumcised?" ¹⁹ So God split open the hollow place that is at Lehi, and water came from it. When he drank, his spirit returned, and he revived. Therefore it was named En-hakkore, which is at Lehi to this day. ²⁰ And he judged Israel in the days of the Philistines twenty years.

Samson's departure in a rage gives his father-in-law the impression that Samson has divorced his daughter. The Hebrew word translated "rejected" (15:2) is often used in a technical sense to mean "divorce." A fair amount of confusion surrounds Samson's marriage. Commentators frequently suggest that the marriage was a particular kind in which the woman continued to live in her father's household, where her husband would visit her from time to time. Such a hypothesis is unnecessary. One would expect the negotiations for marriage to take place at the bride's household. That Samson leaves his wife at her father's after the betrothal festivities is best explained by Samson's rage. He returns once he has calmed down. Indeed, the plot requires us to view Samson's behavior in leaving and then returning to his wife as abnormal, something that the father-in-law could interpret as a divorce while Samson believes he is still married.

Samson's retaliation, tying lighted torches between the tails of three hundred pairs of foxes (or jackals) to burn Philistian fields, is both renowned and outrageous. We are not to evaluate its plausibility. The story is simply a tall tale, intended to entertain at the Philistines' expense.

Vengeance leads to countervengeance. The Philistines' fiery retaliation is highly ironic. They carry out the threat that they had used to force Samson's wife to discover the answer to Samson's riddle. Again, one ought not look too closely at the logic of punishing Samson by killing persons who have wronged him. Perhaps the Philistines blame the father-in-law for angering Samson. The vendetta appears to result in the slaughter of a great many of Israel's enemies.

Even Samson's efforts to retreat from violence lead to further destruction of Israel's enemies. Samson retires to the wilderness of Judah. In a scene characterized by exaggeration, humor, and some anti-Judahite bias, three thousand men of Judah march out to capture the lone, unarmed Samson. The scene is also marked by irony. Samson justifies his aggression against the Philistines in nearly the same words that the Philistines use to justify their vengeance against him.

Samson allows the Judahites to bind him, a seeming defeat that serves as an opportunity for greater vengeance and glory. Meeting the Philistines, the spirit-filled Samson snaps his bonds and reaches for the weapon nearest to hand, a donkey's jawbone. The hyperbole that has characterized all of the Samson episodes reaches new heights. With his ludicrous club, he slaughters one thousand of his opponents.

Samson's victory song (v. 16) includes a wordplay; the Hebrew words for "donkey," "heap," and "ruddy" are homonyms. The Jewish Publication Society translation of the Bible captures something of the pun involved:

> "With the jawbone of an ass, mass upon mass,
> With the jawbone of an ass, I have killed a thousand men."

The story and the victory song are used to explain the name of a hill: Lehi, "jawbone."

The hidden agency of God is very hidden in this part of the Samson story. No reference to Yahweh is made from 15:1 until 15:14, when the "spirit of the LORD" comes over Samson and once again endows him with superhuman strength. The ridiculous inadequacy of Samson's weapon underscores the supernatural quality of his strength. God's agency is hidden, but effective.

Yahweh's work is explicit in the final scene of this set of stories. For the first time, Samson addresses God. Thirsty, he cries out with an exaggerated complaint. God answers his informal prayer by creating a spring. The vignette is used to offer a popular explanation of the spring's name. (The actual meaning of the name was probably "partridge.") The scene has a more profound purpose than explaining a name, however. It demonstrates that God, who works in hidden ways, also works overtly, in answer to prayer. The God who empowers also provides.

The Death and Final Victory of Samson
Judges 16:1–31

16:1 Once Samson went to Gaza, where he saw a prostitute and went in to her. [2] The Gazites were told, "Samson has come here." So they circled around and lay in wait for him all night at the city gate. They kept quiet all night, thinking, "Let us wait until the light of the morning; then we will kill him." [3] But Samson lay only until midnight. Then at midnight he rose up, took hold of the doors of the city gate and the two posts, pulled them up, bar and all, put them on his shoulders, and carried them to the top of the hill that is in front of Hebron.

[4] After this he fell in love with a woman in the valley of Sorek, whose name was Delilah. [5] The lords of the Philistines came to her and said to her, "Coax

him, and find out what makes his strength so great, and how we may overpower him, so that we may bind him in order to subdue him; and we will each give you eleven hundred pieces of silver." ⁶ So Delilah said to Samson, "Please tell me what makes your strength so great, and how you could be bound, so that one could subdue you." ⁷ Samson said to her, "If they bind me with seven fresh bowstrings that are not dried out, then I shall become weak, and be like anyone else." ⁸ Then the lords of the Philistines brought her seven fresh bowstrings that had not dried out, and she bound him with them. ⁹ While men were lying in wait in an inner chamber, she said to him, "The Philistines are upon you, Samson!" But he snapped the bowstrings, as a strand of fiber snaps when it touches the fire. So the secret of his strength was not known.

¹⁰ Then Delilah said to Samson, "You have mocked me and told me lies; please tell me how you could be bound." ¹¹ He said to her, "If they bind me with new ropes that have not been used, then I shall become weak, and be like anyone else." ¹² So Delilah took new ropes and bound him with them, and said to him, "The Philistines are upon you, Samson!" (The men lying in wait were in an inner chamber.) But he snapped the ropes off his arms like a thread.

¹³ Then Delilah said to Samson, "Until now you have mocked me and told me lies; tell me how you could be bound." He said to her, "If you weave the seven locks of my head with the web and make it tight with the pin, then I shall become weak, and be like anyone else." ¹⁴ So while he slept, Delilah took the seven locks of his head and wove them into the web, and made them tight with the pin. Then she said to him, "The Philistines are upon you, Samson!" But he awoke from his sleep, and pulled away the pin, the loom, and the web.

¹⁵ Then she said to him, "How can you say, 'I love you,' when your heart is not with me? You have mocked me three times now and have not told me what makes your strength so great." ¹⁶ Finally, after she had nagged him with her words day after day, and pestered him, he was tired to death. ¹⁷ So he told her his whole secret, and said to her, "A razor has never come upon my head; for I have been a nazirite to God from my mother's womb. If my head were shaved, then my strength would leave me; I would become weak, and be like anyone else."

¹⁸ When Delilah realized that he had told her his whole secret, she sent and called the lords of the Philistines, saying, "This time come up, for he has told his whole secret to me." Then the lords of the Philistines came up to her, and brought the money in their hands. ¹⁹ She let him fall asleep on her lap; and she called a man, and had him shave off the seven locks of his head. He began to weaken, and his strength left him. ²⁰ Then she said, "The Philistines are upon you, Samson!" When he awoke from his sleep, he thought, "I will go out as at other times, and shake myself free." But he did not know that the LORD had left him. ²¹ So the Philistines seized him and gouged out his

eyes. They brought him down to Gaza and bound him with bronze shackles; and he ground at the mill in the prison. [22] But the hair of his head began to grow again after it had been shaved.

[23] Now the lords of the Philistines gathered to offer a great sacrifice to their god Dagon, and to rejoice; for they said, "Our god has given Samson our enemy into our hand." [24] When the people saw him, they praised their god; for they said, "Our god has given our enemy into our hand, the ravager of our country, who has killed many of us." [25] And when their hearts were merry, they said, "Call Samson, and let him entertain us." So they called Samson out of the prison, and he performed for them. They made him stand between the pillars; [26] and Samson said to the attendant who held him by the hand, "Let me feel the pillars on which the house rests, so that I may lean against them." [27] Now the house was full of men and women; all the lords of the Philistines were there, and on the roof there were about three thousand men and women, who looked on while Samson performed.

[28] Then Samson called to the LORD and said, "Lord GOD, remember me and strengthen me only this once, O God, so that with this one act of revenge I may pay back the Philistines for my two eyes." [29] And Samson grasped the two middle pillars on which the house rested, and he leaned his weight against them, his right hand on the one and his left hand on the other. [30] Then Samson said, "Let me die with the Philistines." He strained with all his might; and the house fell on the lords and all the people who were in it. So those he killed at his death were more than those he had killed during his life. [31] Then his brothers and all his family came down and took him and brought him up and buried him between Zorah and Eshtaol in the tomb of his father Manoah. He had judged Israel twenty years.

Like the first section of the adventure tales, the second section begins with Samson's seeing a Philistine woman whom he desires. This time the woman is a prostitute. She resides at Gaza, one of the five major cities comprising the Philistine federation.

The episode (vv. 1–3) presupposes that Gaza was a walled city with only one set of gates, which were locked at night. The men of Gaza would assume that Samson is safely shut within the town's walls until morning, when they could seize him. Samson evades capture by pulling up the city gates and carrying them twenty-four miles to Hebron. The story is nose-thumbing bravado. Samson quite literally "possess[es] the gates of [his] enemies" (Gen. 22:17) (Hamlin, 1990, 136).

The Samson stories pivot upon Samson's dangerous liaisons with three women. The next episode (Judg. 16:4–22) is the third and most lethal of these. This time, the woman is named. The meaning of "Delilah" is uncertain; proposals include "devotee," "coquette," "falling curl," and "small."

In Hebrew, *Lilah* means "night." The name of Samson's lover-betrayer was likely chosen as a play on the meaning of Samson's name: "sunny." "Night" overcomes the "little sun." The story does not specify Delilah's ethnic identity. An inhabitant of the Sorek Valley, Delilah could be Canaanite, Israelite, or Philistine. Given the parallels between Delilah and the Timnite woman, Delilah's readiness to collaborate with the Philistine lords, and Samson's established penchant for Philistine women, Delilah is probably a Philistine.

The story of Samson and Delilah parallels that of Samson and the Timnite woman. As before, Philistine men persuade Samson's paramour to coax a secret from Samson. This time the stakes are higher. Samson has grown into a threat to national security; the Philistine men who solicit Delilah's collaboration are none other than the lords (literally, "tyrants") of the five federated Philistine cities. They want secret information not to best Samson, but to destroy him.

The bribe that the Philistine lords offer Delilah is enormous, over one hundred times the amount that Micah's priest is glad to accept as a yearly stipend (Judg. 17:10). Delilah's strategy for coaxing information from the reticent Samson is similar to that of Samson's former wife. Like the wife, Delilah persistently demands that Samson prove his love by disclosing his secret. Samson repeatedly teases her with a false answer. Delilah's failed attempts to bind Samson recall the Judahites' efforts to turn him over to the Philistines. The first time Delilah binds him, the "fresh bowstrings" snap just as the cords used by the Judahites to bind Samson (15:14) had snapped. The second time, Delilah binds Samson in "new ropes," just as the Judahites had done. Delilah's third attempt is obscure. Verses 13 and 14 include several words that are difficult to translate. They seem to depict weaving Samson's hair into a small loom.

When Samson finally divulges his secret, he refers to his Nazirite status. Samson is set apart for Yahweh by the vow made before his birth. That vow is marked by leaving his hair unshorn. To cut his hair is to annul his Nazirite status, his separateness, to become "like other men."

The story offers a negative picture of Delilah. She illustrates a common biblical and folkloric motif: the "strange" woman who ensnares men. Traditional interpretation portrays Delilah as the quintessential deceptive seductress. In contrast, some recent interpreters suggest that Delilah, like the Timnite woman who betrays Samson to save her life (14:1–20), is a woman who does what she must in order to survive. The story places the Delilah episode after the murder of the Timnite woman. Perhaps Delilah knew that what happened to her predecessor could also happen to her. Others note that from a Philistine perspective, Delilah is like Jael, a heroine celebrated for seducing and killing Israel's enemy (Judg. 4:17–22; 5:24–27).

If it derides Delilah, the episode hardly flatters Samson. Why, after Delilah has tried to bind him three times, does Samson tell her his secret the fourth time she asks? Perhaps we are to imagine that Delilah cries "the Philistines are upon you" in a cajoling, playful tone that Samson interpreted as erotic teasing. More likely, Samson has become overconfident, believing that Yahweh's spirit and the strength it gave are his no matter what he does.

The narrators are careful to guard against a magical interpretation of the Nazirite vow. Samson's strength resides not in his hair, but in his separateness, his consecrated status, and ultimately in God's presence. Yahweh leaves Samson, and so his strength fails.

With Samson's downfall (v. 20b), the tone of the story shifts from ribald humor and erotic teasing to pathos. The Philistines blind, shackle, and imprison Samson. In prison, they set him to grinding grain at a mill, work normally done by an animal, a slave, or a woman.

To all appearances, the Philistines had won. They ascribe their victory to their deity. "Our god has given Samson our enemy into our hand." Samson is subjected to an ultimate humiliation: the Philistines force their captive enemy to dance for them as they celebrate his defeat.

Once again, betrayal and seeming defeat provide an opportunity for Samson to destroy his enemies. Samson, who earlier prayed for water and life, now prays for vengeance and death. Again, his prayer is answered.

The angel's words that Samson would begin to deliver Israel from the Philistines (13:5) and the editorial comment that Yahweh "was seeking a pretext to act against the Philistines" (14:4) established that God was secretly at work in Samson's escapades. Samson's revenge on his captors demonstrates the hidden but victorious purpose of God. The apparent victory of Dagon is actually the will and work of Yahweh. Samson's final act "kills more Philistines" than he had been able to destroy in all of his previous fights. More important, his act is Yahweh's victory over the Philistine deity. Gideon pulled down the altar of Baal; Samson pulls down the entire temple of Dagon.

The concluding note of the cycle, that Samson was buried in his father's tomb between Zorah and Eshtaol, recalls the beginning of his adventures. According to 13:25, all of Samson's escapades began when God stirred him up between Zorah and Eshtaol. The note also provides the story a happier ending than Samson's self-destruction: burial in the tomb of one's father was a desirable fate.

THE PURPOSE OF THE SAMSON STORY

Samson's violent and amorous character has led many commentators to view his story as little more than a negative example of what leadership should not be. The Samson cycle is seen as a cautionary tale of a potential leader who dissipates his strength through amoral behavior and disregard for Yahweh. The ancient Rabbis viewed Samson along these lines, deeming him the "least worthy judge." Some commentators specify Samson's failure more precisely as the violation of his Nazirite status. A Nazirite was prohibited from drinking alcohol, touching a corpse, or cutting his or her hair. Samson does all three. The wedding feast that he holds is (in Hebrew) a "drinking feast." He touches both the corpse of the lion and the fresh bone of a donkey. Finally, of course, his hair is shorn.

As noted above, the disintegration visible in the Gideon and Jephthah accounts can be traced in the Samson stories. Samson neither speaks for God, like Deborah, nor consults God, like Gideon. He does not ratify his actions before God nor speak about God like Jephthah. Rather, he ignores Yahweh except on two occasions when, faced with extreme distress, he calls out. Serving God or God's people appears to play no part in Samson's motivations. The significance of his consecrated status seems to be reduced to abstaining from hair cuts!

Nonetheless, one ought not exaggerate the negative nature of Samson's character. The storytellers do not explicitly censure him. Nor is the motif of the Nazirite vow, found only in chapters 13 and 16, sufficiently integrated with the rest of the Samson cycle to serve as its overall theme. Moreover, Yahweh is thoroughly implicated in Samson's actions. God is behind his passion for a Timnite woman. The spirit of Yahweh empowers Samson to kill not only the lion but also thirty and then one thousand Philistines. God is also involved in Samson's self-destruction. Moreover, the storytellers and compilers seem to relish Samson's audaciousness and physical and sexual prowess. The Samson story was not likely intended merely as a cautionary tale.

A more convincing interpretation views the Samson stories as illustrations of God secretly at work to liberate Israel from its oppressors. The hiddenness of God's agency is stressed by the motif of "knowing/not knowing" that runs throughout the cycle, and by the hidden realities suggested by Samson's riddle.

The "downward spiral" characterizing Israel and its leaders' behavior and the "hiddenness" of God's agency may be related. The two places where God's work is explicitly recognized in the Samson cycle are the two times that Samson prays. Perhaps given the Israelite leader's inattention to the divine will and the weight of the Israelites' apostasy, Yahweh is forced to work behind the scenes, using the tools at hand.

In any case, the cycle does portray God involved in the messiness of human affairs. The stories show Yahweh working secretly, through human actions with all their ambiguity, as well as openly, in direct answer to prayer, in order to defeat Israel's enemies and the enemies' gods.

24. Thieves, Thugs, and Idol Worshipers
Judges 17 and 18

With the end of the Samson stories, the now-familiar cycle—the people sin, God gives them over to their enemies, the people cry out in distress, and God raises up a deliverer—comes to an end. The remaining chapters, Judges 17–21, stand outside of the theological framework that unifies the core of Judges. The book continues to focus on threats to Israel's existence, but now, instead of external enemies, those threats come from within Israel. Moreover, there are no more charismatic leaders. God ceases to deliver the people.

An earlier generation of biblical scholars held that the last five chapters of Judges bore little relationship to the stories of the deliverers. The final narratives were believed to be "filed" after the Samson account because they were set in the time of the judges. More recently, commentators have found thematic continuity between the closing chapters and the earlier stories. They have traced a downward spiral in the stories of the "judges"; the people's apostasy mounts ever higher, while the leaders' characters deteriorate. The final chapters comprise a two-part conclusion in which the downward spiral continues and intensifies, and Israelite society disintegrates. Chapters 17 and 18 illustrate the religious chaos into which Israel has fallen. Judges 19–21, the subject of the following chapter, show the tribes in nearly complete social and political chaos.

The traditions in Judges 17–21 no doubt came from a variety of circles. Editors have unified these various traditions with a refrain: "In those days there was no king in Israel; all the people did what was right in their own eyes," which is found early in the conclusion (17:6) and again as the last words of the book (21:25). Portions of the verse mark the beginning of discrete stories within the conclusion (18:1 and 19:1). The refrain reflects the compilers' promonarchical biases and emphasizes the anarchy into which Israelite society had disintegrated.

In Judges 17 and 18, stories of corrupt worship at the personal and tribal levels serve to illustrate the religious chaos into which Israel had fallen. First, an individual, Micah, creates an idolatrous shrine with purloined silver. Then a tribe, Dan, steals the idol to establish a sanctuary in land they had brutally taken from an unsuspecting people. The editor's evaluative comment—"In those days there was no king in Israel; all the people did what was right in their own eyes" (17:6; cf. 18:1)—makes the stories illustrations of a larger societal breakdown. The problem does not lie with Micah or the Danites alone. "All of the people" Israel have degenerated into anarchy.

The stories of Micah and the Danites may draw on traditions about the founding of the northern sanctuary at Dan. If so, editors have twisted the traditions into an exquisite mockery of the worship site. Judges 18 reflects an antinorthern bias found also in Judges 1. The Micah/Dan story was combined with the traditions in Judges 19–21 to demonstrate the failure of charismatic leadership and the need for a king. Probably still later the materials were placed in the context of the larger book of Judges to illustrate the outcome of Israel's mounting sin.

According to Judges 18, the Danites, unable to gain control of their assigned land in the south, migrated to the far north of Israel where they conquered a city, Laish, for their homeland, renaming it Dan. The tradition of Dan's inability to maintain possession of its territory and subsequent migration is found elsewhere in the Bible. Joshua 19:40–46 locates Dan in a wedge of coastal land bordered by Judah to the south, Ephraim to the north, and Benjamin to the west. The passage goes on to say that the tribe, having lost its territory, conquered a northern city (here called Leshem rather than Laish), and settled there (19:47). The Amorites are blamed for Dan's inability to occupy their southern territory in Judges 1:34–35. The Samson stories suggest that Philistine pressure was a factor in the tribe's migration. All other biblical references to Dan locate the tribe in the northern city. The historicity of traditions about Dan's migration is not certain. The list of Danite cities in Joshua 19 overlaps the list of towns assigned to Judah in Joshua 15; moreover, the southern territory assigned to Dan is defined rather vaguely. Several scholars question whether Dan ever attempted to settle in the south. In any case, the narrative in Judges 18 is less a historical account and more a satirical polemic against Dan on one level, and a statement about the moral and spiritual breakdown of premonarchical Israel on another level.

More is known about the city of Dan than about the tribe's (supposed) migration. Biblical texts speak of Dan as Israel's northern boundary; the nation's ideal territory stretched from "Dan to Beersheba." Dan was the site of one of two worship centers established by Jeroboam I, the first king of the northern tribes after they split away from Judah in the tenth century B.C.E. Jeroboam's aim was to provide northern alternatives to worship in Jerusalem (1 Kgs. 12:25–31), a political move that the Deuteronomistic Historians deplored. The southerners characterize the northern cult sites as idolatrous and call the act of founding them "the sin of Jeroboam."

Archeologists excavating Tell Dan have discovered the remains of a Bronze Age Canaanite city that thrived there for at least a millennium before Israelites settled on the site. "Laish," the name Judges 18 ascribes to the town before Danites occupied it, is found in Egyptian texts.

RELIGIOUS CHAOS ON A PERSONAL LEVEL: MICAH, HIS IDOL, AND HIS PRIEST
Judges 17

17:1 There was a man in the hill country of Ephraim whose name was Micah. ² He said to his mother, "The eleven hundred pieces of silver that were taken from you about which you uttered a curse, and even spoke it in my hearing,—that silver is in my possession; I took it; but now I will return it to you." And his mother said, "May my son be blessed by the LORD!" ³ Then he returned the eleven hundred pieces of silver to his mother; and his mother said, "I consecrate the silver to the LORD from my hand for my son, to make an idol of cast metal." ⁴ So when he returned the money to his mother, his mother took two hundred pieces of silver, and gave it to the silversmith, who made it into an idol of cast metal; and it was in the house of Micah. ⁵ This man Micah had a shrine, and he made an ephod and teraphim, and installed one of his sons, who became his priest. ⁶ In those days there was no king in Israel; all the people did what was right in their own eyes.

⁷ Now there was a young man of Bethlehem in Judah, of the clan of Judah. He was a Levite residing there. ⁸ This man left the town of Bethlehem in Judah, to live wherever he could find a place. He came to the house of Micah in the hill country of Ephraim to carry on his work. ⁹ Micah said to him, "From where do you come?" He replied, "I am a Levite of Bethlehem in Judah, and I am going to live wherever I can find a place." ¹⁰ Then Micah said to him, "Stay with me, and be to me a father and a priest, and I will give you ten pieces of silver a year, a set of clothes, and your living." ¹¹ The Levite agreed to stay with the man; and the young man became to him like one of his sons. ¹² So Micah installed the Levite, and the young man became his priest, and was in the house of Micah. ¹³ Then Micah said, "Now I know that the LORD will prosper me, because the Levite has become my priest."

The story of Micah and his idolatrous shrine sets up the polemical account of Dan's migration and the establishment of a sanctuary (Judges 18). At the same time, the story has its own integrity as a woeful and satirical tale of perverted worship.

The first five verses of the account serve to introduce the protagonist, Micah, not to be confused with the eighth-century prophet who had the same name. The name "Micah" affirms God's incomparability; its longer form, *Micahyahu*, means "Who is like Yahweh." Micah's character as a thief and an idolater unfolds in ironic contrast to his name.

The narrative begins abruptly, presupposing action that has already taken place. Micah's mother has been robbed of eleven hundred pieces of silver. The amount is equivalent to the bribe the Philistine tyrants gave Delilah for betraying Samson (16:5) and is an enormous sum of money, as can be seen by comparing it to the ten pieces of silver that Micah promises his priest for a yearly stipend (17:10).

The woman has cursed whoever stole her silver. Curses, according to Israelite understanding, were not mere words. They were powerful, an effective way of punishing offenders for deeds committed secretly. As the story opens, Micah has apparently been frightened by his mother's curse into confessing his guilt. His mother's blessing of her son may be an expression of a doting parent's affectionate response to a confession. More likely, the blessing is an attempt to avert the curse that she had unwittingly evoked against her own child. Her dedication of the silver to Yahweh is probably a further effort to ward off the effects of the curse.

Ironically, his mother's efforts to undo the curse only serve to compound Micah's guilt. The storyteller raises questions about the integrity of the woman's gesture by having her consecrate all of the recovered silver (eleven hundred pieces) to Yahweh, but actually using only a fraction of it (two hundred pieces) for implements of worship. The real problem, however, is how the woman uses the silver. She has it made into an "idol of cast metal." Making or worshiping idols is a fundamental violation of Israel's faith. Deuteronomy 27:15 curses anyone who makes an idol. Micah and his mother's efforts to avert her curse entail a greater curse.

Two Hebrew terms underlie the phrase "idol of cast metal"; one is often translated "graven image"; the other, "molten image" or "cast idol." Both are anathemas to Israel's God. The Ten Commandments prohibit the making of "graven images." Making molten images is forbidden by another central set of Mosaic laws (Exod. 34:17). "Molten image" is the term used to describe the golden calf Aaron made that nearly provoked God to destroy the Israelites. Text after text asserts that people who make graven or molten images are cursed, cut off, put to shame, or will die.

The issue here is not the worship of other gods, per se, for Micah and his mother intend to worship Yahweh. His mother blesses Micah in Yahweh's name and consecrates the silver to Israel's God, and Micah is confident that Yahweh will prosper him. The issue is that making an image of Yahweh is anathema. Comparing the incomparable God to any created thing is an offense against God's infinite mystery and richness. No single image can adequately portray Yahweh. Micah's name, "Who is like Yahweh," ironically emphasizes this dimension of idolatry.

Prophetic condemnation of using graven or molten images to represent Yahweh also stresses the sinful absurdity of confusing maker and creature. God is the maker; we are the ones whom God has made. The prophets heap scorn on those who bow down to what they have made with their own hands. Three references to the idol as something Micah made emphasize this dimension of the offense. The prophets also condemn those who treat God as an object to be manipulated rather than as the one due all reverence and obedience. Micah is manipulative; he regards worship as a way of making sure that God will give him success (17:13).

Along with his idol of cast metal, Micah makes an ephod and a teraphim. The ephod, a breastplate containing lots used in divination, was an orthodox priestly garment. The compilers of Judges regard the ephod as idolatrous, however; Gideon's ephod was a "snare" that entrapped him and all of Israel. Teraphim appear to be household images perhaps associated with divination. In the early part of Israel's history, teraphim were apparently tolerated; in later periods, teraphim were viewed as idolatrous (2 Kgs. 23:24). In the story of Micah, idolatrous terms such as graven image, molten image, teraphim, and ephod pile up, adding weight to Micah's sin.

Micah's guilt is further compounded when he establishes his own son as his priest. In the early period of Israel's history, this act would have been tolerated. Anyone could function as a priest. According to 2 Samuel 8:18, King David appointed his son as a priest. Later, only members of the priestly caste, the Levites, were allowed to be priests (Deut. 18:1–8). Still later, the priesthood was reserved for an elite subgroup of Levites, the Aaronites.

The earliest versions of the story of Micah probably date back to a period when it was desirable but not necessary for priests to be Levites. The final form of the story would have been told to a later audience, one that believed no one but Levites were eligible for priesthood. This later audience would have viewed Micah's idolatrous worship as an abomination made all the worse by his illegal priest. The storytellers sum up their disapproval of Micah and his shrine in verse 6: "In those days there was no king in Israel; all the people did what was right in their own eyes" (see above, p. 226).

The second half of chapter 17 (vv. 7–13) centers on a Levitical priest whom Micah hires and the Danites later steal. The assertion that the Levite was "of the clan of Judah" (v. 7) is somewhat puzzling. How could he be both a Levite and a Judahite? Some scholars suggest that the term "Levite" came to refer to a priestly class rather than a tribe. Others suggest that the phrase simply refers to the locale where the Levite had been living, not to his tribal affiliation.

In any case, according to the story, the young man had left his home in hope of better employment prospects.

Micah is delighted to hire the Levite; now he will have the very best kind of priest. The choice is orthodox enough, but Micah's motivations in hiring the Levite are as skewed as his idol worship. He wants the right kind of priest so that God will "prosper" him (v. 13). That is, Micah's worship is an effort to manipulate God, to ensure his own prosperity, rather than an effort to please or praise Yahweh.

Micah and his mother do not worship other deities, who have repeatedly led the tribes astray. All that they do, they do in the name of Yahweh. Nonetheless, their worship is perverted, for it seeks to limit and control God, rather than to serve God. Micah and his mother seek to make God serve them.

Micah's story is ironic and perhaps in some ways pathetic. In order to gain divine approval, the penitent thief fashions an idol from stolen and accursed silver. He assumes that his idol and his Levitical priest will guarantee his well-being, an assumption that proves to be utterly wrong. Micah is looking for God in all the wrong places. Such is the chaos into which the tribes' religion had fallen.

RELIGIOUS CHAOS ON THE TRIBAL LEVEL: AN ANTICONQUEST STORY
Judges 18

18:1 **In those days there was no king in Israel. And in those days the tribe of the Danites was seeking for itself a territory to live in; for until then no territory among the tribes of Israel had been allotted to them.** [2] **So the Danites sent five valiant men from the whole number of their clan, from Zorah and from Eshtaol, to spy out the land and to explore it; and they said to them, "Go, explore the land." When they came to the hill country of Ephraim, to** the house of Micah, they stayed there. [3] While they were at Micah's house, they recognized the voice of the young Levite; so they went over and asked him, "Who brought you here? What are you doing in this place? What is your business here?" [4] He said to them, "Micah did such and such for me, and he hired me, and I have become his priest." [5] Then they said to him, "Inquire of God that we may know whether the mission we are undertaking will succeed." [6] The priest replied, "Go in peace. The mission you are on is under the eye of the LORD."

[7] The five men went on, and when they came to Laish, they observed the people who were there living securely, after the manner of the Sidonians, quiet and unsuspecting, lacking nothing on earth, and possessing wealth. Furthermore, they were far from the Sidonians and had no dealings with Aram. [8] When they came to their kinsfolk at Zorah and Eshtaol, they said to them, "What do you report?" [9] They said, "Come, let us go up against them; for we have seen the land, and it is very good. Will you do nothing? Do not be slow to go, but enter in and possess the land. [10] When you go, you will come to an unsuspecting people. The land is broad—God has indeed given it into your hands—a place where there is no lack of anything on earth."

[11] Six hundred men of the Danite clan, armed with weapons of war, set out from Zorah and Eshtaol, [12] and went up and encamped at Kiriath-jearim in Judah. On this account that place is called Mahaneh-dan to this day; it is west of Kiriath-jearim. [13] From there they passed on to the hill country of Ephraim, and came to the house of Micah.

[14] Then the five men who had gone to spy out the land (that is, Laish) said to their comrades, "Do you know that in these buildings there are an ephod, teraphim, and an idol of cast metal? Now therefore consider what you will do." [15] So they turned in that direction and came to the house of the young Levite, at the home of Micah, and greeted him. [16] While the six hundred men of the Danites, armed with their weapons of war, stood by the entrance of the gate, [17] the five men who had gone to spy out the land proceeded to enter and take the idol of cast metal, the ephod, and the teraphim. The priest was standing by the entrance of the gate with the six hundred men armed with weapons of war. [18] When the men went into Micah's house and took the idol of cast metal, the ephod, and the teraphim, the priest said to them, "What are you doing?" [19] They said to him, "Keep quiet! Put your hand over your mouth, and come with us, and be to us a father and a priest. Is it better for you to be priest to the house of one person, or to be priest to a tribe and clan in Israel?" [20] Then the priest accepted the offer. He took the ephod, the teraphim, and the idol, and went along with the people.

[21] So they resumed their journey, putting the little ones, the livestock, and the goods in front of them. [22] When they were some distance from the home of Micah, the men who were in the houses near Micah's house were called out, and they overtook the Danites. [23] They shouted to the Danites, who

turned around and said to Micah, "What is the matter that you come with such a company?" ²⁴ He replied, "You take my gods that I made, and the priest, and go away, and what have I left? How then can you ask me, 'What is the matter?'" ²⁵ And the Danites said to him, "You had better not let your voice be heard among us or else hot-tempered fellows will attack you, and you will lose your life and the lives of your household." ²⁶ Then the Danites went their way. When Micah saw that they were too strong for him, he turned and went back to his home.

²⁷ The Danites, having taken what Micah had made, and the priest who belonged to him, came to Laish, to a people quiet and unsuspecting, put them to the sword, and burned down the city. ²⁸ There was no deliverer, because it was far from Sidon and they had no dealings with Aram. It was in the valley that belongs to Beth-rehob. They rebuilt the city, and lived in it. ²⁹ They named the city Dan, after their ancestor Dan, who was born to Israel; but the name of the city was formerly Laish. ³⁰ Then the Danites set up the idol for themselves. Jonathan son of Gershom, son of Moses, and his sons were priests to the tribe of the Danites until the time the land went into captivity. ³¹ So they maintained as their own Micah's idol that he had made, as long as the house of God was at Shiloh.

The story of Micah's idolatrous shrine becomes intertwined with the story of Dan's establishment of an idolatrous sanctuary. The latter story is structured as a highly satirical conquest narrative. A number of commentators point out parallels between the account of Dan's migration to and capture of the city and the great national saga of Israel's conquest of Canaan. The parallels serve only to highlight Dan's faithlessness, however. God commands Israel to enter and take Canaan, and fights on its behalf; in the Dan narrative, God is conspicuously absent. In the end, the narrative mocks the northern tribe. The storytellers view Dan's conquest not as an act of faith but as an act of brutality; their sanctuary is portrayed as a perversion of Israelite religion.

The compilers' negative assessment of Dan is signaled in the first verse of the account. The note that there was no king in Israel lets the audience know that what follows is an example of anarchy. The promonarchical editors want to show that without a king, society degenerates into chaos.

The account of the Danite spies (vv. 2–10) is the first parallel between Judges 18 and the Israelite conquest narratives. Like Moses (Num. 13–14) and Joshua (Josh. 2), the Danites send warriors to spy out the land that they seek to occupy. Like the Israelite spies, the spies of Dan return with a favorable report of the territory. The main difference between the Danite spies' report and the Israelite spies' report has to do with the strength of the inhabitants of the land. The Canaanites whom Moses and the Israelites faced were "strong, and the towns are fortified and very large" (Num. 13:28). Joshua's army went up against a walled city. Dan's targeted population "lived securely," that is, without walls or fortifications. They were "quiet and unsuspecting." Three times the audience is told that residents of Laish are "unsuspecting" (vv. 7, 10, 27). The threefold repetition evokes sympathy, stressing that the Danite attack is a totally unprovoked assault on an unfortified town.

The vulnerability of Laish is further emphasized by the reference to its distance from Sidon (v. 7). Sidon was a Phoenician city on the Mediterranean coast some thirty miles from Laish, and separated from it by mountains. Laish, according to verse 7, was culturally related to Sidon, but because of the distance, could not rely on it for aid. The text of the last clause in verse 7 is uncertain. Some versions read "Aram," that is, Syria; the Hebrew text reads, "anyone." The point in either case is that Laish is utterly without allies. Unlike the Canaanite cities that Moses and Joshua attacked, Laish is not a worthy opponent but a defenseless, unsuspecting, sympathetic people. Stressing Laish's weakness serves to underline Dan's brutality.

The spy story weaves together the tale of Micah and that of Dan. The spies stay at Micah's house, where they encounter the Levite. The note that the Danites recognize the young man's voice (v. 3) probably means that they recognize his Judean accent, and they go to investigate the presence of another southerner. Their request that the priest "inquire of God" is well within the Levite's job description (Deut. 33:8). They are asking the Levite to use divination, probably by means of the ephod or the teraphim, to determine whether their tribe will win its battle. The answer the priest conveys is exquisitely ambiguous. To be "under the eye of the LORD" could refer to divine approval or to divine judgment. Given the Danite's subsequent brutality, the words "Go in peace" are equally ironic.

The spies' report encourages the Danites to set out on their campaign. The number of Danite warriors involved, six hundred, recalls the six hundred thousand Hebrew men that according to tradition (Exod. 12:37) set out from Egypt toward the promised land.

The ordination of priests and the construction of implements of worship were among the gifts that the Israelites received at Mt. Sinai. As they journey north, the Danites also acquire a priest and worship paraphernalia in a mountainous region (Ephraim). The parallel serves to emphasize the striking difference between the tribes as they were under Moses, and the tribe of Dan as it had become. Moses and his followers established the priesthood and made their worship apparatus at God's command and according to divine instruction. The Danites take Micah's idol and his priest by brute force. The storytellers emphasize that the Danites use intimidation to get what they want. Twice we are reminded that six hundred men armed with weapons of war block the way out as their cohorts steal Micah's idol.

The Levite is not absolved of blame by Dan's intimidating show of strength, however. Offered a bigger, better job, the priest accepts with alacrity. The Hebrew phrase that the NRSV translates "accepted the offer" literally means "his heart was glad." The Levite comes across as an opportunist, willing to collude in the theft of his employer's possessions for the sake of professional advancement.

Dan's theft of Micah's idol, ephod, and teraphim echoes the story of Rachel stealing her father's household gods (Gen. 31:32). Jacob's declaration that whoever stole the gods would be put to death makes the gravity of the offense very clear. The reason that Dan would want Micah's idol and his priest is apparent from the previous chapter; they were seen as guarantees that God would prosper whoever owned them (Judg. 17:13).

The Danites certainly know they are culpable and expect reprisals. They put their children and livestock in front of the armed men, as far from potential pursuers as possible.

Micah's ineffectual attempt to retake the idol and the priest rounds out his story (vv. 21–26). The idol made of silver that Micah had once stolen has now been stolen from him. Micah believed that his Levitical priest guaranteed his prosperity. Now he complains that he has nothing left (v. 24). What goes around comes around. The ancient audiences no doubt enjoyed hearing Micah get his comeuppance.

That Micah deserves no more than he gets does not justify the Danites' behavior, however. The story depicts the tribe as a bunch of thugs, bullies who take what they want by brute force and threats. The tribe acts with increasing brutality as the chapter concludes. The account of Dan's acquisition of territory and establishment of a sanctuary satirically echo the Israelites' conquest of Canaan and their worship at Gilgal (Joshua 5 and 6). The storytellers express disapproval of the conquest of Laish by linking it to the theft of Micah's goods and by reiterating the unprovoked nature of the attack. "Having taken what Micah made," the Danites move on to a greater and more brutal crime. Laish was "a people quiet and unsuspecting " (v. 27) and the Danites slaughter them. The northern sanctuary is also mocked. Twice in five verses we are reminded that the object of Danite worship is an idol, the work of human hands (vv. 27 and 31), and a pilfered one at that.

The identification of Micah (now Dan's) Levitical priest (v. 30) is surprising. A descendant of Moses serving at an idolatrous shrine? Several ancient scribes found the note so disturbing that they altered the genealogy to read "son of Manasseh" rather than "son of Moses."

The final verses of the account fire additional barbs at Dan. In the context of an account of Dan's thuglike behavior, the reference to the northern kingdom's captivity (v. 30) comes across as a judgment. The reference may be to Assyrian assimilation of much of the northern kingdom (including Dan) in 734–32 B.C.E.; it may have to do with the Assyrian conquest and exile of Samaria in 722 B.C.E. The story does not explicitly attribute the "captivity" to Dan's offense; nonetheless, especially in light of Micah's fate, the implication is there.

The reference to the house of God at Shiloh (v. 31) is one last oblique critique of the sanctuary at Dan. The storytellers implicitly contrast the sanctuary at Shiloh, which they view as legitimate, with the stolen idol maintained at Dan.

According to the polemical account of Judges 18, the origin of the sanctuary at Dan occurred as follows: A man steals a huge amount of silver from his own mother. The accursed, pilfered silver is made into an idol, which the Danites, a bunch of thugs, steal. The Danites set the idol up in a city that they have taken by brute force from an unsuspecting, peaceful people. The priesthood at the sanctuary was founded by an opportunistic Levite who colluded in the idol worship and the theft.

Elsewhere, the Deuteronomistic Historians explicitly condemn the Danite sanctuary as a center of idolatry (1 Kgs. 12:28–31). To worship at Dan or Bethel is to "sin the sin of Jeroboam." The account in Judges 17 and 18 does not explicitly condemn the sanctuary; rather, it relies on satire to convey with devastating effect its anti-Danite polemic.

The account is not merely a southern polemic against the rival worship centers in the north, however. The tale of Micah's and Dan's idolatry is linked to the tale of violence and intertribal war involving all of Israel (Judges 19–21). In that context, Micah's and Dan's corrupt worship functions as an illustration of the disintegration of the religious life of Israel as a whole. The repeated assertion that "there was no king in Israel" (not "in Dan") also places Micah's and Dan's degeneracy in the larger context of Israelite disintegration. The tribes' religion has fallen into chaos.

In this chaos, Yahweh is conspicuously absent. Micah, his mother, and the Danites all assume that they are acting in Yahweh's name, but no direct reference to God's speaking or acting appears in the entire narrative. The one inquiry made of God receives a highly ambiguous answer. We have traced the relationship of Israel and its leaders to God throughout the stories of the deliverers. From the story of Deborah, whose words were identified with the words of God, to Samson, who by and large ignores Yahweh, the relationship spirals downward. Now, God appears to have abandoned Israel to a chaos of its own making: "All the people did what was right in their own eyes" (17:6).

25. The Body Severed
Judges 19–21

Israel's downward spiral continues in the final chapters of Judges. The first part of the conclusion, Judges 17–18, exemplifies the religious corruption into which the tribes have fallen. In the second part of the conclusion, Judges 19–21, the breakdown in Israel's relationship to God leads to mass social and political disintegration. A brutal act of gang rape/murder triggers intertribal war and more mass killings and rapes. The account of Israel's escalating disobedience ends with violence and chaos.

A number of literary connections link the tale of the founding of the Danite sanctuary (Judges 17–18) with the account of civil war (Judges 19–21). The first narrative features a Levite going from Bethlehem of Judah to the hill country of Ephraim; the second story begins with a Levite from the hill country of Ephraim journeying to Bethlehem. Both accounts involve breakdowns of relationships within the private sphere, breakdowns that lead to tribal, and eventually intertribal, violence. Both stand under the narrator's negative judgment; as mentioned earlier, the condemning phrase, "In those days there was no king in Israel; all the people did what was right in their own eyes," frames the two-part conclusion (Judg. 17:6; 21:25).

The account in Judges 19–21 is partly political propaganda in favor of David's dynasty. The "villains" are from Gibeah, the hometown of Saul, whose family David displaced. Benjamin, the tribe that fails to hand the miscreants over for judgment, is Saul's tribe. Later, Judah and its allies slaughter the citizens of Jabish-gilead, a town closely associated with Saul. Saul's allies, town, and tribe take a beating in this account.

In its final form, the story's critique is not limited to Saul's people. The Levite brutally sacrifices his wife to protect himself. The avenging tribes bewail the destruction they themselves bring upon Benjamin, and they attempt to aid the enemy they have decimated by annihilating yet another town of Israel. "All the people did what was right in their own eyes." As the book of Judges draws to a close, the fabric of Israelite society utterly unravels.

CONSIDER IT, TAKE COUNSEL, AND SPEAK
Judges 19

19:1 In those days, when there was no king in Israel, a certain Levite, residing in the remote parts of the hill country of Ephraim, took to himself a concubine from Bethlehem in Judah. [2] But his concubine became angry with him, and she went away from him to her father's house at Bethlehem in Judah, and was there some four months. [3] Then her husband set out after her, to speak tenderly to her and bring her back. He had with him his servant and a couple of donkeys. When he reached her father's house, the girl's father saw him and came with joy to meet him. [4] His father-in-law, the girl's father, made him stay, and he remained with him three days; so they ate and drank, and he stayed there. [5] On the fourth day they got up early in the morning, and he prepared to go; but the girl's father said to his son-in-law, "Fortify yourself with a bit of food, and after that you may go." [6] So the two men sat and ate and drank together; and the girl's father said to the man, "Why not spend the night and enjoy yourself?" [7] When the man got up to go, his father-in-law kept urging him until he spent the night there again. [8] On the fifth day he got up early in the morning to leave; and the girl's father said, "Fortify yourself." So they lingered until the day declined, and the two of them ate and drank. [9] When the man with his concubine and his servant got up to leave, his father-in-law, the girl's father, said to him, "Look, the day has worn on until it is almost evening. Spend the night. See, the day has drawn to a close. Spend the night here and enjoy yourself. Tomorrow you can get up early in the morning for your journey, and go home."

[10] But the man would not spend the night; he got up and departed, and arrived opposite Jebus (that is, Jerusalem). He had with him a couple of saddled donkeys, and his concubine was with him. [11] When they were near Jebus, the day was far spent, and the servant said to his master, "Come now, let us turn aside to this city of the Jebusites, and spend the night in it." [12] But his master said to him, "We will not turn aside into a city of foreigners, who do not belong to the people of Israel; but we will continue on to Gibeah." [13] Then he said to his servant, "Come, let us try to reach one of these places, and spend the night at Gibeah or at Ramah." [14] So they passed on and went their way; and the sun went down on them near Gibeah, which belongs to Benjamin. [15] They turned aside there, to go in and spend the night at Gibeah. He went in and sat down in the open square of the city, but no one took them in to spend the night.

[16] Then at evening there was an old man coming from his work in the field. The man was from the hill country of Ephraim, and he was residing in Gibeah. (The people of the place were Benjaminites.) [17] When the old man looked up and saw the wayfarer in the open square of the city, he said, "Where are you going and where do you come from?" [18] He answered him, "We are passing

from Bethlehem in Judah to the remote parts of the hill country of Ephraim, from which I come. I went to Bethlehem in Judah; and I am going to my home. Nobody has offered to take me in. [19] We your servants have straw and fodder for our donkeys, with bread and wine for me and the woman and the young man along with us. We need nothing more." [20] The old man said, "Peace be to you. I will care for all your wants; only do not spend the night in the square." [21] So he brought him into his house, and fed the donkeys; they washed their feet, and ate and drank.

[22] While they were enjoying themselves, the men of the city, a perverse lot, surrounded the house, and started pounding on the door. They said to the old man, the master of the house, "Bring out the man who came into your house, so that we may have intercourse with him." [23] And the man, the master of the house, went out to them and said to them, "No, my brothers, do not act so wickedly. Since this man is my guest, do not do this vile thing. [24] Here are my virgin daughter and his concubine; let me bring them out now. Ravish them and do whatever you want to them; but against this man do not do such a vile thing." [25] But the men would not listen to him. So the man seized his concubine, and put her out to them. They wantonly raped her, and abused her all through the night until the morning. And as the dawn began to break, they let her go. [26] As morning appeared, the woman came and fell down at the door of the man's house where her master was, until it was light.

[27] In the morning her master got up, opened the doors of the house, and when he went out to go on his way, there was his concubine lying at the door of the house, with her hands on the threshold. [28] "Get up," he said to her, "we are going." But there was no answer. Then he put her on the donkey; and the man set out for his home. [29] When he had entered his house, he took a knife, and grasping his concubine he cut her into twelve pieces, limb by limb, and sent her throughout all the territory of Israel. [30] Then he commanded the men whom he sent, saying, "Thus shall you say to all the Israelites, 'Has such a thing ever happened since the day that the Israelites came up from the land of Egypt until this day? Consider it, take counsel, and speak out.'"

The opening words of the narrative, "There was no king in Israel," link the account of the Levite's concubine to the story of Micah and his idol (Judg. 17:6), and the capture of Dan (Judg. 18:1). The phrase, echoed in Judges 21:25, also provides the perspective from which one is to view the remaining chapters: This is anarchy; this is wrong.

"Concubine" refers to a wife whose status is lower than that of a primary wife. Marriage in the ancient Near East normally entailed an exchange of property between the bride's family and the groom's. The exchange of goods not only increased the bride's status; it also made dissolving the marriage costly and difficult. Some scholars plausibly suggest that a "concubine" was a wife who did not bring property into the marriage. The concubine's children would have been considered legitimate heirs if there were no children by a primary wife, and the concubine herself would have had more rights than a slave-wife. She was not chattel. Nonetheless, her status would not have been high. In particular, dissolving the marriage was probably simple, entailing no financial settlement.

The notice that the wife has left her husband is surprising. No other biblical evidence suggests that Israelite women could initiate separation or divorce. Perhaps they had a right to do so unattested elsewhere in the Bible. In a later period, Jewish women in the Egyptian colony Elephantine were able to divorce their husbands. More likely, the story reflects the difference between formal legal rights and informal actual practices. An unhappy wife would have recourse to her father and brothers.

The narrator appears to disapprove of the woman's action. The Hebrew word "anger" (Judg. 19:2) actually means "to play the whore." The verb was probably not intended literally; an ancient Israelite father would hardly have offered shelter to an adulterous daughter, nor would an Israelite husband have sought reconciliation with an unfaithful wife. Rather, the narrator seems to view the concubine's departure, rejecting as it did the authority of her husband, as in and of itself promiscuous.

Verses 3–9 take place in Bethlehem, at the home of the concubine's father, where the Levite goes to fetch her back. "Speak tenderly" (v. 3) literally means "speak to her heart," that is, her will and reason, as well as her emotions. The word "heart" appears five more times in chapter 19. The phrase translated "fortify yourself" literally means "sustain your heart," while the Hebrew underlying the phrase "enjoy yourself" means "make your heart glad." Ironically, after the narrator tells us that the Levite is going to speak tenderly to his wife's heart, the rest of the scene is concerned with the Levite and his father-in-law's hearts, satisfaction, and pleasure.

Indeed, none of the narrative focuses attention on the woman's opinions and feelings. She plays a pivotal role in the story. Her departure serves as a literary device to explain the Levite's lengthy journey, and her gruesome fate is the occasion for all-out civil war. But the woman herself is not among the main characters in the story, nor is her fate among the narrator's chief concerns. In the male-dominated world of the narrator, kingship, tribal war, and male honor are what matter. The concubine is female, she is lower class, and so, in the narrator's eyes, she is of little value.

The exchange between the Levite and his father-in-law is marked by lavish hospitality. Three times the reader is told that the two men "ate and drank" (vv. 4, 6, 8). The host urges his son-in-law to "fortify" himself; twice he tells the son-in-law to enjoy himself. The exaggerated hospitality functions as a foil to the behavior of the Gibeonites who initially fail, then radically violate, the obligation to provide hospitality.

The continued feasting between the father and son-in-law also sheds a negative light on the Levite's character. Having failed to start out at a good hour, he foolishly departs when the day is far gone. Commentators calculate that it must have been late afternoon when the travelers set out. They reach Gibeah, a town about three hours from Bethlehem, at sunset, roughly six o'clock in the evening.

Repeated references to the time call attention to the lateness of the departure; the day has "declined," "worn on," "drawn to a close," until it is "almost evening" (vv. 8–9). Night is a dangerous time for wayfarers; the references to approaching nightfall, repeated in verses 11 and 14, begin to give the story an undercurrent of threat.

As they travel, a brief exchange takes place between the Levite and his servant about "Jebus." The storytellers believed that Jerusalem had been called "Jebus" before Israel conquered it. The name derives from the name of the town's inhabitants, the "Jebusites." In fact, ancient Near Eastern texts from the pre-Israelite period refer to the town as Jerusalem, never as Jebus. The servant proposes staying at Jebus; the Levite prefers to press on to the supposed safety of an Israelite town. Given the events at Gibeah, the Levite's decision is horribly ironic. The supposedly hostile foreign city would have been a better choice than the supposedly safe Israelite town.

Night overtakes the travelers at Gibeah. In the ancient Near East, hospitality to strangers was a sacred obligation, but none of the Gibeonites offer it. Their lack of hospitality comes across as loutish (v. 15). Only an Ephraimite, himself an alien in Gibeah, opens his home to the Levite and his party. That the host is Ephraimite may explain his sympathy for the Levite, who is from Ephraim. His resident alien status also suggests the host's vulnerability; he has no family network to protect himself or his guests from hostile neighbors.

The Ephraimite host's generosity recalls the father-in-law's hospitality. Again, the men "ate and drank" and "were enjoying themselves" (vv. 21–22). It also offers a contrast to the violence of what follows, a contrast that heightens the offense.

The men of Gibeah prove to be utterly depraved. The brutal scene in verses 22–25 parallels a story about threatened gang rape of a stranger in Sodom (Gen. 19:1–11). In both narratives, the town's citizens fail to offer shelter to a stranger (or strangers); in both, hospitality is extended by an outsider, a resident alien. In both, residents of the town demand that the host turn the stranger over to them, so that they might sexually abuse him. In both incidents, the host offers two females to be raped in the place of his male guest. For ancient Israel, Sodom epitomized ungodly violence and indifference to the poor (Ezek. 16:49). God's destruction of Sodom and Gomorrah was a paradigm of divine wrath. The Gibeonites prove to be as wicked as the men of Sodom. Indeed, they are worse, for while the men of Sodom threaten violence, the men of Gibeah carry out their threat. An Israelite town is worse than the non-Israelite Sodom, symbol of wickedness.

The Hebrew phrase translated "perverse lot" (Judg. 19:22) has been the subject of much discussion. The term literally means sons of wickedness or worthlessness, and is used especially of groups who threaten the social order. The perverse lot's double offense—violating hospitality and violent gang rape—are quintessential crimes against the social order.

That the threatened victim is male probably heightened the offense in the eyes of ancient Israelites. The issue is not sexual orientation. The perpetrators of gang rapes of men, far more often than not, consider themselves heterosexual. The kind of violence the "perverse lot" sought to perpetrate is not about sex, per se, but about hostility and domination, a violent demonstration of power over another. Bluntly stated, gang rape of a male would have been considered more atrocious than gang rape of a woman, because within a patriarchal culture, men are more valued than women.

That women were regarded as less valuable and hence more disposable than men explains the Ephraimite host's willingness to sacrifice his daughter and the Levite's wife to save the Levite. Lot's offer of his daughters, in the parallel story of Genesis 19, is often explained as a reflection of the sacred demands of hospitality. The obligation to protect his guest, it is said, requires the sacrifice of what is his, that is, his daughters. In the case of Judges 19, such an explanation is not possible.

The Levite's wife is the Ephraimite's guest. The law of hospitality ought to protect her. But although she is a guest, she is female, and she is lower class. Moreover, having once left her husband, she is stigmatized, sexually suspect. The host's offer discloses his unholy assumptions: such a women is expendable. A female may be sacrificed to save a male. A member of the lower class may be sacrificed to save a higher-class individual.

The language with which the Ephraimite offers the women—"Do whatever you want to them"—echoes the repeated phrase with which the editors condemn the anarchy into which Israel has fallen: "all the people did what was right in their own eyes." The phrase implicitly critiques the Ephraimite's offer. As at Sodom, the ruffians of Gibeah refuse the proffered exchange.

The stories of Sodom and of Gibeah diverge at this point. In Sodom, the guest saves the host by blinding the eyes of the perpetrators. At Gibeah, the guest "saves" the host and himself by pushing his wife out to the vicious mob. The text does not explicitly state whether the host or the Levite shoves the woman outside. Elsewhere in Judges 19, however, the editors use qualifying terms when referring to the father-in-law or the Ephraimite. The phrase "the man" consistently refers to the Levite. The Levite sacrifices his wife to save his own skin. Such an act would be reprehensible even in patriarchal culture. In ancient Israel, when a woman was under a man's authority, she was also under his protection.

The text reports the mob's prolonged rape and eventual release of the woman in one brief verse. The brevity of the report is in stark contrast to the interminable length of the abuse the woman endured "all through the night until morning."

The crass character of the Levite is highlighted in the following verses. The ruffians of Gibeah let the woman go as dawn breaks. She crawls to the door of the house, where she might expect help, and lies there, hands on the threshold in a mute, unheeded plea, until it is fully light. Where is the Levite? Is he awake? Worried? Ready to rescue her as soon as that becomes possible? The answer is found in verse 27. The Levite "got up" to go on his way. Having thrown his wife to a mob of violent men, the Levite went to bed. Now he gets up to go with his wife. His callousness is confirmed in the next verse. The Levite went to Bethlehem to "speak to the heart" of his wife; but he has not addressed her until now. The first word he says to her in this story is a brusque order: "Get up."

The Levite places the woman's inert body on a donkey. The reference to a woman on a donkey recalls the story of Achsah in Judges 1. There, also, a woman is astride a donkey. But Achsah is an articulate, assertive woman who demands and receives from her father springs of life-giving water. The Levite's wife is a speechless, nameless victim who receives only death. The contrast between Achsah and the woman of Judges 19 illustrates the social chaos into which Israel has fallen.

The Levite's final encounter with his wife is an act that Phyllis Trible rightly calls an "extravagance of violence" (Trible, 1984, 65–91). He dismembers her, sending her body parts to the various tribes as a call to war. The Levite's act is a brutal and grotesque parody of Saul, mustering the tribes to rescue their fellow Israelites in 1 Samuel 11. According to that story, when Jabesh-gilead is threatened by Ammonite enemies, Saul butchers an ox, sending pieces of it to the tribes with the message that anyone who fails to respond to the call to rescue Jabesh-gilead will be similarly

butchered. In contrast, the Levite's act is not symbolic. This act of gratu-
itous violence is designed to inspire horror. In a culture where proper
mourning and burial mattered greatly, the act is especially abhorrent.

The text does not explicitly condemn the Levite's action, nor does it
approve it. The NRSV follows the Greek version of the story in Judges
19:29–30. The Hebrew is missing the Levite's instructions to the messengers sent to carry their grisly message throughout Israel. Instead, the words
"has such a thing ever happened" are exclaimed by the tribes upon seeing
the severed parts of the woman's body. The "thing" may be the Gibeanites' violence; it may be the Levite's dismemberment of the woman.

Unlike the Greek version and the NRSV translation, the Hebrew text also
carefully avoids identifying the moment at which the woman dies. Is it at
the threshold? On the donkey? Under the Levite's knife? The storytellers
identify her as a "woman who was murdered" (Judg. 20:4), but do not indicate who murdered her.

"Consider it, take council, and speak out" (19:30) summons Israel to
assemble for deliberations. How shall they respond to such gross immorality, such utter violence? The same question—and the same command—is
issued to the reader. What should we do with such a violent text?

What we should not do is assume that the authors approved of what
happened. The Gibeonites, the Ephraimite host, the Levites, and (later)
the Israelites all stand under the judgment of the text. The storytellers'
purpose is to illustrate the moral and social depravity into which Israel had
fallen in the anarchic period when "there was no king in Israel." This state
of affairs is seen in their failure to explicate who killed the woman, in their
use of parody, and in the political chaos that ensues from the rape and from
the Levite's actions. In the Bible, rape consistently represents a breakdown
in order, and leads to further chaos and bloodshed (Gen. 34; 2 Sam. 13).
The authors and audiences of this text certainly abhorred it.

Nonetheless, the story is shaped by patriarchal assumptions. Like Jephthah's daughter, the woman is expendable. As one commentator notes, the
Levite's indifference to her fate is at least partly shared by the narrator. She
is viewed as a victim, and her fate is seen as an outrage, but she is given no
voice. She acts twice: she leaves her husband's house and she crawls back
to the house where her husband is staying. For the rest, she is an object.
Most of the time, she is ignored.

How should we respond to such a text? The question is challenging.
Over the past decade, women and men concerned about how biblical
interpretation affects the welfare of women have begun to identify helpful
ways to respond to texts of violence against women. A first step is to try to

understand the passage in its historical and its literary contexts. But one must recognize that some stories in the Bible reflect values at variance with the deepest and best ideals and values that the Bible teaches. The patriarchal assumptions shaping Judges 19 conflict with the biblical insistence that God created all humankind, male and female, in God's own image. The Bible bears witness to a God who loves and liberates all humanity. Such a witness calls upon us to name and resist violence against God's daughters and sons, even when the violence is found in the Bible itself. Not to do so is to be complicit in the Levite's and the narrator's indifference, and to risk passing on values that one abhors.

Biblical stories and biblical characters are not always models. They are quite often mirrors that reflect back to the reader life as it is, in all its brokenness and sin, not life as it should be. Tragically, women are raped, even to death. They are murdered by their husbands, or suffer unspeakable mob violence. Phyllis Trible calls upon communities of faith to tell such terrible stories as acts of solidarity with the victims of violence and as acts of mourning for their suffering. She calls on us to tell such stories as acts of repentance and of resistance (Trible, 1984, 1–5). Perhaps the best response is found in the biblical story itself. The last half of verse 30 literally means "Direct your heart to her. Take council. Speak out!" Remember the nameless woman of Judges 19 and all her violated sisters.

THE POLITICAL BODY SEVERED
Judges 20

In Judges 19, Israelite anarchy is exemplified by a brutal gang rape and murder. In Judges 20, all Israel gathers in one body under Yahweh to punish the offenders. At first glance, the description of the tribal assembly in chapter 20 looks positive, even ideal. The Israelites act with unprecedented unity. The assembly and ensuing battle are described in sacred language. The battle has all the characteristics of holy war.

Some scholars view the account as a picture of the ancient tribal assembly as later editors thought it ought to have functioned. Others understand it as a picture of ancient institutions gone terribly awry. This commentary follows the latter tack, interpreting the final chapters of Judges as a parody of sacred assembly and holy war.

The assembly gathers in judgment. But the Levite's testimony is skewed, and the tribes' response is exaggerated. The outcome is devastating. Bent on punishing Gibeah and its tribe, Benjamin, the Israelites suffer a twofold defeat, then win a victory more bitter than defeat. Rape and murder of one woman leads to the near extinction of a tribe—a "breach" in the people Israel that is "repaired" only by mass slaughter and mass rape. The final chapters of Judges paint a picture of utter disintegration of Israelite social, religious, and political life.

20:1 Then all the Israelites came out, from Dan to Beer-sheba, including the land of Gilead, and the congregation assembled in one body before the LORD at Mizpah. ² The chiefs of all the people, of all the tribes of Israel, presented themselves in the assembly of the people of God, four hundred thousand foot-soldiers bearing arms. ³ (Now the Benjaminites heard that the people of Israel had gone up to Mizpah.) And the Israelites said, "Tell us, how did this criminal act come about?" ⁴ The Levite, the husband of the woman who was murdered, answered, "I came to Gibeah that belongs to Benjamin, I and my concubine, to spend the night. ⁵ The lords of Gibeah rose up against me, and surrounded the house at night. They intended to kill me, and they raped my concubine until she died. ⁶ Then I took my concubine and cut her into pieces, and sent her throughout the whole extent of Israel's territory; for they have committed a vile outrage in Israel. ⁷ So now, you Israelites, all of you, give your advice and counsel here."

⁸ All the people got up as one, saying, "We will not any of us go to our tents, nor will any of us return to our houses. ⁹ But now this is what we will do to Gibeah: we will go up against it by lot. ¹⁰ We will take ten men of a hundred throughout all the tribes of Israel, and a hundred of a thousand, and a thousand of ten thousand, to bring provisions for the troops, who are going to repay Gibeah of Benjamin for all the disgrace that they have done in Israel." ¹¹ So all the men of Israel gathered against the city, united as one.

¹² The tribes of Israel sent men through all the tribe of Benjamin, saying, "What crime is this that has been committed among you? ¹³ Now then, hand over those scoundrels in Gibeah, so that we may put them to death, and purge the evil from Israel." But the Benjaminites would not listen to their kinsfolk, the Israelites. ¹⁴ The Benjaminites came together out of the towns to Gibeah, to go out to battle against the Israelites. ¹⁵ On that day the Benjaminites mustered twenty-six thousand armed men from their towns, besides the inhabitants of Gibeah. ¹⁶ Of all this force, there were seven hundred picked men who were left-handed; every one could sling a stone at a hair, and not miss. ¹⁷ And the Israelites, apart from Benjamin, mustered four hundred thousand armed men, all of them warriors.

¹⁸ The Israelites proceeded to go up to Bethel, where they inquired of God, "Which of us shall go up first to battle against the Benjaminites?" And the LORD answered, "Judah shall go up first."

¹⁹ Then the Israelites got up in the morning, and encamped against Gibeah. ²⁰ The Israelites went out to battle against Benjamin; and the

Israelites drew up the battle line against them at Gibeah. [21] The Benjaminites came out of Gibeah, and struck down on that day twenty-two thousand of the Israelites. [22] The Israelites went up and wept before the LORD until the evening; and they inquired of the LORD, "Shall we again draw near to battle against our kinsfolk the Benjaminites?" And the LORD said, "Go up against them." [23] The Israelites took courage, and again formed the battle line in the same place where they had formed it on the first day.

[24] So the Israelites advanced against the Benjaminites the second day. [25] Benjamin moved out against them from Gibeah the second day, and struck down eighteen thousand of the Israelites, all of them armed men. [26] Then all the Israelites, the whole army, went back to Bethel and wept, sitting there before the LORD; they fasted that day until evening. Then they offered burnt offerings and sacrifices of well-being before the LORD. [27] And the Israelites inquired of the LORD (for the ark of the covenant of God was there in those days, [28] and Phinehas son of Eleazar, son of Aaron, ministered before it in those days), saying, "Shall we go out once more to battle against our kinsfolk the Benjaminites, or shall we desist?" The LORD answered, "Go up, for tomorrow I will give them into your hand."

[29] So Israel stationed men in ambush around Gibeah. [30] Then the Israelites went up against the Benjaminites on the third day, and set themselves in array against Gibeah, as before. [31] When the Benjaminites went out against the army, they were drawn away from the city. As before they began to inflict casualties on the troops, along the main roads, one of which goes up to Bethel and the other to Gibeah, as well as in the open country, killing about thirty men of Israel. [32] The Benjaminites thought, "They are being routed before us, as previously." But the Israelites said, "Let us retreat and draw them away from the city toward the roads." [33] The main body of the Israelites drew back its battle line to Baal-tamar, while those Israelites who were in ambush rushed out of their place west of Geba. [34] There came against Gibeah ten thousand picked men out of all Israel, and the battle was fierce. But the Benjaminites did not realize that disaster was close upon them.

[35] The LORD defeated Benjamin before Israel; and the Israelites destroyed twenty-five thousand one hundred men of Benjamin that day, all of them armed.

[36] Then the Benjaminites saw that they were defeated.

The Israelites gave ground to Benjamin, because they trusted to the troops in ambush that they had stationed against Gibeah. [37] The troops in ambush rushed quickly upon Gibeah. Then they put the whole city to the sword. [38] Now the agreement between the main body of Israel and the men in ambush was that when they sent up a cloud of smoke out of the city [39] the main body of Israel should turn in battle. But Benjamin had begun to inflict casualties on the Israelites, killing about thirty of them; so they thought, "Surely they are defeated before us, as in the first battle." [40] But when the cloud, a column of smoke, began to rise out of the city, the Benjaminites looked behind them—and there was the whole city going up in smoke toward the sky! [41] Then the main body of Israel turned, and the Benjaminites were dismayed, for they saw that disaster was close upon them. [42] Therefore they turned away from the Israelites in the direction of the wilderness; but the battle overtook them, and those who came out of the city were slaughtering them in between. [43] Cutting down the Benjaminites, they pursued them from Nohah and trod them down as far as a place east of Gibeah. [44] Eighteen thousand Benjaminites fell, all of them courageous fighters. [45] When they turned and fled toward the wilderness to the rock of Rimmon, five thousand of them were cut down on the main roads, and they were pursued as far as Gidom, and two thousand of them were slain. [46] So all who fell that day of Benjamin were twenty-five thousand arms-bearing men, all of them courageous fighters. [47] But six hundred turned and fled toward the wilderness to the rock of Rimmon, and remained at the rock of Rimmon for four months. [48] Meanwhile, the Israelites turned back against the Benjaminites, and put them to the sword—the city, the people, the animals, and all that remained. Also the remaining towns they set on fire.

According to 1 Samuel 11:7, the tribes respond to Saul's summons, conveyed by a dismembered ox, with unity. They "come out" "as one." In Judges 20, the allied tribes respond to the grisly summons conveyed by the woman's dismembered body with unified, horrified zeal. The tribes "came out" as "one body." Their unity is emphasized by the geographic note in Judges 20:1. "Dan to Beersheba" marks out the ideal extent of Israelite territory. Dan is the religious sanctuary in the far north of Israel (see chapter 18); Beersheba is a religious sanctuary in the southern tip of Judah. Gilead is Israel's land east of the Jordan; Dan to Beersheba plus Gilead comprises all of Israel. "All of the people," "all of the tribes," gather as "one body."

Normally in the Bible, unified Israelite action is desirable. In the context of Judges, however, it may be more ominous than positive. The Israelites act in concert only two other times in the book; both are negative. "All the Israelites" gather and weep at the angel's indictment in Judges 2:4. "All Israel" prostitute themselves to Gideon's ephod in Judges 8:27.

The tribes' response in Judges 20 is stated in religious language. They gather before Yahweh at Mizpah, a sanctuary on the boundary between Benjamin and Ephraim. (Again one notes an anti-Saul twist to the story; Mizpah is the site of Saul's coronation.) The Israelites are referred to as the "people of God." The words "assembly" and "congregation" are religious terms.

As depicted by the Deuteronomistic authors, one function of the tribal assembly is to bring to trial and to punish individual or communal wrongdoers. In Judges 20, the assembly gathers to hear the Levite's complaint. For the reader, discrepancies between the Levite's testimony and the narrator's version of the events discredit the Levite. The Levite indicts the leaders of Gibeah, its "lords," rather than a criminal element of the town, a "perverse lot." He claims that these lords "tried to kill" him rather than that the men threatened to rape him. Perhaps he wants to avoid repeating the humiliating threat; perhaps he is highlighting the danger to himself in order to excuse his failure to protect his wife. Moreover, he omits any reference to his own role in the events, that is, to his pushing his wife out to the mob. The Levite's testimony gives the impression that he narrowly escaped with his life and was unable to save his wife.

The tribes' response to the Levite's testimony is as unified as their response to the summons. They get up "as one" and gather "against the city, united as one." The eleven allied tribes give Benjamin a chance to avoid battle by surrendering the offenders. (The term "scoundrels" in verse 13 is the same word translated "perverse lot" in Judg. 19:22.) Their demand recognizes Benjaminite authority over and accountability for tribal members.

Benjamin's rejection of the demand is not unexpected. Their response to an armed threat in this story is consistent with their reputation as a proud and warlike tribe.

The reference to seven hundred left-handed (or, better, ambidextrous) elite fighters is a link with an earlier ambidextrous assassin, Ehud (Judges 3). Here, the phrase describes a whole contingent of crackerjack shots, partly explaining how the vastly outnumbered Benjaminites are able to resist the Israelites.

The account of the war against Benjamin is highly schematized. Three battles take place, each beginning with the tribes going to Bethel to "inquire" of Yahweh, to seek God's will by divination. Bethel is located on the Benjaminite-Ephraim boundary. Like Dan, it was designated a royal sanctuary by the northern kingdom's first king.

Before the first battle, the Israelite tribes "inquire" not whether to go to war, but who is to go first. Perhaps the reader is to understand that they are overconfident, given their numerical superiority. The inquiry also recalls the opening verses of Judges, where the tribes inquire who is to go first (Judg. 1:1). But in Judges 1, the battle is against the Canaanites. Here, it is against their kinsmen. The answer is the same as in Judges 1:2; Judah is to go first. But while God promises to give Judah victory in Judges 1:2, no such promise is voiced in the opening of this civil war.

Each of the three battle scenes moves from inquiry at Bethel to battle itself. Little description of the first campaign is offered (Judg. 20:19–21) except to say that it is a rout, resulting in twenty-two thousand Israelite casualties, or (as some would translate the phrase) the loss of twenty-two contingents. After the battle, the people weep, as they wept at Bochim (Judg. 2:1–5).

The second battle also begins with inquiry of Yahweh at Bethel. This time, the Israelites do ask whether to go into battle. The answer is "yes" but, again, no promise of victory is forthcoming. And again, the Israelites are defeated.

A third time, the united tribes go to Bethel. Again they weep. This time, they also fast and make sacrifices. Again they inquire of God whether or not to continue the battle. This third time, the tribes' inquiry presents the alternative possibility of refraining from war. But the answer again is "go up," this time accompanied by a promise of victory worded similarly to the promise in Judges 1:2.

The tribes' victorious battle against Benjamin, narrated in verses 29–48, seems muddled. Auld aptly compares the passage to two slides of a scene simultaneously projected onto a screen. The main outline is clear enough, but the details are fuzzy (Auld, 1984, 245).

The Israelites' strategy resembles the tactics that brought them victory at Ai (Joshua 8). A small group of warriors lies hidden, ready to ambush the city, while the main Israelite army lures the Benjaminite troops away from the town walls. As at Ai, the strategy is successful. The Benjaminites, falsely confident that they will once again win, pursue the Israelites feigning retreat. The men lying in ambush take the undefended town, slaughter its citizens, and torch the city. Then both they and the main army turn and attack the Benjaminite army in a pincerlike trap.

The parallels between the battle at Gibeah and the battle at Ai serve to point out the difference in the two stories. At Ai, Israel defeats a Canaanite city. At Gibeah, they decimate one of their own tribes.

The editors seem to have juggled the numbers in Judges 20:44–46 to match the tally in verse 35. In any case, both suggest overwhelming casualties. Only a small remnant survive. The rest of the population not only of Gibeah but of the whole of Benjamin is slain (v. 45). Although the storytellers do not use the word, the Israelite destruction of Benjamin looks like *herem*, the ban. They put to the sword the people, the animals, all.

The battle against Gibeah is not the first instance of intertribal strife in the Deuteronomistic History. Already in Joshua 22, the western tribes threaten war against the tribes east of the Jordan. There, war is averted. Gideon diplomatically averts civil war with Ephraim, but carries out a vendetta against two towns that are either Israelite or allies of Israel. Jehpthah does engage in battle against Israelites; his Gileadites kill Ephraimites. The escalating strife between the tribes culminates in chapter 20 in all-out civil war, and the disaster is nearly total. Only six hundred Benjaminites survive.

To modern sensibilities, "holy war" against non-Israelites is as disturbing as civil war within the tribal league. That opinion would not hold for an ancient Israelite audience, as is made clear by the emphasis that the Benjaminites are kin (Judg. 20:13, 23, 28) and especially by the tribes' bitter lament that there is "one tribe lacking in Israel" (Judg. 21:3). The rip in the social fabric of Israel appears irreparable. Despite the unity of the tribal action and the religious language in which the deliberations and the battle are couched, the story illustrates the disintegration of Israelite social and political structures. The assembly accepts the half-truths of the Levite's testimony. Their response, slaughtering twenty-five thousand warriors and murdering thousands more women and children, is totally disproportionate to the crime, horrific though it was. The people war against their own, making a "breach in the tribes of Israel" (Judg. 21:15). Judges 2 had warned that worship of other gods would lead Israel into a downward spiral, with each generation worse than those who went before. What was warned about comes to pass. Apostasy leads to social chaos.

There remains an unanswered question: How is one to understand the role of God in this story? Twice, God answers the Israelite inquiry and the tribes go out to battle, only to face defeat. The third time, things appear to work as they are supposed to. After weeping and sacrifice, the tribes' inquiry carefully refrains from limiting God's response; it includes the option of resuming battle or desisting from war.

The answer, "go up," is accompanied by a promise of victory couched in nearly the same language as divine assurance to Joshua and to Judah before the Israelites commit apostasy. Moreover, the promise is made good. God gives Israel victory. But the victory is more grievous than defeat. After their losses, the tribes weep at Bethel (Judg. 20:23, 26). After they win, they weep "bitterly" (Judg. 21:2).

Commentators suggest different explanations for God's role in this narrative. Some argue that the tribes carry out their inquiries improperly. Initially they ask not "should we go up," but "who should go up first." The second time, they ask the right question, but only the third time do they offer sacrifices. That time they receive a trustworthy answer.

This explanation falters, however, in that the fulfillment of the divine promise proves bitter. Moreover, believing that the writers want to depict God as playing a kind of "Simon says" game with Israel is difficult. Perhaps the most likely explanation is that the defeats and the victory should be seen as divine chastisement. One commentator notes that the Gibeanites are not only Benjaminite; they are also Israelites. All are implicated in the guilt.

Possibly the Israelites' minds are made up and battle is a forgone conclusion before the tribes ever consult Yahweh. They "came out" against Benjamin; "come out" is often a military term. Moreover, they came out armed, determined to act. They appoint quartermaster corps and go armed, to give Benjamin an ultimatum before they consider inquiring of God. The initial inquiry is not open to the possibility that their plans do not reflect divine will. Possibly the Israelites' minds are so set that they can no longer hear a contrary word.

Is it also possible the tribes' repeated apostasy has so violated their relationship with God that they are no longer able to discern false words from true oracles?

In Ezekiel 14:3, the prophet, speaking on behalf of God, warns that Israel cannot worship idols, then turn and expect to hear a word from Yahweh: " . . . these men have taken their idols into their hearts, and placed their iniquity as a stumbling block before them; shall I let myself be consulted by them?" Ezekiel goes on to say,

> For any of those of the house of Israel, or of the aliens who reside in Israel, who separate themselves from me, taking their idols into their hearts and placing their iniquity as a stumbling block before them, and yet come to a prophet to inquire of me by him, I the LORD will answer them myself. I will set my face against them; I will make them a sign and a byword and cut them off from the midst of my people; and you shall know that I am the LORD. (Ezek. 14:7–8)

Perhaps the account of Israel's battle against Benjamin conveys in story form the reality that Ezekiel declares as divine speech. One need not believe in a punitive God to recognize that entrenched behaviors, attitudes, and habits can distort perceptions of God's will, can make wrong look right, and right look ungodly. Perhaps the people's relationship to God had so deteriorated that it was no longer possible for them to hear the divine word.

BITTER FRUITS
Judges 21

The Israelites have killed all but six hundred Benjaminite men and have slaughtered all of the women and children of that tribe. In chapter 21, the reader learns that the tribes have also sworn not to intermarry with the Benjaminites. The threatened extinction of a tribe that the Israelites have brought about is now a source of bitter grief to them. Chapter 21 narrates two parallel Israelite efforts to circumvent the consequences of their actions. Each effort entails further violence and violation.

21:1 Now the Israelites had sworn at Mizpah, "No one of us shall give his daughter in marriage to Benjamin." ² And the people came to Bethel, and sat there until evening before God, and they lifted up their voices and wept bitterly. ³ They said, "O LORD, the God of Israel, why has it come to pass that today there should be one tribe lacking in Israel?" ⁴ On the next day, the people got up early, and built an altar there, and offered burnt offerings and sacrifices of well-being. ⁵ Then the Israelites said, "Which of all the tribes of Israel did not come up in the assembly to the LORD?" For a solemn oath had been taken concerning whoever did not come up to the LORD to Mizpah, saying, "That one shall be put to death." ⁶ But the Israelites had compassion for Benjamin their kin, and said, "One tribe is cut off from Israel this day. ⁷ What shall we do for wives for those who are left, since we have sworn by the LORD that we will not give them any of our daughters as wives?"

⁸ Then they said, "Is there anyone from the tribes of Israel who did not come up to the LORD to Mizpah?" It turned out that no one from Jabesh-gilead had come to the camp, to the assembly. ⁹ For when the roll was called among the people, not one of the inhabitants of Jabesh-gilead was there. ¹⁰ So the congregation sent twelve thousand soldiers there and commanded them, "Go, put the inhabitants of Jabesh-gilead to the sword, including the women and the little ones. ¹¹ This is what you shall do; every male and every woman that has lain with a male you shall devote to destruction." ¹² And they found among the inhabitants of Jabesh-gilead four hundred young virgins who had never slept with a man and brought them to the camp at Shiloh, which is in the land of Canaan.

¹³ Then the whole congregation sent word to the Benjaminites who were at the rock of Rimmon, and proclaimed peace to them. ¹⁴ Benjamin returned at that time; and they gave them the women whom they had saved alive of the women of Jabesh-gilead; but they did not suffice for them.

¹⁵ The people had compassion on Benjamin because the LORD had made a breach in the tribes of Israel. ¹⁶ So the elders of the congregation said, "What shall we do for wives for those who are left, since there are no women left in Benjamin?" ¹⁷ And they said, "There must be heirs for the survivors of

Benjamin, in order that a tribe may not be blotted out from Israel. [18] Yet we cannot give any of our daughters to them as wives." For the Israelites had sworn, "Cursed be anyone who gives a wife to Benjamin." [19] So they said, "Look, the yearly festival of the LORD is taking place at Shiloh, which is north of Bethel, on the east of the highway that goes up from Bethel to Shechem, and south of Lebonah." [20] And they instructed the Benjaminites, saying, "Go and lie in wait in the vineyards, [21] and watch; when the young women of Shiloh come out to dance in the dances, then come out of the vineyards and each of you carry off a wife for himself from the young women of Shiloh, and go to the land of Benjamin. [22] Then if their fathers or their brothers come to complain to us, we will say to them, 'Be generous and allow us to have them; because we did not capture in battle a wife for each man. But neither did you incur guilt by giving your daughters to them.'" [23] The Benjaminites did so; they took wives for each of them from the dancers whom they abducted. Then they went and returned to their territory, and rebuilt the towns, and lived in them. [24] So the Israelites departed from there at that time by tribes and families, and they went out from there to their own territories.

[25] In those days there was no king in Israel; all the people did what was right in their own eyes.

The eleven tribes return to the sanctuary at Bethel where they had twice lamented their defeat. Now they lament their victory. Their question in Judges 21:3 is less an effort to obtain information than a protest against the outcome of the war. The lamentation is ironic. "Why, O Lord, why?" they cry. The answer is obvious. They themselves went to war; they engaged in the massive slaughter of noncombatants, killing all of the Benjaminite women and children as well as most of the Benjaminite men; and they made an oath that would prevent the survivors from rebuilding the tribe. In a collective buck-passing gesture, the Israelites blame the consequences of their actions on God. Not surprisingly, God is silent.

As they had previously done, the Israelite tribes weep and offer sacrifices at Bethel. (Why they build a new altar is unclear.) Unlike the previous assemblies at the sanctuary, this time the tribes make no inquiry of God.

Rather, they determine their own plans for obtaining wives for the surviving Benjaminite men. The plans involve first battle with Jabesh-gilead and then enabling the Benjaminites to kidnap young female dancers at Shiloh for wives. The two strategies may have been alternate versions of the same basic tradition. In the final form of the text, they are presented as sequential stories.

The battle at Jabesh-gilead is prompted by the Israelites' recollection that they had vowed to put to death anyone who failed to answer the initial summons to fight the Benjaminites. Such an oath is not implausible. Saul is said to make a similar vow when he summons the tribes to aid Jabesh-gilead in 1 Samuel 11. But in Judges 21, the Israelites appear to recall their vow only because they discover a need for a supply of young virgins, not for the sake of the oath itself.

With bitter irony, the story tells that the Israelites seek to prevent one tribe from extinction by exterminating a city. Their justification for doing so is distorted. Out of compassion for Benjamin, their kin (Judg. 21:6), lest they be exterminated, the tribes slaughter the people of Jabesh-gilead, also their kin, on the grounds that Jabesh-gilead had not sent warriors to help kill the Benjaminites.

The number of soldiers sent to take the city, like the number of Israelites and Benjaminites earlier mustered, is greatly exaggerated. The command given to the soldiers, to kill all but the marriageable girls of the town, is reminiscent of Moses' instructions in the war against the Midianites (Num. 31:15–18). The storytellers seem to have used that tradition as a source. "Devotion" of enemy populations "to destruction" is an element of "holy war" ideology (see pp. 49–53). Only in these two passages and in the story of battle against Sihon (Deut. 2:34) does the ban explicitly include Israelite slaughter of "the little ones." Only in Judges 21 are the murdered little ones Israelite.

Murder begets murder in the first effort to secure wives for the Benjaminites. In the second effort, rape leads to additional rape. The elders' plot to get around their oaths by conspiring with Benjamin to kidnap dancers at Shiloh is exquisite sophistry.

The narrative appears to be a late addition. Parenthetical remarks giving Shiloh's location (v. 19) suggest that the site was no longer well-known. The location connects Judges 21 with the story of Hannah and Samuel in 1 Samuel 1, which also takes place at the yearly festival at Shiloh.

Commentators agree that the tradition of Benjaminites's kidnapping their brides is a fictionalized account. The compilers seem to have developed the story of the seizure of the girls of Shiloh to connect the final scene of the book with the rape at Gibeah. The story demonstrates spreading social chaos as violence begets violence.

The language in which the story is told is more violent in the Hebrew than it appears in the NRSV translation. Three Hebrew terms are particularly worth noting. The phrase translated "lie in wait" is the same word used to describe the ambush of Gibeah in Judges 20:37. Apart from military situations, the verb is found in contexts of violence and wickedness. One "lies in wait" to take a life or to commit adultery. The verb translated "carry off" is found only twice in the Bible, here and in Psalm 10:9, where it is also connected with the verb "lie in wait" to describe the behavior of "the wicked": "They lurk in secret like a lion in its covert; they lurk that they may seize the poor; they seize the poor and drag them off in their net." Just so, the elders of Israel advise the Benjaminite men to "lurk" and "seize" the young girls of Shiloh.

The final verb used to describe the Benjaminites' actions in verse 23, translated "abducted," is a common verb meaning "rob" or "plunder" when used of a thing; it is described as a trespass against God in Leviticus 6:2. Abducting a person usually involves a different verb. In any case, abduction is a grave offense. Torah provides the death penalty for kidnapping an Israelite (Exod. 21:16; Deut. 24:7).

In ancient Israel, the rape of a girl or woman was considered primarily an offense against her father, brother, or (if she were married) her husband. The act dishonored the males who had authority over the female. The tribal elders anticipate that the abduction of the young women of Shiloh is liable to inflame their fathers and brothers. They prepare a justification of the violence, framing the rape of the virgins as an act of grace for the men of Shiloh, who did not have to break their oaths and incur guilt. The justification is another example of blatant hypocrisy.

The storytellers' evaluation of the closing chapters of Judges is conveyed by the final verse: "In those days there was no king in Israel; all the people did what was right in their own eyes." The chaos and rebellion hinted at in chapter 1 is rampant. Israel is disintegrating at all levels: the personal and public spheres, the households, cities, and tribes; all are in chaos.

Israel's downward spiral is reflected in the treatment of the women. The book begins with the stories of Achsah and of Deborah, women who act forcefully and effectively; Judges ends with the rape/murder of the Levite's wife and the kidnapping and rape of the daughters of Shiloh. The life of the "people of God" in their promised land appears to have degenerated into spiritual, moral, and political bankruptcy.

For an exilic audience, the downward spiral that characterizes Judges provided an explanation for the judgment that they had suffered. Apostasy, turning from God, undoes the basis of Israelite identity. The fabric of the community unravels. Israel had been warned again and again. Joshua said it would be so. The messenger of God at Bochim left no room for doubt. Judgment follows apostasy.

What mercy is there, then? What hope? In the concluding chapters of Judges, none. But the story of God's ways with God's people does not end with Judges 21. Given the repeated warnings issued to Israel, the disintegration the tribes suffered is expected. What is unexpected is that apostasy, violence, and anarchy are not the final words.

Mercy and hope are found precisely in the fact that the story of Israel continues. It continues in two ways, depending on what version one consults. In the Hebrew text, 1 and 2 Samuel come immediately after Judges. The failure of charismatic leadership is followed by the rise of the monarchy. The Deuteronomistic History includes divergent views of kingship. One view is that the king is given by God to mediate divine blessing and governance. The word to the exiles is that divine mercy extends beyond judgment. When all familiar structures are at an end, God opens up new, unexpected ways into the future.

The breakdown of the old era of charismatic leadership ends with violence against women. Perhaps it is not accidental that the story of the new era, the monarchy, begins with an account of a strong, faithful woman, Hannah—a barren woman whose miraculous pregnancy brings new life to Israel.

The NRSV and other Protestant Bibles follow the ancient Greek versions, placing Ruth after Judges. The story provides a model of covenant faithfulness and loyalty, illustrating how communal life is intended to be lived.

The story of Ruth is not overidealized. Famine, bereavement, and economic destitution are all present. But the story moves from emptiness to fullness, from death to life. The story of apostasy leading to social chaos and violence in the book of Judges is followed by a story of covenantal faithfulness leading to harmony and blessing in Ruth. Acting with integrity and faithfulness in the daily struggle for survival, Ruth and her mother-in-law, Naomi, find redemption.

Ruth

Introduction to the Book of Ruth

The book of Ruth, which is meant to be read or heard at one sitting, is a beautifully composed work whose themes are woven through the whole of the book. If you have not already read the story, you would do well to read it before consulting this commentary.

THE STYLE, GENRE, LOCATION, AND DATING OF RUTH

Like Joshua and Judges, Ruth is part of ancient Israel's conversation about its origins. Within that conversation, the book speaks with a voice that is quite distinguishable from the Deuteronomistic History. Its vocabulary and structure differ from the flowery prose and collagelike character of Joshua through Second Kings. With the exception of the last five verses, the book of Ruth seems to be the work of a single storyteller, one highly skilled at crafting a tale.

Ruth is also a different kind of literature than the Deuteronomistic History. Joshua and Judges are theology in the guise of history. Its compilers focus attention on public issues and events. Most commentators consider Ruth a "novella," that is, a short story made up of several scenes. It has to do with a single family, and especially with two women in that family: Naomi and Ruth. The story has public implications, but its focus is not public events but rather God at work in human relationships, as people treat one another faithfully.

(It should be noted that to call Ruth a story rather than history is not to say that it is somehow less than true. Great literature discloses truths unavailable through historical reports. Novels like *The Brothers Karamazov* or *The Color Purple*, for example, use the language of metaphor, fiction, and poetry to speak truths far more profound than, say, the committee minutes sitting on my desk, even though the committee minutes are more historically factual.)

Originally, Ruth may not have been located with the books comprising the Deuteronomistic History. The Jewish Bible follows ancient Hebrew manuscripts in placing Ruth in the Writings, that is, the section of the canon that includes Psalms, Proverbs, Job, and the like. The Christian tradition of putting Ruth after Judges also has ancient roots; it follows ancient Greek and Latin versions of the Bible. But most commentators believe that the placement of Ruth among the Writings came first.

Ruth may have been written around the same time period as Joshua and Judges. While the dating of Ruth is very uncertain, Frederic Bush's recent study comparing the features of the language of the book with early and late Hebrew suggests that Ruth was written just before, during, or soon after the Babylonian exile of the sixth century B.C.E., which is when the Deuteronomistic Historians compiled their work (Bush, 1996, 18–30). Nonetheless, it represents a different voice from that period.

THE MESSAGE OF THE BOOK OF RUTH: AN ONGOING CONVERSATION

Ruth is a brief book, containing only eighty-five verses. Moreover, the book displays a level of coherence that is rarely found in the Hebrew Bible, and it presents remarkably few translation issues. Nonetheless, the book has given rise to an amazing array of interpretations.

For many biblical theologians, Ruth is a book about *hesed*, that is, loving faithfulness. Ruth, Naomi, and Boaz extend loyalty and care toward one another that goes beyond what is socially expected or legally required. That approach to the book is often linked to an emphasis on the powerful, though hidden, providence of God, working through faithful human beings to bring about blessing. In contrast, other biblical interpreters see the actions of the characters in Ruth as ambiguous; at least a few recent interpreters argue that Boaz and Naomi, at least, act with mixed motives and vested interests.

For a number of commentators, the story of Ruth, which honors a Moabite heroine in a culture that often disparaged foreigners, is a voice for inclusiveness. Ruth, the Moabite, is a model of Israelite faithfulness. Others take an opposite point of view. They argue that the story urges assimilation. According to that view, Ruth is presented first as a convert who renounces her own heritage, and who is then erased from the story altogether. A major stream of Jewish interpretation of the book also views Ruth as a story of assimilation in which Ruth is an ideal convert but sees her conversion as a good thing.

In the past two decades, Ruth has been the subject of many feminist and womanist interpretations. After all, only two biblical books are named for a woman, but interpreters arrive at differing assessments of the treatment of women in the story. Some laud the book as a women's story, in which female characters make decisions, act with strength, and show radical unconventional loyalty toward one another. The latter characteristic has led a number of lesbian interpreters to embrace the story as a model for women whose first commitment is to another woman.

In contrast, other feminist women and men argue that the story inculcates patriarchal values. According to that view, the storyteller presents Ruth as a model of self-sacrifice, giving up her homeland, her religion, her best chance for security, and even her child for the sake of the family.

Why do interpreters of Ruth reach such wide-ranging conclusions? I will name three factors; no doubt there are others.

First, the storyteller has crafted a tale in which the listener has to fill in many gaps. We are not told why the characters act the way they do. Indeed, more than half of the story consists of dialogue. Of eighty-five verses, conversations take up fifty-five verses. The audience is supposed to deduce the characters' motives from what they say and do.

Interpreters fill the gaps in different ways, depending on their own experiences. So a number of indigenous interpreters, whose people have been forced to endure centuries of assimilation to their conqueror's religion and culture, legitimately critique the story. They hear Ruth's vow to Naomi—"Your people will be my people, your God, my God"—as a text of terror, and Ruth as a story that lauds rejecting one's own heritage. Women thirsty for biblical stories that depict women's friendships and portray women's agency may equally legitimately celebrate Ruth's loyalty to Naomi.

Interpreters' backgrounds and intellectual or faith commitments shape what they regard as appropriate or legitimate readings. Some believe that the character's words should be taken at face value, or that the storyteller's intention is decisive for our interpretation. Others allow for the possibility of duplicity in the characters' speech or read against the grain; that is, they deliberately interpret the text in a way counter to the purpose of the narrator.

A second factor contributing to the range of readings is our ignorance about a number of legal, familial, and social customs presupposed by the narrative. The storyteller naturally assumed that the audience was aware of the cultural background of Ruth. She or he did not have to explain why the kinsman who redeemed Elimelech's field also had to marry Ruth, for example. The audience would have been familiar with Israelite laws and customs and would not have given them a second thought. That familiarity has been lost over the centuries. Biblical scholars are no longer able to understand many of the legal and social underpinnings of the story. Commentators differ in how they construe those practices, which in turn leads them to understand the message of the book in diverse ways. I will note plausible positions as issues arise, but want to acknowledge from the start that much is uncertain.

A third factor that contributes to the range of readings is the artistry of the storyteller who composed the book of Ruth. Several different themes are woven into the story. As I read it, Ruth is about economic survival *and* about loyalty *and* about accepting foreigners *and* about the loyalty of one woman to another. Although Ruth seems to represent the voice of a single storyteller, that storyteller has put a number of ideas into conversation with one another. The conversation continues through centuries of interpretation.

Such diversity does not mean that anything goes. Some interpretations do not adequately take into account key features of the story. Others are unlikely in light of what is known about ancient storytelling. Some perspectives are not adequate with respect to the interpreter's own context. Still, within the boundaries set by the text, and by the ancient and modern contexts, a wide range of views of the story of Ruth are plausible.

THE MESSAGE OF THE BOOK OF RUTH: ONE READING

While recognizing the validity of alternative interpretations of Ruth, my comments do reflect a particular interpretation. In common with numerous biblical theologians, I understand the book as a story of God working through faithful relationships to bring about blessing. The relationships are between particular individuals: it matters that Ruth is a Moabite, an ethnic group that the Israelites despised. It matters that she is a woman and that her fierce loyalty is to a woman. And it matters that Naomi and Ruth, though without material resources, strategize not only for their own individual welfare but also for each other's. Boaz, a prominent man determined to do more than required and see more than is obvious, is the third character through whom God works to bring blessing out of emptiness and to turn bitterness into joy.

26. Loss and Loyalty
Ruth 1

The book of Ruth is often called an "idyll," a lovely pastoral story with a "rags to riches" ending, and indeed the narrative tells of faithful action and ultimate blessing. But the blessing is worked out in the midst of harsh realities: famine, barrenness, and death. And the loyalty is expressed through complex relationships that cross ethnic and religious boundaries and fly in the face of social conventions. The first chapter of Ruth focuses on the harsh reality of Naomi's loss and on Ruth's fierce, redemptive commitment.

The chapter has a three-part structure. Section one (vv. 1–5) sets the stage. In section two (vv. 6–18), dialogue between Naomi and her daughters-in-law discloses Naomi's grief and the countervailing note of Ruth's loyalty. Naomi's bitter despair overshadows the homecoming scene in section three (vv. 19–22).

SETTING THE STAGE
Ruth 1:1–5

1:1 **In the days when the judges ruled, there was a famine in the land, and a certain man of Bethlehem in Judah went to live in the country of Moab, he and his wife and two sons. ² The name of the man was Elimelech and the name of his wife Naomi, and the names of his two sons were Mahlon and Chilion; they were Ephrathites from Bethlehem in Judah. They went into the country of Moab, and remained there. ³ But Elimelech, the husband of Naomi, died, and she was left with her two sons. ⁴ These took Moabite wives; the name of the one was Orpah and the name of the other Ruth. When they had lived there about ten years, ⁵ both Mahlon and Chilion also died, so that the woman was left without her two sons and her husband.**

In verses 1–5, the storyteller quickly sets the stage, introducing six of the characters and establishing the facts necessary for the story to unfold.

Verse one identifies the period and place in which the story is set. The opening words set Ruth in the time before the monarchy, linking it with the stories in the book of Judges. That setting would have created distance between the story and its later audience. Geographically, the story is set in two places: Bethlehem of Judah and Moab. Movement between the two locales structures the chapter. The scene begins with a journey from Bethlehem to Moab and ends with Naomi and Ruth's return from Moab to Bethlehem.

Bethlehem and Moab are not arbitrary settings. Bethlehem, a village near Jerusalem, has positive associations in ancient Israel because of its ties to the great King David. Like Elimelech, the Israelite monarch was said to be an Ephrathite from Bethlehem in Judah (1 Sam. 17:12). (The term "Ephrathah" has various meanings; in Ruth and 1 Samuel 17, it appears to refer to either a subgroup of the tribe of Judah, or a region in or around Bethlehem.) Later, of course, Bethlehem became famous as the birthplace of Jesus. For all these positive associations, as the story begins, Bethlehem, the "House of Bread," is a place of famine.

Moab also would have conjured up an array of associations for its ancient audience, most of them bad. Israel was often at odds with its neighbor Moab (a kingdom located to the east of the Dead Sea). One Israelite tradition derides the Moabites as offspring of an incestuous union (Gen. 19:30–38). According to Numbers 25:1–9, consorting with Moabite women is highly dangerous. Israelite men became sexually involved with Moabite women, who led them to worship an idol; twenty-four thousand Israelites died of the plague God sent as judgment! Territorial disputes over land east of the Jordan often led to hostilities between Moab and Israel; Judges 3:12–30 casts Moab in the role of oppressor and the Moabite King Eglon in the role of buffoon. Hostility toward Moab was enshrined in a biblical law; Deuteronomy 23:3–4 prohibits Israel from allowing Moabites to become part of the assembly of Yahweh, no matter how long they lived among them.

The author of Ruth does not seem to criticize Elimelech and his family for seeking food in Moab. A number of biblical stories tell of famine pushing Israelites, including Abraham and Jacob, to hostile foreign lands in search of food. Setting the opening of the story in Moab does sound an ominous note, however. Can any good come out of Moab? The negative associations are first challenged—Moab, not Judah, is a source of food. Then they are reinforced. Death and barrenness overwhelm the family in Moab. Finally, the stereotype is overturned. Ruth's ethnic identity is stressed in the story. As the story unfolds, the Moabite heroine represents a surprising reversal of exclusivistic attitudes.

The first section quickly introduces most of the story's characters. Six of the story's nine actors are named in verses 2–4. The men, Elimelech, Mahlon, and Chilion, have no speaking parts. The storyteller introduces them in order to note that they have died, leaving Naomi bereft of her husband and her sons. Orpah, a Moabite daughter-in-law, stays in the story long enough to function as a foil, or at least an alternative, to Ruth. The story pivots around Naomi and Ruth.

The storyteller stresses the relationship of the characters. As commentators frequently point out, chapter 1 is full of familial terms: "his wife," "her husband," "his sons," "her sons," "wives," "daughters-in-law," "mother-in-law." The book has to do with a family—its near-demise and ultimate survival.

In the process, the shape of that family changes. In verse 1, it is male-centered. The storyteller first introduces "a certain man," then mentions "his" wife and "his" sons. Ruth's world is a man's world. Like most biblical accounts, the book of Ruth presupposes that a woman's economic security and legal/social status depend upon her place in a male-headed household. The deaths of her menfolk leave Naomi as the head of what is left of the family. Verse 5 speaks of "her" sons and "her" husband. Set in a man's world, the book is, nonetheless, a woman's story. Naomi and Ruth are the agents whose needs, loyalties, and determined efforts to survive shape the plot.

The women, Naomi, Ruth, and Orpah, make decisions and take action independent of any man not because they choose to but because they must. Already verse 1 suggests the harshness of the world in which the story is set. There was famine; the refugee family finds food, but it also finds death. In three short verses, the storyteller reports the loss of the family's three men. Reference to Mahlon and Chilion living for ten years after their marriages without their wives bearing a child suggests an additional hardship. Ruth and Orpah are barren. Despite its matter-of-fact tone, the first section of the story establishes a mood of death and deprivation. By the end of the chapter, Naomi will fully acknowledge the bitterness of her loss.

GOING BACK HOME
Ruth 1:6–18

1:6 **Then she started to return with her daughters-in-law from the country of Moab, for she had heard in the country of Moab that the LORD had considered his people and given them food. ^{7} So she set out from the place where she had been living, she and her two daughters-in-law, and they went on their** way to go back to the land of Judah. [8] But Naomi said to her two daughters-in-law, "Go back each of you to your mother's house. May the LORD deal kindly with you, as you have dealt with the dead and with me. [9] The LORD grant that you may find security, each of you in the house of your husband." Then she kissed them, and they wept aloud. [10] They said to her, "No, we will return with you to your people." [11] But Naomi said, "Turn back, my daughters, why will you go with me? Do I still have sons in my womb that they may become your husbands? [12] Turn back, my daughters, go your way, for I am too old to have a husband. Even if I thought there was hope for me, even if I should have a husband tonight and bear sons, [13] would you then wait until they were grown? Would you then refrain from marrying? No, my daughters, it has been far more bitter for me than for you, because the hand of the LORD has turned against me." [14] Then they wept aloud again. Orpah kissed her mother-in-law, but Ruth clung to her.

[15] So she said, "See, your sister-in-law has gone back to her people and to her gods; return after your sister-in-law." [16] But Ruth said,

"Do not press me to leave you
    or to turn back from following you!
Where you go, I will go;
    where you lodge, I will lodge;
your people shall be my people,
    and your God my God.
[17] Where you die, I will die—
    there will I be buried.
May the LORD do thus and so to me,
    and more as well,
if even death parts me from you!"

[18] When Naomi saw that she was determined to go with her, she said no more to her.

As many interpreters have noted, the dialogue between Naomi and her daughters-in-law centers on the word "go back." The Hebrew verb *shuv*, translated "go back," "return," "turn back," recurs twelve times in this chapter, ten times in verses 6–18. At stake is the location of each woman's "home." Where is the place to which each will "return"? Will Ruth and Orpah "go back" to Bethlehem or to Moab?

Naomi's destination is not in question; she will "go back" to Judah. For Naomi, the issue is whether hope lies at the end of her journey. Naomi goes back "empty." Her hopelessness is increasingly clear as the dialogue progresses.

The section begins with Naomi's decision to return to Judah. She has heard that Yahweh provided the people food. This reference to God in the book of Ruth is one of only two times that God acts directly in the story. Yahweh gives food (1:6) and conception (4:13). The two references frame the story with the divine gift of fertility (bread and babies), which makes human life possible. The deity is not silent or absent in the rest of the book. There are twenty-four explicit references to God, Almighty, or LORD in the eighty-five verses of Ruth. But except for Ruth 1:6 and Ruth 4:13, references to God are found in the context of human words. The focus is on human action, human initiative, human commitments. God is found within the blessings, vows, and even complaints of one person to another.

Naomi sets out to go back to Judah, accompanied by her two daughters-in-law. The departure is recounted twice. After the journey is underway, Naomi tells the younger women to "go back." Why she does not instruct them to return before they start out is not clear. Perhaps Naomi assumed that Ruth and Orpah were simply going with her for the first leg of her journey, as was customary in ancient times (cf. Gen. 18). Perhaps the responsibility of providing for her daughters-in-law became an increasingly heavy burden as they traveled on, and Naomi changed her mind. In any case, sometime into their journey back to Judah, Naomi tells her daughters-in-law to return to their families in Moab. Three exchanges take place between Naomi and the daughters-in-law. Each begins with the older woman's command, "Go back," followed by Orpah's and Ruth's responses.

In the first exchange, verses 8–10, Naomi follows the dismissal, "go back," with a farewell prayer. It is the first of many times in the book that Yahweh's name is invoked in blessing. Naomi's blessing of Ruth and Orpah is rooted in the concept *hesed* (translated "deal kindly"). The concept is central to Israelite understanding of covenantal relations and is a pivotal theme in the book of Ruth. Katharine Doob Sakenfeld's definitive study of the term identifies *hesed* as kindness or mercy that (a) takes place within the context of an ongoing, positive relationship; (b) responds to a genuine need on the part of the recipient; and (c) goes above and beyond what is required of the one showing kindness (Sakenfeld, 1985, 131). The term can refer to the mercy and faithfulness of God toward human beings or of people to one another.

Naomi grounds her prayer that God deal kindly with Ruth and Orpah in the loving faithfulness the young women have modeled. The correspondence between divine action and human action is a theme that runs throughout the book of Ruth.

We have said that the story is set in a man's world. Within that world, the only shape of *hesed* that Naomi can envision for her daughters-in-law is the security of marriage. (The word translated "security" is frequently translated "rest" and refers to being settled, free from want and from harassment.) Naomi prays that the younger women will find husbands.

The text is silent about Naomi's motives for sending Orpah and Ruth back. Interpreters fill in the silence in different ways. Some believe that Naomi found her sons' marriages to Moabite women an embarrassment. Others suggest that the young women reminded her of all she had lost; Naomi did not want them around. The most frequent interpretation of Naomi's motives is that she sends them away for their own sakes: their mothers might be able to provide for them; Naomi cannot. In my opinion, the last explanation is most plausible. Naomi sees no possibilities for her future. Verse 8 hints at her despair; she identifies herself with those who are already dead. In any case, both Orpah and Ruth resist their mother-in-law's attempt to send them away from her. They are resolved to "go back"—but to Judah, not to Moab.

Verses 11–14 recount the second exchange between Naomi and her daughters-in-law. Naomi again insists that they return to their families. This time, her argument is explicit. She cannot give her daughters-in-law the only security that she can imagine for young women. She is too old to bear sons. The far-fetched scenario in verse 13 emphasizes the utter impossibility of Naomi providing husbands for Orpah and Ruth.

Biblical scholars debate whether or not Naomi's speech reflects the practice of levirate marriage. Deuteronomy 25:5–10 requires the brother of a man who dies childless to marry the deceased brother's widow. By a legal fiction, the first child born to the widow and her brother-in-law is counted as the dead man's son and heir. From a male perspective, the aim of levirate marriage is to establish the deceased man's "name," that is, his lineage, reputation, achievement, indeed, the ongoing significance of his life. A second purpose of the law is to provide the widow with economic security, a place in society, and protection. If levirate marriage is behind Naomi's words, it is the second purpose that she has in mind. Naomi's expressed concern is providing security for the living women, not offspring for the deceased men.

The last words in Ruth 1:13 express Naomi's despair over her own lot, as well as her frustration that she cannot provide for her daughters-in-law. Her hopelessness is explicit. Orpah and Ruth may yet remarry and have sons. Naomi cannot. We do not know exactly how old Naomi is. Assuming that an Israelite woman was married in her teens to a man in his late twenties, and adding ten years for the time the family spent in Moab, Naomi would have been somewhere in her fifties. Given the harshness of ancient subsistence farmers' lives, that was old. Naomi is well past child-bearing age.

The young women's response to Naomi again involves weeping and a kiss. But while Ruth and Orpah had originally responded in unison, resisting Naomi's appeal to leave, now they make their own individual choices. Orpah's kiss is her farewell, signaling her acceptance of Naomi's instructions. She will obey and go back.

Orpah illustrates a choice that Ruth rejects. She ought not be seen as irresponsible or bad. The ancient Rabbis condemned Orpah, but the storyteller does not. Orpah has shown Naomi and the men of the family *hesed*; she obeys Naomi's instruction. In verse 15, Naomi holds Orpah up as a model for Ruth to emulate.

At least one indigenous interpreter identifies Orpah as a sign of hope for native peoples. Laura Donaldson reads "against the grain," celebrating the fact that Orpah holds to her heritage and her sacred ancestors rather than assimilating (Donaldson, 1999, 130–44). Most recent interpreters find Orpah's choice responsible and sensible, but not as worthy as Ruth's. Orpah serves as a foil to highlight Ruth's extraordinary love.

The passion of Ruth's commitment is suggested by the word "clung." The verb is most frequently found in the context of marriage, such as the famous words from the garden scene in Genesis 2:24. "Therefore a man leaves his father and his mother and clings to his wife, and they become one flesh." Ruth clings to her mother-in-law as a man clings to his wife.

Naomi makes one last attempt to send Ruth away. This time she holds up Orpah as an example and draws on Ruth's ties to her own people and her own gods. Ruth's response is among the most radical statements of commitment in the Bible. Often quoted at weddings, the words of Ruth 1:15–16 take the form of a covenant, but a covenant that goes against all social expectations. Naomi has urged Ruth to seek security in a husband. Ruth chooses to commit herself to Naomi. She binds herself unconditionally not only to a woman rather than a man, but, in an act of radical solidarity, to a woman in near desperate circumstances.

Ruth's pledge goes beyond "until death do us part." Burial was extremely important in the ancient Near Eastern world. A full generation younger than Naomi, Ruth can expect to outlive her mother-in-law by many years; surely she would be free to return to her native land after Naomi's death. Nonetheless, Ruth vows that her bones will rest with Naomi's, not in Moab.

Ruth's motives, like Naomi's, remain unspoken. Traditionally, commentators have focused on the words "your God shall be my God" and viewed Ruth's commitment as conversion. Recent interpretations of Ruth's decision diverge wildly. Some have understood Ruth as acting at least in part out of self-interest; she burned her bridges by marrying a non-Moabite. Some hold her up as a model for strong women-identified women. Others suggest that Ruth embodies values of self-sacrifice or assimilation that support patriarchy or colonization.

As I read the story (filling in the silences from my particular point of view), Ruth acts out of love for the woman who has been her mother the past ten years. Over and over she addresses herself to Naomi: "I will not leave you." The repeated "you" shows that her commitment is for the sake of Naomi, not Naomi's religion or people. Her commitment is not made out of weakness or self-abnegation. We are told Ruth is a "woman of valor," a "woman of strength" (see comments on 3:11). As I understand her, Ruth acts out of that strength, making a conscious, determined choice. Ruth does not accept Naomi's definition of Ruth's life; that is, that Moab is her home, and a Moabite husband her only hope for the future. Naomi is Ruth's family. Moreover, Ruth knows that she is the only family that Naomi has left. The word translated "leave" in verse 16 often carries the meaning "abandon." Ruth will not abandon Naomi to the hopelessness that Naomi envisions for herself.

Naomi, seeing Ruth's fierce determination, says "no more to her." The text says nothing about Naomi's emotions. Again, commentators interpret Naomi's silence in widely varying ways. Some say that Naomi is too overwhelmed by Ruth's love to speak; others, that she is irritated and frustrated by Ruth's disobedience. Naomi's expression of bitterness in verses 20–21 indicates that she is not yet able to appreciate fully Ruth's radical kindness. Nonetheless, it is better not to overread Naomi's silence. The text probably means simply that Naomi gives up trying to persuade Ruth to go home to her mother's house. Readers learn nothing about Naomi's feelings or the two women's interactions on the long journey back to Judah.

A BITTER RETURN
Ruth 1:19–22

> 1:19 **So the two of them went on until they came to Bethlehem. When they came to Bethlehem, the whole town was stirred because of them; and the women said, "Is this Naomi?"** 20 **She said to them,**
>   **"Call me no longer Naomi,**
>   **call me Mara,**
>   **for the Almighty has dealt bitterly with me.**

²¹ **I went away full,**
   but the LORD **has brought me back empty;**
why call me Naomi
   when the LORD **has dealt harshly with me,**
   and the Almighty has brought calamity upon me?"
²² **So Naomi returned together with Ruth the Moabite, her daughter-in-law, who came back with her from the country of Moab. They came to Bethlehem at the beginning of the barley harvest.**

The final verses of chapter 1 round out the scene. The chapter opened with the family journeying from Bethlehem to Moab. It ends with the completion of the journey back to Bethlehem. But how different the ending of the chapter is from the beginning! As the scene begins, there is no food, but there is an intact family. As it ends, there is food, but the grieving Naomi sees herself as "empty," without family.

The women's exclamation, "Is this Naomi?" may convey shock at how changed Naomi is; more likely, the question expresses their excitement that Naomi has returned. Naomi responds with a wordplay to voice her sense of utter destitution. She is not Naomi, "Delight"; she is Mara, "Bitter."

Naomi lays the responsibility for her suffering squarely on God. Her complaint is very sharp. Four times Naomi names the deity as the one who has brought her to grief. "Shaddai," "Yahweh" (traditionally rendered "Almighty" and "LORD"), has afflicted her, done evil to her. The verb translated "dealt harshly" can be translated "afflict" or "oppress," as Pharaoh afflicted the Hebrews (Exod. 1:10, 11). The verb underlying "brought calamity upon me" can be rendered even stronger "Shaddai has done evil to me."

"Naomi" ("pleasant, delight") is probably a short form of a name referring to the deity: "[God is] my delight." If so, the complaint is even more pointed: "Why call me '[God is] my delight' when the LORD has dealt harshly with me, and the Almighty has brought calamity upon me?"

As sharp as it is, Naomi's complaint is not faithlessness. Israel affirmed that God makes "weal and woe." Naomi stands with Job, Jeremiah, Jonah, and the psalmists in complaining against God.

Naomi has lost much. From her perspective, she is "empty." Many commentators describe Naomi as ungrateful for what Ruth has done, but Ruth's declaration of loyalty cannot immediately erase the desolation of widowhood and her sons' deaths.

Though Naomi cannot yet appreciate it, the importance of Ruth's loyalty does not escape the narrator's perspective. Naomi does not return alone, but "together with Ruth." The final words of the chapter provide an additional glimmer of hope. After years of famine comes "the beginning of the barley harvest."

The audience must wait until the end of the story for hope to be fulfilled. The last verses of Ruth 1 help to bracket the entire book. The women of Bethlehem clamorously greet Naomi's return. When the story ends, the same women will celebrate the birth of Ruth's son, a son "born to Naomi" (4:14–17).

27. A Provisional Resolution
Ruth 2

The initial chapter of Ruth introduced us to two impoverished widows. In a world where women depend on men for social status, protection, and provision, Naomi and Ruth have no husbands, fathers, or sons. In a world where the very meaning of existence is tied to children and grandchildren, Naomi has lost her only offspring, and Ruth, after ten barren years, has no husband. As Ruth 2 begins, two questions loom large. How will Ruth and Naomi survive? And if they survive, what hope can the future possibly offer?

In this chapter, Ruth's initiative and labor, together with the unexpected introduction of a kindly disposed and wealthy kinsman, Boaz, combine to provide the two widows with food. The narrative also offers hints that the resolution is not a final one; gleaning, scavenging in the fields, is not the whole of Ruth and Naomi's futures. In and through the human actions and human dialogue, one senses another agency at work. Coincidences, blessings, and human acts of *hesed*, kindness, point to the hidden activity of God. (See p. 269 for a discussion of the concept of *hesed*.)

The structure of the chapter includes three parts. The first scene (vv. 1–3), set in the village, introduces the rich relative, Boaz, and establishes Ruth's determination to glean. The second scene (vv. 4–17), set in a barley field, focuses on Boaz and Ruth, and particularly on Boaz's increasing interest in and kindness toward the young widow. Scene three (vv. 18–23) returns to Bethlehem and to dialogue between Ruth and Naomi.

AS LUCK WOULD HAVE IT
Ruth 2:1–3

2:1 Now Naomi had a kinsman on her husband's side, a prominent rich man, of the family of Elimelech, whose name was Boaz. ² And Ruth the Moabite said to Naomi, "Let me go to the field and glean among the ears of grain,

behind someone in whose sight I may find favor." She said to her, "Go, my daughter." ³ So she went. She came and gleaned in the field behind the reapers. As it happened, she came to the part of the field belonging to Boaz, who was of the family of Elimelech.

The scene begins with an aside, in which the narrator introduces the third of the story's three main characters. The man is a kinsman, although it is not clear how close a relative he is. The meaning of the word translated "kinsman" is uncertain. Twice we are told that he is a member of Elimelech's family, but the Hebrew word translated "family" encompasses a large number of people. One should think of "family" in the sense of a "family reunion," not in the sense of a nuclear family, or even a family extending to all the grandchildren of one grandparent. Boaz's kinship to Naomi and Ruth is not likely to be close enough to entail any legal obligations for the women. Had there been a claim to be made, presumably Naomi would have made it.

Still, the three references to Boaz as family or kin of Elimelech raise expectations. The family is the safety net for ancient Israelite society. Male family members were a woman's primary source of aid and protection.

Moreover, this male relative is "rich" and "prominent." The Hebrew words underlying "prominent rich man" literally mean "a man mighty in power, wealth, ability." Boaz has land; he also has honor and standing. Danna Nolan Fewell and David M. Gunn, playing on the fact that "Boaz" is also the name of one of the pillars in Solomon's temple, aptly refer to him as a "pillar of the community" (Fewell, 1990, 83). The sense of Boaz's prominence in Bethlehem is reinforced by his very name. The popular understanding of "Boaz" is "in him is strength." The reader now knows (though Ruth does not) that the two women have a strong, wealthy kinsman, a potential source of assistance.

After the narrative aside, the story line continues. Ruth asks Naomi's permission to glean. "Gleaning" was an ancient Israelite provision for the landless poor to obtain food. Leviticus 19:9–10 enjoins farmers *not* to strip their fields clean at harvest time. They were to leave some of the crop at the edges of their fields and to refrain from going back over fields, vines, or olive trees to get the grain and fruit they missed the first time, so that the poor and the sojourners could gather what remained. Deuteronomy 24:19–22 adds widows and the fatherless to the groups entitled to glean. According to the biblical injunctions, the poor had a right to glean. They could not take that right for granted, however. In practice, their access to the crop depended upon a landowner's goodwill. Ruth hopes to "find favor" with some farmer; that is, she hopes that someone will give her permission to glean.

Ruth's determination to glean illustrates her commitment and initiative. It also underscores the two widows' poverty. Gleaning was a hard and uncertain way of seeking food. As in Ruth 1, the story unfolds within the context of harsh realities; this time, the hardships are economic. With no menfolk and no land, the women's best available means of survival is dependency on others' willingness to allow one of them to gather what has been left behind.

The existence of a rich kinsman hints at one possible factor in Ruth and Naomi's survival. But Ruth's initiative and hard labor will be a second, vital factor in preserving the women's lives. The phrase "as it happened" points to a third element in the women's survival: chance. As luck would have it, Ruth "happens" to come to glean in just that section of the village's lands that belonged to Boaz. As luck would have it, Boaz comes to his field at just the right moment (v. 4).

Some interpreters believe that the coincidences in the story of Ruth are no more than chance. According to their perspective, the tale focuses entirely on human agency. God has no role until Ruth and Boaz marry and God gives Ruth conception (Ruth 4:13). A majority of commentators, however, view such coincidences as evidence of the hidden activity of Providence. The storyteller does not spell out what is behind events in the book of Ruth but describes encounters and conversations. The right person appears on the scene at just the right moment. People utter blessings and prayers, and the prayers are answered. Human beings act with great generosity and commitment. Each reader can decide if Providence is at work in all of this, or if things simply happen as luck would have it. In this commentator's view the story points to God at work in and through ongoing events and human encounters, providing opportunities and bringing human efforts to fulfillment. The tale may suggest an image of God that more resembles a gardener, providing what is necessary for the plants to grow, than it resembles a monarch, issuing commands.

BOAZ AND RUTH IN THE BARLEY FIELD
Ruth 2:4–17

> 2:4 **Just then Boaz came from Bethlehem. He said to the reapers, "The LORD be with you." They answered, "The LORD bless you." 5 Then Boaz said to his servant who was in charge of the reapers, "To whom does this young woman**

belong?" [6] The servant who was in charge of the reapers answered, "She is the Moabite who came back with Naomi from the country of Moab. [7] She said, 'Please, let me glean and gather among the sheaves behind the reapers.' So she came, and she has been on her feet from early this morning until now, without resting even for a moment."

[8] Then Boaz said to Ruth, "Now listen, my daughter, do not go to glean in another field or leave this one, but keep close to my young women. [9] Keep your eyes on the field that is being reaped, and follow behind them. I have ordered the young men not to bother you. If you get thirsty, go to the vessels and drink from what the young men have drawn." [10] Then she fell prostrate, with her face to the ground, and said to him, "Why have I found favor in your sight, that you should take notice of me, when I am a foreigner?" [11] But Boaz answered her, "All that you have done for your mother-in-law since the death of your husband has been fully told me, and how you left your father and mother and your native land and came to a people that you did not know before. [12] May the LORD reward you for your deeds, and may you have a full reward from the LORD, the God of Israel, under whose wings you have come for refuge!" [13] Then she said, "May I continue to find favor in your sight, my lord, for you have comforted me and spoken kindly to your servant, even though I am not one of your servants."

[14] At mealtime Boaz said to her, "Come here, and eat some of this bread, and dip your morsel in the sour wine." So she sat beside the reapers, and he heaped up for her some parched grain. She ate until she was satisfied, and she had some left over. [15] When she got up to glean, Boaz instructed his young men, "Let her glean even among the standing sheaves, and do not reproach her. [16] You must also pull out some handfuls for her from the bundles, and leave them for her to glean, and do not rebuke her."

[17] So she gleaned in the field until evening. Then she beat out what she had gleaned, and it was about an ephah of barley.

The focus of scene two is the "chance" encounter between Boaz and Ruth. The storyteller depicts Boaz's increasing interest in and benevolence toward Ruth. The storyteller portrays Ruth as hardworking and humble; her humility reflects the social and gender hierarchy of ancient Israel. Nonetheless, a few double meanings and ambiguities in Ruth's speeches hint at less deferent possibilities.

The section begins with Boaz and his workers exchanging blessings. Their words are probably conventional forms of greetings. As many commentators note, English-speakers also exchange greetings with little awareness of their meanings: "good-bye," that is, "God be with ye" or "farewell." Nonetheless, the brief exchange does establish a sense of well-being. The relationship between Boaz and the reapers is as it ought to be; people bless one another. More important, the storyteller makes Boaz's first words a form of prayer. Each of the three main characters of the story invokes the name of Yahweh in her or his first speech (1:8; 1:17; 2:4). God is close to the thoughts and the lips of these people.

Boaz's second comment, a question to the supervisor, discloses the patriarchal assumptions of ancient Israelite society. In a small village, strangers are conspicuous. Seeing an unknown woman, Boaz asks not who she is, but to whom she belongs. Except the heads of household, normally free male landowners, ancient Israelites normally were identified by the family or household to whom they belonged. Women in particular were identified by their relationship to their father, husband, master, or possibly brother or grown son. Boaz wants to know where Ruth fits in the village society. His question does not assume that she is chattel, but that she is a dependent member of a patriarchal family.

The overseer's answer is also revealing. He first identifies Ruth's nationality. She is the Moabite . . . from Moab. It may be that aliens, whose clan relationships would have little meaning to Israelites, were identified first by their homeland. The emphatic repetition of Ruth's nationality suggests that more is going on here. Ruth is called "Moabite" seven different times in the book. Katharine Doob Sakenfeld is probably correct when she suggests that the overseer's words reflect the pejorative view the community had of Ruth; she is "that foreigner" (Sakenfeld, 1999, 41). The overseer then identifies Naomi, the head of the family to whom Ruth "belongs."

The remainder of the overseer's speech presents a number of problems for translators and interpreters. As translated by the NRSV, Ruth's request, "to glean and gather among the sheaves" seems to preempt Boaz's permission for her to work among the sheaves, given in verse 15. It would also be a presumptuous request for Ruth to make; gleaners were allowed to gather in those parts of a field that had already been harvested, not in the sections where the reapers were still working. Perhaps, as Frederic Bush argues, Ruth asks "to glean and gather into sheaves" (Bush, 1996, 114). Perhaps, with several ancient manuscripts and several modern commentators, we should omit the phrase "gather among the sheaves" altogether.

Translators have to change the Hebrew of the last half of verse 7 to make any sense of it at all. The changes that the NRSV translators have made are as plausible as any. The overseer praises Ruth's diligence.

Having learned who she is, Boaz addresses Ruth, inviting her to glean in his fields throughout the harvest. While not all commentators agree, most hear in Boaz's speech allusions to dangers faced by young women going out alone. Boaz's assurance that he has ordered the young men "not to bother" Ruth more literally reads, "I have ordered the young men not to touch you." The words can mean "not to interfere with you," but spoken to a young woman, they at least raise the possibility of sexual abuse. The threat is explicit in Naomi's advice to Ruth at the end of the chapter, as Naomi counsels her to stay close to Boaz's women, lest she be "bothered" in another field. The verb translated "bother" in verse 22 is very strong; it frequently has to do with physical violence.

A young woman in the open countryside was at risk. Ruth is a young woman who, as a widow, is known to have no male protector; as a foreigner, she is without connections or resources in Bethlehem. Ruth seemingly has three strikes against her.

Boaz invites Ruth to remain in his fields throughout the harvest, and offers her advice and reassurance. She is to stay with his young women and keep her eyes down, and he will see to it that the young male workers leave her alone. Added to concern for her safety is concern for her needs. Ruth may drink water provided for Boaz's servants.

In a threatening and alien situation, the protection Boaz offers Ruth is no small thing. Ruth falls to her knees, touching her forehead to the ground. This posture is most often made by human beings to God. From one person to another, the gesture expresses both humility and thankfulness.

Ruth's question to Boaz also bespeaks her humble gratitude (v. 10). The storyteller again reminds us that Ruth is a vulnerable foreigner. The deference of her posture and her words to Boaz underline her powerlessness and dependence on the patronage of this wealthy landowner. The story takes for granted a social hierarchy in which there is a wide gap between a man and a woman, a rich landowner and a poor gleaner, a "pillar of the community" and a foreigner.

Boaz's next words to Ruth go some distance towards bridging the gap. In verse 11, he praises Ruth with words that echo and honor her commitment to Naomi (1:15–16). His words "you left your father and your mother and your native land" also recall the call of Abraham: "Go from your country and your kindred and your father's house . . ." (Gen. 12:1). Boaz implicitly compares Ruth's courage to that of Israel's great ancestor. As Sakenfeld notes, Boaz's speech reinterprets Ruth's foreignness. She is not "that outsider"; she is a woman who, like Abraham, was willing to leave all she knew (Sakenfeld, 1999, 44).

Like Naomi (1:8), Boaz invokes God's blessing on Ruth; like Naomi, he grounds the blessing in Ruth's own faithfulness. Ruth's response in Ruth 2:13 again displays grateful deference. It may do more, however. Boaz hopes that God will reward Ruth. Ruth expresses hope that she will continue to find favor in Boaz's eyes. Boaz says that Ruth has sought refuge under God's "wings." Ruth states that Boaz has offered her comfort. Later, Ruth draws the connection between divine refuge and Boaz's protection more explicitly. The word translated "wings" also means "cloak" or "skirt." Ruth will ask Boaz to spread his "cloak" (wings) over her (3:9). In the most delicate possible manner, Ruth calls on Boaz to act upon his prayers for her.

Another possible dimension exists to Ruth's speech. The phrase rendered "spoken kindly" literally means "spoken to my heart." To "speak to the heart" can mean "to encourage" or "to comfort." Used of a man speaking to a woman, however, the phrase elsewhere means "to woo." The storyteller offers a hint of what is to come. Boaz will be more than a generous patron or even a protective kinsman. The final words of Ruth's response may convey a similar hint (v. 13). The phrase literally reads, "I will not be as one of your servants." In context, their primary meaning is, as the NRSV rightly translates, "even though I am not one of your servants." But another translation is also possible: "I will not be [merely] one of your servants." Perhaps the storyteller is pointing toward things to come?

Some time elapses between verses 13 and 14. At lunchtime, Boaz calls for Ruth to join his workers. He invites the "foreigner" into his circle and gives her more food than she can finish. Given Ruth and Naomi's poverty, a long time may have passed since Ruth has been able to eat her fill.

Boaz's increasing benevolence goes far beyond what society expected or law required. After lunch, he instructs his workers to allow her to gather grain in the part of the field they are still harvesting, and even to pull grain out of the barley that they have already cut and bound. The reader is again reminded of the importance of Boaz's protection. The verb translated "reproach" most often means "disgrace" or "shame."

Boaz's kindness makes a huge difference to Ruth and Naomi's welfare. The daily ration for a hired laborer was slightly more than two pounds of cereal. Presumably, a typical gleaner would gather significantly less. In contrast, Ruth has gleaned an ephah: twenty to thirty pounds (Hamlin, 1996, 35). Boaz's *hesed* ensures that Naomi and Ruth have adequate provision, at least while the harvest lasts.

PROVISIONAL BLESSING
Ruth 2:18–23

> 2:18 **She picked it up and came into the town, and her mother-in-law saw how much she had gleaned. Then she took out and gave her what was left over after she herself had been satisfied.** [19] **Her mother-in-law said to her, "Where did you glean today? And where have you worked? Blessed be the man who took notice of you." So she told her mother-in-law with whom she**

had worked, and said, "The name of the man with whom I worked today is Boaz." [20] Then Naomi said to her daughter-in-law, "Blessed be he by the LORD, whose kindness has not forsaken the living or the dead!" Naomi also said to her, "The man is a relative of ours, one of our nearest kin." [21] Then Ruth the Moabite said, "He even said to me, 'Stay close by my servants, until they have finished all my harvest.'" [22] Naomi said to Ruth, her daughter-in-law, "It is better, my daughter, that you go out with his young women, otherwise you might be bothered in another field." [23] So she stayed close to the young women of Boaz, gleaning until the end of the barley and wheat harvests; and she lived with her mother-in-law.

The chapter closes as it began, with a conversation between Ruth and Naomi. The older woman, seeing the quantity of grain Ruth has gleaned, and receiving the cooked food Ruth has brought home from her lunch, rightly realizes that Ruth could not have garnered that much without help. Before Naomi knows the identity of the helpful landowner, she blesses him for noticing Ruth. (The word "notice" in Naomi's blessing is the same verb that Ruth uses in verse 10.) The abundant food and the attention that led to it begin to pull Naomi out of her despair.

Ruth's identification of the man who had aided her is a turning point for Naomi. Earlier, the grieving widow/mother had seen God's hand behind her losses (1:21). Now she sees the work of God in the "chance" that brought Ruth to Boaz's field, and in the kindness Boaz has shown. Once again, she blesses Boaz.

The blessing raises a question. Whose kindness to the living and the dead does Naomi praise? Grammatically, the sentence is ambiguous. Perhaps she is referring to Boaz's kindness; perhaps it is Yahweh's. Most likely, it is both. Human activity and divine agency are intertwined throughout the book of Ruth. The narrator may well intend the audience to hear Naomi's blessing as praise of both Yahweh's and Boaz's *hesed*. Indeed, the blessing may reflect the view that Boaz's kindness is the kindness of God. God acts in and through deeds of human faithfulness to meet Ruth's and Naomi's needs.

Ruth gave Naomi information that she did not have: the name of her benefactor. Now Naomi responds by telling Ruth what she did not know; the benefactor, Boaz, is a near relative, one of their "nearest kin." The phrase "nearest kin" can also be translated "one of our redeemers." In ancient Israel, a "redeemer" was a male relative responsible for the welfare of family members. According to the laws of Leviticus, a redeemer's obligation includes buying back land that impoverished family members had been forced to sell to outsiders, and purchasing the freedom of kin forced to sell themselves into slavery (Lev. 25:25, 47–49). The redeemer also appears to be responsible for protecting family members in a more general sense, the context in which Naomi uses the word.

Boaz does not appear to have any legal obligations to Naomi and Ruth. Nonetheless, Naomi appears confident both that he has a moral obligation toward them and that he will act on that obligation. In Boaz's kindness, and in the "coincidence" of Ruth's "happening" onto Boaz's field, Naomi glimpses the *hesed* of God. Naomi begins to turn from bitter emptiness to hope.

In the final verses, Ruth recounts Boaz's encouragement to stay in his portion of the village's field. Implicit in his offer is an invitation to continue gleaning among the sheaves. Ruth reassures her mother-in-law that their provisions will continue as long as the harvest lasts and for some time thereafter.

As the chapter ends, the barley and wheat harvests are over. The note that Ruth "lived with her mother-in-law" could also be translated: "Ruth stayed at home with her mother-in-law." That is, she no longer went out to glean.

Boaz's lavish assistance allowed Ruth to glean extraordinary amounts of grain. Nonetheless, even twenty to thirty pounds of barley was only enough to feed two women for five to seven days (Hamlin, 1996, 35), not enough to provide for them through the long months until next year's harvest season. Ruth 2 offers a provisional solution to Ruth and Naomi's situation. Boaz's *hesed* and Yahweh's *hesed* address the women's immediate need. They have enough to eat, for several months. But the solution is only temporary, offering no long-term security. The storyteller's notice that the harvest is over and Ruth stays at home with her mother-in-law prepares the reader for the women to take steps to secure a more long-term solution.

28. Scandalous Valor
Ruth 3

As Ruth 3 opens, the harvest season is over. Assuming Boaz's benevolence toward Ruth continued, Ruth would have gleaned enough to feed Naomi and herself for several months. But gleaning offers only temporary assistance. Moreover, hope that Boaz's apparent interest in Ruth or his sense of responsibility as Naomi's near kinsman would lead him to take further action dims as the seven weeks of harvest passed. The women are in a precarious position.

In light of the end of the harvest and its possibilities, Naomi seeks a more permanent security for Ruth. In Naomi's thinking, as we learned in Ruth 1, that means a husband and a home. In a sexually charged, risky encounter, Ruth, following Naomi's instructions, takes the initiative that Boaz had not taken. Courage is rewarded; a home secured.

The chapter is problematic. Contemporary readers may well shake their heads at a woman's security depending on finding a husband. Moreover, Ruth uses sexual wiles to get him. We would not want to teach our daughters or nieces that their best road to success is to dress up seductively and go to the threshing floor (or bar) to catch themselves wealthy men.

A number of interpreters understand the chapter as a story of frank seduction and even entrapment. Others believe that the conduct of characters as righteous as Ruth and Boaz must have been aboveboard. The gaps left for readers to fill in are large; moreover, in keeping with a private tryst in the middle of the night, the storyteller has chosen to cloak the scene with deliberately ambiguous language. The reader must decide how he or she will interpret the encounter.

As I interpret the story, it is about women in a man's world doing what they have to do in order to survive. Naomi is a realist. In patriarchally structured ancient Israel, women were dependent upon men for access to economic resources. By that reading, Ruth 3 has to do with loyalty and courage, with acting upon what one has prayed for, and with survival. The story also addresses a God who works through both socially marginalized and socially prominent people and through events that might be deemed scandalous.

The structure of Ruth 3 parallels that of Ruth 2. Both chapters open and close with conversations between Naomi and Ruth. In the initial dialogue, one of the women sets forth a strategy and the other concurs. In the final exchange, Ruth and Naomi discuss what has transpired. The middle sections of both chapters describe encounters between Ruth and Boaz.

Marked differences are also obvious in how the story unfolds in the two chapters. In Ruth 2, Ruth takes initiative, proposing to go out and glean. Naomi consents with the fewest possible words. Perhaps Ruth's successful gleaning heartens her mother-in-law; perhaps Ruth's hard labor piques Naomi's sense of responsibility for her. In any case, in Ruth 3, Naomi takes the initiative to seek Ruth's security.

The characters exchange roles in the central scenes, also. Surrounded by his workers in the barley field, Boaz takes the initiative to address and to aid Ruth. In the private world of the threshing floor, Ruth acts first.

In Ruth 2, Ruth's labor and Boaz's kindness, while stopgap, secure the women's survival. In Ruth 3, Naomi's shrewdness, Ruth's courage, and Boaz's caring lead to a permanent resolution that benefits all three.

WHAT WAS SHE THINKING?
Ruth 3:1–5

> 3:1 **Naomi her mother-in-law said to her, "My daughter, I need to seek some security for you, so that it may be well with you. ² Now here is our kinsman Boaz, with whose young women you have been working. See, he is winnowing barley tonight at the threshing floor. ³ Now wash and anoint yourself, and put on your best clothes and go down to the threshing floor; but do not make yourself known to the man until he has finished eating and drinking. ⁴ When he lies down, observe the place where he lies; then, go and uncover his feet and lie down; and he will tell you what to do." ⁵ She said to her, "All that you tell me I will do."**

In her opening speech, Naomi urged her daughters-in-law to return to their families, and prayed that each might find "security" in her husband's house (1:9). Now Naomi does what she had asked Yahweh to do; she seeks Ruth's security by helping her to obtain a husband. Some interpreters suggest that Naomi's motives are not as selfless as they appear, that she is willing for her daughter-in-law to take huge risks in order to achieve security for herself. Such an interpretation, while possible, reads "against the grain" of Naomi's speech. The motive she explicitly states is that things may be well for Ruth. Moreover, Naomi may already have some security. In Ruth 4, we learn that Naomi is selling a field of Elimelech's. Presumably whoever purchased the field would be responsible for Naomi's maintenance. In that case, Ruth is the one whose future is most at risk. Naomi cannot imagine Ruth's well-being apart from marriage. Her assessment of the possibilities her culture offered unmarried, childless, destitute women may be accurate.

In Ruth 2, the narrator drew attention to Boaz as a possible solution to the women's poverty. As Naomi looks for a husband for Ruth, Boaz is the obvious candidate. He is a near-kinsman, a pillar of the community, and he has shown considerable interest in the younger woman. But seven weeks have passed since he first met Ruth, and he has not acted on that interest. Naomi apparently decides to give him a jump start.

Naomi spells out her plan for Ruth in verses 2–4. The phrasing of her speech resembles Boaz's instructions to Ruth in 2:8–9. Both address Ruth as "my daughter" and use rhetorical questions to drive home their points. A literal translation of verse 3:2 begins, "Now, isn't Boaz our kinsman. . . ?" Boaz's speech in 2:8 begins, "Have you not heard. . . ?" The storyteller never brings Naomi and Boaz together in the book. Nonetheless, their similarity of speech points to their shared concern for Ruth.

Naomi goes on to note that Boaz is winnowing barley. "Winnowing" involves tossing the threshed mixture of barley, chaff, and straw into the air, so that the breeze, which regularly arises in Palestine in the late afternoon, will blow the chaff away. The heavier grain falls to the threshing floor. Commentators note that it is odd that Boaz is winnowing barley after the end of the wheat harvest some weeks later. Sakenfeld suggests that farmers were able to protect the crop until they were freed from the pressure of harvest to winnow it (Sakenfeld, 1999, 52).

For the story's plot, what matters is that Boaz's activity provides Ruth an opportunity to approach him privately. She could hardly go alone to his house. She can hope to meet him away from others' eyes under the cover of darkness at the threshing floor.

Boaz is at the threshing floor; Ruth is to go to him. Naomi's advice on how Ruth is to approach him and what she is to do once she arrives there is sexually charged. The chapter is full of innuendo. The storyteller repeatedly employs ambiguous verbs. "To know," "to uncover," and "to lie down" can all be used euphemistically. The story is set at a threshing floor, a locale associated with prostitution (Hos. 9:1). Reading Naomi's speech to Ruth as anything except instructions on how to seduce Boaz is hard to do.

Commentators debate the significance of Naomi's directions that Ruth wash, anoint herself, and change clothes. Despite the NRSV translation, the Hebrew text does not say Ruth should put on her "best" clothes; it simply indicates that she is to change garments. Nonetheless, she is to come to Boaz clean and fresh.

Naomi tells Ruth to make herself as attractive as possible and to wait until Boaz, if not actually drunk, is feeling no pain. Ruth is then to uncover part of his lower body and to lie down at his side. Just how much of Boaz's body Ruth is to uncover is not clear. Aside from Ruth 3, the word translated "feet" is found only in Dan 10:6, where it means "legs." The word is related to the term more commonly used for "feet," a term sometimes employed as a euphemism for genitals. Regardless of what or how much Ruth is to uncover, the gesture is more than a little suggestive. Ruth is not told to offer any verbal explanation that might mitigate her action's erotic impact. Boaz will tell her what to do. Naomi hopes that this will lead to marriage.

The plan is risky. However, unlike Boaz's ancestress Tamar, who risked capital punishment for the sake of perpetuating her husband's lineage (Gen. 38), Ruth was not in danger of legal punishment. Biblical law defines sexual offenses as violations of the rights of a woman's father, husband, or, in certain cases, father-in-law or brother-in-law over her sexuality. The husband had exclusive rights of possession; the father, rights of control. There was no father, father-in-law, husband, or brother-in-law to exert claims over Ruth. Legally, she was a free agent.

Nonetheless, Naomi's plans involved personal and social risks. I see nothing that would have prevented Boaz from taking advantage of Ruth's offer without assuming further responsibility for her or Naomi. Interpreters who argue that he would face social pressure to marry Ruth overlook the fact that, except for Naomi, no one but Boaz knows that she is there. In any case, there do not appear to have been strictures on a man having sex with a woman, so long as he does not violate another man's rights in the process. Moreover, his response to Ruth's advances (v. 10) is hardly that of a man who has been entrapped. Ruth risks exploitation.

She also risks scandal. A woman who was not under any man's authority may not have been subject to sexual offense laws, but she was not supposed to sleep around. Ruth put her reputation on the line. Presumably Naomi knows the dangers and believes that they are necessary and that the goal is worth it. She wants Boaz to marry Ruth and hopes that Ruth's alluring approach will lead to the desired end.

Perhaps in the absence of property concerns and of male rights to a woman's sexuality, marriage was an informal affair. Biblical and other ancient Near Eastern laws offer some hints that a man could marry a woman who had no family ties simply by having sex with her. Perhaps Naomi expected Boaz to take Ruth as his wife then and there. Alternatively she may have hoped the encounter would lead to marriage later on.

Perhaps Naomi assessed the risks and found them less threatening than the danger of starvation, or of Ruth being forced to sell herself into slavery, or being forced into prostitution. Perhaps she had great confidence in Boaz to behave honorably. We do not know what Naomi was thinking.

The storyteller provides even fewer clues to Ruth's thoughts or feelings. The only hint the narrative gives of Ruth's motivation comes in Ruth's reply to her mother-in-law's final instruction. Naomi says that Boaz will tell Ruth what to do. Ruth replies, "All that you say, I will do." Ruth will act because Naomi tells her to, not because Boaz does.

Two women do what they have to do in order to provide for the other. Two women do what they have to do so that both may survive.

SCANDAL AND VALOR
Ruth 3:6–15

3:6 **So she went down to the threshing floor and did just as her mother-in-law had instructed her.** [7] **When Boaz had eaten and drunk, and he was in a contented mood, he went to lie down at the end of the heap of grain. Then she came stealthily and uncovered his feet, and lay down.** [8] **At midnight the man was startled, and turned over, and there, lying at his feet, was a woman!** [9] **He said, "Who are you?" And she answered, "I am Ruth, your servant; spread your cloak over your servant, for you are next-of-kin."** [10] **He said, "May you be blessed by the LORD, my daughter; this last instance of your loyalty is better than the first; you have not gone after young men, whether poor or rich.** [11] **And now, my daughter, do not be afraid, I will do for you all that you ask, for all the assembly of my people know that you are a worthy woman.** [12] **But now, though it is true that I am a near kinsman, there is another kinsman more closely related than I.** [13] **Remain this night, and in the morning, if he will act as next-of-kin for you, good; let him do it. If he is not willing to act as next-of-kin for you, then, as the LORD lives, I will act as next-of-kin for you. Lie down until the morning."**

[14] **So she lay at his feet until morning, but got up before one person could recognize another; for he said, "It must not be known that the woman came to the threshing floor."** [15] **Then he said, "Bring the cloak you are wearing and hold it out." So she held it, and he measured out six measures of barley, and put it on her back; then he went into the city.**

The scene at the threshing floor can be divided into two parts. In verses 6–9, Ruth carries out Naomi's instructions. Verses 10–15 comprise Boaz's response.

The narrator reinforces Ruth's agreement to "do just as her mother-in-law had instructed" (v. 6). The description of how the plan unfolds adds details to the bare bones of Naomi's instructions. Ruth does wait until Boaz has eaten and drunk his fill. The narrator adds that he was feeling mellow, and presumably, susceptible. The note that he lay down at the end of the heap of grain ensures that the encounter will be private; Boaz is lying apart from any other workers who may be sleeping at the threshing floor.

Apparently Ruth lies beside Boaz for a number of hours, until midnight. The middle of the night is a time of danger and possibility. In the middle of the night, Boaz wakes, startled. The verb is strong; it usually refers to a startled fear response. Boaz shudders, then sees a woman lying next to him. Not surprisingly, he asks who she is.

In the public space of the barley field, Boaz had asked an intermediary "to whom does this young woman belong?" (2:5). In the privacy of the nighttime encounter, he speaks to Ruth directly: "Who are you?" In response, Ruth mentions neither her household nor her nationality. Ruth 3 is the only chapter that does not refer to Ruth as a Moabite. She simply gives her name. In this one-on-one encounter, she is not the Moabite woman, nor Mahlon's widow, nor even the one who came back with Naomi. She is Ruth.

And she is Boaz's "servant." The Hebrew term, 'amah, is a different word than the word translated "servant" in 2:13. While not certain, apparently the term Ruth uses to describe herself now refers to a handmaid with a higher status than the "servant" of Ruth 2. Moreover, an 'amah could become a wife.

Interpreters debate the meaning of Ruth's request to Boaz to spread his cloak over her. Some commentators believe that it is an invitation to engage in sex, rather than a proposal of marriage. That seems unlikely. Ezekiel 16:8 uses the phrase metaphorically to refer to marriage. Moreover, Naomi's determination and Boaz's agreement that Ruth and Boaz should marry supports understanding the phrase as a marriage proposal. The phrasing echoes Boaz's prayer (Ruth 2:12). There, he speaks of the God of Israel, under whose "wings" Ruth has sought refuge. The word translated "wings" is the same as that translated "cloak" in 3:9. Ruth asks Boaz to make good on his prayer.

Ruth grounds her request in the fact that Boaz is "next of kin"; that is, Boaz is a redeemer. The term "redeemer" has a technical meaning in biblical law; the redeemer is to buy back property that a member of the family is forced by poverty to sell, or buy back destitute persons who sell themselves or are sold into slavery. The word is also often used in a more general sense, however, to refer to a kinsman's obligation to care for family members in need. Ruth uses it in that more general way.

Boaz's response is enthusiastic. He is neither embarrassed nor displeased by Ruth's initiative. Indeed, he interprets her request for redemption as a generous offer, and responds with a blessing and with praise.

Boaz's blessing echoes Naomi's in Ruth 1:8–9. Commentators agree that Ruth's "first *hesed*," "loyalty," is her commitment to Naomi, and possibly to Elimelech and Mahlon. Her second and better act of loyalty is her marriage proposal. What is not clear is why Boaz finds the latter act of *hesed* better than the first. Is his reaction that of an old man, grateful for a younger woman's attentions? That interpretation finds support in the following statement, that Ruth could have gone after a younger man. Alternatively, perhaps her *hesed* is her concern for her family. By marrying Boaz, she will provide security to Naomi. Indeed, marrying one of Elimelech's near-kinsmen is probably the only way Ruth can stay with Naomi. As suggested above, provision for Naomi is probably the responsibility of whichever of Elimelech's near-kinsmen redeems the land. If Ruth had "gone after" a husband outside of Elimelech and Naomi's kinship circle, she would probably have been separated from Naomi. Her second husband would have had no obligations to provide for the mother of her first husband. Boaz may also have levirate marriage in mind. He may interpret Ruth's act as intended to "establish the name of the deceased."

Clearly Ruth and Naomi are not concerned about preserving their deceased husbands' lineage. They seek security and well-being for themselves and each other. Boaz quite possibly has a different view of the matter than do the women. The author of Ruth delights in presenting the characters' differing perspectives. In Ruth 4, Boaz publicly states that he is acquiring Ruth to establish Mahlon's name. He may well have already interpreted Ruth's proposal along those lines.

In any case, Boaz views Ruth's sexual advance as loyalty. Her scandalous behavior is actually faithfulness, not offense. Boaz's praise of Ruth recalls the story of Tamar and Judah. After Tamar dresses up as a prostitute in order to trick Judah into fulfilling his levirate obligation, Judah declares that she is more righteous than he is. Like Tamar, Ruth is "more righteous."

The encounter also recalls the pejorative legend of Moabite origins found in Genesis 19:30–36. After Lot and his daughters flee from the destruction of Sodom and Gomorrah, his daughters fear there are no other men left alive. In order to preserve their lineage, the daughters encourage their father to become drunk; when he is too inebriated to know what is happening, the eldest daughter has sex with him. The resulting baby is Moab, the father of all Moabites. The myth finds echoes in Ruth's visit to the threshing floor. There, Ruth approaches a father figure who is at least slightly drunk.

Deeming Ruth's sexual invitation as "loyalty" and even loyalty "better than the first," Boaz subverts the stereotypical view of Moabite women's sexual immorality. In Boaz's earlier blessing (2:11–12), he reinterprets the meaning of Ruth's foreignness as loyalty. In his second blessing (3:10), he reinterprets Israelite understanding of Moabite women's sexuality. Ruth is not licentious; she is loyal.

Boaz accepts Ruth's proposal. He will do "all" that she asks. Naomi had concluded her instructions to Ruth with the assertion that Boaz would tell her what to do. In fact, Ruth ends up telling Boaz what to do, and Boaz agrees to do it. His assurance that he will do all Ruth asks uses the same language as Ruth's answer to Naomi, that she would do all Naomi asks. The only difference is the addition of the words "for you." The parallel language seems to function as assurance that each of the characters approaches the others with a mutual effort to serve, to do what the others ask.

Boaz grounds his willingness to marry Ruth in her valor. He declares that everyone knows she is a woman of worth. The term translated "worth," *hayil*, is the same word translated "rich" when it is used of Boaz in Ruth 2:1. *Hayil* has to do with substance, virtue, valor. Like Boaz himself, Ruth is a person of *hayil*. With that one word, the social and economic gap between the two characters is bridged. They are fit partners for each other, for each is a person of valor. Ruth and Naomi's problem seems resolved. They will have security in Boaz's household.

But, wait. There is a problem: an even closer kinsman with the right to redeem. What Boaz means by the expression "act as next-of-kin" is not clear. Ruth used the term "redeemer" in a general sense. Boaz's fivefold repetition of the word in verses 12–13 suggests that he is using the word in its more technical sense. Just what that entails, and how "redemption" relates to marriage, is uncertain; some possible interpretations will be sketched in the next chapter. In any case, Boaz reassures Ruth that she will be cared for by one of the next-of-kin.

Boaz then tells Ruth to stay the night; Ruth lies down until the early morning hours. Does the word "lie down" have sexual overtones here? Probably not. With the introduction of a nearer kinsman, Ruth is no longer available. The proper, upright Boaz will observe custom. Given the existence of the nearer kinsman, Boaz appears relieved that Ruth leaves the threshing floor before it is light. Her reputation, and his own, are safeguarded.

As at the end of Ruth 2, Boaz sends Ruth home with a sizeable amount of barley. It may be that here the barley seed symbolizes offspring. In Ruth 2, Boaz sent home the grain in answer to Ruth and Naomi's immediate need for food. In Ruth 3, Boaz may well send the seed home as a symbol of fertility, responding to Ruth and Naomi's long-term need for family and offspring.

AN END TO EMPTINESS
Ruth 3:16–18

> 3:16 **She came to her mother-in-law, who said, "How did things go with you, my daughter?" Then she told her all that the man had done for her,** [17] **saying, "He gave me these six measures of barley, for he said, 'Do not go back to your mother-in-law empty-handed.'"** [18] **She replied, "Wait, my daughter, until you learn how the matter turns out, for the man will not rest, but will settle the matter today."**

The chapter circles around to end as it started, that is, with a conversation between Ruth and Naomi. The symmetry gives that story a satisfying sense of completion.

Naomi's question to Ruth in verse 16 echoes Boaz's question in verse 9. The Hebrew phrase underlying her question is "Who are you, my daughter?" Unlike Boaz's query, Naomi does not mean the question literally. Rather, she appears to be asking about Ruth's status: What happened? Are you a widow or a wife?

Ruth's answer hints at the meaning of the encounter with Boaz for her. She speaks not of Boaz's willingness to marry her, but of the food he has sent to Naomi. Boaz's assertion that Ruth should not return to her mother-in-law empty-handed has not been mentioned before. Several commentators argue that Ruth invents the phrase in order to include Naomi in the "redemption." Possibly, too, the phrase is to be heard as a quote, included only now in order to avoid repetition. Boaz and Ruth incorporate Naomi into the security that she helped Ruth find.

The phrase echoes an earlier scene. In 1:21, Naomi laments that she is "empty." In Ruth 3, Ruth and Boaz ensure that Naomi will be empty no more.

The chapter began with Naomi's telling Ruth to "go." It ends with her telling Ruth to "wait." Once again, Naomi witnesses to her confidence in Boaz's integrity.

The chapter ends with assurance; Ruth and, through Ruth, Naomi will be redeemed. Narrative tension emerges at the end of the chapter, however. Whether the women will have a provider is not in question, but whether they will have the right provider is. The scene ends with that question unresolved. Who will be Ruth's husband? The nearer kinsman or the man of substance and valor, the "strong man" Boaz?

29. Negotiations and Blessings
Ruth 4

The laments and tensions Naomi and Ruth have faced find glad resolution in this final act of the story. They move from precarious poverty to secure abundance, from bereavement and barrenness to the longed-for birth of a son, from bitter complaint to delighted celebration. Ruth's fierce, unconventional loyalty, Naomi's calculated risks, and Boaz's determination to do and find more than is expected, blessed by the hidden workings of God, lead to a conclusion fuller than any of the human characters could have envisioned.

The resolution is not without ambiguity. The book of Ruth is a women's story played out on a patriarchal stage. Moreover, the prominence of the Jewish Naomi over her Moabite daughter-in-law leads some interpreters to call it an assimilationist tale, one that all but erases its foreign heroine. The story can support patriarchal or assimilationist ends, but a more hopeful interpretation is also available. For if the book of Ruth is shaped by a patriarchal culture, it is nonetheless a story of human faithfulness beyond what laws or custom dictate and a story of blessing that exceeds all expectations.

Modern readers may feel the distance between themselves and ancient Israelite culture when they come to Ruth 4. The scenes, especially verses 1–12, presuppose knowledge of family customs, laws, and social practices that the storyteller no doubt shared with the ancient audiences, but that have been lost over time. Biblical scholars debate at great length what assumptions about inheritance, redemption, and levirate marriage underlie Boaz's encounter with the "nearer kinsman." Lack of evidence may prevent scholars from ever resolving questions arising from this text. The debates are highly technical and extremely complex. The comments below will not attempt to summarize them, but will identify some of the key questions, and, where possible, set forth one or two plausible answers. Readers interested in a fuller discussion of the legal and familial issues may consult Frederick Bush's commentary (Bush, 1996, 243–48).

Structurally, the chapter divides into three sections: verses 1–12, Boaz's legal maneuvering; verses 14–17, celebration of the child "born to Naomi"; and verses 18–22, a genealogy. Verse 13 is a transitional verse that serves as the culmination of the negotiations in scene 1 and the cause of celebration in the subsequent verses.

Many commentators find a parallel between the structure of Ruth 4 and that of Ruth 1. The genealogy of 4:18–22 corresponds to the introduction of 1:1–5, in that both sections quickly convey family information. Shared actors and vocabulary link 4:13–17 and 1:19–22, dialogues between Naomi and the women of Bethlehem. Ruth 4:1–12 and 1:6–18 each consist of dialogues negotiating family bonds.

Similarities in their structures underline the striking contrasts between the opening and concluding chapters of Ruth. Both chapters reflect the ambiguities of a woman's story told in a man's world. As the book opens, Naomi, Ruth, and Orpah negotiate their family bonds; the women determine their own futures (1:6–12). In the scene at the gate (4:1–12), men determine Ruth's and Naomi's futures. But the decisions that the women face in Ruth 1 are agonizing; Orpah and Ruth must choose between the security of marriage and their love of Naomi; whichever choice they make, they face risk and loss. The negotiations at the gate allow Ruth a future that includes both marriage and Naomi.

The contrast between Naomi's dialogue with the women of Bethlehem in 1:19–22 and those same women's encounter in 4:14–17 could not be stronger. In the earlier scene, Naomi bitterly complains that Yahweh has "dealt harshly" with her. As the story closes, the Bethlehemite women joyously bless Yahweh who has not left Naomi bereft.

The family information provided by 1:1–5 involves the deaths of the family's three men and ten years of barrenness. Ruth 4:18–22 reports ten generations of births, tracing the lineage of the Elimelech's family, so nearly extinguished, forward until it culminates in the birth of King David. That Ruth, a women's story, ends with an all-male genealogy is regrettable. Nonetheless, the genealogy represents a thrust toward life and an insistence on the public significance of personal integrity and faithfulness.

AT THE GATE
Ruth 4:1–12

4:1 **No sooner had Boaz gone up to the gate and sat down there than the next-of-kin, of whom Boaz had spoken, came passing by. So Boaz said,**

"Come over, friend; sit down here." And he went over and sat down. [2] Then Boaz took ten men of the elders of the city, and said, "Sit down here"; so they sat down. [3] He then said to the next-of-kin, "Naomi, who has come back from the country of Moab, is selling the parcel of land that belonged to our kinsman Elimelech. [4] So I thought I would tell you of it, and say: Buy it in the presence of those sitting here, and in the presence of the elders of my people. If you will redeem it, redeem it; but if you will not, tell me, so that I may know; for there is no one prior to you to redeem it, and I come after you." So he said, "I will redeem it." [5] Then Boaz said, "The day you acquire the field from the hand of Naomi, you are also acquiring Ruth the Moabite, the widow of the dead man, to maintain the dead man's name on his inheritance." [6] At this, the next-of-kin said, "I cannot redeem it for myself without damaging my own inheritance. Take my right of redemption yourself, for I cannot redeem it."

[7] Now this was the custom in former times in Israel concerning redeeming and exchanging: to confirm a transaction, the one took off a sandal and gave it to the other; this was the manner of attesting in Israel. [8] So when the next-of-kin said to Boaz, "Acquire it for yourself," he took off his sandal. [9] Then Boaz said to the elders and all the people, "Today you are witnesses that I have acquired from the hand of Naomi all that belonged to Elimelech and all that belonged to Chilion and Mahlon. [10] I have also acquired Ruth the Moabite, the wife of Mahlon, to be my wife, to maintain the dead man's name on his inheritance, in order that the name of the dead may not be cut off from his kindred and from the gate of his native place; today you are witnesses." [11] Then all the people who were at the gate, along with the elders, said, "We are witnesses. May the LORD make the woman who is coming into your house like Rachel and Leah, who together built up the house of Israel. May you produce children in Ephrathah and bestow a name in Bethlehem; [12] and, through the children that the LORD will give you by this young woman, may your house be like the house of Perez, whom Tamar bore to Judah."

At the conclusion of Ruth 3, Naomi assured Ruth that Boaz would settle the matter of her marriage that very day. Naomi is right. The narrative moves directly to Boaz, seated at the gate, preparing to carry out his promise to Ruth (3:13).

The "gate" was the ancient equivalent of the town hall, courthouse, and perhaps the stock exchange. Rather than a simple entryway, ancient Israelite gates were elaborate two-story structures with multiple chambers and a large, bench-lined plaza. There would have been ample space for meetings and hearings. Since the village fields were located outside of the town walls, nearly everyone in the town would pass through the gate sometime during the day. The gate was the place to conduct business deals, try cases, and conduct legal transactions. The story shifts from the nighttime, private sphere of the threshing floor to the daylight, public world of the gate.

Boaz, the "prominent rich man" (2:1), is in his element in the public, male world of the gate. He issues instructions and his instructions are followed. Boaz quickly gathers the parties necessary for his negotiations: the nearer kinsman and the requisite witnesses.

Boaz addresses the nearer kinsman not by name but with a phrase that NRSV translates "friend" but that is more accurately translated "so and so" (v. 1). (Nielsen aptly renders the phrase "you there." [Nielsen, 1997, 81].) Boaz surely knew the man's name; they were, after all, part of the same kinship circle. By having Boaz call the man "so and so," the storyteller stresses his anonymity, subtly devaluing the nearer kinsman.

"So and so" plays a role in the narrative that is structurally parallel to Orpah (Ruth 1). The nearer kinsman and Orpah are foils. Their unexceptional responses to difficult situations highlight the extraordinary actions of Boaz and Ruth. The storyteller distinguishes the two, however. Naomi praises Orpah for her kindness, her *hesed*. The narrator affirms her by giving her a name. "So and so" is law abiding, but he does not rise to the occasion. He does not do *hesed*; that is, he does not go beyond what is required to provide for the needs of Ruth, Naomi, and their deceased husbands. Unwilling to "maintain the name of the dead man" by marrying Ruth, "so and so" himself remains nameless.

After calling "so and so" to sit down, Boaz summons ten witnesses. He takes his witnesses from the village "elders," presumably men with property who were empowered to make, witness, and execute legal decisions (see, for example, Deut. 21:18, 19). The number of witnesses, probably more than was legally required, ensured that their testimony would be irrefutable. At each step of the proceedings, Boaz sees to it that the transaction is scrupulously correct.

In addition to the three identified parties—Boaz, the nearer kinsman, and the group of witnesses—perhaps another actor is in this scene. The phrase "no sooner" (4:1) points to the same "chance" seen when Ruth "happened" to glean in the field of Boaz, who came to the field "just then" (2:3–4). As noted on p. 277, some interpreters argue that the storyteller intended the audience to understand the striking coincidences in Ruth as just that, coincidences or chance. Others see in the coincidences signs of Providence, as human *hesed* opens up the possibility of divine action.

Verses 3–6 describe the negotiations. Boaz engages in a two-part gambit. First, he announces the opportunity for the nearer kinsman to redeem Elimelech's field. Land was a scarce and valued resource in ancient Israel;

the man accepts (vv. 3–4). Then Boaz confronts the kinsman with an unexpected condition for acquiring the property. Ruth goes with the field. To gain one, the man must marry the other. "So and so" cannot do this and relinquishes his rights and his obligations as next of kin to Boaz. The threat is resolved; Ruth will have the right husband.

The exchange between Boaz and "so and so" raises a tangle of problems for biblical scholars. First, the very existence of a field that Naomi has the right to sell comes as a surprise. The audience has heard nothing about this land until now. The storyteller has portrayed Ruth and Naomi as paupers, forced to survive by gleaning. Now the audience learns that Naomi has rights to a field. How can this be?

Some interpreters suggest that Elimelech sold his field before the family migrated to Moab. In ancient Israel, family land was a sacred trust. Israel recognized God as the true owner of the land; the family who possessed the land was its tenant and steward. Leviticus 25:23–28 mandates that fields sold outside the extended family or clan could be "redeemed," that is, repurchased by the original owner or one of his kin. Perhaps Naomi is selling, or, rather transferring, the right to redeem the property. (The Hebrew verb translated "selling" does not always involve an exchange of money. For further discussion of this theory, see Bush, 1996, 211–15).

Possibly Naomi still legally possessed the land or its produce but had not been able to reclaim it from squatters. A number of commentators note that arable land would not be allowed to lie fallow during its owner's prolonged absence. And it is likely that people who labored to plant and tend the field would have had a right to its produce. In that case, Naomi would not have been able to reclaim the field until now that the harvest was over (2:23). It may even be that Naomi had to sue to recover the property (see 2 Kgs. 8:5–6). If the field remained Naomi's legal possession, we must assume she was unable to work the field, so she was selling her rights to it. Naomi did not join Ruth in gleaning; she may have been too old for field work.

Besides being surprising in terms of the plot of the story, Naomi's rights over a field are unexpected in light of what is known about ancient Near Eastern legal customs. It comes as some surprise that Naomi, a widow with no living children, would have the legal right to sell her husband's field. The Bible does not provide much evidence about the inheritance rights of widows. What little evidence there is suggests a childless widow would not normally inherit her husband's land. It was too important to keep the property within the man's clan.

One scenario set forth by a number of scholars is that a widow, including Naomi, had rights to the produce of her husband's land until she remarried or died, when the field would revert to her husband's kinsmen. Naomi then would be selling not the land itself, but rights to farm it during her lifetime. Other commentators suggest that Naomi was a trustee or executor, overseeing the process by which the field passed to one of her husband's kinsmen. It is likely that, in either of those two cases, whoever acquired the field was responsible for Naomi's maintenance.

A link between acquiring Elimelech's field and providing for his widow, Naomi, sheds light on another question raised by the passage: Why did Boaz open negotiations with "so and so" by bringing up the field? In Ruth 3, Boaz was concerned about Ruth's well-being and agreed to see that she secured the protection of marriage. Why, then, are his first comments about property, not about marriage? Boaz does not mention marriage until after the nearer kinsman agrees to serve as redeemer.

The logic of the chapter requires interpreting Boaz's opening gambit as a clever strategy designed to move the kinsman to relinquish his right to redeem the field. Boaz wants to ensure that the field that had belonged to Elimelech and then to his sons remained in the family of his son's widow. Moreover, if the redeemer of the property was obligated to provide for Naomi, then the only way Ruth and Naomi could remain together was for the same man who redeemed the field to marry Ruth. Only thus could Ruth fulfill her vow: "Where you lodge, I will lodge."

That conclusion leads to a further much-debated question. Why is the man who redeems the field required to marry Ruth? Legally, he probably isn't. Morally, he is obligated to marry the widow to provide an heir for the deceased owner of the field. Although the matter is debated, Boaz's statement in verse 5 probably relates to a practice called levirate marriage. Levirate marriage was a legal fiction that provided a son for a man who had died childless. In ancient Israel to die childless was an evil fate. The meaning of a man's life and possibly even his ongoing existence after death depended upon his fathering a son who would inherit his land. To do so was to establish his name. The word "name" is not to be taken literally; in the two biblical narratives having to do with levirate marriage, the sons are neither named for their fictive deceased father nor reckoned to him in the genealogies. Rather, "name" in this sense has to do with lineage and with being remembered.

Even now, for many people, children represent the ongoing meaning of life. Perhaps people whose family has farmed the same land for generations can understand the Israelite sense of the importance not only of having children and grandchildren, but also of those offspring living on one's land.

In any case, levirate marriage was a practice whereby if a kinsman of the deceased man married his widow, the firstborn son was counted as the deceased man's child and would inherit his land, thus providing him with a name. To marry the widow and establish his name was a moral obligation, or at least a righteous act, on the part of the nearer kinsman.

(The sole legal case in the Bible that deals with levirate marriage, Deut. 25:5–10, enjoins it only on the deceased man's brother, and only in cases where the brothers had not yet divided their father's property.)

Some scholars believe that redeeming the field and marrying the widow were linked legally. That perspective is possible, but it would not explain why Boaz's assertion that he had to marry Ruth caught the nearer kinsman off-guard. It seems more likely, as Bush argues, that Boaz counted on social pressure to force "so and so" either to marry Ruth or to relinquish his rights to redeem the field. When Boaz publicly challenges "so and so" to marry Ruth, the kinsman is in a tough spot. Having agreed to act as next of kin in redeeming the land, an act that would benefit him, he will look very bad if he then refuses to act on his obligation as next of kin by marrying his childless kinsman's widow. Boaz has maneuvered the nearer kinsman into a position where to save face he must either relinquish his legal rights to redeem the field or fulfill his moral obligation to marry Ruth. (Bush, 1996, 243–46).

But if the nearer kinsman marries Ruth, he will have to feed not only Naomi but also Ruth, the firstborn son, and any other children Ruth might bear. And the field will not belong to his children (presumably already born to another wife) but to an as-yet-unconceived child, reckoned to Mahlon's line. The nearer kinsmen would not do this because such a move would jeopardize the inheritance of his own children, as well as his own lineage and his own name.

The nearer kinsman takes the option that allows him to maintain his honor and to protect his children's inheritance. He relinquishes to Boaz both the rights to redeem the field and the obligation to marry Ruth.

The negotiations lead to the desired outcome. Ruth had described Boaz as her "redeemer" in the general sense of a kinsman obligated to help or deliver family members who were in need. Boaz sees additional possibilities in Ruth's assertion and acts as "redeemer" in a technical sense. He uses redemption of Elimelech's field to keep the family intact and to maintain the land within Naomi and Ruth's family. Once again, Boaz sees and does more than he is expected to do.

When the negotiations are completed, Boaz publicly ratifies the agreement. In the ancient Near East, symbolic acts often had legal significance.

The gesture of drawing off a sandal symbolized and enacted Boaz and the kinsman's agreement. The details of the gesture are unclear. Did Boaz give the sandal to the kinsman as a payment? Did the nearer kinsman take off his sandal as a sign that he had relinquished a right? The only other time drawing off a sandal occurs in the Scriptures is in the Deuteronomic law of levirate marriage [25:9]. Despite the fact that both that law and the exchange between Boaz and "so and so" concern levirate marriage, the gesture of removing a sandal does not seem to have the same significance in the two texts. Deuteronomy does not shed light on the symbolism of the act in Ruth. What is clear is that the transfer of the right to redeem the land and to marry Ruth is publicly enacted.

To make doubly sure, Boaz then declares the outcome before a superfluous number of witnesses. The rights of a nearer kinsman are incontrovertibly his. The proprieties are well and duly observed. The desired outcome is achieved. Boaz has a wife of valor, Ruth. Naomi is part of the family circle. The family maintains its land. Even the deceased are blessed by the arrangement. Elimelech and Mahlon will have names in Israel.

The people at the gate respond to the happy outcome with an enthusiastic, three-part blessing. The townspeople compare Ruth to Rachel and Leah, women who bore eight of Jacob's twelve children. With Zilpah and Bilhah, they are the mothers of the tribes of Israel (Gen. 30:1–24). The significance of the marriage extends beyond Boaz, Ruth, and Naomi to include Bethlehem and even Israel.

The NRSV has probably translated the second part of the blessing too narrowly. The phrase rendered "produce children" is "do *hayil*." "Do *hayil*" can indeed mean to have the power to father children, but it can also refer to honor and wealth as well as offspring. The word *hayil* plays off of the descriptions of Boaz as a "prominent man of *hayil*" (a "prominent rich man," 2:1) and Ruth as a "woman of *hayil*" (a "worthy woman," 3:11). The phrase translated "bestow a name" apparently can also refer to renown. The townspeople thus bless Boaz with prosperity, progeny, honor, and renown.

In their third wish for Boaz, the people compare Ruth to Tamar. As noted on p. 290, Tamar and Ruth have similar stories. Both are childless widows. Both, after much risk, bear a child (or, in Tamar's case, children) who establish the names of their deceased husbands. Tamar and Perez are Boaz's ancestors; he thus highly values their house, their lineage. The people hope that Ruth and he will have an equally important house.

The final blessing includes a touch of irony. Previously, Boaz has given seed to Ruth. The word translated "children" in verse 12 literally means "seed." In this verse, Ruth brings seed to Boaz. The townspeople's blessing will be fulfilled in the closing genealogy.

The scene is a satisfying resolution of the tale. The loss, hardships, and risk that Naomi and Ruth go through in the first three chapters give way to security and hope for a future. References to the "house of Israel" hint that their story is more significant than the protagonists can know.

Despite its happy conclusion, this passage is not without difficulties for the modern reader. Set in a man's world, the gate, the scene is thoroughly shaped by patriarchal values, reflecting male interests and male perspectives. The outcome of the negotiations intimately concerns Ruth and Naomi. Nonetheless, the women have no part in the scene; they are not even there. Moreover, the negotiations are couched in a male perspective. In the private world of the threshing floor, Boaz's expressed concern is Ruth's welfare. In the public world of the gate, Boaz speaks of the need to "maintain the dead man's name on his inheritance." Boaz uses explanations and language that the male elders will hear. Like Naomi and Ruth before him, Boaz "works the system." Nonetheless, his words underline the patriarchal character of the system.

Boaz even speaks of "acquiring" Ruth, which is not purchasing her. Ruth is not chattel. In fact, the choice of the verb, which is not found with the meaning "marry" elsewhere in the Scriptures, may be a matter of style rather than substance. Nonetheless, in this exchange Ruth is an object, not a subject, and if she is not chattel, she is subordinate.

The blessing also reflects a male perspective. It alludes to Ruth at the beginning and the end, but it never gives her name. Moreover, the blessing explicitly locates Ruth's value in her ability to bear sons. The townsmen do not explicitly bless Ruth. They bless the man, Boaz.

MARRIAGE AND A CHILD
Ruth 4:13

4:13 **So Boaz took Ruth and she became his wife. When they came together, the LORD made her conceive, and she bore a son.**

In the opening chapter of the book, Naomi expresses hope that Ruth will find security in the house of a husband (1:9). The introduction of Boaz as a rich, prominent kinsman stirs up expectations (2:1): perhaps Boaz will solve Ruth and Naomi's dilemma. By the time Ruth approaches Boaz at the threshing floor, the story is firmly aimed at bringing the two together in marriage. Finally, the anticipated outcome takes place. Naomi's hopes and strategies, Ruth's determined courage, and Boaz's negotiations lead to the desired conclusion. The storyteller reports the events in a surprisingly brief statement. In Hebrew, verse 13 requires only fifteen words to announce that Boaz and Ruth marry, the marriage is consummated, she conceives, and a son is born.

The text refers to Yahweh's direct action for the second and last time in the book. In 1:6, Naomi heard that Yahweh had given the Judeans food. Now Yahweh has given Ruth conception. In the book of Ruth, God acts directly to ensure the fertility that makes human life possible; elsewhere in the book, the work of God is seen in human words and actions.

A SON IS BORN TO NAOMI
Ruth 4:14–17

> 4:14 **Then the women said to Naomi, "Blessed be the LORD, who has not left you this day without next-of-kin; and may his name be renowned in Israel! ¹⁵ He shall be to you a restorer of life and a nourisher of your old age; for your daughter-in-law who loves you, who is more to you than seven sons, has borne him." ¹⁶ Then Naomi took the child and laid him in her bosom, and became his nurse. ¹⁷ The women of the neighborhood gave him a name, saying, "A son has been born to Naomi." They named him Obed; he became the father of Jesse, the father of David.**

The story moves from the gate, a male-dominated arena, to the birthing room, a women's sphere. As noted in the introduction to this chapter, the scene celebrating Obed's birth echoes the scene describing Naomi's return to Bethlehem (1:19–22).

Both involve Naomi and the women of Bethlehem. But where Naomi had spoken in bitter lament, now the women of Bethlehem cry out in joyous celebration. In chapter 1, Naomi described herself as "empty" and railed against God, whom she held responsible for the death of her husband and sons. Now the women bless Yahweh, who has not withheld a redeemer, a male kinsman, from Naomi. In both scenes Ruth is silent. But while Naomi, in the bitterness of her grief, ignored Ruth in her speech to the townswomen (1:19–22), now the neighboring women offer a more just assessment of Ruth's value to Naomi: she is worth more than seven sons, for she "loves." Ruth's radical *hesed*, her loving-kindness, was ignored in 1:19–22; it is recognized now.

The women's words form a counterpart to the townsmen's blessing (4:11–12). Their perspective is strikingly different from the men's point of

view. Boaz is the focus of the townsmen's blessing. For them, the importance of the upcoming marriage is that it will provide Boaz with a household, a lineage. They wish for him many sons. The townsmen allude to
Ruth at the beginning and end of their speech, but value her for her capacity to bear children. In contrast, the townswomen focus their speech tightly
on Naomi. They rejoice in the birth of the baby, precisely because of the
care he will give to Naomi as she ages, and because of his maternity. For
the women of Bethlehem, Ruth is not valued for her children; her child is
of value because he is born of her. The women value Ruth not for her fertile womb, but for her love.

The scene has two parts. The marriage and birth (v. 13, discussed separately, because it looks both backwards and forwards) evoke the women
of Bethlehem's blessing (vv. 14–15). The narrative description of Naomi
tenderly cradling her newborn grandson (v. 16) is followed by neighbor
women's speech (v. 17).

The townswomen bless Yahweh for what Yahweh has done for Naomi,
giving her a "next of kin." The Hebrew word is that same one used of Boaz
and of the nearer kinsman. The newborn baby is a redeemer for Naomi, a
male relative who can provide for her in her old age. The phrase "restorer
of life" consists of the same two words, in slightly different forms, that are
found in Psalm 23:3, "he restores my soul." As he grows, Obed will nourish Naomi both physically and emotionally. Already, as a newborn infant,
he restores the older woman's hope and happiness. The use of the word
"restore" (literally, to "bring back") is particularly poignant because that
verb is used in Naomi's complaint: "The LORD has brought me back
empty" (1:21). In her grief, Naomi misunderstood God's role. Yahweh was
not set against her but was working for her restoration. Now God has given
Naomi a kinsman, who will "bring back" life.

The wording of the women's blessing includes an ambiguous phrase not
unlike the ambiguity in an earlier blessing by Naomi (2:20). Naomi's
words, "whose kindness has not forsaken the living or the dead," could
apply to either Yahweh or to Boaz. Here, the women exclaim, "May his
name be renowned in Israel!" "His name" may refer either to the infant
next of kin or to Yahweh. We do not need to decide between the two; the
townswomen extol both. As was the case in 2:20, the ambiguity is theologically significant. God is extolled through human beings. Verses 17–18
show that the women's prayer will be fulfilled. The baby will be renowned
in Israel, for he will become the grandfather of the great King David.
Through Obed's offspring, King David, and through Jesus, David's Son,
God will be renowned, God's name declared in praise.

Naomi, like any doting grandmother, cradles the baby (4:16). Naomi's act has been interpreted as an indication that Naomi adopted Obed, but that view has not been widely accepted. The phrase "became his nurse" simply means she cared for him, not that she took Ruth's place, anymore than the presence of a caring grandmother now means that the mother no longer plays a parental role.

The neighbor women, recognizing that the baby will "nourish Naomi" in her old age, name him "Obed," "servant." Why the neighbors are said to name the child is not clear. Elsewhere in the Bible, a baby is named by the mother or, less frequently, the father. Perhaps the storyteller wants to stress that Obed's birth is significant for more than his immediate family. Perhaps the women reflect on the meaning of his name, rather than actually naming him.

Their final words, "a son is born to Naomi," celebrate the end of Naomi's bitterness and her renewed hope. This widowed woman who lost her two sons is no longer childless, no longer empty. The significance of the baby's birth for Israel becomes apparent in the last half of verse 17. One can almost imagine the storyteller saying, "Wait for it!" This is the father of Jesse, the father of David.

Numerous interpreters have criticized the scene for eclipsing Ruth. Indigenous interpreters who read the book of Ruth as a story that urges assimilation find its focus on Naomi dangerous. According to that reading, Ruth has already given up her Moabite heritage to adopt Naomi's people and deity. Now she is erased altogether. The storyteller gives baby Obed a "good Jewish mother," Naomi. Katharine Doob Sakenfeld notes that the scene is also problematic in cultures where the paternal grandmother has authority over her grandchildren, so that the actual mother has little or no say in their upbringing. The story of Ruth can be read as legitimizing the mother's circumscribed role (Sakenfeld, 1999, 83).

In light of such critiques, as Sakenfeld notes, it is important to recognize that the storyteller says nothing about the roles Naomi and Ruth play in raising Obed. Moreover, the story should not be taken as a prescription for families. It is the celebration of the survival of one particular family. And it celebrates the restoration of one suffering woman. The book of Ruth can be interpreted in ways that undergird oppressive power relationships. But interpreting the storyteller's focus on Naomi in another way is also possible. Unlike the paternal grandmothers in the cultures that Sakenfeld describes, Naomi does not hold a powerful position in her family circle. She is not the mother of the male head of household, nor is she his mother-in-law. She is the mother of his wife's first husband. Presumably by redeeming Elimelech's field, Boaz has assumed responsibility to provide Naomi with food and shelter, but Naomi's status in the family circle depends upon Ruth and Boaz's commitment. Of the three main actors in this story, Naomi is the most vulnerable. Moreover, she has suffered not only the loss of her husband but also the loss of two sons. Naomi stands most in need of redemption. The women's glad cries, "a son is born to Naomi," attest that she finds that redemption.

A SON IS BORN TO ISRAEL
Ruth 4:18–22

4:18 **Now these are the descendants of Perez: Perez became the father of Hezron,** [19] **Hezron of Ram, Ram of Amminadab,** [20] **Amminadab of Nahshon, Nahshon of Salmon,** [21] **Salmon of Boaz, Boaz of Obed,** [22] **Obed of Jesse, and Jesse of David.**

After the dramatic, romantic, and tender scenes of the story of Ruth, its closing verses come as something of a surprise. The closing verses raise two overall questions.

First, what is this archival material doing here? Until recently, scholars almost unanimously assessed the genealogy as a late addition to the book of Ruth. The verses sound very much like genealogies in Genesis composed by the priestly writers, who could well have added an appendix to Ruth. Moreover, it isn't the kind of ending one expects the tale to have. None of the similar stories in the Bible end with a genealogy.

More recently, scholars have begun to take seriously the final form of biblical texts and are no longer given to discarding parts of scripture simply because they were probably written later than the surrounding text. Moreover, current opinion is more divided about whether the verses are original to the story. In fact, a number of interpreters believe that the Davidic genealogy is key to the purpose of the book; that Ruth was written in order to cast David's Moabite ancestry in the best possible light. In my opinion, that interpretation is not finally persuasive; the story focuses on Ruth, Naomi, and Boaz, not on David. Nonetheless, the genealogy makes an important contribution to the theology of the book.

The second question raised by genealogy is an ethical one. Ruth is one of the few biblical narratives in which women's actions and voices drive the plot. Boaz plays a key role, but it is Naomi whose "emptiness" stands as the central problem in the story and Ruth who functions as her redeemer. Ruth's faithfulness is the foundation of the glad resolution of this tale.

Without question, the women work out their futures in a man's world, but they do work them out. And Ruth is worth more to Naomi than seven sons.

For a story so focused on women to conclude with a genealogy comprised entirely of men's names seems incongruous. Are Ruth and Naomi subordinated to male interests after all? Is their story subsumed under the narrative of the "great man," David?

The ambiguity is real. Nonetheless, alternative ways of looking at the genealogy are available. First, the lineage given in verses 18–22 does not stop with David. The royal genealogy continues and is taken up in the Gospel of Matthew (1:1–17). One strategy for dealing with the patriarchal character of the final verses of Ruth is to trace the development of the genealogy in Matthew. There, we find that among the many fathers of Jesus that text names are three mothers: Tamar, Rahab, and Ruth.

The choice to include just those three "mothers of Messiah" has intrigued commentators. Why Tamar, Rahab, and Ruth, but not Rebekah? Not Sarah? Not any of the queen mothers? As Raymond Brown has shown, the three women share two characteristics (Brown, 1977, 71–74). First, they are non-Israelites. Genesis 38 does not identify Tamar's nationality, but by New Testament times, tradition held that she was Canaanite. Rahab is Canaanite. Ruth, of course, is a Moabite. Second, each of the three women is sexually suspect. Tamar dressed as a prostitute to seduce her father-in-law in order to trick him into fulfilling his levirate obligation. Rahab was a prostitute. Ruth seeks out the sleeping Boaz in the middle of the night, uncovers his "feet," and lies down. Yet they, like Mary, the young unwed mother of Jesus, are agents through whom God chooses to work. Judah declares that Tamar is more righteous than he is. Rahab rescues Israelite spies from the Canaanite king; she is, moreover, the first person in the promised land to confess faith in the sovereignty of Yahweh. Ruth is a woman of *ḥayil*, a woman of valor and worth. She models *ḥesed*, covenantal love.

The presence of the names of just these three women in the genealogy of Jesus challenges any overly narrow notion of ethnic or sexual purity. These women did not conform to what their society defined as normative behavior, yet they are precisely the ones whom God chooses to bring about divine deliverance and divine blessing. Many churches have single mothers in their congregations. Some members of the congregation have mixed feelings about their presence. Other churches have enacted increasingly rigid policies banning sexually suspect persons from ordination. The presence of the names of three foreign, sexually suspect women is hardly a basis for constructing a sexual ethic. But it is a biblical basis for caution about absolutizing our opinions about sexual morality, and it does challenge ethnocentricity. Human conventions and norms do not bind God.

Another way of approaching the genealogy notes that feminist scholars have long insisted that there can be no final separation of the private and the public, the personal and the political, spheres of life. The genealogy makes a statement about the significance of personal faithfulness for the larger community. Ruth, Naomi, and Boaz each show *hesed*. The concluding genealogy is a strong statement that their personal integrity and faithfulness have public, political significance. Without Ruth's love for Naomi, without Naomi's daring, and without Boaz's stratagems and willingness to take on more than is required, there would be no David.

The faithfulness of the three characters has led to blessing for each of them. The circle of blessing expands to include the past when Boaz finds a way to keep Elimelech and Mahlon's land in the family, so that the son he and Ruth have will establish their names. Even the dead are blessed. The speeches of the townsmen and women show that the faithful lives of these three persons have significance for their broader community. The genealogical conclusion shows the circle of blessing expanding to include generations yet unborn. Indeed, the whole of Israel is blessed by Ruth and Naomi and Boaz's *hesed*. From a Christian perspective, that blessing extends yet further, as David's lineage continues and his son Jesus' blessing enfolds the world.

The story of Ruth, like all stories and all texts, is enfleshed, shaped by the assumptions and interests of the storyteller's culture. Nevertheless, this short book offers a testimony that rings true. God works in and is made known through loving, faithful relationships to offer blessing beyond anything that those struggling to keep faith could ever imagine.

Works Cited

Auld, A. Graeme. *Joshua, Judges, and Ruth*. Philadelphia: Westminster Press, 1984.

Bird, Phyllis A. "The Harlot as Heroine: Narrative Art and Social Presupposition in Three Old Testament Texts [Gen 38:1–26: Josh 2:1–24; 1 Kgs 3:16–27]." *Semeia* 46 (1989): 119–39.

Boling, Robert G. *Judges: A New Translation with Introduction, Notes, and Commentary*. Anchor Bible. Garden City, N.Y.: Doubleday, 1975.

Brown, Raymond E. *The Birth of the Messiah: A Commentary on the Infancy Narratives in Matthew and Luke*, 71–74. Garden City, N.Y.: Doubleday, 1977.

Bush, Frederic William. *Ruth, Esther*. Waco, Tex.: Word Books, 1996.

Campbell. Edward F. *Ruth: A New Translation with Introduction, Notes, and Commentary*. Anchor Bible. Garden City, N.Y.: Doubleday, 1975.

Day, Peggy L. "From the Child Is Born the Woman: The Story of Jephthah's Daughter." In *Gender and Difference in Ancient Israel*, 58–74. Minneapolis: Fortress Press, 1989.

Donaldson, Laura E. "The Sign of Orpah: Reading Ruth through Native Eyes." In *Ruth and Esther: A Feminist Companion to the Bible*, 2d ser., ed. by Althalya Brenner, 130–44. Sheffield: Sheffield Academic Press, 1999.

Exum, J. Cheryl. "Aspects of Symmetry and Balance in the Samson Saga: [Judg 13–16]." *Journal for the Study of the Old Testament* 19 (1981): 3–29.

Fewell, Danna Nolan, and David Miller Gunn. *Compromising Redemption: Relating Characters in the Book of Ruth*. Louisville, Ky.: Westminster/John Knox Press, 1990.

Fretheim, Terence E. *Deuteronomic History*. Nashville: Abingdon Press, 1983.

Hamlin, E. John. *At Risk in the Promised Land: A Commentary on the Book of Judges*. Grand Rapids: Wm. B. Eerdmans Publishing Co., 1990.

————. *Surely There Is a Future: A Commentary on the Book of Ruth*. Grand Rapids: Wm. B. Eerdmans Publishing Co.; Edinburgh: Handsel Press Ltd., 1996.

Harrelson, Walter J. *The Ten Commandments and Human Rights*. Philadelphia: Fortress Press, 1980.

Lohfink, Norbert. "The Deuteronomistic Picture of the Transfer of Authority from Moses to Joshua." In *Theology of the Pentateuch: Themes of the Priestly Narrative and Deuteronomy*, 234–47. Minneapolis: Fortress Press, 1994.

Miller, Patrick D. *Deuteronomy*. Interpretation. Louisville, Ky.: John Knox Press, 1990.

————. *The Divine Warrior in Early Israel*. Cambridge, Mass.: Harvard University Press, 1973.

Nielsen, Kirsten. *Ruth: A Commentary*. Louisville, Ky.: Westminster John Knox Press, 1997.

Nelson, Richard D. *Joshua: A Commentary*. OTL. Louisville, Ky.: Westminster John Knox Press, 1997.

Olson, Dennis. "Deuteronomy." In *The New Interpreter's Bible*, Vol. 2 Nashville: Abingdon Press, 1998.

Sakenfeld, Katharine Doob. *Ruth*. Interpretation. Louisville, Ky.: Westminster John Knox Press, 1999.

————. *Faithfulness in Action: Loyalty in Biblical Perspective*. Philadelphia: Fortress Press, 1985.

Stone, Lawson G. "Ethical and Apologetic Tendencies in the Redaction of the Book of Joshua." *Catholic Biblical Quarterly* 53 (January 1991): 25–36.

Trible, Phyllis. *God and the Rhetoric of Sexuality*. Philadelphia: Fortress Press, 1978.

————. *Texts of Terror: Literary-Feminist Readings of Biblical Narratives*. Philadelphia: Fortress Press, 1984.

Webb, Barry G. *The Book of Judges: An Integrated Reading*. Sheffield, Eng.: JSOT Press, 1987.

For Further Reading

Joshua

Cetina, Edesioo Sanchez. "Joshua." In *The International Bible Commentary: A Catholic and Ecumenical Commentary for the Twenty-first Century*, ed. by William R. Farmer, 525–47. Collegeville, Minn.: Liturgical Press, 1998.

Fretheim, Terence E. *Deuteronomic History*. Nashville: Abingdon Press, 1983.

Nelson, Richard D. *Joshua: A Commentary*. OTL. Louisville, Ky.: Westminster John Knox Press, 1997.

Rowlett, Lori. "Inclusion, Exclusion and Marginality in the Book of Joshua." *Journal for the Study of the Old Testament* 55 (1992): 15–23.

Soggin, J. Alberto. *Joshua: A Commentary*. London: S.C.M. Press, 1972.

Judges

Auld, A. Graeme. *Joshua, Judges, and Ruth*. Philadelphia: Westminster Press, 1984.

Exum, J. Cheryl. "Judges." In *Harper's Bible Commentary*, ed. by James L. Mays, 245–61. San Francisco: Harper & Row, 1988.

Olson, Dennis. "Judges," *The New Interpreter's Bible*. Vol. 2. Nashville: Abingdon Press, 1998.

Soggin, J. Alberto. *Judges: A Commentary*. Philadelphia: Westminster Press, 1981.

Webb, Barry G. *The Book of Judges: An Integrated Reading*. Sheffield, Eng.: JSOT Press, 1987.

Ruth

Bush, Frederic William. *Ruth, Esther*. Waco, Tex.: Word Books, 1996.

Campbell, Edward. *Ruth: A New Translation with Introduction, Notes, and Commentary*. Anchor Bible. Garden City, N.Y.: Doubleday, 1975.

Farmer, Kathleen. "Ruth," *The New Interpreter's Bible*. Vol. 2. Nashville: Abingdon Press, 1998.

Sakenfeld, Katharine Doob. *Ruth*. Louisville, Ky.: Westminster John Knox Press, 1999.

Trible, Phyllis. *God and the Rhetoric of Sexuality*. Philadelphia: Fortress Press, 1978.

Weems, Renita. *Just a Sister Away: A Womanist Vision of Women's Relationships in the Bible*. San Diego: LuraMedia, 1988.